D1742517

Converging Evidence

Human Cognitive Processing (HCP)

Cognitive Foundations of Language Structure and Use

This book series is a forum for interdisciplinary research on the grammatical structure, semantic organization, and communicative function of language(s), and their anchoring in human cognitive faculties.

For an overview of all books published in this series, please see
http://benjamins.com/catalog/hcp

Volume 33

Converging Evidence. Methodological and theoretical issues for linguistic research
Edited by Doris Schönefeld

Converging Evidence

Methodological and theoretical issues for linguistic research

Edited by

Doris Schönefeld
Universität Leipzig

John Benjamins Publishing Company
Amsterdam / Philadelphia

TM The paper used in this publication meets the minimum requirements of American National Standard for Information Sciences – Permanence of Paper for Printed Library Materials, ANSI Z39.48-1984.

Library of Congress Cataloging-in-Publication Data

Converging evidence : methodological and theoretical issues for linguistic research / edited by Doris Schönefeld.

p. cm. (Human Cognitive Processing, ISSN 1387-6724 ; v. 33)

Includes bibliographical references and index.

1. Linguistics--Research--Methodology. I. Schönefeld, Doris, 1953-

P126.C676 2011

410.72--dc23 2011029002

ISBN 978 90 272 2387 6 (Hb ; alk. paper)

ISBN 978 90 272 8451 8 (Eb)

John Benjamins Publishing Co. · P.O. Box 36224 · 1020 ME Amsterdam · The Netherlands

John Benjamins North America · P.O. Box 27519 · Philadelphia PA 19118-0519 · USA

Table of contents

Contributors

Ad Backus
Tilburg University
A.M.Backus@uvt.nl
Postal address:
Faculty of Humanities
P.O. Box 90153
5000 LE Tilburg, The Netherlands

Anke Beger
Flensburg University
ankebeger@web.de
Postal address:
Englisches Seminar
Auf dem Campus 1
D-24943 Flensburg, Germany

Réka Benczes
Eötvös Loránd University
rbenczes@gmail.com
Postal address:
School of English and American Studies
H-1088 Budapest
Rákóczi út 5, Hungary

Susanne Borgwaldt
University of Braunschweig
s.borgwaldt@tu-braunschweig.de
Postal address:
Institut für Germanistik
Technische Universität Carolo Wilhelmina
zu Braunschweig
Bienroder Weg 80
D-38106 Braunschweig

Silke Brandt
University of Basel
silke.brandt@unibas.ch
Postal address:
Englisches Seminar
Nadelberg 6
CH-4051 Basel, Switzerland

Thomas Egan
Hedmark University College
Thomas.Egan@hihm.no
Postal address:
P.b. 4010 Bedriftssenteret
2306 Hamar, Norway

Stefan Th. Gries
University of California, Santa Barbara
stgries@linguistics.ucsb.edu
Postal address:
South Hall 3431/3432
University of California, Santa Barbara
Santa Barbara, CA 93106-3100, USA

Silke Höche
University of Hannover
silke.hoeche@engsem.uni-hannover.de
Postal address:
Englisches Seminar/Englische Sprachwissenschaft
Königsworther Platz 1
D-30167 Hannover, Germany

Gunther Kaltenböck
University of Vienna
gunther.kaltenboeck@univie.ac.at
Postal address:
Institut für Anglistik
und Amerikanistik
Spitalgasse 2-4
A-1090 Wien, Austria

Evan Kidd
University of Manchester
evan.j.kidd@manchester.ac.uk
Postal address:
School of Psychological Sciences
Coupland 1
Oxford Road M13 9PL
Manchester, UK

Maria Mos
Tilburg University
maria.mos@uvt.nl
Postal address:
Department of Communication
and Information Sciences
Room D 411
P.O. Box 90153
5000 LE Tilburg, The Netherlands

Nina Reshöft
University of Bremen
n.reshoeft@uni-bremen.de
Postal address:
FB 10 Sprach- und
Literaturwissenschaften
GW2 Raum A3380
Bibliothekstr. 1
D-28359 Bremen, Germany

Doris Schönefeld
University of Leipzig
schoenefeld@uni-leipzig.de
Postal address
Institut für Anglistik
Beethovenstraße 15
D-04107 Leipzig, Germany

Sven Staffeldt
University of Würzburg
sven.staffeldt@uni-wuerzburg.de
Postal address:
Lehrstuhl für deutsche
Sprachwissenschaft
Am Hubland
D-97074 Würzburg, Germany

Gerard J. Steen
University of Amsterdam
gj.steen@let.vu.nl
Postal address:
Faculty of Arts, 11A–35
Department of Language
and Communication
VU University Amsterdam
De Boelelaan 1105
1081 HV Amsterdam, The Netherlands

Rasmus Steinkrauss
University of Groningen
E-mail: r.g.a.steinkrauss@rug.nl
Postal address:
Center for Language and Cognition
Oude Kijk in 't Jatstraat 26
9712 EK Groningen

Alexander Ziem
University of Düsseldorf
ziem@phil-fak.uni-duesseldorf.de
Postal address:
Heinrich-Heine-Universität Düsseldorf
Germanistische Sprachwissenschaft
Universitätsstr. 1
D-40225 Düsseldorf, Germany

Preface

This volume contains a selection of papers that are based on presentations given at the 3rd International Conference of the German Cognitive Linguistics Association held at Leipzig University, September 25–27, 2008. The conference was titled 'Converging evidence', and aimed at discussing and opening up research perspectives that can promote and produce new insights in the field of cognitive (usage-based) linguistics. The focus was on the presentation of (cognitively oriented) research resulting from the application of empirical methods, more specifically, from corpus-linguistic methods and experimental work.

The 13 papers collected in the volume demonstrate exactly this research agenda. They all report on findings obtained from corpus analyses and experimental tasks, and can be seen as textbook examples of how to conduct (empirical) research within the cognitive-linguistic framework. The papers have gone through a selective peer-review process intended to yield a high quality research product.

Credit for the quality of the papers goes first and foremost to the authors. They contributed a great deal of effort and creativity to produce this work, and I would very much like to thank them for their excellent cooperation in writing and re-writing their inspiring texts.

Credit also goes to the 30 reviewers, who donated time from busy schedules to carefully read and evaluate the submissions, each of which underwent two reviews. The appointed reviewers were (in alphabetical order): Kirsten Abbot-Smith, Michel Achard, Inbal Arnon, Johanna Barðdal, John Barnden, Silke Brandt, Cristiano Broccias, Paula Chesley, Alan Cienki, Timothy Colleman, Alexis Dimitriadis, Dagmar Divjak, Susanne Gahl, Volker Gast, Dirk Geeraerts, Gaetanelle Gilquin, Stefan Gries, Beate Hampe, Martin Hilpert, Willem Hollmann, Florian Jaeger, Celeste Kidd, Andreas Langlotz, Cornelia Müller, Sae Oshima, Klaus-Uwe Panther, Neal Snider, Benedikt Szmrecsanyi, Stefanie Wulff, and Arne Zeschel. I cannot thank them enough for writing thoughtful reviews on the contributions' strengths and weaknesses alike, thus stimulating a creative phase of revision.

Credit for the final polish and acceptance of the volume as a whole goes to the HCP series editors Linda Thornburg and Klaus-Uwe Panther. Without their constructive and helpful criticism the book would not have come into existence.

Doris Schönefeld
Leipzig, Germany
May 2011

Introduction

On evidence and the convergence of evidence in linguistic research*

Doris Schönefeld
University of Leipzig

1. Introduction

The kind of evidence employed in linguistic research is determined by the researcher's linguistic orientation and adherence to a particular theory, along with its respective methodological commitments. This also holds for the requirement of converging evidence, that is, of evidence or findings that converge on one and the same conclusion. Commonly, converging evidence is assumed to emerge when a phenomenon is analyzed from more than one methodological perspective (cf. Gries, Hampe, and Schönefeld 2005, 2010). In a discussion of evidence arising from such multi-methodological research, Arppe et al. (2010) elaborate on the benefits and the problems of such a research strategy and make a strong case for the combination of different types of evidence in the analysis of language. At the same time they point at a major challenge in this respect: to ensure the comparability of the concepts and constructs under analysis as well as of aspects considered to be informative about these, such as various types of frequency, reaction times, or ratings. Steen (2007: 21, this volume) identifies a second type of converging evidence that results from 'phenomenological pluralism'. The second type encompasses evidence gained from analyses of an allegedly identical phenomenon in different domains and is problematic in that it needs to be ensured that the phenomena are the same indeed (cf. below and Steen, this volume).

The concern with methodological issues, in particular the question of what kinds of evidence can and should be used in linguistic research, has been an almost constant companion in discussions about the definition of linguistics and its

* I would like to thank the two anonymous referees and the two series editors for their extensive and stimulating feedback on earlier versions of this chapter, which made it possible to improve it in a substantial number of respects. Any remaining insufficiencies are entirely my own.

philosophical position. The notion of converging evidence is a fairly recent one, and the question of what it may add to linguistic research was raised as a result of the application of empirical research methods in linguistics where the formulation of testable hypotheses and their verification are of central concern.

This introductory chapter aims at specifying some of the major issues and problems connected with evidence drawn from various sources. They are discussed in connection with the linguistic frameworks preferably employing them, keeping a constant eye on situations in which the convergence of evidence may become an issue. As a necessary prerequisite for such an endeavor, Section 2 specifies the notion of converging evidence. Section 3 looks at introspective evidence, favored in Generative Linguistics. Included there is a discussion of empiricism in Generative Linguistics, which may come as a surprise, since this connection seems to be a contradiction in terms from the perspective of the paradigm's rationalist origin. Section 4 is concerned with empirical evidence, which is discussed in connection with the linguistic framework of cognitive linguistics, as an essential characteristic of corpus-linguistic work and for its role in truly usage-based cognitive linguistics. This Section is central to the book, with the chapters collected here focusing on and demonstrating the use of empirical data in (cognitively oriented) linguistic analyses. Section 5 proceeds to summarize what kinds of "facts" and experience – data in the broadest sense – are at the linguist's disposal for making discoveries, before – as a kind of wrap up of the discussion – Section 6 motivates the need for evidence to converge. Section 7 gives a brief overview of the case studies assembled in this book in support of the argument about converging evidence. Finally, Section 8 considers some prospects for future research.

2. The potential of evidence to converge

In addition to the distinction of converging evidence according to its source (gained by different methods, or gained from different domains), it is necessary to discuss briefly and specify when the convergence of evidence is an issue.[1] The methods available in linguistic research are, roughly speaking, the employment of speaker intuitions and introspection, corpus data, experimentally elicited data, physiological data, and statistical methods (for more details see Section 5).

Looking at the first, 'non-empirical', method from the perspective of convergence of evidence, we can conceive of two situations where it matters. This is, firstly, when the analysis of a linguistic phenomenon does not rest on the linguist's

1. I am grateful to one of the reviewers for pointing out this requirement and for addressing the aspects that are being considered here.

intuitions alone, but when other people's intuitions are taken into account as well, as is common practice when theorizing is tested against grammaticality judgments. Secondly, convergence will definitely become an aspect to consider when analysts are willing to test their intuitions against (empirical) facts of the language under analysis, usage data, and experimental facts.

As far as 'empirical' methods are concerned, e.g. the use of corpus data and the elicitation of experimental data, the question of their comparative value arises in a way that is similar to the way evidence arises from phenomenological pluralism: Just as we must be careful in deciding whether evidence from different domains can be understood to stand for the same phenomenon tested (cf. below and Steen, this volume), corpus evidence and experimental evidence found or elicited for 'the same' hypothesis are not automatically about the same phenomenon either. Thus, convergence is not necessarily the default situation when corpus and experimental data are drawn on in hypothesis testing. We may also be faced with non-convergence, which, nevertheless, need not always falsify the hypothesis at issue. This may have various reasons. Firstly, such diverging evidence may be due to the different nature of the two types of data: corpus data reflect language as product, whereas experimental data, tapping language processing online, more directly reflect language as process. Hence, if a hypothesis/prediction is concerned with the status as a mental construct of a particular (linguistic) unit/phenomenon, it is the latter kind of data that has more weight and can be taken as evidential in this respect, and corpus data need not necessarily converge on that. On the other hand, if corpus data allow for the verification of a hypothesis, experimental evidence may diverge, if, for example, the factors assumed to account for the data are not the ones actually involved. Beger, in the final chapter of this volume, reports on a case where the results obtained from a corpus analysis and experimentally elicited data diverge. In such a situation, the experiment can be considered as diagnostic and as a valuable corrective. It potentially allows for the discovery of more plausible explanations for the data observed, and thus serves its purpose as a hypothesis tester, too. Secondly, divergence may result from testing language use at two different levels of generality. One method, data analysis, usually looks at the usage in a corpus. This, if it is meant to reflect a speech community's usage at a particular time (or over time), contains data that represent the use of language by many speakers, thus revealing intersubjective linguistic behavior (at aggregate level). Experimental data do not necessarily generalize over speakers so that what is tested is individual usage. That is why experimental results may, of course, be different from what is found in more 'general' usage, where individual differences may just average out.

Thirdly, the fact that experimenting allows for the control of factors that go uncontrolled in observed usage data can also account for results that do not converge on exactly the same conclusion. In such cases, divergence does not necessarily falsify one's hypothesis either, but it may indicate the need for the hypothesis to be refined. A situation like this represents an almost classical case of an empirical research agenda, illustrating the idea of the empirical cycle (elaborated in Section 4). Conversely, experimental findings may also be tested against corpus data, and as the study by Gries (this volume) shows, corpus analyses – in combination with sophisticated statistical techniques – can add to what has been found on the basis of experiments, too. Hence, in such scenarios, what at first may seem to be cases of divergence turn out to be cases of complementation and mutual cross-fertilization.

Against the background of the above clarifications, the following sections discuss various types of evidence linguistic research may draw on, with reference to the linguistic theories and models that favor them.

3. Introspective evidence

Sometimes, introspection is considered equivalent to intuition, though both concepts differ from each other in that they focus on subtly different aspects of using one's knowledge: intuition is concerned with gaining rational insight, grasping or seeing what something is or that something is true, and, hence, is a matter of processing information. Introspection is a kind of self-observation and rather a matter of making oneself aware of one's activities when grasping something. It can be paraphrased as observing, examining and describing one's thoughts (for a brief argument about the distinctions see e.g. Schütze (1996: 48–52)). In this sense of self-observation, introspection meets one criterion of empirical methods, where analyses are also based on observation, though admittedly on other-oriented observation. Itkonen (2003) sets introspection and intuition apart more clearly.[2] Understanding linguistics as a human science that is concerned with normative facts (cf. also López-Serena 2009), he attributes language to Popper's world 3 (cf. below) and postulates that investigations into language be based on intuition. He describes the essence of intuition as drawing on speakers' abilities to remember what they know of their language, what the norms of their language are (cf. Itkonen 2003: 41), and sets it apart from introspection and observation by linking each of them to one of the three Popperian ontological levels:

> [...] i.e. ontology divided into the 'worlds' of physical states/events, of psychological states/events, and of social concepts and/or norms. The labels for these worlds are 'w–1', 'w–2', and 'w–3'. Each of these worlds requires its own characteristic act of knowledge: w–1 = observation, w–2 = introspection, w–3 = intuition. [...] All three types of acts are potentially conscious; and, as subjective psychological acts,

2. I thank one of the reviewers for bringing this publication to my attention.

> they all emanate from w–2. (...) [...] There is an obvious conceptual interdependence between acts of knowledge and their objects. Observation is that which pertains to material or physical entities, and vice versa. [...] Similarly, intuition qua subjective act is that which pertains to social or intersubjective concepts/norms, and vice versa. (Itkonen 2003: 44–45)

As Itkonen emphasizes the social nature of language, it follows that intuition, "pertain[ing] to concepts or rules existing in an intersubjective normative reality" (Itkonen 1981: 128)), suffices for the description of a speaker's knowledge of a language, whereas introspection, being concerned with subjective sensations mainly caused by physical events, does not seem to play a part in linguistic analysis. This is at least a possible conclusion from Itkonen's understanding of language and the absence of this cognitive act in Itkonen's further elaboration. Observation is the method of data analysis, since data as results of material events associate with the intersubjective physical world (cf. Itkonen 1981: 128). Considering the relation between intuition (of norms) and observation (of corpus occurrences), Itkonen (2005: 359–360) points out "observation is connected to the quantitative analysis of actual utterances whereas intuition is connected to the qualitative analysis of conceptual possibilities". He gives prominence to intuition, since data analysis does only work on the basis of a speaker's/analyst's intuitive knowledge of the rules of the language (cf. Itkonen 2005: 361). Moreover, regarding our knowledge of norms, observation (or quantitative analysis) does not tell us what the norms are, exactly because norms, the entities of normative reality, are not observable (cf. Itkonen 1981: 128).

Geeraerts (2005: 171–182) discusses Itkonen's concept of intuition critically, and notes that, in practice, it is almost identical to that of introspection (in the understanding of Generative Linguistics) in that the latter also draws on a speaker's knowledge of linguistic conventions.

In this chapter, I do not distinguish between intuition and introspection; both terms are used interchangeably for methods of analysis that draw on the (native) speaker's knowledge of her or his language.

3.1 Introspective evidence – the (sole) source of insight in Generative Linguistics

In Generative Linguistics, the linguistic paradigm dominant in the second half of the twentieth century, studying language and modeling it is always equivalent to studying and modeling linguistic competence, i.e. native speakers' tacit knowledge of the grammar of their language. The generally accepted method to make this knowledge accessible and explicit is to consult the native speakers' intuitions about expressions or strings of words of their language. These intuitions are about the well-formedness of sentences and about sentence structure, and it is assumed that they can be unearthed by means of grammaticality judgments, where native speakers are asked to say whether a given sentence is well-formed or not and whether it has a particular structure or not (cf. also Radford 1988: 9). The judgments are used as evidence in the process of testing the hypotheses formulated, the theory or model constructed by the linguist. Once researchers have gained some affirmative evidence for the phenomena they postulate, they may proceed deductively to develop hypotheses of what it is to know a language into a more complex model or theory of language. For testing such (deduced) hypotheses, e.g. about a particular structure or structural principle of the language under analysis, expressions that either exhibit or deviate from the hypothesized principle can be constructed and again be tested for their grammaticality. As soon as these expressions are judged to be well-formed, this is taken as sufficient evidence for the correctness of the extrapolated structure or principle, and the judgment represents evidence in support of the theory from which the predictions have been generated. If they are judged to be ill-formed, the hypothesis must be revised or even discarded. From such a perspective, the ideal person for linguistic theory construction is a linguist who is also a native speaker of the language s/he studies. This is because the study of language is theory-driven and intuition-based, and the linguist would then profitably and conveniently represent the expert with respect to both (theoretical) linguistic knowledge and speaker intuition. When constructing a model/theory of some linguistic phenomenon and elaborating the predictions it generates, the linguist can simultaneously draw on intuitions of well-formedness.

Hence, hypothesis formation and testing in this framework draws on introspective evidence alone, it is the sole kind of evidence used in the process of constructing linguistic theory and is – for the sake of its acknowledgement and general acceptance – not required to converge with any other kind of evidence. By implying that competence can be known on the basis of intuition alone, or by deduction from intuited notions, the generative framework places itself in the philosophical tradition of rationalism, where, as Lehmann (2004: 188) puts it,

> [...] linguistic data play no role whatsoever, since the linguist only externalizes what is already in his mind. Representations of speech events are neither needed as a basis of inductive generalizations nor as touchstones of empirical verification or falsification of hypotheses deduced from the theory, since it is not an empirical theory.

A second explanation, suggested by one of the reviewers, for the generative linguists' lack of interest in performance data could be their understanding of grammar as a model generating all *possible sentences* of a language. These can indeed be inferred from grammaticality judgments by extrapolating the linguistic knowledge underlying them. Such a procedure is, however, in stark contrast with empirical approaches to linguistics, which are concerned with *actually occurring sentences*, from which grammatical knowledge is assumed to arise.

Hence, it does not come as a surprise that criticism of the restriction to, and the confidence in, introspection alone has been leveled from other, more empirically oriented, theoretical positions, such as functional and cognitive linguistics. Concerning the method of extracting the intuitions of native speakers the problem arises that grammaticality judgments are notorious for not being uniform.[3] Different speakers may disagree on the grammaticality of a particular structure just as well as one and the same speaker may feel different about the grammaticality of one structure at different times or in different situations, which indeed questions their diagnostic value. It is far from clear whether such judgments can be taken as direct measures of linguistic competence, because they seem to be influenced by a considerable number of other factors, such as the subjects' metalinguistic skills, which are not controlled for in the usual practice of eliciting the judgments. Hence, they need to be handled with care as regards their diagnostic significance (for a convincing demonstration thereof see Schütze 1996 (Chapters 3–5 in particular) and Keller 1998, for example).

The rejection of performance data for linguistic analyses within this framework follows from the assumption that they reflect competence imperfectly. They may be defective or ungrammatical, due to attention or memory lapses or other psychological factors such as tiredness or boredom, and must therefore be understood as contaminated by non-linguistic factors. Such 'flawed' performance phenomena as slips of the tongue, false starts or restarts, anacolutha, incomplete utterances, repetitions, and the like are not revealing about a speaker's linguistic knowledge: "Linguistic theory is concerned primarily with an ideal speaker-listener, ... who knows its [sic] language perfectly and is unaffected by such grammatically irrelevant conditions as memory limitations ... in applying his knowledge of the language in actual performance" (Chomsky 1965: 3).

Moreover, from the assumption that the set of sentences of a language is infinite, Chomsky (1957: 15) concluded that it is "obvious that the set of grammatical sentences cannot be identified with any particular corpus of utterances obtained by the linguist in his field work". A third argument against the suitability of corpora for linguistic description is that

3. This problem will not be discussed in detail. Suffice it to say that such concepts and factors as acceptability, context-sensitivity, and the understanding of grammaticality as a dichotomy (with the values + or -) or a continuum add to the complexity of grammaticality judgments and the feasibility of their 'translation' into a speaker's tacit knowledge of his language (for a discussion of the concept of grammaticality see e.g. Schütze 1996: 19–53, Fetzer 2004).

> [t]he problem for the linguist [...] is to determine from the data of performance the underlying system of rules that must have been mastered by the speaker-listener and that he puts to use in actual performance. [...] [T]his [information about the speaker- hearer's competence, D.S.] is neither presented for direct observation nor extractable from data by inductive procedures of any known sort. (Chomsky 1965: 4, 18; see also Itkonen's argument rendered in Section 2)

It is a logical consequence of the assumed impossibility of extracting the underlying rule system from real performance data that introspective judgments are required in generative theorizing (for a similar argument, cf. Riemer 2009: 661).

3.2 Generative Linguistics in more recent times – broadening the methodological spectrum

Even in Generative Linguistics, the discussion about research procedures and the value of particular types of evidence to be produced in support of one's ideas and claims, empirical data in particular, is enjoying a revival. In 2009, Volume 28.1 of the *Zeitschrift für Sprachwissenschaft* provided a platform for a debate on the issue of evidence from within the generative framework and from an external perspective. The general debate is about the relationship between empirical work and theory formation in linguistics, more particularly, the focus is on the kind of data employed in linguistic research, their nature, elicitation and interpretation.

First of all (and not surprisingly from a generative perspective), in most of the (framework-internal) papers, the relation between theory and empirical work is elaborated in one direction: it is a matter of the empirical foundation of (generative) grammar theory (cf. Fanselow 2009: 133). As a consequence of the priority given to deductive theory formation, the discussion about empiricism is qualified as not being of central concern, and if data are to be employed, this is only fruitful if the analysis is theory-driven, so that appropriate questions can be asked (cf. Fanselow 2009: 134).

A second point made is that the empirical methods currently available are insufficient and inadequate for the main goal of linguistic research (i.e. the formation of a theory modeling competence), and the argument is basically in favor of employing acceptability judgments. The judgments themselves would generate sufficient data for theory testing, the more so, when the data show variation which would need to be accounted for by the theory under construction. This procedure would represent a good method of empirical foundation, and the 'new' empirical methods could be employed in the clarification of the nature of differences in acceptability judgments in problematic cases (cf. Fanselow 2009: 136–137). Hence, it is not surprising that acceptability judgments and the concept of well-formedness are placed center stage. Meyer (2009: 141–150) elaborates on the latter and emphasizes its multi-dimensional nature, including such aspects as a linguistic unit's occurrence (in language use, incorporating the dimension of language variation), the frequency of occurrence, and its correspondence to a linguistic rule or regularity. He argues that this multi-dimensional approach is required if empirical facts, such as different data types, scalar values, sample effects, and the like are supposed to be accounted for, simultaneously pointing to the empirical challenge of appropriate operationalizations.

Meyer's article shows that the methodological discussion within the generative framework is no longer restricted to introspection, as, for example, information on occurrence and frequency of a linguistic unit can only be drawn from usage data. As far as their role in linguistic research is concerned, Schütze (2009) argues that data collected from corpora (the Web in this case) should supplement judgments. Just briefly commenting on 'idea-sparking' uses, he is more concerned with an 'evidentiary scenario', corresponding to the theory-driven procedure when corpus data are used as evidence for particular theoretical claims. He qualifies this procedure by saying that "merely having found instances of a construction of interest should not be construed as evidence of anything ipso facto" (Schütze 2009: 152), a qualification with which we could not agree more (cf. also Section 4.2). In addition, Schütze illustrates that the sole reliance on corpus examples has its drawbacks, concluding that search data cannot stand as evidence on their own:

> My view is that evidentiary uses of Web data require checking those data against the intuitions of live human speakers of the language. In case such verification fails, considerations should be given to how the exemplars might have arisen *other than* as genuine instances of use of the language in question, and how their frequency compares to relevant base rates. (Schütze 2009: 155)

This emphasizes and specifies a point also made by Sinclair (1991: 39) and McEnery and Wilson (1996, cf. also Section 4.2), that data need to be interpreted and evaluated, and that the rightful place of introspection is just there.

4. Empirical evidence

Before going into detail regarding the employment of empirical data in specific linguistic theories, we will look at what is common practice in empirical linguistic research in general.[4] With the proclamation of doing empirical research, linguists commit themselves to the 'empirical cycle', a methodological manual or programme first propagated for doing empirical research in the field of psychology by

4. For a complex argument on empirical linguistics see Sampson (2001).

Adriaan D. de Groot (1969). Following the steps suggested there, the linguist inductively produces generalizations and formulates hypotheses regarding particular phenomena on the basis of what he has observed and collected. These hypotheses are meant to explain the phenomena at issue and are simultaneously the ground from which to deduce consequences in the form of further (more general) testable predictions. Hypothesis formulation always needs to be accompanied with hypothesis testing – either by further observations, or by simulation or testing for specific factors in experiments and evaluating the results. The practice to be applied here is to look for data and/or design experiments for refuting the null hypotheses H_0 (rather than for verifying one's own, or alternative, hypotheses (H_1)). Such a procedure presupposes that the hypotheses formulated must be testable.

In short, the research agenda can be summarized to (ideally) comprise the following phases:

- observation
- descriptive research of what has been observed
- exploratory research (using inductive and deductive reasoning) resulting in the formation of (testable!) hypotheses
- analytical research of empirically testing these hypotheses and
- evaluation.

On the basis of such a strategy, the model envisaged by the researcher for the description and explanation of a particular linguistic phenomenon can be put on firm ground. When further elaborating and extending the model to cover more data, the researcher will traverse the cycle again, collecting more data, forming more general hypotheses, running experiments to test them, etc.

Empirical research in linguistics is most obvious in usage-based approaches, where, by definition, usage data are the prime source of linguistic discovery: they represent the observed facts from which hypotheses are inductively constructed and generalizations made which allow for predictions about further data. At the same time, data are an important source of evidence in that they are employed as the test case for the hypotheses made: New data must be in accordance with one's claims, and as soon as some data disconfirm them, the claims must be reconsidered and adapted so that they cover also the new data, or alternative explanations must be looked for, covering both the original and the new 'facts'. In some studies collected in this volume the usage data employed converge on the hypotheses to be tested (cf. Backus and Mos, Egan, Höche, Reshöft). In others, the data analyses result in a modification or refinement of the hypotheses made (cf. Beger; Borgwaldt and Benczes; Brandt and Kidd; Kaltenböck; and Steinkrauss). This situation is indicative of the potential of data analyses in general and for hypothesis testing in particular.

A second source of evidence associated with empirical research is elicited data, that is data available as a result of employing questionnaires and running experiments, where the elicitation may also be triggered by non-linguistic stimuli. The former data can either be categorized with introspective data (though in a more objective form, since they represent the intuitions of many speakers), or with empirical data. This depends on what the questions are intended to elicit: grammaticality judgments or the subjects' 'linguistic behavior' (e.g. as in translation or gap-filling tasks).[5]

Experimentation, which allows for the controlled elicitation of data, has its place in the phase of empirical hypothesis testing, where predictions following from intuition or the generalizations over usage data are put to the test. The study by Borgwaldt and Benczes is a case in point. Against the backdrop of the standard practice to formulate testable hypotheses, these may (but need not) also provide a pointer to the design of experimental studies. If an experiment can produce results refuting H_0, this adds to the validity of the alternative hypothesis. If the results do not corroborate the model envisaged, an explanation must be looked for, for example by checking all the (other) factors potentially involved in the experimental activity and controlling for them accordingly. If nothing can be identified, this should feedback to theory construction and give rise to re-thinking one's model.

In other words, traversing the empirical cycle is actually concerned with collecting evidence that converges on the same assumption(s). That is, a procedure in which a hypothesis was formulated on the basis of usage data and is tested in an experiment represents a showpiece of converging evidence in that results of two methodologically different analyses point to the same explanation of the observed phenomenon. The studies by Backus and Mos; Beger; and Brandt and Kidd pretty much follow such a strategy and reveal its usefulness and potential. Working through the phases of the empirical cycle, it is obvious that researchers will – deliberately or unconsciously – also consult their own knowledge of the language, their intuitions. The generalizations made and the interpretations given to the data do not come about independently of a researcher's theoretical orientation and presuppositions; hypothesis construction does not work without logical deduction from the facts AND predetermined conceptions. Even 'corpus-driven grammar', a radically empiricist approach to language description mainly developed by Hunston and Francis (2000, for example), where corpus data are analyzed for distributional patterns with a minimum of theoretical presuppositions, is not 'theory-free'. For, the identification of these patterns rests on the recognition of such notions as word categories, and, although these seem to be pre-theoretical at first sight, it must be noted that in the categorization process different criteria are susceptible to

5. This difference was brought to my attention by one of the reviewers.

different weightings – depending on the linguist's conviction: does one take notional, morphological and/or a distributional aspects as decisive for a word's category? That is the linguist's intuitions and theoretical predilections cannot be blocked completely. The important point to make from the perspective of empiricism is that the generalizations and hypotheses made by the linguist should indeed be data-based rather than theory-driven (which is in contrast to the practice in Generative Linguistics (cf. Section 3.2)) and that they must have been ascertained by a rigorous search for all available evidence and a judicious assessment of its probative value (for a more detailed discussion about different types of evidence to be used in linguistic theorizing see Schönefeld 2001: 110–113).

4.1 Empirical evidence – evidence naturally employed within Cognitive Linguistics

As has been shown, Generative Linguistics places itself in the logical tradition of linguistic research, mainly relying on deductive reasoning and introspection. Since the late 1980s, a competing linguistic paradigm has been emerging, cognitive linguistics, which, exactly as elaborated by Kuhn (1970) for the development of science on the basis of his studies of theories in physics and astronomy, clashes with much of the 'received wisdom' of Generative Linguistics.

Cognitive linguistics sees itself as a usage-based approach to the analysis of language. Hence, it is only natural that the research questions asked and tackled within its framework should also be approached from the perspective of language use or performance (from which also the grammatical knowledge (the competence) of a speaker is assumed to arise). Unlike the generative practice of eliciting intuitions by means of grammaticality judgments in order to test or validate their theoretical claims, usage-based research is empirical. This implies that theory construction starts out from the description and analysis of observable facts in the first place. The observable facts for the construction of a linguistic model are what we hear people say and see them write, i.e., it is performance data from which any generalization should be made. It is, however, crucial to note here again that also observational data are not 'pure' in the sense of theory-free. For, as soon as observations are processed and described, the observer needs to categorize and to make judgments as to what it is that has been observed, and this is always shaped by preceding experience, such as the observer's linguistic knowledge, the ideas he has about language (that is, the model he adheres to), his research tradition, other observations, and the like. We need to be aware of these influences that might skew observation (cf. Section 6), and one way to counteract this danger of 'seeing what one expects to see' or 'overlooking what one does not expect' is to look for converging evidence. Moreover, saying that theory formation in cognitive linguistics is data-based does not exclude introspection/intuition at all, but it will certainly have its place in the interpretation of the data and in the determination of their theoretical significance. Intuition is also important to cognitive linguistics for another reason, which follows from its central concern with meaning (understood as conceptualization). It is widely acknowledged that the analysis of a linguistic unit's conceptual content is most naturally and successfully accomplished by employing one's intuition. In Talmy's (2007: xiii) view, introspection is the only methodology allowing for direct access to meaning: "Meaning is a consciousness phenomenon and, if it is to be taken on as a target of research, introspection – itself a process occurring in consciousness – is the relevant instrumentality able to reach its venue". Harder (2007: 1248) argues along similar lines "since mental content is only accessible to human subjects, there is no way of getting at the central data without them [intuitions D.S.]". On the other hand, if meaning is understood as an effect of contextualized use, as function in context, it is mandatory to consult the corpus. Such a view of meaning was hold by Firth (1957: 11, 14), for example, who claims that a word's meaning is known by the company it keeps, and it eventually reflects in collocational analyses (e.g. Sinclair 1991), one of the first forms of corpus-linguistic work.[6] In cognitive-linguistic research, the interaction between a word's meaning and context is explicitly drawn on when the meanings of constructions are investigated by applying collostructional analyses (cf. Gries and Stefanowitsch (2004), Stefanowitsch and Gries (2003), (2005)). The focus on use is also present in modern cognitive-linguistic theorizing about the concept of meaning and is pushed quite far by Croft and Cruse (2004: 97), who propagate an approach "where neither meanings nor structural relations are specified in the lexicon, but are construed 'on-line', in actual situations of use", with the actual expressions figuring as just one of several components contributing partial clues to the construal (cf. Croft and Cruse 2004: 98).

Hence, unlike the introspective evidence considered sufficient in Generative Linguistics, drawing on (converging) evidence of different types suggests itself as essential for doing research within a data- or usage-based framework, which Cognitive Linguistics evidently adheres to.

In addition to the implicit methodological anchoring provided by the label 'usage-based', cognitive linguists have explicitly discussed methodological issues from the start. Lakoff (1990: 46) summarizes and generalizes for the methodology

6. Such an understanding of 'meaning' can be traced back to Malinowski, who – according to Steiner (1983: 57–58) – defines 'meaning' by referring to both 'function' and 'context': Meaning is function in context, it is use of language and not concept. The same concept of meaning is taken up and further elaborated by Halliday.

to be applied in cognitive linguistics that it needs to reflect the *generalization commitment* and the *cognitive commitment*:

> From my perspective, the generalization commitment is a commitment to linguistics as a scientific endeavor, a commitment to seek general principles. The cognitive commitment is a commitment not to isolate linguistics from the study of the mind, but to take seriously the widest range of other data about the mind. Neither of these commitments, in themselves, imposes a particular form on the answer. As such, they are methodological, not substantive commitments.

It is the latter commitment that hints at the requirement for evidence to converge on one conclusion, though the evidence Lakoff had in mind is of a different type from what has been discussed thus far. He was more concerned with the compatibility of claims made for linguistic phenomena with findings, or evidence, produced in neighbouring fields, such as psychology, neurology and biology, that is evidence as a product of 'phenomenological pluralism'.

Assessing the cognitive-linguistic enterprise, Langacker (1999: 23–37) makes a statement on 'some methodological principles', too. He argues for such basic principles (shared with functional linguists) as "... concern with the integrity of one's data, the need for precise formulations leading to testable hypotheses, the desirability of accounting for a wide range of phenomena with a limited set of constructs" (Langacker 1999: 24). The latter, corresponding to Lakoff's generalization commitment, he sees embodied in Cognitive Grammar's assumption that any linguistic unit is symbolic, i.e. a form-meaning pairing. Following from this, grammar and lexicon are 'the same' in that they represent symbols. They are nevertheless distinguishable in that they exhibit different degrees of symbolic specificity, complexity and entrenchment (cf. Langacker 1991: 44).

Regarding the formulation and testing of hypotheses, Langacker specifies as the most fundamental methodological principle "to look for converging evidence from multiple sources" (Langacker 1999: 26). He illustrates this commitment for particular linguistic constructs (such as profiling and search domain, for example) by drawing on evidence from three different sources. The constructs

> are shown to be necessary for the adequate semantic description of multiple phenomena in various languages. ... [to be] commensurate with (if not identical to) independently observable cognitive abilities. ... [to be] critical for the explicit characterization of varied grammatical phenomena. (Langacker 1999: 27)

This, again, is an appeal to look for evidence for allegedly the same constructs from different domains of investigation. Or, to put it differently, the researcher is invited to consult evidence from different domains and test whether it can be assumed to converge on the same conclusion. Again, this is the type of evidence described and discussed as a product of 'phenomenological pluralism'.

From a more external perspective, the one of a psychologist, Gibbs (2007) critically evaluates cognitive-linguistic research with a particular focus on the way the researchers arrive at their theories and hypotheses. In the (cognitive) psychologists' view, cognitive linguistics is not yet really empirical, because objective scientific experiments are not common practice. They criticize cognitive linguistic work for a lack of objective evidence in the form of objective, replicable data gained from experimental tests:

> What is needed [...] is for cognitive linguists to be more sensitive to some of the important properties of framing experimental hypotheses (e.g. constructing falsifiable hypotheses, considering alternative hypotheses), and trying to articulate their ideas, and empirical findings in ways that may be tested by scholars in other disciplines. (cf. Gibbs 2007: 17)

Even if we take this to be a rather pessimistic description of the situation, it seems to hint at a gap between aspirations and reality in cognitive-linguistic research, and Gibbs's criticism needs to be taken seriously. So it does not come as a surprise that criticism is leveled at a quantitatively (and at times also qualitatively) unsatisfactory use of empirical methods also from within the cognitive-linguistic paradigm. Geeraerts (2006) elaborates on the tensions between the inclination towards empirical methods (almost 'inherent' to a usage-based form of linguistic investigation) and the reality of the still dominant traditional introspective methodology of conceptual analysis. He argues against this suboptimal situation (cf. Geeraerts 2006: 39–44) and encourages the application of empirical methods, also in the field of semantic analysis. Successful attempts at analyzing such outspoken semantic-conceptual phenomena as metaphor on the basis of corpus data (cf. Stefanowitsch and Gries 2006) make it obvious that this is a promising way to go. However, for the current situation, it must be admitted that neither empirical methods nor the consultation of different types of evidence can be rated as the default situation in cognitive-linguistic research.

All in all, the work done by linguists who feel affiliated to the cognitive framework, shows no restriction in their methodology to the sole employment of just one type of evidence, namely that of introspective reasoning. As proponents of a usage-based approach to language, cognitive linguists draw on the analysis of performance data, and should primarily do so: they search data for regularities and more general patterns, and draw conclusions as to their motivation(s) and what they mean with respect to our linguistic and cognitive functioning. They also take data as the test case for their theoretical claims. It has also been shown that there is considerable demand for improvement both in the phases of the formation of (testable) hypotheses and (empirical) testing. This needs to be added to the list of desiderata in cognitive-linguistic research. Accordingly, testable hypotheses and their testing are in the focus of most of the contributions to this volume.

4.2 Empirical evidence – an essential characteristic of corpus linguistics

In parallel with, but independently of, the developments in the cognitive-linguistic paradigm, the discussion of methodological issues was also provoked by corpus-linguistic work, which defines itself on the basis of the methodology employed: the observation of naturally occurring data. As the label makes obvious, corpus linguistics is usage-based by definition. It takes its discoveries and findings from the observation of actual usage and introspection – the collected data need to be interpreted. The use of corpora as the principal source for describing language marks corpus linguistics as a field adhering to an empiricist view of scientific inquiry (cf. also Leech 1992: 107–111), placing it in the philosophical framework of empiricism. Knowledge is drawn from observable data, the data are replicable and allow for verification/falsification on the basis of further data. In the wake of this empirical orientation, Stubbs (1993: 8) requires that "[l]anguage should be studied in actual, attested, authentic instances of use, not as intuitive, invented, isolated sentences". In accordance with Schütze (cf. Section 3.2), it needs to be emphasized that it does not suffice to rely for testing one's hypotheses on a small number of authentic instances only, but that a representative inventory of data needs to be employed.[7] McEnery and Wilson (1996: 1–19) likewise characterize corpus linguistics as resting on (computer-aided) empiricism, which makes it a systematic and rigorous approach, but they also make a strong point of its affinity to cognitive rationalism. They suggest that the best possible research strategy is to view corpus- and introspection-based approaches to linguistics as complementary:

7. I am aware of the problem of the concept of 'representativeness' of corpora and corpus data. The former is topicalized in almost any publication about corpus linguistics (e.g. Sinclair 1987; Biber 1992 (2005); McEnery and Wilson 1996; Biber, Conrad, and Reppen 1998), and will not be discussed here. Suffice it to say that representativeness as such is so multi-faceted a phenomenon that, though it can be checked or achieved for particular parameters, it is extraordinarily difficult to achieve in full. In this respect, the concept compares to that of 'equivalence' in translation studies. The consequence arising from this was spelled out by one of the reviewers, commenting that the desideratum of a representative corpus leaves us with two options, the first of which is more preferable: (i) either representativeness is regarded as a challenge to be faced, or (ii) linguists should restrict themselves to making claims about corpora rather than about mental representations of linguistic data. The question of 'representativeness' (or rather significance) of corpus data is taken up in Section 4.3.

> [...] artificial data can have a place in modern corpus linguistics. Yet it should always be used with naturally occurring data which can act as a control, a yardstick if you will. Corpus linguistics is, and should be, a synthesis of introspective and observational techniques, relying on a mix of artificial and natural observation.
> (McEnery and Wilson 1996: 16)

In practice this means that text corpora serve as the empirical foundation on which the analysis of linguistic units, their properties and relations rests. The automatic, systematic and quantitative analysis of corpora is seen as the prerequisite for hypothesis formation and hypothesis testing (though not to the exclusion of introspection and logical extrapolation), since they represent both the linguistic material over which to generalize and an objective test case for the researcher's hypotheses. In the first case, hypothesis formation, corpus analyses aim at the identification and exploration of linguistic entities and regularities. In this phase, the analyst's theoretical background assumptions will, as has already been hinted at in Section 4, play a role and it is important that they be made explicit. In particular, when the corpora used are tagged, parsed and/or semantically annotated, the information that can be gathered from them will be affected by theoretical preconceptions and decisions linked with the tagging, parsing and annotation procedures respectively. Theory and introspection will have to enter the scene in exploratory research, when assumptions are made as to which theoretical constructs the identified linguistic facts are indicative of.

In the second case, hypotheses – no matter if formed on the basis of corpus-linguistic analyses or deduced by extrapolation – are tested against corpus data and, if confirmed, can be made the basis for making further testable hypotheses. Two things require special care in this phase: It is important to formulate potentially falsifiable hypotheses (cf. the argument in 4.1), and it is decisive for the proper functioning of the test that the variables of one's hypothesis are operationalized in a way that what is measured or counted actually represents a factor involved in the theoretical construct being tested. For the decision of how the variables in the researcher's hypothesis can or need to be investigated in corpus-based research, Gries (2009: 177–178) suggests, "you answer two interrelated questions. Firstly, 'what will I perceive when I perform our study and observe the values/levels of the variable involved?' Secondly, 'which mathematical concept will I use – counts/frequencies, averages, dispersions, or correlations?'" The second question makes it obvious that in corpus linguistics the corpus is not just used for the identification of interesting linguistic phenomena, but is systematically and exhaustively searched so that frequencies of occurrence can (easily) be calculated and be analyzed for what they could mean for the construction of a linguistic model. A careful quantitative evaluation of the data elicited from a representative corpus opens the analysis to the incorporation of probabilistic aspects, if data variation can be shown to relate to particular contextual and co-textual factors, for example. These are aspects notoriously difficult to capture on the basis of introspection alone, as was pointed out by Sinclair (1991: 39) from early on:

> The problem about all kinds of introspection is that it does not give evidence about usage. The informant will not be able to distinguish among various kinds of language patterning – psychological associations, semantic groupings, and so on. Actual usage plays a very minor role in one's consciousness of language and one would be recording largely ideas about language rather than facts of it.

He concludes from this that the rightful place of introspection is in the evaluation of evidence rather than in its creation.

In much the same way corpus analyses are also carried out when results of earlier studies need to be confirmed or replicated, or when the results of studies having drawn on data other than those collected from corpora are to be validated.

Since almost all the case studies collected in this volume incorporate corpus analyses (in the sense of systematic and exhaustive searches allowing for quantitative evaluation), they exactly fit this methodological pattern: the authors' own (or other) hypotheses are tested against (new) corpus data. The (more general and deeper) insights following from such a strategy may trigger suggestions and questions for further experimental investigation, as is shown by Backus and Mos; Beger; and Brandt and Kidd (cf. also Section 4).

4.3 Empirical evidence – towards a truly usage-based approach in cognitive linguistics

Since the methodological aspirations of cognitive linguistics obviously coincide with what has been received practice in (computer) corpus linguistics for quite some time, it is not surprising that, quite recently, there have been successful attempts at an explicit unification of cognitive-linguistic theorizing and corpus-linguistic methodology. Studies exemplifying this procedure were encouraged, promoted and collected by Gries and Stefanowitsch in two volumes (2006), and they make a convincing case for the fruitfulness of corpus-linguistic techniques for the analysis and explanation of phenomena that are of central interest within the cognitive-linguistic framework, namely the lexicon-grammar continuum and metaphor and metonymy. The explicit turn to corpus-linguistic methodology (as the most likely form of usage-based approaches applied there) in cognitive linguistics is also discussed by Tummers, Heylen, and Geeraerts (in different orders, 2005, 2008). It is basically three points that need to be taken up here to complete the picture of the types of evidence designed so far: quantification, significance testing, and multifactorial analyses. The first two activities are associated naturally in that significance testing presupposes quantification. They are required in corpus-based studies to evaluate the position and relevance of the discovered phenomena in the language under analysis and a model thereof. Raw frequencies and percentages, however, are difficult to evaluate and interpret. For example, for an interpretation of the frequency of two co-occurring words, we would need to know what the expectation for their co-occurrence is on the basis of the total occurrences of both words at issue. In technical terms, we need to have a baseline frequency against which the observed frequency can be evaluated and tested for its significance. In Tummers's et al. (2005: 235) words, this is a general requirement in corpus-based research: "In order to identify the relevant, i.e. significant, features of language use, descriptive and inferential statistical techniques have to be used". Significance tests tell us whether it is justified to extend one's findings from the sample analysis to the total population, i.e. to the language under analysis. In this respect, they are indispensable in order to be able to tell apart pseudo-findings from real findings, with the former turning out to be accidental coincidences in a corpus and the latter representing the meaningful relations or phenomena which are important for the theoretical modeling of the language under analysis.

As Tummers et al. (2005: 242) point out, frequency counts have another shortcoming, namely that of not allowing for the control of other factors potentially involved in the distribution of the phenomenon analyzed. Though it is conceivable to consider all the potentially relevant factors in separate analyses, this would not help in the identification of possible interactions between them. That is why multifactorial analyses have been introduced to usage-based analyses, allowing for the simultaneous analysis of the impact on the dependent phenomenon of several factors as well as of the interaction between them (as shown by Gries 2003, this volume, and publications of the research team *Quantitative Lexicology and Variational Linguistics* at Leuven University, for example).[8] Heylen et al. (2008) elaborate at length and in great detail and discuss critically the use of several types of multivariate statistics in cognitive-linguistic research. For details, the interested reader is referred to this text.

To conclude, the current situation in usage-based cognitive-linguistic analysis can be described as gradually extending its methodology from frequency-oriented systematic and exhaustive corpus analyses (for the recognition of probabilities and trends in language use) to the more sophisticated statistical testing of explanations for the findings made.[9] The more advanced studies also take into account the

8. The people most prominently involved in the group's research activities are Dirk Geeraerts, Dirk Speelman, and Stefan Grondelaers.

9. 'Exhaustive' is meant in the sense of searching the complete corpus for the phenomenon at issue and drawing on the full list of extracted data.

complexity of language by looking for – and also developing – multifactorial methods so that as many variables as have been found to be influential on the phenomenon under analysis can be incorporated into the analysis. The studies in this volume can be situated in this area: usage-based cognitive linguistics. The most advanced study in this respect is the one by Gries, who discusses and demonstrates more sophisticated statistical testing and the employment of multifactorial analyses in linguistic research.

5. Data in linguistic research – a summary and overview

In the previous sections, various types of evidence employed in linguistic research were introduced and discussed, introspective data and corpus data in particular. Experimentally elicited data were also mentioned, though in passing, and statistical methods for determining the significance of empirically triggered findings.

Haspelmath (2009: 158) takes an even broader perspective, listing and discussing eight different types of data systematically in relation to the questions they could help to answer. He notes that all data having been used in linguistic analyses have shown to be relevant in principle. We will add to our data survey those that have been referred to only briefly or not at all. Experimental data (elicited in psycholinguistic tests) were already mentioned as evidence used when testing hypotheses following from generalizations over usage data (see Section 4) and they are shown to be informative by the studies of Backus and Mos; Beger; and Brandt and Kidd. Haspelmath points to another function experimental data may have in linguistic research: they are required for research into the regularities of a speaker's mental grammar, because the mere encounter in corpora of a particular linguistic unit or construction does not say anything about its mental representation (cf. the argument in Section 2). Another type of data adds to exactly this kind of research question: physiological data, such as fMRI and ERP, resulting from neuro-linguistic investigations. However, the problem with physiological and experimentally elicited data alike consists again in the potential interference of other factors. Since both in experiments and in the observation and measurement of people's physiological reactions to particular stimuli many factors must be assumed to be involved in the cause and effect relation to be tested, the results produced and observed can only be interpreted with great caution. Effects (the dependent variable) attributed to the factor assumed to be tested (the independent variable) may just as well be caused by one or more factors not even known to be involved in the experimental task. It is exactly here that the need for converging evidence becomes straightforwardly obvious: if the results of several experiments and/or measurements allow for the same conclusions, this adds to their explanatory power.

Schlesewsky (2009: 177) argues in a similar vein, focusing on the discrepancy between multidimensional data and unidimensional interpretations in current psycholinguistic research. Interestingly, he sees in this discrepancy a potential reason for the felt gradient character of many data, which may simply follow from a negligence of factors that are also part and parcel of the issue under analysis. The solution he envisages is methodological pluralism. The development and installment of multifactorial analyses also in cognitive linguistics (cf. Section 5 and the study by Gries) is a promising way to go and improve the quality of empirical research in this field. Notable examples include Gries (2003: blurb), whose aim is to "demonstrate the superiority of corpus-based, multifactorial and probabilistic approaches towards grammatical phenomena over traditional analyses based on acceptability judgments and minimal pair tests", and the publications by the QLVL research team. In Heylen et al. (2008), the authors broadly and critically discuss the approaches by both Gries and colleagues and the QLVL group, exploring "how they can complement each other", and arguing that "these two approaches have the potential to converge into a single promising methodology for empirical usage-based research" (Gries 2003: 93).

A second point raised (and bemoaned) by Schlesewsky is an asymmetrical interaction between theory and empirical work. The latter would always be aimed at experimentally validating theoretical assumptions, without theory-incompatible data having repercussions in theory formation (cf. Schlesewsky 2009: 175–176). However, this asymmetry is naturally counterbalanced in usage-based accounts, where data are not only the test case for hypotheses but also the basis from which these are formulated in the first place. Moreover, the studies by Kaltenböck and Brandt and Kidd also serve as examples of how 'theory-incompatible' data can and should be handled in an approach that is responsive to the data and takes them seriously.

From all this and from what has been found in the more general discussion of introspective and empirical evidence in linguistic research, it turns out that neither introspection nor empirical data can be used to the exclusion of the other. Rather, linguists seem to use the two types of data at different stages of their research agendas and, hence, for different purposes, depending on the research tradition they work in. This is what makes Gast (2006: 114) conclude that "'empiricism' and 'rationalism' should be regarded as scalar rather than complementary opposites, and what we should really talk about is the way responsibility can be apportioned between observation and reasoning for an accurate description and analysis of language".

6. Conclusion to the discussion

6.1 Why evidence is needed to converge

Concluding the discussion of the types of evidence linguistic theorizing should draw on and the merits and problems inherent in the individual types, I argue lastly – from a usage-based perspective – that all types are required: usage data, introspection, and experiment, and that a converging evidence approach suggests itself as the order of the day, for various reasons.

First of all, as has been made explicit, each of the types is particularly suitable for particular phases in the empirical cycle. Typically, the analysis of usage data is prominent in descriptive and exploratory research, where it may be complemented by (the analyst's and/or his subjects') introspection. Experimentation is prominent in analytical research, where also multifactorial analyses may be employed and significance testing has its place. It is, however, also not uncommon to use further usage data here, for the replication of previous findings or their corroboration in different conditions, for example. A research algorithm relying on just one sort of evidence and neglecting the others will always imply the risk of being insufficient in that certain aspects or factors might be wrongly interpreted or totally overlooked.

This already implies that, secondly, there is no restriction to one particular type of evidence to be drawn on in the respective phases of the research cycle. It is especially useful to employ different types of evidence produced by different methodologies in the phase of hypothesis testing. If in this phase, (comparable) evidence resulting from methodological pluralism can be shown to converge on one and the same conclusion, this adds to the probability of the tested hypothesis being correct or true. Diverging evidence should start an investigation into potential causes, before actually refuting the hypothesis tested (see Section 2). The usefulness and potential of such a procedure becomes apparent in the majority of the studies collected here: Backus and Mos; Beger; Brandt and Kidd; Borgwaldt and Benczes; Egan; Höche; Kaltenböck; Reshöft; and Steinkrauss. These studies cover a wide variety of linguistic phenomena, above all from the fields of semantics and language acquisition, and prove both the practicality and the effectiveness of this research strategy.

Evidence arising from phenomenological pluralism may also be employed in the verification process of a claim, though with due care only, namely if the phenomena brought into a relationship can be shown to actually relate in the way assumed in independent analyses.

In addition to this practice, which can be considered as a general recommendation for usage-based research, a number of concrete situations and examples have been mentioned in the course of the argument in which the search for converging evidence is indicated:

- Evidence converging on the same conclusion would reduce the risk of generalizations and hypotheses being skewed by the researcher's linguistic experience and predilections.
- Searching for converging evidence is appropriate for the analysis and explanation of such a complex and multi-faceted phenomenon as language. The many factors being involved in any verbal activity need to be recognized and controlled for, and there are at least two strategies the researcher can adopt: multifactorial analyses and checking the effect of (at least some of) the factors assumed to be responsible for the verbal behavior under analysis in a number of different experiments. Compatible results would definitely buttress the researcher's hypotheses and conclusions respectively. Gries' study (this volume) puts forward a convincing case for the importance of and the gain to be achieved from deciding on the appropriate type of multi-factorial analysis that fits the research question best.
- Along similar lines, converging evidence adds to the weight of a hypothesis, i.e. to the probability of a hypothesis to be true. This would be the case if, for example, a data-based hypothesis can be corroborated by results elicited in experiments probing the same phenomenon in a more controlled way.
- Converging evidence is needed to determine the significance of a finding: Since all usage-based research works on the basis of samples only, inferential statistics is required in addition to (simple) frequency counts to separate accidental findings from (theoretically) informative ones.

Furthermore, there are also other scenarios in which the search for a convergence of evidence should be put on the research agenda:

- Converging evidence is desirable to avoid unjustified generalizations: individual observations or analyses do not allow for generalizations or the postulation of a theoretical construct, if they are not backed up by at least further observations of the same type (replication studies). They would have much more explanatory power, if they could be corroborated as a result of employing other methodologies.
- Converging evidence is desirable to guard the researcher against what is known as the confirmation bias. It is natural that observations that coincide with the researcher's theoretical assumptions are taken as confirming evidence and are given great mental weight. On the other hand, observations that contradict these assumptions are taken as exceptions and hardly leave a mental trace. In an even stronger form, such a bias can result in a selection

bias, so that the researcher dismisses evidence that disconfirms his hypothesis (or rather confirms the null hypothesis). In such a situation, the theory becomes more important than the question being investigated, so that the evidence is made to fit, instead of being used to test, the theory. In the 'worst-case scenario', the neglect of contradictory observations may cause untenable ideas to become 'received wisdom' and lead to the construction of false theories. Schlesewsky (2009: 173) reports such a case from the realms of neurolinguistics, where the initial interpretation of neuro-physiological data was maintained and drawn on in later studies, although meanwhile data had been produced which disprove it. A more widely known example to emphasize the reality of this danger is the adherence of generative grammar theory to transformations (up to the development of the Minimalist Program), although experiments designed in the 1960s to produce evidence for the cognitive costs of such operations could not corroborate their psychological reality.

- Converging evidence is desirable in situations in which the data at issue may be interpreted by several hypotheses. The decision between such competing hypotheses can be promoted by further, independent evidence. Such a strategy was shown to be effective by Gries, Hampe, and Schönefeld (2005, 2010) for example, who approached the question of what is the better predictor for the association between a word and a construction, frequency or collostruction strength, from both a corpus-based and an experimental perspective.
- Converging evidence is desirable when testing hypotheses resorting to (conditioning) factors from the field of language processing. To be sure, corpus data can suggest assumptions regarding language-processing procedures, but they should not be made the only evidence in the verification process. For, the corpus does not give first-hand information on what was actually going on in the formulation process of the written and spoken text respectively. In order to tap the procedures going on in language production and comprehension, experimentation should follow in the research agenda to test whether the hypotheses formulated on the basis of corpus findings can be corroborated (cf. Section 2).

6.2 Converging evidence in practice

In the contributions to the volume at hand, converging evidence is lived in practice. From a (predominantly) cognitive-linguistic perspective, all of them illustrate a research strategy that draws on at least two different methodologies. Thus, they demonstrate a pluralism of methods in one project and study respectively rather than giving a general survey of the methodological potential available to (cognitive) linguists. This feature sets the present volume apart from another book-length study explicitly concerned with methods in cognitive linguistics, González-Márquez et al. (2007: xxii), a volume "intended as a handbook to exploring the empirical dimension of the theoretical questions raised by C[ognitive] L[inguitics]". That book may be seen as a prerequisite to the book at hand.[10] Whereas the former discusses the broad spectrum of empirical methods available to cognitively oriented linguistic research, the focus in the present volume is on the use of corpus data, not least because corpus-based approaches are currently enjoying a heyday, also in (cognitive) linguistics. Most of the contributions collected in this volume can be located within this context. They report on studies in which corpus data were employed in combination with the various other methodological tools discussed above. The corpus data are processed and evaluated either in more 'traditional' qualitative analyses based on raw frequencies or in quantitative corpus analyses. This way the studies show how corpus data can be systematically searched, analyzed, and interpreted for the elucidation of linguistic problems, also using statistical methods and techniques. In addition, the present volume also illustrates how experimentally elicited findings and those from other domains can be employed as evidence for the claims one makes with respect to a particular linguistic phenomenon. A brief summary of each contribution is presented in Section 7.

7. The contributions to this volume

As has been seen, this introductory chapter has taken a theoretical stance on the issue of evidence and its convergence. It has considered what counts as evidence in linguistic research in general and in usage-based (cognitive) research in particular and has located the chapters collected in this volume within this debate.

In the lead chapter that follows, **Gerard Steen** takes a reverse perspective, starting out from a central research question raised in cognitive linguistics (the nature of metaphor) and developing an argument about the value of the method of converging evidence in cognitive linguistics. Steen argues that metaphor constitutes a showcase for the method, but that it equally constitutes a showcase for the difficulties involved in handling converging evidence. In Steen's view, the notion of converging evidence typically displays a conflation between two phenomena, which he labels 'phenomenological pluralism' and 'methodological pluralism' (cf. Steen 2007). The latter is acknowledged for its potential to produce converging

10. The foreword, in which Talmy (2007) discusses different types of evidence for their pros and cons and for their suitability to the investigation into particular research phenomena or questions, is of special importance also to the concern here.

evidence, the former is characterized as exciting and attractive, but problematic, which is explicated in detail.

The body of this volume is subdivided into three parts that focus on investigations into different linguistic phenomena: meaning, language acquisition, and discourse. As specified by the book's theme, the studies are concerned with evidence from more than one source, seeking to test their hypotheses against at least two types of evidence: introspectively gained evidence and evidence gained from the analysis of empirical data in the form of corpus data or experimentally elicited data. When a third methodology is incorporated into a study, it is the experimental elicitation of data in order to test individual factors assumed to be involved in the phenomenon under analysis in a controlled way.

7.1 Part 1: Multi-methodological approaches to constructional and idiomatic meaning

Chapters 3–9, constituting Part 1 of the volume, examine the role of corpus-based and experimental evidence in the analysis of constructional and idiomatic meanings. Two are concerned with cognition verb constructions.

In the first, **Thomas Egan** uses corpus data to test introspective interpretations of the '*see* x *to be* y' construction proposed in the 1970s, and finds his data to converge on these intuitive hypotheses, thus contradicting earlier findings based on work with smaller corpora.

Gunther Kaltenböck's chapter investigates the syntactic status of clause-initial *I think* followed by a so-called complement clause and in doing so illustrates how quantitative and qualitative corpus analysis can be used to gain insights into syntactic structure. The analysis of syntactic and prosodic aspects of a construction yields various types of evidence, which at first glance seem incompatible but can be accounted for in a grammar that allows for a dynamic relationship between usage and structure and incorporates a diachronic dimension.

The second sub-group in Part 1 contains three chapters that focus on constructional alternatives.

Silke Höche looks at similarities and differences of the '*be about to* V' and the '*be going to* V' patterns from a cognitive-linguistic, usage-based perspective, incorporating several sources of insight. Her comparative investigation of the two patterns demonstrates the successful integration of two sources of evidence: introspection in conjunction with prior attempts at spelling out formal and functional features of the constructions, and corpus investigation in conjunction with inferential statistical analysis.

Using the dative alternation as an example, **Stefan Th. Gries** investigates syntactic priming on the basis of corpus data from the British component of the

International Corpus of English. The methodological point of this chapter is the use of an 'unusual' source of evidence, as syntactic priming is a phenomenon almost exclusively investigated through experimenting. He finds that the results of his analyses do not only converge on those gained from experimental data, but also go beyond them, making additional factors visible that are significantly involved in priming.

Ad Backus and **Mario Mos** analyze two Dutch constructions expressing likelihood and possibility for their productivity and semantic overlap. The analysis of the '*is tee* V' construction and the 'V-*baar*' construction exploits two sources: it draws on both corpus data in conjunction with inferential statistical analysis and experimental data in the form of acceptability judgments. The results of both types of analysis converge on the identification of the same similarities and differences of the constructions and speak for the existence of the constructions as entrenched patterns.

The final two chapters in Part 1 use the respective methodologies for the investigation of idioms and creative language use.

Alexander Ziem and **Sven Staffeldt's** chapter is concerned with the analysis of idiomatic uses of a body-part term, *finger*, on the basis of corpus data and extrapolations from a basic tenet of cognitive linguistics, that meaning is grounded in experience. On the basis of evidence from corpus data, they suggest that the hypotheses following from the 'embodiment' position need to be refined.

Susanne Borgwaldt and **Réka Benczes** study word formation strategies in two typologically different languages (German and Hungarian) by eliciting data from native speakers in a novel-object naming task. Apart from replicating results from studies of German they carried out earlier, their findings require the refinement of hypotheses made for Hungarian.

7.2 Part 2: Multi-methodological approaches to language acquisition

The three chapters in Part 2 focus on the collection and use of empirical evidence in the investigation into language acquisition, another field that is prominently represented in usage-based research. Again relying on at least two types of evidence, two studies enquire into the L1 acquisition of particular constructions.

Rasmus Steinkrauss uses longitudinal data from a German child's acquisition of a group of wh-questions in order to test the assumption that acquisition is largely determined by the input frequency with which the child experiences the respective constructions. His results show that further factors need to be considered to account for what happens in acquisition, namely the function(s) of the constructions at issue and what has already been acquired before.

Silke Brandt and **Evan Kidd** provide evidence for truly usage-based strategies in children's acquisition and use of relative clauses. Comparing corpus data of such constructions with the results from two experimental tasks, they find that children perform best with those types of relative clauses that are the most frequent exemplars in usage data, reflecting that children give careful consideration to subtle factors of the input they are exposed to.

Nina Reshöft seeks to identify typological differences in the expression of motion events by Romance learners of English. The analysis of corpus data reveals that these learners show a tendency to transfer their L1-specific lexicalization patterns for the expression of motion events to their interlanguage, thus producing evidence for the assumed distinction between verb-framed and satellite-framed languages.

7.3 Part 3: Multi-methodological approaches to the study of discourse

Part 3 is represented by one study. **Anke Beger** turns to an analysis of experts and laymen's use of emotion metaphors in the discourse of counseling. What she finds from the analysis of corpus data is then tested against data elicited in a guided interview. The latter data turn out to be complementary to the former in that they reveal a new factor to be causally related to the use of the respective metaphors. This speaks for the efficiency of a research strategy that uses evidence from multiple sources.

8. Convergence of evidence: Prospects for future research

The studies collected in this book give proof of the feasibility and usefulness of multi-methodological analyses of linguistic phenomena, recommending them as an endeavor worth pursuing. In the conclusion to the discussion (Section 6.1), the increased power and efficiency of using multi-source evidence was pointed out, but it also needs to be kept in mind that such a research strategy is not without its pitfalls and challenges, one of which is the broad methodological expertise required for pursuing it. For example, the researcher must be aware of the exact nature of the different types of evidence obtained, so that the comparability of the evidence can be assumed if not ensured (cf. also Arppe et al. 2010: 4–5). As far as evidence resulting from phenomenological pluralism is concerned, it is strongly suggested that the respective expert knowledge is pooled and shared. That is, future research will, in all probability, benefit from collaborative and interdisciplinary work. For usage-based research into language, potential collaborators are – besides psycholinguists – psychologists and sociologists, for example, who could contribute both their expertise in their fields and their methodological know-how. For, in social research, the (multi-methodological) sociological approach, also known as the triangulation (of methods) has been practiced for some time (cf. Olsen 2004: 103), and in psychology it is also gaining ground (cf. Flick 2004).

A second aspect to guide future research, addressed in Section 4.3, is elaborated and discussed by e.g. Gries 2003, Tummers et al. (2005), and Gries (2006) and concerns quantification in empirical/usage-based research. The former two argue for the use of quantitative techniques in usage-based linguistics. More particularly, they advocate the use of multivariate statistics for the explanation of language phenomena, because such statistics make it possible to consider the manifold factors involved in language use in their complex interaction (cf. Tummers et al. 2005: 243). The latter (cf. Gries 2006: 198, 200) emphasizes the necessity for (corpus) linguists to use more powerful statistical tools (than raw frequencies), to do rigorous statistical testing, and to employ such measures as effect size and confidence intervals in the validation of their empirical results.

From these considerations, the cornerstones for future research in empirical linguistics are evident: more multi-methodological research and more quantification.

References

Arppe, Antti et al. 2010. Cognitive corpus linguistics: Five points of debate on current theory and methodology. *Corpora* 5: 1–27.

Biber, Douglas. 2005. Representativeness in corpus design. In Geoffrey Sampson & Diana McCarthy, eds., *Corpus Linguistics. Readings in a Widening Discipline*, 17–197. New York: Continuum.

Biber, Douglas, Susan Conrad, & Randi Reppen. 1998. *Corpus Linguistics. Investigating Language Structure and Use.* Cambridge: CUP.

Chomsky, Noam. 1957. *Syntactic Structures.* The Hague: Mouton.

Chomsky, Noam. 1965. *Aspects of the Theory of Syntax.* Cambridge, MA: MIT Press.

Croft, William & D. Alan Cruse. 2004. *Cognitive Linguistics.* Cambridge: CUP.

De Groot, Adriaan D. 1969. *Methodology: Foundations of Inference and Research in the Behavioural Sciences.* The Hague: Mouton.

Fanselow, Gisbert. 2009. Die (generative) Syntax in den *Zeiten der Empiriediskussion. Zeitschrift für Sprachwissenschaft* 28: 133–139.

Fetzer, Anita. 2004. *Recontextualising Context: Grammaticality Meets Appropriateness.* Amsterdam & Philadelphia: Benjamins.

Firth, John R. 1957. A synopsis of linguistic theory, 1930–1955. *Studies in Linguistic Analysis* Special Volume. Philological Society: 1–32.

Flick, Uwe. 2004. *Triangulation. Eine Einführung.* Wiesbaden: VS Verlag für Sozialwissenschaften.

Gast, Volker. 2006. Introduction. *ZAA* 54.2: 113–120.

Geeraerts, Dirk. 2005. Lectal variation and empirical data in Cognitive Linguistics. In Francesco J. Ruiz de Mendoza & Sandra Peña Cervel, eds., *Cognitive Linguistics: Internal Dynamics and Interdisciplinary Interaction*, 163–189. Berlin: Mouton de Gruyter.

Geeraerts, Dirk. 2006. Methodology in Cognitive Linguistics. In Gitte Kristiansen, Michel Achard, René Driven, & Francisco J. Ruiz de Mendoza Ibánez, eds., *Cognitive Linguistics: Current Applications and Future Perspectives*, 21–49. Berlin: Mouton de Gruyter.

Gibbs, Raymond W. 2007. Why cognitive linguists should care more about empirical methods. In Monica Gonzalez-Marquez, Irene Mittelberg, Seana Coulson, & Michael J. Spivey, eds., *Methods in Cognitive Linguistics*, 2–18. Amsterdam & Philadelphia: Benjamins.

González-Márquez, Monica, Irene Mittelberg, Seana Coulson & Michael J. Spivey. eds. 2007. *Methods in Cognitive Linguistics.* Amsterdam & Philadelphia: Benjamins.

Gries, Stefan Th. 2003. *Multifactorial Analysis in Corpus Linguistics: A Study of Particle Placement.* New York: Continuum.

Gries, Stefan Th. 2006, Some Proposals towards a More Rigorous Corpus Linguistics, *ZAA* 54 (2): 191–202.

Gries, Stefan Th. 2009. *Quantitative Corpus Linguistics with R: A Practical Introduction.* New York: Routledge.

Gries, Stefan Th, Beate Hampe & Doris Schönefeld. 2005. Converging evidence: Bringing together experimental and corpus data on the association of verbs and constructions. *Cognitive Linguistics* 16 (4): 635–676.

Gries, Stefan Th, Beate Hampe & Doris Schönefeld. 2010. Converging evidence II: More on the association of verbs and constructions. In John Newman & Sally Rice, eds., *Experimental and Empirical Methods in the Study of Conceptual Structure, Discourse, and Language*, 59–90. Stanford, CA: CSLI.

Gries, Stefan Th. & Anatol Stefanowitsch. 2004. Covarying collexemes in the into-causative. In Michel Achard & Suzanne Kemmer, eds., *Language, Culture and Mind*, 225–236. Stanford: CSLI Publications.

Gries, Stefan Th. & Anatol Stefanowitsch. 2006. *Corpora in Cognitive Linguistics: Corpus-Based Approaches to Syntax and Lexis.* Berlin: Mouton de Gruyter.

Harder, Peter. 2007. Cognitive Linguistics and Philosophy. In Dirk Geeraerts & Hubert Cuyckens, eds., *The Oxford Handbook of Cognitive Linguistics*, 1241–1265. Oxford: OUP.

Haspelmath, Martin. 2009. Welche Fragen können wir mit herkömmlichen Daten beantworten? *Zeitschrift für Sprachwissenschaft* 28: 157–162.

Heylen, Kris, José Tummers & Dirk Geeraerts. 2008. Methodological issues in corpus-based Cognitive Linguistics. In Gitte Kristiansen & René Dirven, eds., *Cognitive Sociolinguistics: Language Variation, Cultural Models, Social Systems*, 91–128. Berlin: Mouton de Gruyter.

Hunston, Susan & Gill Francis. 2000. *Pattern Grammar: A Corpus-Driven Approach to the Lexical Grammar of English.* Amsterdam: Benjamins.

Itkonen, Esa. 1981. The concept of linguistic intuition. In Florian Coulmas, ed., *A Festschrift for Native Speaker*, 127–140. Mouton: The Hague.

Itkonen, Esa. 2003. *What is Language? A Study in the Philosophy of Linguistics.* Turku: Abo Akademis tryckeri.

Itkonen, Esa. 2005. Concerning the synthesis between intuition-based study of norms and observation-based study of corpora. *SKY Journal of Linguistics* 18: 357–377.

Keller, Frank. 1998. *Grammaticality Judgments and Linguistic Methodology.* Retrieved on 18 May 2009 from http://biblioteca.universia.net/ficha.do?id=41569708 & http://citeseerx.ist.psu.edu/viewdoc/summary?doi=10.1.1.52.2559.

Kuhn, Thomas. 1970. *The Structure of Scientific Revolutions.* Chicago: The University of Chicago Press.

Lakoff, George. 1990. The invariance hypothesis: Is abstract reason based on image-schemas? *Cognitive Linguistics* 1: 39–74.

Langacker, Ronald W. 1991. *Foundations of Cognitive Grammar 2.* Stanford, CA: Stanford University Press.

Langacker, Ronald W. 1999. Assessing the cognitive linguistic enterprise. In Theo Janssen & Gisela Redeker, eds., *Cognitive Linguistics: Foundations, Scope and Methodology*, 13–59. Berlin: Mouton de Gruyter.

Leech, Geoffrey. 1992. Corpora and theories of linguistic performance. In Jan Svartvik, ed., *Directions in Corpus Linguistics*, 105–122. Berlin: Mouton de Gruyter.

Lehmann, Christian. 2004. Data in linguistics. *The Linguistic Review* 21 (3–4): 275–310.

López-Serena, Araceli. 2009. Intuition, acceptability and grammaticality: A reply to Riemer. *Language Sciences* 31: 634–648.

McEnery, Tony & Andrew Wilson. 1996. *Corpus Linguistics*. Edinburgh: EUP.

Meyer, Markus. 2009. Sprachliche Wohlgeformtheit – eine kritische Bestandsaufnahme. *Zeitschrift für Sprachwissenschaft* 28: 141–150.

Olsen, Wendy. 2004. Triangulation in Social Research: Qualitative and Quantitive Methods Can Really Be Mixed. *Developments in Sociology* 20: 103–121.

Radford, Andrew. 1988. *Transformational Grammar. A First Course*. Cambridge: CUP.

Riemer, Nick. 2009. On not having read Itkonen: Empiricism and intuitions in the generative data debate. *Language Sciences* 31: 649–662.

Sampson, Geoffrey. 2001. *Empirical Linguistics*. London: Continuum.

Schlesewsky, Matthias. 2009. Linguistische Daten aus experimentellen Umgebungen: Eine multiexperimentelle und multimodale Perspektive. *Zeitschrift für Sprachwissenschaft* 28: 169–178.

Schönefeld, Doris. 2001. *Where Lexicon and Syntax Meet*. Berlin: Mouton de Gruyter.

Schütze, Carson T. (1996) *The Empirical Base of Linguistics: Grammaticality Judgments and Linguistic Methodology*. Chicago: The University of Chicago Press.

Schütze Carson T. 2009. Web searches should supplement judgments, not supplant them. *Zeitschrift für Sprachwissenschaft* 28: 151–156.

Sinclair, John McH. 1987. *Looking up: An Account of the Cobuild Project in Lexical Computing*. London: Collins ELT.

Sinclair, John McH. 1991. *Corpus, Concordances, Collocations*. Oxford: OUP.

Steen, Gerard. 2007. *Finding Metaphor in Grammar and Usage*. Amsterdam & Philadelphia: Benjamins.

Steiner, Erich. 1983. *Die Entwicklung des Britischen Kontextualismus*. Heidelberg: Julius Groos.

Stefanowitsch, Anatol & Stefan Th. Gries. 2003. Collostructions: Investigating the interaction between words and constructions. *International Journal of Corpus Linguistics* 8: 209–243.

Stefanowitsch, Anatol & Stefan Th. Gries. 2005. Covarying collexemes. *Corpus Linguistics and Linguistic Theory* 1.1: 1–43.

Stefanowitsch, Anatol & Stefan T. Gries. 2006. *Corpus-based Approaches to Metaphor and Metonymy*. Berlin: Mouton de Gruyter.

Stubbs, Michael. 1993. British traditions in text analysis: From Firth to Sinclair. In Mona Baker, Gill Francis, & Elena Tognini-Bonelli, eds., *Text and Technology*, 1–33. Amsterdam & Philadelphia: Benjamins.

Talmy, Leonard. 2007. Foreword. In Monica González-Márquez, Irene Mittelberg, Seana Coulson & Michael J. Spivey, eds., *Methods in Cognitive Linguistics*, xi–xxi. Amsterdam & Philadelphia: Benjamins.

Tummers, Jose, Kris Heylen & Dirk Geeraerts. 2005. Usage-based approaches in Cognitive Linguistics: A technical state of the art. *Corpus Linguistics and Linguistic Theory* 1–2: 225–261.

Issues in collecting converging evidence

Is metaphor always a matter of thought?*

Gerard J. Steen
VU University Amsterdam

In empirical research, metaphor constitutes a showcase for the difficulties involved in handling converging evidence, which typically displays a conflation between two scientific phenomena, 'phenomenological pluralism' and 'methodological pluralism'. Phenomenological pluralism is exciting but problematic, and involves the evaluation of evidence produced by different methods of data collection and analysis across distinct areas of research, pertaining to distinct phenomena of investigation. Methodological pluralism, by contrast, is widely accepted as able to produce converging evidence – it pertains to using different methods of data collection and analysis within one distinct area of research, so that evidence may be legitimately claimed to point to the same conclusion about the same phenomenon.

Keywords: data analysis, data collection, methodological pluralism, phenomenological pluralism

1. Introduction

Cognitive linguists present their work as being about thought. The most brazen expression of this position can be found in Fauconnier and Turner's (2002) *The Way We Think*. Other titles are equally explicit, but always emphasize the connection between thought and language (e.g. Coulson and Lewandowska-Tomaszczyk 2005; Dirven and Pütz 1996; Fauconnier 1997; Panther and Radden 1999; Turner 1996). This is because the basic idea of cognitive linguistics is that central features of language, including metaphor and metonymy, are essentially a matter of thought, which is meant to suggest that these phenomena arise out of largely general

* I am grateful to the Netherlands Organization for Scientific Research, NWO, for grant 277-30-001, "Metaphor in discourse: Linguistic forms, conceptual structures, cognitive representations", which made this research possible.

cognitive processes which may also be reflected in other modalities than language, such as gesture and visuals (cf. Langacker 1987, 1991). Thus metonymy has been defined as "a cognitive process in which one conceptual entity, the vehicle, provides mental access to another conceptual entity, the target, within the same cognitive model" (Radden and Kövecses 1999: 21). And metaphor is *understanding* one thing in terms of another (Lakoff and Johnson 1980: 4). The question whether metaphor is a matter of thought is therefore a non-issue in cognitive linguistics.

If metaphor is a matter of thought, it should always be a matter of thought. Yet recent psycholinguistic discussion suggests that this depends on what you mean by 'thought'. If you mean the conceptual system of the abstract idealized native speaker of a language, then it might be true that metaphor can always be seen as a matter of thought: in the style of some of the most prolific cognitive-linguistic writers, there is plenty of evidence which suggests that, in our culture, 'we' tend to 'think' of love as a journey, time as money, ideas as objects, or happy as up. The postulation of these so-called conceptual metaphors is a hypothesis about the abstract conceptual system and its use by the idealized native speaker of a language, and it may be able to explain much of the structure of metaphor in language.

However, if 'thought' is taken as referring to the psychological processes of concrete individuals when they produce or receive linguistic expressions of metaphor, or when they acquire and maintain a particular language, then we have a different situation. Then it looks as if not every metaphor triggers a cross-domain mapping or non-literal comparison in the way predicted and widely assumed by cognitive linguists. If 'thought' is taken as processing, psycholinguists now assume that there is too much counter-evidence against the hypothesis that metaphor is always a matter of thought. That hypothesis has been rejected and replaced by the following, more precise question: under which conditions does a metaphor trigger a cross-domain comparison, and when does it not (Glucksberg and Haught 2006: 215; cf. Gentner and Bowdle 2008; Glucksberg 2008)?

In this paper I will suggest that answering this question is obviated by the two distinct meanings of the term 'thought' briefly invoked just now, and that cognitive linguists need to be more careful in their use of the term. First, there is the notion of thought as the conceptual structure that is an abstract representation of the knowledge of the idealized native speaker of some language. This definition may be employed either from a systematic perspective, which is concerned with the abstract world knowledge of that idealized native speaker, and which may be connected to the abstract linguistic knowledge of that same idealized native speaker. Or it may be employed from a usage-oriented perspective, which deals with instantiations of that conceptual system in specific (sets of) linguistic expressions. This is another way of invoking the old linguistic distinction between competence and performance, which is still a useful opposition that is not restricted to generative linguistics and can be connected without difficulty to cognitive-psychological work on performance versus competence.

Second, there is the notion of thought as a concrete, situated psychological process and its products, some mental representation(s). This is a matter of the cognitive behavior of individual people. This is a psychological notion of thought that may equally well be employed from a system-oriented or a use-oriented perspective, which in turn would lead us into a consideration of issues about psychological competence versus performance.

The difference between these two notions of thought can be characterized theoretically and empirically. Theoretically, when 'thought' refers to the conceptual system of the abstract idealized native speaker of a language, we are dealing with a semiotic (or some prefer 'symbolic') approach to thought. Such an approach looks at concepts in the same way as linguists look at linguistic constructions as part of the linguistic system of an abstract idealized native speaker of a language. Both concepts and linguistic forms and expressions can be seen as part of sign systems and their use, as has been well explained by for instance semiotician Umberto Eco (1976) and his main source of inspiration, Charles Sanders Peirce. This would have to be aligned with a linguistic interpretation of the notions of competence and performance.

By contrast, but still theoretically, when 'thought' refers to the psychological processes that are part of concrete people's competence and performance, we are dealing with a behavioral (in this case psychological) approach to thought. Such an approach looks at concepts in the same way as psycholinguists look at linguistic constructions in cognitive processes such as production, reception, and language acquisition. Concepts are then seen as part of individual people's conceptual systems called their mental encyclopedia, just as words can be studied behaviorally as part of people's mental dictionaries. Examples of this approach may be found in Markman (1999) and Murphy (2002). Such a psychological approach to thought includes attention to the underlying system of knowledge which has to be acquired and maintained by human beings, which is also referred to as competence; and it also includes attention to the utilization of that system in events of usage, which is also referred to as performance. That human beings display individual differences in these areas is a well-known fact that is essential to the psychological study of competence and performance (cf. Blasko 1999).

Empirically, the semiotic description of the knowledge of the abstract idealized native speaker is not identical with the psychological description of the cognitive processes and products that are displayed by individual language users (e.g. Gibbs 2006). The cognitive-linguistic analyses of metonymy and metaphor, whether as language or thought, are typically semiotic and based on analyses of linguistic forms and their presumably connected concepts; speculative accounts of cognition are offered by many cognitive linguists, but these do not necessarily capture what may be observed about the genuine psychological products in individual people's cognition, or the processes that have led up to them. That type of research requires the analysis of behavioral data. Metaphor may be a matter of thought from a semiotic perspective, but that does not make it into a matter of thought from a psychological perspective.

The distinction between the semiotic and psychological conceptualizations of thought has often been played down or ignored in cognitive linguistics. This has initially been productive because it led to an encompassing and ambitious research agenda in which many different phenomena that had been somewhat neglected for a long time were re-connected and placed at the centre of the stage. For instance, the innovative theoretical notion of conceptual metaphor in the idealized language user's encyclopedia could only have been proposed and developed in this way; the same goes for the postulated relations between metaphorical conceptual structures in the encyclopedia and their corresponding linguistic forms in the lexico-grammar; diachronic metaphor, or the role of metaphor in language change, is another product of this combination or conflation of the semiotic and the psychological approach; and all of these proposals also produced a framework for testable models for cognitive processing.

These wide-ranging developments led to the accumulation of evidence pointing to the possibility that these semiotic analyses also capture the psychological nature of metaphor. This has triggered much exciting work in cognitive linguistics, along the lines referenced in the opening paragraph above. Yet this possibility is regarded as a theoretical proposal, at most, by most psychologists. Indeed, Murphy (1996, 1997) and Boroditsky (2000) have complained that the cognitive-linguistic models of metaphor processing are not even precise enough for experimental testing (cf. McGlone 2007). And the psycholinguist most sympathetic to the cognitive-linguistic enterprise, Ray Gibbs, has proposed no fewer than four alternative interpretations of the possibility that metaphor is a matter of thought, most of which do not involve 'thought' in the psychological conceptualization adumbrated here (e.g. Gibbs 1999). In cognitive psychology and psycholinguistics it is therefore not a fact that metaphor is a matter of thought in the sense of individual people's long-term knowledge and its short-term use in language processing; at most it counts as an interesting theoretical proposal that needs much more work. That metaphor would be a matter of thought is therefore not a non-issue at all.

In this paper I argue that the perceived discrepancy between metaphor-as-thought in abstract conceptual structure versus metaphor-as-thought in actual cognition does not mean that the original cognitive-linguistic ideas about metaphor in thought need to be abandoned. What the discrepancy does point to is a need for more precision about what is theory and what precisely may be accepted as established fact. Moreover, the gap also points to the need for more precision about the interpretation of the cognitive-linguistic theory and its predictions about metaphor in thought for distinct areas of research. These two consequences affect the interpretation of various types of evidence as potentially converging, or not. It may also influence the practice of those cognitive linguists who like to refer to their work as having to do with thought.

2. Metaphor in symbolic structure and practice versus in cognitive process and product

The two distinct interpretations of metaphor as thought are the joint result of the cognitive turn in metaphor studies. In the late seventies of the twentieth century, a number of key publications appeared which signaled the definitive shift from taking metaphor as a mere matter of language to taking metaphor as a matter of thought (Ortony 1979; Honeck and Hoffman 1980; Lakoff and Johnson 1980). This shift of perspective from language to thought includes newly forged connections between thought on the one hand and, on the other hand, metaphor in usage and metaphor in grammar (Steen 2007). Thus, conventionalized metaphorical meanings have been systematically described at all levels of lexico-grammar, notably morphological, lexical, phraseological, and more abstractly constructional. The application of these conventionalized metaphorical meanings in concrete events of usage involving text and talk has also been widely studied. Moreover, the grammatical model was extended to the study of sign language, while usage oriented studies spread to include metaphor expressed by visuals and gesture. All of these linguistic phenomena in grammar and usage have been analyzed in cognitive linguistics as 'motivated' by underlying patterns of 'metaphorical thought', in which conceptual structures were mapped from one domain onto another irrespective of their material mode of expression (cf. Gibbs 2008).

The cognitive-linguistic findings present a case for the ubiquitous and natural existence of 'metaphor in thought' if that is interpreted as the conceptual system and its use in symbolic practice (of the idealized native speaker, that is). It also constitutes a case for the presence of metaphor in several semiotic codes such as language, visuals, and gesture, as a reflection of 'metaphorical thought'. The impact of all of this has clearly been revolutionary (even though the insights were not original but dependent on a long line of intellectual inquiry, going back all the way to Nietzsche and Vico – cf. Jäkel 1999). New applications included the study of polysemy, 'inference patterns', language change, cross-linguistic patterns, and so on (cf. Lakoff and Johnson 1999), and these have yielded exciting new ideas and insights.

However, the ubiquitous presence of metaphor in our symbolic systems and practice does not entail that *all* metaphor has now *always* become a matter of *thought* if this is taken to refer to what individual people do. This would mean that the metaphorical mappings that may be observed in the semiotic analyses of conceptual structures should also be observable in individual behavior. For grammar, then the conventionalized metaphorical meanings at all levels of lexico-grammatical structure should be attached to conventionalized metaphorical mappings in people's individual conceptual systems. And for usage, any metaphorical meaning at all levels of lexico-grammatical structure in a usage event should be attached to metaphorical mappings in people's individual working memory during processing. Only then can it be maintained that metaphor in thought analyzed as symbolic structure and practice is the same as metaphor in thought analyzed as individual cognitive behavior (Steen 2007).

Psycholinguistic evidence about metaphor in processing (usage) does not support this equation between symbolic practice and psychology. The first stage of the research shows that Gibbs (1994) and others presented evidence that was compatible with the idea that metaphor in usage required the activation of two domains that then needed to be bridged by a cross-domain mapping. Since the early nineties, however, Sam Glucksberg and his associates have contested this position and presented evidence that metaphor does not work via cross-domain mapping but via abstraction, which goes via superordinate categorization (Glucksberg 2001). Moreover, Glucksberg also showed that, when metaphors cease to be novel and become conventional, they do not require such abstraction by superordinate categorization anymore and simply become polysemous (e.g., 2008). Glucksberg's alternative to the cognitive-linguistic position has more recently been combined with the cognitive-linguistic position of metaphor as cross-domain mapping in one encompassing theory of metaphor processing advanced by Gentner and Bowdle (2001, 2008; Bowdle and Gentner 2005), called the Career of Metaphor. Experimental evidence shows that the question whether metaphor can be observed in thought during processing depends on the interaction between metaphor's conceptual structure (conventionality versus novelty) and its linguistic form (metaphor versus simile).

The most important conclusion from both the work by Glucksberg and his associates and by Gentner and Bowdle is that it is only novel metaphor that always gets processed as metaphor in thought, that is, by the activation of two domains of which one is the original source domain. Most other metaphor does not need this type of cross-domain mapping, simply because it involves conventionalized figurative meaning that is directly available from the individual's mental lexicon. Thus when people talk about argumentation and use 'war' terms such as *attack* or *defend* to do so, they would typically use the conventionalized and already available argumentation senses of those 'war' terms instead of accessing their war knowledge and utilizing that to set up an argumentation sense.

The exception to the rule uncovered by the Career of Metaphor researchers is when conventional metaphor is expressed as a simile, not a metaphor. In that case, the original source domain meaning of the metaphorically used term is relevant again, as in *That business is like a goldmine*. In such a case, we are asked to set up a metaphorical comparison between the business and a goldmine, instead of only retrieving the conventionalized figurative meaning of the word *goldmine* ('an activity which brings you lots of money').

This is the type of exception that may be able to account for some of the positive evidence previously produced by Gibbs and others, which was compatible with the idea that metaphor in thought as symbolic structure and practice was indeed predictive of metaphor in thought in cognitive processing. I have suggested that this may in fact have to do with a much broader issue which does not relate to simile alone: the deliberate nature of simile and other forms of metaphor, which, by their linguistic form, posit an ineluctable invitation to the addressee to construct a metaphorical mapping (2008; 2010).

Another issue in the classic cognitive-linguistic proposals about metaphor as thought is the questionable priority assigned to basic or concrete meanings of words in individual processing. Why should language users always go to all the trouble of accessing concrete meanings that have to do with physical defending and attacking and so on, if the argumentation senses of the same words are readily available? It would mean that language users would naturally prefer to take a detour, by-pass available conventional meanings, set up conceptual structures in a war domain and only then project onto the target domain of argumentation. This would fly in the face of another basic tenet in cognitive linguistics, that the use of conventionalized lexico-grammar is highly usage-based (Barlow and Kemmer 2000; Bybee and Hopper 2001; Tomasello 2003). Language users tend to learn in order to improve their performance and competence; their learning process is not just restricted to conceptual metaphors, but also includes figurative senses of words and other language forms. Moreover, their individual learning process does not mimic the history of the language: they are offered linguistic expressions that already have particular conventionalized meanings, which they do not have to reconstruct from scratch (Tomasello 1999, 2003).

In this connection it is important to remember that it has been empirically shown that people cannot ignore metaphors (Glucksberg, Gildea, and Bookin 1982). When people have encountered a metaphorical meaning sufficiently often for them to store it in their mental lexicon, as opposed to or next to their encyclopedia, they can use it directly. The conventionalized metaphorical sense can even become more salient and accessible than the original more concrete basic meaning (Giora 2003). Again, in special circumstances, for instance deliberate metaphor use, people may indeed take a detour in order to follow the instructions of the writer or speaker; but this precisely means that in other cases they do not have to do so. This is why the research issue in psycholinguistics has now become 'when is metaphor processed metaphorically' – instead of assuming that metaphor is always processed metaphorically and therefore a matter of thought in both the psycholinguistic and the cognitive-linguistic sense (Steen 2008).

The Career of Metaphor offers the beginning of a psycholinguistic account of metaphor's relation to thought that is compatible with the usage-based perspective that is essential to cognitive linguistics. It posits that metaphor in thought begins as a genuine cross-domain mapping, requiring some form of comparison, when it is novel. But then metaphor can get stored and conventionally used by means of a process of superordinate categorization in thought, and by metaphorically motivated polysemy in language. This holds unless metaphor is expressed as a simile, which prompts for the use of a cross-domain mapping in thought again. This complex position formulated by Gentner and Bowdle (2008) can be seen as one specific variant of one of the four alternative hypotheses presented by Gibbs (1999) about the relation between metaphor in language and thought. And it needs to be further developed by attending to the issue of deliberate metaphor use (Steen 2008; 2010).

One possible counter-argument to this view might come from those who favor the embodied nature of metaphorical meanings, such as Gibbs (2006) and others. Yet, the evidence presented in those types of studies does not necessarily mean that we always understand language via basic, typically concrete meanings first. That connections between metaphorical and basic meanings are preserved in the brain is one thing. They may even facilitate some deliberate uses of conventional metaphor. However, the activation of concrete senses of words that are used metaphorically does not need to guide the complete understanding process. In particular, it does not force the language user to access a complete conceptual domain in order to set up a source that is then needed to project unto a target. The difference between lexical access with temporary activation of metaphorical and concrete meanings, on the one hand, and the actual process of conceptual mapping when it does in fact take place, on the other, needs to be examined much more closely before any far-reaching conclusions can be drawn in this respect.

3. Phenomenological pluralism

We have seen that 'metaphor-as-thought' can mean more than one thing, and that the two theoretical definitions discussed so far do not necessarily lead to identical approaches and therefore characterizations of reality 'out there'. I have described the underlying methodological differences that play a role here with reference to three dimensions (Steen 2007):

I. Language versus thought
II. Grammar versus usage
III. Symbol versus behavior (or semiotic analysis of signs versus psychological analysis of cognitive processes and products)

When it comes to observing 'metaphor in thought', these dimensions produce a three-dimensional space in which distinct cells require slightly different types of data and observations. What counts as metaphor in one area does not necessarily count as metaphor in another. An overview of these differences is shown in Table 1.

Table 1 shows that the notion of metaphor as thought can refer either to row 2, or to row 4, or to rows 2 and 4 together. Cognitive linguists like to take rows 2 and 4 together, claiming that both rows can present converging evidence for what they claim is the same thing. Psycholinguists, by contrast, take row 4 as their home territory. To them row 2 does not involve empirical research that is comparable to what happens in row 4, simply because it is not research about cognitive processes and products (behavior) but about conceptual symbols, which represent a different reality to psychologists as long as such symbols stay abstracted away from real people's minds. To most psycholinguists, row 2 can at most be used as theoretical input for behavioral models pertaining to row 4.

Table 1. Areas of research for cognitive-linguistic approaches to metaphor in language

		Metaphor in grammar	**Metaphor in usage**
Approached as symbolic structure	*Approached as language*	When does a conventionalized linguistic form-meaning pairing count as metaphorical?	When does any linguistic form-meaning pairing in text and talk count as metaphorical?
	Approached as thought	When does a conceptual structure related to a conventionalized linguistic form count as metaphorical?	When does a conceptual structure related to any linguistic form in text and talk count as metaphorical?
Approached as behavior, whether process or product	*Approached as language*	When does the storing, acquisition or even loss of a conventionalized linguistic form-meaning pairing count as metaphorical?	When does the production or reception in text or talk of any linguistic form-meaning pairing count as metaphorical?
	Approached as thought	When does the storing, acquisition, or even loss of a conceptual structure related to a conventionalized linguistic form count as metaphorical?	When does the production or reception in text or talk of a conceptual structure related to any linguistic form count as metaphorical?

The crucial question for cognitive linguistics in the present context is whether the cognitive-linguistic definition of metaphor as thought, that is, metaphor as always involving a mapping between two conceptual domains, can now be maintained. I would like to submit that the answer to this question can be affirmative, as long as we recall that metaphor as thought is a matter of theoretical definition, or 'conceptualization', not necessarily of fact. This means that the single theoretical definition does not have to lead to the same kind of research in different areas and, what is more, the same kinds of outcome for every area on the map displayed in Figure 1. This is best explained with reference to the various stages of the empirical cycle of research (cf also Schönefeld, this volume), which work differently for diverging areas and, concomitantly, phenomena in the field.

I have argued that the empirical cycle in metaphor research (and elsewhere) may be profitably divided into five stages (Steen 2007). These mutually affect each other, but they need to be kept apart from a functional, methodological perspective. Figure 1 shows how this may be schematically depicted.

Even when cognitive linguists and psycholinguists adhere to the same conceptualization of metaphor as a matter of a cross-domain mapping, this identical theoretical definition can lead to distinct operational definitions for research. This is because translating such a conceptualization into an operational definition involves the selection of variables that can be observed and measured in distinct areas of research. Since the areas are different, the variables are different, too.

Concentrating on metaphor as a matter of 'thought', we should look at rows 2 and 4 of Table 1. As for row 2, we need an operational definition for observing metaphor in thought approached as conceptual structure from a semiotic perspective

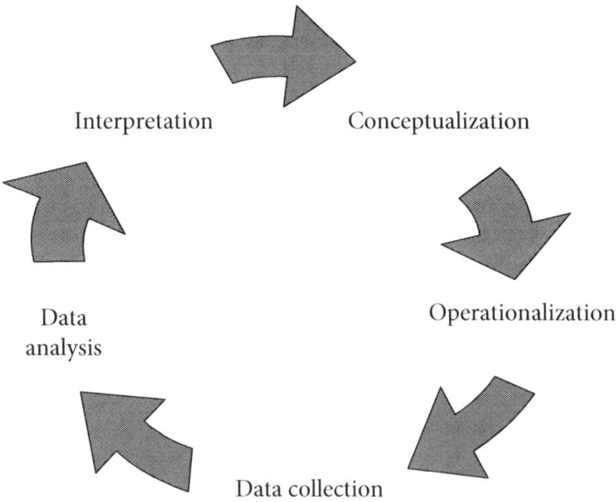

Figure 1. The empirical cycle

– whether this applies to grammar or to usage. This means that we need evidence for the presence of at least two distinct concepts that are related by a cross-domain mapping (non-literal comparison) in abstract conceptual (symbolic) systems and their use. The best objectification of this phenomenon may be found in computational conceptual networks such as WordNet (e.g. Lönneker-Rodman 2008).

As for row 4, we need an operational definition for observing metaphor in thought approached as conceptual structure from a behavioral perspective – again, irrespective of whether this applies to grammar or to usage. This means that we need evidence for the activation and use of distinct concepts that are related by a cross-domain mapping in on-going psychological processes and their products – typically long-term for grammar, and short-term for usage. This objective involves observing people in action, either in their natural environments or in a lab. For instance, when people consciously and deliberately use aspects of one domain to talk about another domain by means of non-literal comparison, then it may be concluded that they have activated both domains in their cognitive processes. (How it can be determined that this is what we see is a rather different and difficult matter.)

When psychologists test their theories about cognitive processes and their products, they typically prefer observation of manipulated behavior in the lab because it gives them more control about the behavior that is studied. To put this differently, if this control is lacking, there are typically too many alternative explanations of the behavior that is observed, so that the research cannot give clear answers to the question under examination. This is why psychological research on metaphor in thought is typically experimental. It is also why psychologically oriented research on metaphor in thought by means of observation, as in discourse analysis and applied linguistics, is hesitant to draw conclusions from what people say and do about what people think (e.g. Cameron and Low 1999).

More important, however, is the difference in purport of the evidence collected for metaphor in thought conceptualized as in row 4 versus in row 2. The point is that evidence about metaphor in conceptual structures in symbolic or semiotic approaches concerns the knowledge of the abstract idealized native speaker of a language. This is not identical with the knowledge and its use by real people engaged in observable tasks. What may be reconstructed in the semiotic approach may not exist or play a role in the same way in genuine psychological behavior.

Let us now move on to the even more complicated matter of metaphor as 'thought' as it is reflected in language. This takes us to rows 1 and 3 in Table 1. For row 1, we are looking for an operational definition that can find metaphor in linguistic forms approached from a linguistic (semiotic) perspective. This requires presenting linguistic evidence for distinct form-meaning pairings in abstract linguistic systems and their use. This may again be best imagined by turning to computational linguistic networks, such as lexicons for dictionaries. These will contain many lexical items that have one form and at least two senses of which one is metaphorically related to the other, including *attack, defend,* and so on.

This is evidence for metaphor in language, approached as semiotic or symbolic structure. But it is a moot point whether this type of evidence always constitutes evidence for metaphor in thought, even if that is limited to the domain of symbolic or semiotic enquiry that is depicted by the upper half of Table 1, in row 2. The basis on which this argument of a connection between rows 1 and 2 has been made in cognitive linguistics is typically located in systematic polysemy. It suggests that metaphorical meanings of individual lexical items are not accidental but systematic, and may therefore be due to some pattern of thought. Technically, this entails postulating a productive semantic relationship between two lexical fields that is conceptually driven, for instance the ones that have to do with argumentation and war, or love and journeys, or emotions and vertical orientation. But this also raises the question what counts as a productive semantic pattern. How many items need to be involved? Does the productive pattern still need to be in operation, or does historical change also still count as evidence for contemporary productivity? These are questions about the potential relation between row 1 and row 2, and this still does not address the question about metaphor in thought as cognitive behavior (row 4). Moreover, these are also questions about the potential relation between row 1 and row 3, since it is not clear whether the symbolic evidence captures all or even any of the cognitive processes and resulting structures that are part of row 3.

When we move to row 3 itself, this does take us into processes and products of cognition, but to the level of language again. In order to observe metaphor at this level of reality, we need evidence for the activation of two distinct linguistic meanings paired to one linguistic form in the relevant psycholinguistic processes and their products. It means that the activation of both the source and target-domain senses of for instance *defend* and *attack* or *high* and *low* should be observable in concrete situations of use. (One complication with psycholinguistic research is that competence, or lexico-grammar, can only be studied by examining – sometimes whole series – of usage events, or performance – cf. Winner 1988).

Again, this is evidence for metaphor in language from a processing perspective. (Indeed, this may be taken as yet another definition of 'thought', for instance by those psychologists who take all of cognition as thought, including linguistic as opposed to conceptual processing. However, we will leave this further complication aside here.) What we need to ask instead is whether this behavioral approach to metaphor in language can also count as evidence for metaphor in conceptual processing itself.

This is a natural assumption for cognitive linguists, since they do not make a sharp distinction between the mental lexicon and the mental encyclopedia and assume that lexical knowledge is embedded in world knowledge. However, this position is not universally shared, neither within cognitive linguistics, where for instance Vyv Evans is working on an alternative model which does make a distinction between lexical and conceptual knowledge (Evans 2006; Evans and Zinken, in press), nor in psychology, where a distinction is made between the construction of a number of different mental models for discourse, in which a linguistic surface text can be distinguished from a conceptual text base and situation model (e.g. Kintsch 1998; Van Oostendorp and Goldman 1999). Thus, it is well possible that lexical units can be accessed in such a way that they facilitate speedy lexical disambiguation between metaphorical and non-metaphorical senses; in such a scenario, the predicted metaphorical mappings between presumably corresponding conceptual (as opposed to lexical) structures do not have to arise. Note that this holds even if metaphorically motivated polysemous lexical units do activate the two comparable senses in the early stages of processing. Evidence for metaphor in row 3 therefore does not necessarily constitute evidence for metaphor in row 4.

This is how the same theoretical definition of metaphor as a cross-domain mapping can lead to a quest for evidence in diverse areas of experience, yet the evidence collected consequently cannot have the same purport. Semiotic evidence for metaphor as thought (in row 2) does not constitute evidence for the same thing as processing evidence for metaphor-as-thought (in row 4). And semiotic evidence for metaphor-as-thought reflected in language (row 1) is not necessarily evidence for the same thing as processing evidence for metaphor-as-thought reflected in language (row 3; cf. Sandra and Rice 1995; Croft 1998). Finally, evidence for metaphor in linguistic processing (row 3) is not sufficient for saying that we may also conclude that there is metaphor in conceptual processing (row 4). These points now bring us to the first fundamental claim about converging evidence.

If two types of evidence are not evidence for the same phenomenon, they cannot be said to be converging, i.e., 'pointing towards the same conclusion'. What can be said, though, is that the same theoretical definition of metaphor-as-thought (the definition of metaphor as a mapping between two domains in conceptual structure, located in row 2) guides research into related but different phenomena, which at least makes for consistency and compatibility. Different types of evidence may hence be compatible with a more complex encompassing picture across phenomena, as in several of the distinct areas in Table 1. They may be interpreted as suggestive evidence for the more complex, encompassing picture. But the term 'evidence' in that connection would remain too strong until that more encompassing picture has been made explicit as an encompassing model, with concrete and testable claims about the relations between the distinct areas. And it is precisely this aspect of Conceptual Metaphor Theory that has been criticized by psycholinguists Murphy (1996, 1997), Boroditsky (2000), McGlone (2008), Gentner and Bowdle (2008), and Giora (2008).

The conclusion that should follow is therefore the following claim (Steen 2007):

- Phenomenological pluralism is exciting but problematic

"Converging evidence" presented about *distinct phenomena*, such as metaphor in grammar versus usage, or metaphor in language versus thought, or metaphor in symbols versus behavior, or their more specific configurations, is exciting but problematic, unless clear models of the relation between the distinct phenomena can show how the evidence for one type of phenomenon can be said to point to the same conclusion as the evidence for another type of phenomenon.

These ideas are not new, and some have been expressed in various places by other researchers, as I have indicated. The point here is that they can be connected to three essential dimensions of cognitive-linguistic research: the division between language and thought, the contrast between grammar and usage, and the opposition between semiotic and behavioral approaches. These fundamental distinctions create their own research realities, and these areas cannot be reunited without additional theory that explains the empirical connections between them. If these principles are respected, this has the above consequences for what can and cannot count as converging evidence between these areas.

4. Methodological pluralism

Fortunately, there is a second consequence that follows from the above analysis. It may also be formulated in the form of a methodological claim. The contrast between that claim and the more cautionary position put forward above can throw into relief how cognitive linguistics may and may not benefit from collecting converging evidence.

- Methodological pluralism is exciting and attractive

"Converging evidence" presented about the same phenomenon, whether metaphor in grammar versus usage, metaphor in language versus thought, metaphor in symbols versus behavior, or their more specific configurations, is exciting and attractive, provided the same norms of data collection and analysis are adhered to in evaluating the evidence obtained with one type of method as with the other type of method.

In what follows I discuss this thesis in connection with the strongest possible interpretation of metaphor as thought, that is, that metaphor always requires a cross-domain mapping in cognitive processing and its products, whether in usage (production, reception, and interaction) or in grammar (acquisition, maintenance, and attrition). After all, this is the typical interpretation of metaphor as thought in cognitive linguistics. I will return to the relation with metaphor in thought taken as a matter of symbolic knowledge structures in competence and performance in the conclusion.

The methodological pluralism claim makes a distinction between methods of data collection and methods of data analysis. I have distinguished between three methods of data collection in my methodological analysis of metaphor research (Steen 2007), to which a fourth should be added here for the sake of completeness. The four basic methods of data collection are introspection, observation, manipulation, and simulation. They may be briefly characterized as follows:

- Introspection: observation of cognitive processes and products in elicited behavior of self
- Observation: observation of cognitive processes and products in natural behavior of others
- Manipulation: observation of cognitive processes and products in manipulated behavior of others
- Simulation: observation of semiotic processes modeled and run by computational means

The general advantages and disadvantages of using these methods of data collection can be found in any handbook of methodology. Discussions of these methods in the context of cognitive linguistics have been offered by Gries, Hampe, and Schönefeld (2005) and by González-Marquez et al. (2006). More detailed methodological discussions in connection with research on metaphor in thought approached as genuine cognition include Hoffman and Kemper (1987), Murphy (1996, 1997), Low (1999), Gibbs (2006), McGlone (2007), Barnden (2008), and Cameron (2008).

The general drift of all of these discussions is that introspection and observation are problematic when it comes to collecting data that can throw light on the question whether people think metaphorically when they process metaphor in language. Introspection cannot count as a useful method because most of metaphorical thought has been claimed to be largely unconscious by cognitive linguists themselves, which by definition prevents access to this cognitive behavior by the introspecting analyst. Observation can only examine what people do and say, which offers a very limited window on what they think as they speak or write and act. In some cases, observation may suffice, but in most cases, its findings will simply be too unreliable and open to alternative explanations. That both observation and introspection are of limited use is due to the nature of the phenomenon under study, largely unconscious and fast processes of cognition, which, in other areas, such as visual perception, also require different methods than introspection and observation.

This severely restricts the possibilities for obtaining converging evidence by methodological pluralism, at least in the area of metaphor as genuine thought, that is, as on-going cognitive processes and their products. In psychology and psycholinguistics, the term converging evidence is consequently encountered only in those cases where off-line and online measurements of experimentally manipulated behavior are brought together, or where different measures of either of the two are compared. In the latter case, the same phenomenon is measured by more than one method, as may be illustrated by the three experiments reported in Gentner, Imai, and Boroditsky (2002), or by that study as a whole, on the one hand, and another study by McGlone and Harding (1998) on the other (Boroditsky 2000: 7). In the former case, the process (on-line) and product (off-line) are measured as parts of one encompassing model of cognition, as may be illustrated by Gentner and Bowdle (2001: 234).

In itself, it appears to be a daunting enough task within experimental psychology to collect this type of converging evidence. Given the lack of reliability of other evidence deriving from introspection and observation, these can at most be called consistent or compatible with the experimental evidence. The strongest claim that can be made about such positive introspective and observational evidence is that it does not undermine the experimental evidence. Whether it can be said to strengthen it, because it would converge towards the same conclusion, is a moot point. True convergence might be restricted to only some very clear cases of metaphor in thought, such as deliberate metaphor, including simile, extended comparison, and allegory.

Evidence collected by simulation is yet another matter. What it does is show that a particular computational model has been successfully implemented, to the extent that it can produce the predicted results of the computational mechanism. This is an achievement in its own right. It makes explicit how a particular model of cognition might work. This may be interpreted as presenting converging evidence for a particular theory. But this will only hold if experimental behavioral evidence can show that the system adequately mimics people's cognitive processes and their products (cf. Barnden 2008).

If psychological research on metaphor in thought is so dependent on manipulation, it might be expected that data analysis is typically quantitative, not qualitative. In general this is true. Behavioral measures can be used to collect reading times (Gentner and Bowdle 2008), lexical decision latencies (Giora 2008), event-related brain potentials (ERPs) (Coulson 2008) and other comparable data such as distances covered on a racetrack and times needed to do so (Gibbs and Matlock 2008). All of these are quantities that can be recorded and analyzed as such. The same holds for off-line tasks based on semantic differential scales or Likert scales requiring participants to give scores or true-false judgments to distinct items.

However, even in quantitative experimental work, qualitative analysis may play an important role. For instance, when people are asked to think out loud (Steen 1994) or write up their interpretations of metaphorical stimuli (Glucksberg and McGlone 1999), the data come in the form of verbal protocols that need qualitative analysis by means of a coding scheme. This may eventually turn the data into quantifiable categories, but the qualitative stage of data analysis requires special attention in terms of reliability. Agreement between independent analysts who follow an explicit protocol or procedure for analysis needs to be sufficient and requires statistical testing before a claim can be made that it is. Quantitative analysis of verbal data that have been converted into countable categories does not make sense unless the conversion is accurate and does not contain too much error.

In sum, converging evidence for metaphor in thought in the psychological interpretation of the phrase typically requires data collection by distinct techniques of manipulation, not introspection or observation. It also requires quantitative data analysis, or qualitative analysis of verbal data that can be shown to be reliable. These are high demands. Collecting converging evidence interpreted as this kind of methodological pluralism for metaphor as thought is therefore a huge enough challenge as it is.

5. Conclusion

Is metaphor always a matter of thought? The answer to this question depends on whether the question is taken as a question about theory or research. If the question is about theory, the answer can be affirmative, as it will be in cognitive linguistics, for then metaphor may always be relatable to some cross-domain mapping simply because it is defined in that way. But in that case, care should be taken that this position should not be presented as if it were fact. Instead, this is a claim that is theoretical, a hypothesis, and one that should be tested by empirical research for which converging evidence may be collected.

Empirical research about metaphor in thought may be of two kinds at least, semiotic and psychological. If the question about metaphor in thought is about empirical research, therefore, the answer depends on what is meant by 'thought'. If 'thought' is intended to refer to the abstract knowledge of the idealized native speaker of a language, as happens in semiotic approaches, then metaphor can again, even empirically, be always seen as a matter of thought. The recent history of cognitive linguistics has shown that the empirical answer to this interpretation of 'thought' is still a matter of considerable difficulty, given, for instance, the difference between primary and complex metaphors.

However, if thought is taken as the concrete cognitive processes and products of competence and performance of human beings, then metaphor is not always a matter of thought. Instead, the question should then be reformulated into: when is metaphor a matter of thought? This is how psycholinguists and psychologists have approached and currently are approaching the question. They raise serious empirical doubts about the general cognitive linguistic tenet that metaphor is a matter of thought.

When mention is made of converging evidence for metaphor as a matter of thought, it should be clear that this is a claim about research, not the theoretical issue distinguished above. In empirical research, metaphor constitutes a showcase for the difficulties involved in handling converging evidence. The notion of converging evidence typically displays a conflation between two scientific phenomena, 'phenomenological pluralism' and 'methodological pluralism', as I have attempted to demonstrate above.

Phenomenological pluralism is exciting but problematic. It involves the evaluation of evidence produced by different methods of data collection and analysis across distinct areas of research, pertaining to distinct phenomena of investigation. I have illustrated these differences with reference to semiotic versus psychological approaches to metaphor in both language and thought, and emphasized that many researchers object to taking semiotic evidence as pertaining to the same phenomenon as behavioral evidence. Methodological pluralism, by contrast, is widely accepted as able to produce converging evidence – it pertains to using different methods of data collection and analysis within one distinct area of research, so that evidence may be legitimately claimed to point to the same conclusion about the same phenomenon.

Since psycholinguists are working hard on collecting converging evidence for metaphor in thought as psychological process and product, I believe that cognitive linguists might wish to concentrate on producing converging evidence for metaphor in language and thought as semiotic or symbolic structure. The evaluation of converging evidence for conceptual metaphor could therefore profitably focus on the semiotic approach to metaphorical thought in grammar and usage that is so characteristic of cognitive linguistics (row 2). This task, if it wishes to attain the same levels of validity and reliability as the ones strived for in psychology, is already problematic, challenging, and exciting enough, as I have shown at length in Steen (2007).

If this objective is adopted, cognitive linguists should also be more careful with their meta-talk. They should be quite precise about their intentions when they say that metaphor is a matter of thought. They should first of all make it clear whether they talk about the theoretical definition (or conceptualization) of metaphor, as a cross-domain mapping, or whether they make an empirical claim. The theoretical claim should not be confused with a finding or a fact. And second, if the claim that metaphor is a matter of thought is meant to be an empirical claim, it should be clear whether this is meant within the semiotic framework of investigation that is predominant in cognitive linguistics, which largely pertains to the knowledge about grammar and usage of the abstract, idealized language user, on the one hand, or whether it is meant within the behavioral framework of the concrete cognitive processes and products that have been studied by psychologists. Only then will it be fully clear what it means to say that metaphor is a matter of thought.

References

Barlow, M. & S. Kemmer, eds. 2000. *Usage Based Models of Language*. Stanford, CA: CSLI publications.

Barnden, J. 2008. Metaphor and artificial intelligence: Why they matter to each other. In R. W. Gibbs, ed., *The Cambridge Handbook of Metaphor and Thought*, 311–338. Cambridge: CUP.

Blasko, D. 1999. Only the tip of the iceberg: Who understands what about metaphor? *Journal of Pragmatics* 31: 1675–1683.

Boroditsky, L. 2000. Metaphoric structuring: Understanding time through spatial metaphors. *Cognition* 75(1): 1–28.

Bowdle, B. F. & D. Gentner. 2005. The career of metaphor. *Psychological Review* 112(1): 193–216.

Bybee, J. & P. J. Hopper, eds. 2001. *Frequency and the Emergence of Linguistic Structure*. Amsterdam: John Benjamins.

Cameron, L. 2008. Metaphor and talk. In R. W. Gibbs, ed., *The Cambridge Handbook of Metaphor and Thought*, 197–211. Cambridge: Cambridge University Press.

Cameron, L. & G. Low, eds. 1999. *Researching and Applying Metaphor*. Cambridge Applied Linguistics. Cambridge: Cambridge University Press.

Coulson, S. 2008. Metaphor comprehension and the brain. In R. W. Gibbs, ed., *The Cambridge Handbook of Metaphor and Thought*, 177–194. Cambridge: CUP.

Coulson, S. & B. Lewandowska-Tomaszczyk, eds. 2005. *The Literal and Nonliteral in Language and Thought*. Frankfurt am Main: Peter Lang.

Croft, W. 1998. Linguistic evidence and mental representations. *Cognitive Linguistics* 9(2): 151–173.

Dirven, R. & M. Pütz, eds. 1996. *The Construal of Space in Language and Thought*. Berlin: Mouton de Gruyter.

Eco, U. 1976. *A Theory of Semiotics*. Indianapolis: Indiana University Press.

Evans, V. 2006. Lexical concepts, cognitive models, and meaning-construction. *Cognitive Linguistics* 17 (4): 491–534.

Evans, V., & J. Zinken, in press. Figurative language in a cognitive theory of meaning construction. In R. Chrisley & C. Makris, eds., *Art, Body, Embodiment*. Cambridge: Cambridge Scholars Press.

Fauconnier, G. 1997. *Mappings in Thought and Language*. Cambridge: Cambridge University Press.

Fauconnier, G. & M. Turner. 2002. *The Way We Think: Conceptual Blending and the Mind's Hidden Complexities*. New York: Basic Books.

Gentner, D. & B. F. Bowdle. 2001. Convention, form, and figurative language processing. *Metaphor and Symbol* 16(3 & 4): 223–248.

Gentner, D. & B. F. Bowdle. 2008. Metaphor as structure-mapping. In R. W. Gibbs, ed., *The Cambridge Handbook of Metaphor and Thought*, 109–128. Cambridge: Cambridge University Press.

Gentner, D., M. Imai, et al. 2002. As time goes by: Evidence for two systems in processing space time metaphors. *Language and Cognitive Processes* 17(*): 537– 565.

Gibbs, R. W. 1994. *The Poetics of Mind: Figurative Thought, Language, and Understanding*. Cambridge: Cambridge University Press.

Gibbs, R. W. 1999. Researching metaphor. In: L. Cameron & G. Low, eds., *Researching and Applying Metaphor*, 29–47. Cambridge: Cambridge University Press.

Gibbs, R. W. 2006. Introspection and cognitive linguistics: Should we trust our own intuitions? *Annual Review of Cognitive Linguistics* 4: 135–152.

Gibbs, R. W., ed., 2008. *The Cambridge Handbook of Metaphor and Thought*. Cambridge: Cambridge University Press.

Gibbs, R. W. & T. Matlock. 2008. Metaphor, imagination, and simulation: Psycholinguistic evidence. In R. W. Gibbs, ed., *The Cambridge Handbook of Metaphor and Thought*, 161–176. Cambridge: CUP.

Giora, R. 2003. *On Our Mind: Salience, Context, and Figurative Language*. New York: Oxford University Press.

Giora, R. 2008. Is metaphor unique? In R. W. Gibbs, ed., *The Cambridge Handbook of Metaphor and Thought*, 143–160. Cambridge: Cambridge University Press.

Glucksberg, S. 2001. *Understanding Figurative Language: From Metaphors to Idioms*. Oxford and New York: Oxford University Press.

Glucksberg, S. 2008. How metaphors create categories–quickly. In R. W. Gibbs, ed., *The Cambridge Handbook of Metaphor and Thought*, 67–83. Cambridge: Cambridge University Press.

Glucksberg, S., P. Gildea, et al. 1982. On understanding nonliteral speech: Can people ignore metaphors? *Journal of Verbal Learning and Verbal Behavior* 21: 85–98.

Glucksberg, S. & C. Haught. 2006. On the relation between metaphor and simile: When comparison fails. *Mind & Language* 21: 360–378.

Glucksberg, S. & M. McGlone. 1999. When love is not a journey: What metaphors mean. *Journal of Pragmatics* 31(*): 1541–1558.

Gonzalez-Marquez, M., I. Mittelberg, et al., eds. 2006. *Methods in Cognitive Linguistics*. Amsterdam & Philadelphia: John Benjamins.

Gries, S., B. Hampe, & D. Schönefeld. 2005. Converging evidence: Bringing together experimental and corpus data on the association of verbs and constructions. *Cognitive Linguistics* 16(4): 635–67.

Hoffman, R. R. & S. Kemper. 1987. What could reaction-time studies be telling us about metaphor comprehension? *Metaphor and Symbolic Activity* 2(2): 149–186.

Honeck, R. & R. R. Hoffman, eds. 1980. *Cognition and Figurative Language*. Hillsdale, NJ: Lawrence Erlbaum.

Jäkel, O. 1999. Kant, Blumenberg, Weinrich: Some forgotten contributions to the cognitive theory of metaphor. In R. W. Gibbs & G. J. Steen, eds., *Metaphor in Cognitive Linguistics*, 9–27. Amsterdam: John Benjamins.

Kintsch, W. 1998. *Comprehension: A Paradigm for Cognition*. Cambridge: Cambridge University Press.

Lakoff, G. & M. Johnson. 1980. *Metaphors We Live By*. Chicago: The University of Chicago Press.

Lakoff, G. & M. Johnson. 1999. *Philosophy in the Flesh: The Embodied Mind and its Challenge to Western Thought.* New York: Basic Books.

Langacker, R. W. 1987. *Foundations in Cognitive Grammar, Vol. I: Theoretical Prerequisites.* Stanford: Stanford University Press.

Langacker, R. W. 1991. *Foundations in Cognitive Grammar, Vol. II: Descriptive Application.* Stanford: Stanford University Press.

Lönneker-Rodman, B. 2008. The Hamburg metaphor database. Issues in resource creation. *Language Resources and Evaluation* 42. 293–318.

Low, G. 1999. Validating metaphor research projects: Researching and applying metaphor. In L. Cameron & G. Low, eds., *Researching and Applying Metaphor*, 48–65. Cambridge: Cambridge University Press.

Markman, A. 1999. *Knowledge Representation.* Mahwah, NJ: Erlbaum.

McGlone, M. 2007. What is the explanatory value of a conceptual metaphor? *Language & Communication* 27: 109–126.

McGlone, M. & J. Harding. 1998. Back (or forward?) to the future: The role of perspective in temporal language comprehension. *Journal of Experimental Psychology: Learning, Memory and Cognition* 24(*): 1211–1223.

Murphy, G. 1996. On metaphoric representation. *Cognition* 60(*): 173–204.

Murphy, G. 1997. Reasons to doubt the present evidence for metaphoric representation. *Cognition* 62(*): 99–108.

Murphy, G. 2002. *The Big Book of Concepts.* Cambridge, MA & London: MIT Press.

Ortony, A., ed. 1979/1993. *Metaphor and Thought.* Cambridge: Cambridge University Press.

Panther, K.-U. & G. Radden, eds. 1999. *Metonymy in Language and Thought.* Amsterdam: John Benjamins.

Radden, G. & Z. Kövecses. 1999. Towards a theory of metonymy. In K.-U. Panther & G. Radden *Metonymy in Language and Thought*, 17–59. Amsterdam: John Benjamins.

Sandra, D. & S. Rice. 1995. Network analyses of prepositional meaning: Mirroring whose mind– the linguist's or the language user's? *Cognitive Linguistics* 6(1): 89– 130.

Steen, G. J. 1994. *Understanding Metaphor in Literature: An Empirical Approach.* London: Longman.

Steen, G. J. 2007. *Finding Metaphor in Grammar and Usage: A Methodological Analysis of Theory and Research.* Amsterdam: John Benjamins.

Steen, G. J. 2008. The paradox of metaphor: Why we need a three-dimensional model of metaphor. *Metaphor and Symbol* 23(4): 213–241.

Steen, G. J. 2010. When is metaphor deliberate? In N.-L. Johannesson, C. Alm-Arvius, & D. C. Minugh, *Selected Papers from the Stockholm 2008 Metaphor Festival.* Stockholm: Acta Universitatis Stockholmiensis.

Tomasello, M. 1999. *The Cultural Origins of Human Cognition.* Cambridge, MA: Harvard University Press.

Tomasello, M. 2003. *Constructing a Language: A Usage-based Theory of Language Acquisition.* Cambridge, MA: Harvard University Press.

Turner, M. 1996. *The Literary Mind: The Origins of Language and Thought.* Oxford: Oxford University Press.

Van Oostendorp, H. & S. Goldman, eds. 1999. *The Construction of Mental Representations During Reading.* Mahwah, NJ: Lawrence Erlbaum.

Winner, E. 1988. *The Point of Words.* Cambridge, MA & London: Harvard University Press.

PART 1

Multi-methodological approaches to constructional and idiomatic meaning

1.1 Cognition verb constructions

Perception and conception

The '*see* x *to be* y' construction from a cognitive perspective*

Thomas Egan
Hedmark University College

This chapter revisits a construction discussed by Bolinger (1974), investigating whether his intuitive interpretation of it holds in the light of robust corpus data. Bolinger's interpretation has been disputed, notably by Noël (2003), on the basis of what he takes to be diverging evidence from the British National Corpus. A careful examination of all instances of the '*see* x *to be* y' construction in three large corpora provides converging evidence showing that Bolinger was basically correct when he stated that when followed by a *to*-infinitive complement, perceptual verbs are being used in a conceptual sense. This interpretation of the *see* construction with the *to*-infinitive complement is related to a more general schematic interpretation of the meaning of the *to*-infinitive form.

Keywords: concept, construction, infinitive complement, percept, perceptual verbs

1. Introduction

Thirty-five years ago Dwight Bolinger published a paper in which he maintained that verbs like *see*, which are normally used to code percepts, can be used with *to*-infinitive complements to code concepts. Bolinger distinguished between one construction containing a bare infinitive complement that codes percepts, and another construction containing a *to*-infinitive complement that codes concepts. He claimed that when a verb such as *see*, which normally occurs in the first type of construction, is used in the second type, the profile of the construction overrides

* I would like to thank the editor of this volume and two anonymous referees for helpful comments and suggestions. I would also like to thank Mark Davies, the compiler of the Corpus of Contemporary American English, and Antoinette Renouf and her team at Birmingham City University, who developed WebCorp, for making these resources freely available. Without their generosity, collecting the sort of data essential to this paper would have been impossible.

that of the verb, with the result that the complement clause codes a concept rather than a percept. Bolinger's contention was based on introspective evidence, as was the norm at the time. Noël (2003) argues that corpus evidence undermines Bolinger's thesis to some extent. According to Noël, corpus tokens from the British National Corpus (BNC) lead to conclusions that diverge from those reached by Bolinger on the basis of intuitive evidence. In this chapter I revisit Bolinger's arguments and seek for converging evidence in three large-scale corpora, in this case the BNC, the Corpus of Contemporary American English (COCA) and WebCorp. The size of the corpora chosen for the study was necessitated by the comparative rarity of the '*see* x *to be* y' construction. Its very rarity also dictates that the methodology employed is as much qualitative as quantitative.

Section 2 presents Bolinger's thesis and Section 3 Noël's counterarguments. In Section 4, I present corpus data showing that the '*see* x *to be* y' construction codes either concepts pure and simple, or percepts subject to conceptual reworking in the form of a comparative, and possibly a revised, construal. In Section 5, I argue that the *to*-infinitive is best interpreted globally as coding the targeted of several possible alternative situations and that the particular interpretation of the '*see* x *to be* y' construction presented in Section 4 is a reflex of this semantic component of the *to*-infinitive. Finally in Section 6, I conclude that the corpus evidence is actually converging rather than diverging and thus tips the scales in favor of Bolinger's original analysis.

2. Bolinger's thesis

In a paper published in 1974 Bolinger discusses two types of constructions in English, one of which is predominantly used to code conceptual data, the other sense data. He writes:

> This essay is about the contrast between two opposing constructions in English, and the two classes of verbs that are used in them. It is also about the blending and homonymic conflicts that occur at their borders. One class is conceptual. It refers to our hold on *facts* and includes knowing, believing, proving, judging, understanding, discovering, assuming, inferring, saying, and similar meanings. The other class is perceptual. It refers to our *laying* hold of *sense data*, and includes seeing, hearing, observing, perceiving, and the like. The corresponding constructions both contain infinitive complements, but they differ. With concepts [...] the infinitive carries *to*; with percepts it does not. (Bolinger 1974: 65)

Bolinger provides many illustrations of both types of construction, including those cited here as (1)–(4).

Concepts:
(1) I *know* you to be a kind person.
(2) We *hold* these facts to be self evident.

Percepts:
(3) They *saw* it happen.
(4) I have *viewed* them pass in full parade.

(Bolinger 1974: 65, my numbering)

Sentences (1)–(4) instantiate two constructions, both of which share the structure [Subject-Verb-Object-Object Complement] (hereafter SVOC). In (1) and (2) the object complement is a *to*-infinitive, in (3) and (4) a bare infinitive. The situations in the complement clauses in (1) and (2) belong to the mental domain. They are mental objects of belief or judgment with the matrix verb subject coded as the possessor of the belief in question. They thus belong to the second-world in Popper's (1972) three-fold classification. The situations in the complement clauses in (3) and (4), on the other hand, clearly belong to Popper's first world, the world external to the matrix verb subject. In their case the matrix verb codes the subjects' registering these external situations. Bolinger points out that verbs like those in (1) and (2) cannot occur with the bare infinitive:

> The bare infinitive is not used with verbs that are lexically conceptual [...]. But the opposite – the *to* with verbs that are lexically perceptual – is quite normal. The perceptual verbs are being used in a conceptual sense, roughly equivalent to the same verbs with a *that* clause: **I saw it to be true** = **I saw that it was true**.
>
> (Bolinger 1974: 66)

Tokens cited by Bolinger in support of his contention that perceptual verbs may be used in a conceptual sense include (5)–(9).

(5) I *see* this to be the next logical step.
(6) We *felt* it to be essential that all take part.
(7) The guide *sensed* it to constitute a certain risk.
(8) I *saw* them to be obnoxious.
(9) I *felt* him to possess the necessary qualifications.

(Bolinger 1974: 66, my numbering)

In (5), for example, something's being the next logical step is not asserted to pertain in a world external to the matrix verb subject. Rather it is coded as existing in that subject's mental domain. All five tokens code judgments on the part of the matrix verb subjects and in this respect they resemble tokens (1) and (2) rather than (3) and (4). Bolinger points out that the distinction between the two types had already been drawn by Jespersen.

> Jespersen (*Modern English Grammar* V 18.2) notes the distinction, and says, of the verb to see, 'This *to* is chiefly used when see does not indicate immediate perception but an inference: **I see this to be true...**' Inference is one form of cognitive data. (Bolinger 1974: 87)

Examples (1)–(9) are all products of Bolinger's introspection. By relying on such evidence he is typical of his era. This is not to say that Bolinger is blind to the value of attested tokens. He cites several in the footnotes to the 1974 paper, but typically these illustrate exceptions, unusual usages. When it comes to what he perceives as more prototypical cases, he relies on made-up examples. The conclusions he draws on the basis of such examples have been subjected to criticism by Noël (2003), as demonstrated in the next section.

3. Noël's criticism of Bolinger

Noël (2003) deals with *to*-infinitive and *that* complements as these are interpreted in the work of Wierzbicka (1988), Verspoor (1990) and Langacker (1995). It is in his discussion of Verspoor's work that Noël refers to Bolinger's distinction between concepts and percepts, although he refers to Bolinger himself in his introduction where he characterizes what he terms 'semantic extremism'.

> Of course, the core idea behind [models like Cognitive Grammar and Construction Grammar] – that all form signals meaning, that every grammatical choice has a meaning behind it, that there is no syntax without semantics – is not so new: Anna Wierzbicka, one of the most outspoken defenders of the doctrine points back to a quote from Dwight Bolinger dating from 1968: "a difference in syntactic form always spells a difference in meaning"
> (Bolinger 1968: 127, cited in Wierzbicka 1988: 25). (Noël 2003: 347–348)

Noël goes on to state, "Bolinger's had always been a fairly lonely and 'eccentric' voice in the proverbial dark, whereas his (what I would call) 'semantic extremism' is now no longer very special" (Noël 2003: 348). Noël's criticism of those he perceives to be "semantic extremists" is supported by a discussion of finite and non-finite complement clauses. In his discussion he reviews the conclusions reached by Bolinger, Wierzbicka, Verspoor, and Langacker on the basis of introspection in the light of the evidence of tokens taken from the British National Corpus. In this chapter I am concerned with just one of these conclusions, Bolinger's division of complements into two types, those coding concepts and those coding percepts. Of these Noël writes, "Contrary to what others have claimed in connection with perception verbs, these complements do not necessarily engender a semantic shift from the perceptual to the conceptual" (Noël 2003: 363). As evidence for this contention he maintains:

The following examples suggest that immediate perception can just as well be expressed with a *to*-infinitive:

(10) Other boys and girls were flitting hither and thither among the trees, singly, without a word or a sign of communication with one another. A few were older, many were younger, than I. Some like myself were looking about them. Others had found what they sought. These, when I passed them, I *saw to be sitting or kneeling* beside cradles, rocking them, or singing, or gazing intently. (BNC ABL 734)

(11) My fingers ache and I *feel my face to be beetroot-red.* (BNC G02 46)

(12) But for /E/, thc short variant can be a low vowel ([a, ae]) and the long variant is a mid vowel that *is easily heard to be qualitatively distinct.* (BNC FAD 269)

(13) Allow the patient to speak of what they *notice to be wrong* with themselves and try not to put words into the patient's mouth. (BNC B1R 262)

(14) Suppose, for example, that up until today I have observed a large number of ravens under a wide variety of circumstances and *have observed all of them to have been black* and that, on that basis, I conclude, "All ravens are black". (BNC FBE 233)

(15) As soon as he left the car he *sensed the air to be damper and colder* than in London, musty with the scent of the distant North Sea, whose breakers were grinding the beach a few miles away at Felixstowe. (BNC GUP 1193)

(Noël 2003: 360, my numbering and italics)

The discussion in the next section focuses on the '*see* x *to be* y' construction exemplified in (10), as an instantiation of SVOC. I return to the other tokens, with the exception of (12), at the end of the section. The reason for omitting (12) from the discussion is the passive form of the matrix verb. The *to* form of the infinitive is overwhelmingly favored after passive verbs in present-day English, regardless of the semantics of the matrix construction.

4. The '*see* x *to be* y' construction revisited

That the verb *see* can code conception rather than perception is not at issue. In the lexicalized phrase *I see what you mean* it is the faculty of understanding rather than that of vision that is referred to. The issue is not even whether the '*see* x *to be* y' construction can be used to code concepts. Noël (2003: 362) admits that this is the case. The issue is whether the construction can be used to code perception pure and simple, as is the case with the bare infinitive construction in (3) and (4).

Noël's rejection of Bolinger's hypothesis is based on just six tokens from the BNC, one of which, (12), is irrelevant to the point at issue as the matrix verb is passive.[1] The BNC contains 100 million words. Yet it only throws up a handful of relevant tokens. In an effort to unearth a larger relevant sample of tokens, I conducted a search of COCA, which contains over 400 million words, and used WebCorp to search the World Wide Web.

As mentioned in the previous section the focus of this chapter is on constructions containing the matrix verb *see*. Accordingly, I first searched for the string 'see/sees/saw/seeing/seen * to be' in both the BNC and COCA. The total number of tokens returned for the BNC was 51 and for COCA 114. Of these 27 (BNC) and 36 (COCA) were tokens in which the item filling the open slot coded the object (landmark) of the matrix verb and the clause headed by 'to be' an object predicative.[2] Many of the tokens returned by the search were not of the SVOC type. To give some idea of the sorts of tokens deemed irrelevant to the study, a selection of these is cited as (16)–(19).

(16) It's a very dangerous pride, you *see, to be* what they called 'colored.'
(COCA: Bartell David: *Misquoting the Star*)

(17) To the colonists, the Adirondack region was nothing but a "dismal wilderness" – a vast, impenetrable barrier of trees, extending unbroken as far as the eye could *see and to be* avoided during the westward expansion. (COCA: Ketchledge, Edwin H.: "The Adirondacks: Born-Again Forest". In *Natural History*)

(18) It requires the *seen object to be matched* with stored memories of the usual appearance of known objects, the retrieval of information about the object's function and our associations with it, and the retrieval of information about the object's name. (BNC HHY 4376)

(19) But we *saw enough to be grateful* that so much is being done to protect and conserve this rich heritage and, driving on lead free petrol, we felt comfortable knowing that we were doing our bit. (BNC CFT 4494)

In (16) *see* is part of a comment clause, the open slot being filled by a comma. In (17) *see* is a constituent of one postmodifier of *barrier* and *to be* of a second

1. One reviewer points out that the semantic analysis of the other examples from Noël proposed at the end of this section also works for (12). While this is true, since there is no possible alternative form of infinitival complementation in the form of the bare infinitive, tokens with passive matrix verbs cannot be included in the data.

2. One should note that six of the tokens in the BNC with the relevant structure are from Patrick J. Duffley's (1992) book on the English infinitive. It is a moot point whether these can be considered genuine usage tokens and, if not, whether they should be included in the data. I decided to include them, with some misgivings.

conjoined postmodifier. In (18) *seen* is a premodifier of *object* and in (19) the *to*-infinitive clause is an adverbial of result and not an object predicative.

As there is no reason to suspect that the landmark in the '*see* x *to be* y' construction should be coded in a single word, a search was also made in both the BNC and COCA for the string 'see/sees/saw/seeing/seen * * to be'. The number of tokens returned was almost double the number returned in the first search, 319 as opposed to 165 for the two corpora combined, but the percentage of relevant tokens was much lower, 13% as opposed to 38%. The reason for this is that the two word open slot allows for the insertion of more types of constituents, such as agents of passive matrix verbs, than is possible in the case of the single word slot. The likelihood of ever greater diminishing returns with more wild cards led to my decision not to search for longer strings in these two corpora.

The WebCorp searches differed from the BNC and COCA searches in that ten separate strings were searched for, 'see * to be', 'see * * to be', 'sees * to be', etc. The reason for this was that by conducting ten separate searches it was possible to access as many as 5,000 web pages. WebCorp can currently access up to 500 web pages per query using AltaVista/Yahoo as input (as opposed to only 62 using Google for searches with wild cards). The ten searches returned a total of 2736 hits, of which 511 had the relevant form.[3] Table 1 contains details of the results for all three corpora.

Table 1 reveals a clear difference between the BNC and the other two corpora in the percentage of relevant hits returned. This difference is significant at the level of p = 0.0001. The difference between COCA and WebCorp with respect to the

Table 1. Overview of corpus data for 'SEE * to be' and 'SEE * * to be'

Corpus	Hits returned	Relevant tokens: % of total hits	Passive matrix verb: % of relevant tokens	Active purely conceptual: % of active tokens	Active involving perception: % of active tokens
BNC	168	58	42	15	1
		35%	72%	88%	13%
COCA	316	48	16	27	5
		15%	34%	84%	16%
WebCorp	2736	511	56	418	37
		19%	11%	92%	8%
Total	3220	617	114	460	43
		19%	18%	91%	9%

3. WebCorp includes a function whereby one can restrict returns to one hit per site. I made use of this option in my search. My reason for doing so was a wish to avoid threads in which the same item is repeated dozens of times, in question and answer form, for instance.

proportion of relevant hits is not statistically significant (Pearson's χ^2 with 1 degree of freedom = 2.30: p= 0.13). It is not possible to say whether the higher return for the BNC is due a greater degree of accuracy being achieved by the custom-built search engine, SARA, which was used in the search, or whether it is related to the variety of text types in the corpus. The difference between the incidence of passive matrix verbs in the BNC and the other two corpora is no doubt related to differences in the text types in the various corpora. In addition the comparatively low percentage for the passive in WebCorp is due to the fact that the form *seen* only occurred in two of ten search strings, thus restricting possible passive forms to a maximum of 20% of the total number of hits returned. Most interesting with reference to the topic of the present chapter are the final two columns of the table, which show the number of tokens with active matrix verbs that code purely conceptual predications and predications involving an element of visual perception, respectively. The difference between the three corpora in terms of the number of tokens involving perception is not statistically significant (Pearson's χ^2 with 2 degrees of freedom = 2.26: p= 0.32).

As shown in Table 1, there are in all 43 tokens involving an element of visual perception. Before considering these, let us first look at a handful of tokens in (20)–(23) in which the complement is clearly a concept.

(20) That ranch is all that he *sees himself to be*: rugged, real and thoroughly Texan. (COCA: John F. Dickerson: *Home On The Range*)

(21) Perhaps parents did not *see peer relationships to be* as important at the younger age levels but significant at the high school level.
(COCA: Hertzog, Nancy B./Bennett, Tess: "In Whose Eyes? Parents' Perspectives on the Learning Needs of Their Gifted Children". *Roeper Review*)

(22) I *saw it to be* the will of God that all should be filled.
(http://www.seeking4truth.com/margaret_mcdonald.htm)[4]

(23) More tartly, he wrote that if you *see a lie to be* a lie, "you have already dealt it its mortal blow."
(COCA: Widmer, Ted: "Arthur of Camelot". *American Scholar*)

In none of these tokens is the subject engaged in an action of visual perception. Thus in (20), although *rugged* may code an attribute visible to the naked eye, this cannot be the case for *real*. In (21) the relative importance of peer relationships is a matter for mental evaluation. Similarly in (22) the will of God is subject to individual interpretation and in (23) the ascription of untruthfulness to individual judgment.

In the three corpora investigated in this study 91% of the tokens of '*see* x *to be* y' resemble (20)–(23) in that there is no question of the visual faculty being

4. All tokens from the Web were downloaded using WebCorp on 24 and 25 September 2009.

involved in the situation coded. There remain, however, 43 tokens in which the eyes are definitely active instruments in the predication. Let us start by considering tokens (24)–(26).

(24) As they approached, Reni rose from his seat at a table near the large rectangular pool which was the centrepiece of what – as Huy now *saw it to be* – was an unconventionally asymmetrical garden. (BNC H84 2027)

(25) *The precipices and peaks on my left* which I had imagined to be tempestuous and stormy I now *saw* fleetingly *to be* a vast lovely and elevated place of feasting recreation and enjoyment behind mountains that were adorned and pleasant. (http://www.pearls.org/content/view/805/56/)

(26) It could have been the dazzling sunlight, or his eyes playing tricks on him; but, for a moment, Lucian thought they were half-horse, half-human [...] As they galloped closer, Lucian *saw them to be* men and women dressed alike in fringed tunics and trousers of soft leather.
(COCA: Lloyd Alexander: *The Arkadians*)

The question is whether (24)–(26) are to be understood as coding purely perceptual predications. I would argue that these tokens, while they definitely code the exercise of the visual faculty, nevertheless also imply an element of revised construal, of re-perception after the mists have cleared, so to speak. Thus in (24) Huy's perspective on the garden changes and he realizes that it is asymmetrical. This act of realization is conceptual, though prompted by perceptual evidence. Similarly in (25) the subject's perspective on the mountain range changes. In (26) Lucian first perceives the riders to be centaur-like. As they come into focus he perceives their outline more closely and the new input leads to a recategorization of the objects of his perception. This recategorization is a cognitive operation. The point at which the revision occurred is signaled by the underlined adverbial *as they galloped closer*, as it is in (24) and (25) by *now*. The construction instantiated by all three tokens may be assigned the following schematic characterization: "In the dark/from a distance, we imagined x to be y: we later saw it to be z" (See Egan 2008: 152).

The '*see* x *to be* y' construction is not the only English construction used to code this form of revised construal. Consider in this respect (27)–(30).

(27) One day as he was walking through the Wild Woods he tripped over a thick tree root. As he picked himself up, cursing, he *saw that the root was actually* the outstretched leg of a red-hairedcreature who was lying happily against a tree trunk, sipping a beer.
(http://daiquiribird.philsites.net/saiyuki/fanfics/sanzoubyhimself.php)

(28) Tired from the long Oregon to Boston flight, I was standing at the front desk of my hotel doing a routine check-in. Suddenly, the main doors burst open,

and a small army of 15 very tall beavers swept into the lobby in a curiously synchronized fashion. Upon closer inspection, I *saw that the beavers were actually* humans who had evidently survived Extreme Fur Makeovers.
(http://www2.computer.org/portal/web/buildyourcareer/fa002)

(29) Some women gathered bamboo shoots, sat on a log, and began paring them. But they noticed the trunk exuded drops of blood with each cut of their knives. Some men came by and *saw that the trunk was actually* a giant, torporous boa constrictor.
(http://www.crystalinks.com/floodstories3.html)

(30) Thick grey smoke began rising out of the opening in the ground, the farmers felt the heat rising along with it and *saw that the smoke was actually* filled with ash.
(http://www.paricutin.com/paricutin_story_002.htm)

Sentences (27) and (28) resemble (24)–(26) in that they explicitly code both the original perception and the revised classification of the perceived object. Thus in (27) what was originally perceived as a tree root turns out to be the leg of a beer-sipping giant. Similarly in (28) what were originally perceived to be beavers turn out to be fur-clad humans. Example (29) differs from (24)–(28) in that the experiencers of the original perception, the women, are not identical to the experiencers/agents of the revised construal, the men. The fact that in this case the act of reconstrual is carried out by different participants to the original perceivers does not alter the fact that it is presented to the reader as a recategorization. The adverb *actually* signals the contrast, just as it does in (30), in which the original perception is not explicitly coded. Here the contrast is between *smoke* as normally perceived, prototypical smoke as it were, and smoke containing ash. In all four tokens (27)–(30) *actually* signals the presence of an alternative perception, which is to be understood as the correct alterative relative to one that may or may not be explicitly coded. I argue in Section 5 that the intimation of such an alternative is part of the schematic meaning of the *to*-infinitive.

Of a total of 43 tokens of '*see* x *to be* y' that involve visual perception, 23 contain, in the immediate co-text, explicit alternatives to what is predicated as being seen (see Table 2). However, not all of these code revised perception in the '*see* x *to be* y' clause in the manner of (24)–(26).

(31) They were not all as neatly round as I had first *seen them to be.*
(COCA: Goldman, E S.: *Yellow Jackets*)

(32) Yes, we do *see galaxys to be closer* to us and each other than they actually are.
(http://www.physicsforums.com/archive/index.php/t-59595.html)

(33) Illusions such as that of *seeing something to be other* than it is, however, are treated as experiences that involve the theories of both veridical perception and hallucination.
(http://www.oxfordscholarship.com/oso/public/content/philosophy/9780195381344/acprof-9780195381344-chapter-6.html)

(34) This is analogous to an ant looking very closely at a curved surface and *seeing it to be flat* – it doesn't see the curvature.
(http://www.learner.org/courses/mathilluminated/units/8/textbook/07.php)

The revised perceptions coded in the '*see* x *to be* y' clauses in (24)–(26) code what the speaker profiles as the correct construal of the situation perceived by the subject. It is the *actual* state of affairs. The exact opposite is the case in (31)–(34). Each of these tokens codes a construal on the part of the subject, which is coded by the speaker as *false*. Thus in (31) the adverbial *first* in the *seen* clause refers to the locus of an original misperception, rather than that of the revision. Examples (32) and (33) both contain a comparative phrase, *than they actually are* and *than it is*, in which the speaker communicates that the subject's perception is false. In (34) the surface that is seen as flat by the ant has already been said by the speaker to be curved. As is shown in Table 3, 18 of the 43 tokens of '*see* x *to be* y' are similar to (32)–(34) in that they occur in texts of a scientific or philosophical nature which problematize visual perception. In these tokens '*see* x *to be* y' could not be replaced by '*see that* x *is* y', as suggested by Bolinger (1974). The point, of course, is precisely that in these tokens x *is not* y! To be more precise, what is *perceived* by the subject as being *true* is *conceived* by the speaker as being *false*. However, while Bolinger is incorrect in suggesting that the *to*-infinitive predication could be replaced by a finite clause (with positive polarity), he is undoubtedly correct in that these sentences involve concepts as well as percepts. In these tokens, '*see that* x *is* y' does not code a revised construal, as in the case of (24)–(26), but an alternative construal. The construal of the subject is undermined in each case by that of the speaker.

Hitherto all the tokens we have looked at have contained explicit alternatives. There are also, as may be seen in Table 2, 17 tokens, such as (35)–(37), that contain implicit alternatives.

Table 2. Semantics of '*see* x *to be* y' constructions in terms of coding alternative situations

Explicit alternatives	Implicit alternatives	Neither explicit nor implicit alternatives	Total
23	17	3	43

(35) "And the boat is missing. And Helsse as well, " said Traz. Reith *saw this to be the case.* (COCA: Vance, Jack: *Planet of Adventure*)

(36) The really strange thing about time dilation is that it is symmetrical: if you and I have relative motion, then I *see your clock to be running slow*, and you *see mine to be running slow*.
(http://www.phys.unsw.edu.au/einsteinlight/jw/module4_twinparadox.htm)

(37) I went to Mr. Crew's and thence to the Theatre, where I saw again "The Lost Lady," which do now please me better than before; and here I sitting behind in a dark place, a lady spit backward upon me by a mistake, not seeing me, but after *seeing her to be a very pretty lady*, was not troubled at it at all.
(http://beebo.org/quotes/pepys/34)

Example (35) resembles (24)–(26) in that it could be paraphrased by *saw that this was actually the case*. The subject perceives that the boat is no longer at its moorings. The implied alternative is the situation expected by both participants in the dialogue, that it should be in its usual place. (36), on the other hand, resembles (31)–(34) in that the coded perceptions are implied to be false. Neither clock is actually running slow. The implied alternative is that they are both keeping perfect time. Finally, in (37), which is an extract from Pepys' diaries, the implied alternative to the spitter's being a very pretty lady is her being a less pretty one, in which case Pepys would no doubt have taken umbrage at her transgression. Six of the 43 tokens that code visual perception are from early or late modern English as opposed to present-day English. Although all six contain either explicit or implicit alternatives, it is debatable whether they should be included in a study such as the present one, the focus of which is how the '*see* x *to be* y' construction is used in contemporary English. On the one hand, these six tokens were originally produced in an earlier era. On the other hand, they have been *re*produced in our day. They have been included in the totals in Tables 1 and 2, but are listed by themselves in Table 3, which contains details of the text types in which the various tokens occur.

As seen in Table 3 the text type in which one most often finds the '*see* x *to be* y' construction in contemporary sources in my data is scientific or philosophical. These include both academic papers and popularized texts. In each case the situation perceived by the subject is implied by the speaker to be false and it is contrasted either explicitly or implicitly with another situation, this being the situation

Table 3. '*see* x *to be* y' constructions according to text types

Older texts	Science/Philosophy	Other non-fiction	Fiction/Narrative	Total
6	18	6	13	43

actually pertaining in the speaker's conception. Only one of the other six non-fiction tokens is of this type, the other five being of the revised construal type. Ten of the fictional/narrative tokens are of the latter type with only three of the *false construal* type.

All tokens of '*see* x *to be* y' examined thus far have contained either an explicit or implicit alternative. The object predicative in all of these 40 tokens can therefore be characterized as the focused alternative of several possible situations. This focused alternative is taken by the referent of the clausal subject to be in accordance with the state of affairs pertaining in the domain in question. In 22 of 43 cases this perception is undercut by the conception of the speaker. There remain, however, three tokens, as seen in Table 2, in which an alternative situation to the one in the complement clause is neither explicitly mentioned nor obviously implied. These are (38)–(40).

(38) The doctor shone a light into both eyes, *seeing them to be healthy green colour*, "You don't seem to be sensitive to light."
(http://www.fanfiction.net/s/4742686/1/)

(39) The roomba was set to automatically clean the house, and I *saw it to be stuck*. The roomba managed to get between a fan stand and the virtual wall and could not get out.
(http://www.youtube.com/watch%3fv=a99O5xKFMDw)

(40) The blue haired, tanned skinned ninja boy grinned and took something from his trouser pocket. Kid *saw it to be another note*, the lettering just as neat as the first, second, third, fourth and fifth note.
(http://www.fanfiction.net/s/5324650/1/Notes)

The question at issue is whether these three tokens can be assimilated to one of the two schematic interpretations of '*see* x *to be* y' involving implicit alternative situations. May they perhaps be viewed as peripheral members of a category whose prototype is either 'perceive that x is actually y' or 'misperceive x as y'? As there is no implication of misperception in any of the three tokens, it is only the first of these two senses that need be considered. Although there is no obvious implication in (38) that the eyes might have an unhealthy color, the very fact that the doctor is examining them surely leaves open the possibility of their being diseased, thus licensing the employment of the alternative-implying construction. Similarly in (39) there is an obvious alternative to the roomba's being stuck. It could be moving about cleaning in the intended fashion. In (40) there is nothing in the co-text to indicate that *Kid* expected something else to be produced from the pocket of the ninja boy. There is, however, another possible motivation for this extension from the prototypical sense. Example (40) resembles (24)–(26) and (35) in coding the revelation of something hidden. Even though there is no obvious alternative to the production of the note, this element of revelation may be sufficient to trigger the semantics associated with this construction.

Having looked at the 43 tokens in the three corpora, and assigned (at least 40 of) them to one of two semantic classes, I now return to Noël's examples from the BNC, reproduced here for convenience. The question is whether any or all of these tokens code some sort of alternative construal, perhaps in the form of a revised construal, or whether they may be more appropriately understood as coding predications of perception pure and simple.

(10) Other boys and girls were flitting hither and thither among the trees, singly, without a word or a sign of communication with one another. A few were older, many were younger, than I. Some like myself were looking about them. Others had found what they sought. These, when I passed them, I *saw to be sitting or kneeling* beside cradles, rocking them, or singing, or gazing intently. (BNC ABL 734)

(11) My fingers ache and I *feel my face to be beetroot-red.* (BNC G02 46)

(12) But for /E/, the short variant can be a low vowel ([a, ae]) and the long variant is a mid vowel that *is easily heard to be qualitatively distinct.* (BNC FAD 269)

(13) Allow the patient to speak of what they *notice to be wrong* with themselves and try not to put words into the patient's mouth. (BNC B1R 262)

(14) Suppose, for example, that up until today I have observed a large number of ravens under a wide variety of circumstances and *have observed all of them to have been black* and that, on that basis, I conclude, "All ravens are black". (BNC FBE 233)

(15) As soon as he left the car he *sensed the air to be damper and colder* than in London, musty with the scent of the distant North Sea, whose breakers were grinding the beach a few miles away at Felixstowe. (BNC GUP 1193)
(Noël 2003: 360, my numbering and italics)

Example (10) resembles (25). As the speaker approaches the children, they come more clearly into focus and he can see what they are actually doing. It is clearly compatible with the interpretation of the 'see x *to be* y' construction as implying an element of revised construal. Although (13) does not code a revised construal as such it contains an explicit comparison between two possible perceptions, the clause beginning *and try not to* implying that the patients' own perception of their conditions is to be preferred to the alternative of the doctor's making up their minds for them. Example (15) resembles (13) in this respect, the comparative phrase *than in London* signaling an explicit comparison that involves a recalibration of the subject's internal thermometer, as it were. It resembles both (32) and (33) in containing a *than* comparative phrase. Example (11) resembles (13) and (15) except for the fact that, in its case, the alternative is implicit rather than explicit. The latent alternative to *being beetroot-red* is the more usual facial complexion. This leaves (14), which describes a process involving the ascription of blackness to the class of ravens on the basis of visual evidence. In this situation the writer might equally well have written *and observed that all of them were black*, given that this was indeed the case. Reformulating it in this manner, however, would lead to a loss of the intimation of a possible alternative inherent in the *to*-infinitive complement construction. The latter leaves open the possibility of the subject's observing ravens that are not black, even though that possibility has not been realized in the present case. Moreover, the fact that this possibility exists is actually noted by the writer, who goes on to state 'But there is no logical guarantee that the next raven I observe will not be pink' (BNC FBE 236). The crucial point in relation to Bolinger's thesis is that the observations referred to in (14) do not merely involve the visual faculty. The subject is engaged in a process of cumulative recording of sense impressions with a view to arriving at a valid generalization.

All five tokens cited as evidence by Noël against Bolinger's thesis have now been shown to code a comparative, and in some cases a revised, construal. In each case the perceived situation is construed as one of several possible alternatives and in each case it is the alternative actually observed. In the next section this interpretation of the *to*-infinitive when it occurs as a complement of perception matrix verbs is related to the schematic sense of the *to*-infinitive form, which I also take to involve the coding of a targeted alternative.

5. Goal as targeted alternative: The semantics of the *to*-infinitive

There is little doubt that the *to* of the infinitive is historically derived from the preposition *to*. Fischer (2003: 451) writes: "It is generally acknowledged in the literature that the allative preposition *to* (or its equivalent in other Germanic languages) developed into an infinitival marker when it became combined with an infinitive". Many linguists have therefore assumed that *to* is a variant of the preposition and that it instantiates a 'path towards goal' schema. As Smith and Escobedo (2001: 550) put it: "[...] the meanings of matrix predicates preferring *to*-infinitival complements usually evoke some aspect of the path-goal sense associated with prepositional *to*".[5]

Figure 1 illustrates a basic path-goal schema. For the purposes of this chapter the source is ignored. In other words, the whole *from-to-goal* relation is not in focus, just the *to-goal* portion of the schema.

5. One should point out that not all cognitive linguists agree that *to* evokes a path-goal sense. Tyler and Evans (2003: 149), for instance, maintain that *to* codes mere orientation towards a goal.

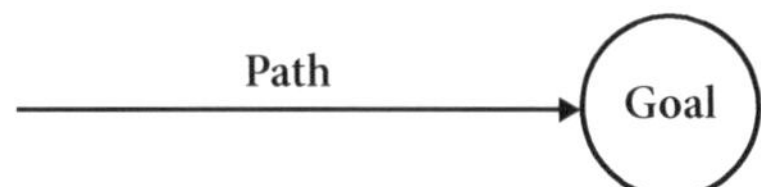

Figure 1. A basic path-goal schema

What exactly is illustrated in Figure 1? Clearly it contains at least two crucial components in *distance* and *direction*: a certain *distance* is traveled along the path before arriving at the goal and this path goes in a certain *direction*. Both of these components have been emphasized by cognitive linguists working on the *to*-infinitive, the first by Smith and Escobedo (2001), the second by Verspoor (1998). However, given these two components, I would maintain that it only really makes sense to construe a situation in terms of the schema illustrated in Figure 1 if the goal in question is profiled either

- as uncertain of being attained, as in Figure 2, or
- as one of several potential targets, as in Figure 3.

Figure 2 incorporates variations in the distance traversed along the path towards the goal. The arrows to the right in the figure are meant to include those to the left. The figure thus illustrates three consecutive possible stopping-points on the path towards the goal.

The *employment* of *to* carries no guarantee that the goal coded in the complement of the preposition will actually be reached. Lack of achievement may be seen in examples (41)–(44) and is illustrated in Figure 2 by the three arrows, indicating varying degrees of progress towards the goal.

(41) Lower your body *to the floor* but do not touch it, and repeat. (BNC A0W 1)

(42) Barbara Coleman made a little jump backwards, a shaking hand went *to her lips* but not fast enough to cut off her cry of fear. (BNC GV2 2533)

(43) I drove the car under an arch leading *to another wing* of the motel and parked in front of my own room. (BNC ABS 564)

(44) Though a military race, the Celts, unlike the Spartans, were not controlled by women, because they inclined *to homosexuality*; but, like the Spartans, they brought up their children austerely. (BNC H0K 175)

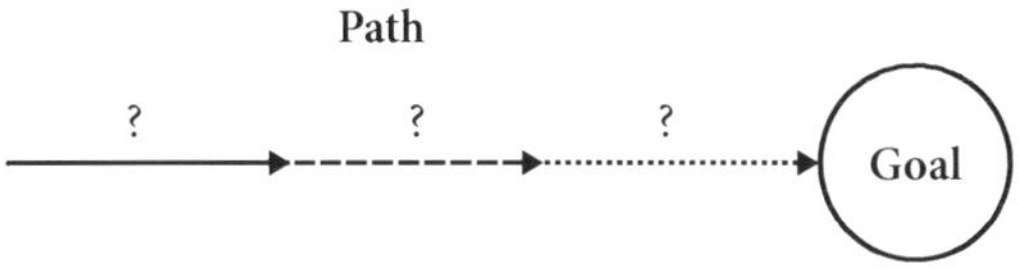

Figure 2. A path-goal schema with alternative lengths of path traversed

In (41) the body traces a path towards the floor, but without ever reaching that goal. In (42) the subject raises her hand in the direction of her lips but has not reached them at the point at which she cries out. In (43) *to* does not code motion in the general direction of a target, but rather a static relationship of orientation (or one of subjective, fictive motion) between the arch and the wing. This is the sense of *to* taken to be schematic by Tyler and Evans (2003). Example (44) also differs from (41) and (42). It does not code physical motion, but rather emotion. The Celts are not coded as being completely homosexual – after all, they have children! – but as having leanings in that direction. In all four examples *to* is to be interpreted as 'in the direction of' (i.e. 'towards') rather than 'right up to'.

Whereas Figure 2 brings out the element of *distance* inherent in the path-goal schema, Figure 3 illustrates the other key component, that of *direction*. In this figure the actual goal is contrasted with various unrealized alternatives. Although the figure only incorporates two latent alternatives, the number of these may in theory vary from just one to an infinite number.

The concept of alternative unrealized goals, illustrated in Figure 3, is exemplified in (45)–(49).

(45) You must tell your doctor if you're allergic *to certain antibiotics not penicillin*, or to rabbits. (BNC A0J 1339)
(46) The divine promises are made *to Jacob* and *not to Esau*. (BNC ACG 994)
(47) Your body belongs *to you* and *not to anyone else*. (BNC ARA 56)
(48) Then he turns *to God, not away from Him*. (B1X 1289)
(49) Britain's church life has been compared *not to a virgin landscape but to a garden* which has been planted already. (BNC C8L 125)

In (45) the targeted goal of *antibiotics* is contrasted with the alternative of *penicillin*. Similarly in (46) and (47) the targeted goals of *Jacob* and *you* are both contrasted with just one alternative, *Esau* and *anyone else*, respectively. Example (48) differs from (45)–(47) in that it is the actual direction of the alternative path, rather than the alternative goal itself, that is contrasted with the targeted goal of *God*. In (45)–(48) the actual goal is stated before the dispreferred alternative. In (49) on the other hand, it is the incorrect alternative of *a virgin landscape* that is mentioned first.

In all five tokens (45)–(49) the alternative goals to the targeted goal are coded explicitly. Indeed, these tokens were chosen for exemplification for this very reason. In other cases, however, one or more of the alternatives may be backgrounded. They may be implicit in the co-text or context, as in (50)–(52), or they may not be, as in (53).

(50) For instance, he had been particularly close *to his mother*. (BNC A6B 1675)

(51) It resists the will of a tyrant wholeheartedly but never by resorting *to hatred or violence*. (BNC C9B 641)

(52) In the door leading *to the kitchen* Pumfrey noticed a girl of ten or so. (BNC H8Y 2979)

(53) At nine o'clock he left his room and went down *to the bar*. (BNC C86 2591)

In (50) the targeted goal is coded as *his mother*. In this case our encyclopedic knowledge of family relationships points to other close relatives as implicit alternative loci of his (actually T.S. Eliot's) confidence. In (51) it is the two discarded alternatives of *hatred* and *violence* that are coded. Again we can make use of our world knowledge to infer that the targeted alternative in this case is peaceful protest. In (52) the *kitchen door* is implicitly contrasted with other doors. This contrast may, of course, be of no great import in the actual communicative situation, in which case one would expect addressees to filter it out. This is even more the case in a token like (53), in which it would be far-fetched to presume that *the bar* is being contrasted with specific implicit alternative goals. Unless the actual goal is the unique one of *home*, one has to use a preposition in English to identify the goal of a motion verb like *go*. Note in this connection that an English verb coding exit from a location, such as *leave* in (53), does not require a preposition to code the location in question. This is for the obvious reason that we can only be in one place at a time, and can thus only leave one place at any one time. However if there are alternative exits from the location we can *leave by* one of them. We can also, for example, *leave from Terminal 1*, but only in an airport with at least two terminals.

Common to the predications illustrated in Figures 2 and 3 is the fact that they open for the possibility of alternatives. In Figure 2 the alternative of *not reaching* the goal is *reaching* it. In Figure 3 the alternative is the presence of at least one

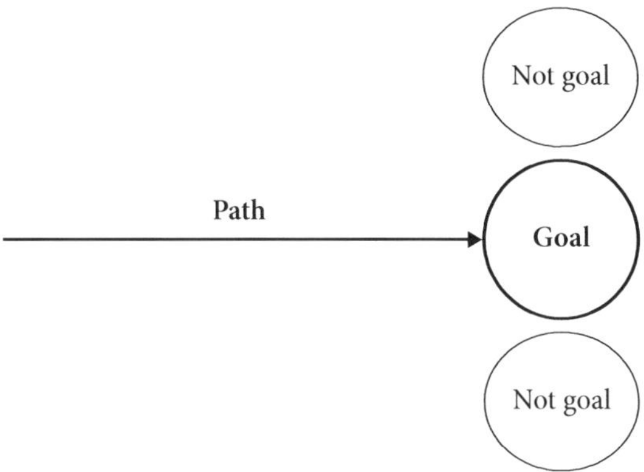

Figure 3. A path-goal schema incorporating unrealized alternative goals

other (latent) theoretically possible goal. To accommodate both these readings I propose that the preposition *to* should at the maximally schematic level be defined as coding *the targeted of several alternative goals*. The alternative in the first case is getting closer to, or actually reaching the goal. In the second case it is the presence in the background of some possible alternative goals. I have argued elsewhere that this schematic sense of the preposition *to* may be extended to infinitival *to*, yielding the following schematic definition for *to*-infinitive complements.[6]

> A schematic definition of *to*-infinitive complements
> "A situation, viewed as a whole, is profiled as the more/most likely of two or more alternatives in some (specified) domain." (Egan, 2008: 99)

This definition is taken to subsume all sorts of *to*-infinitive complements. There are three main classes of these, coding Judgment predications, General Validity predications and Forward-oriented predications. All three are illustrated briefly below.

In the case of perceptual verbs with *to*-infinitive complements, discussed in the previous section, the domain referred to in the schematic definition is specified as the mental one incorporating acts of judgment that, by their very nature, admit of alternatives. They resemble in this respect more prototypical judgment matrix verbs, like *guess* in (54), *assume* in (55) and *judge* in (56).

(54) Trent had been correct in *guessing their destination to be* on the north fork of the Belpan River. (BNC AMU 907)

(55) He *assumed the pigtail to be* her own, but it wasn't. (BNC FSP 569)

(56) Nevertheless, in a 'matched guise' test which I administered to a class of fourteen to fifteen year-old adolescents in the speaker's own home area, seven out of eleven black pupils *judged her to be* black on the basis of an extract from the story above (see Chapter 4 for a discussion). (BNC HXY 226)

Judgment constructions code a conjecture on the part of the matrix verb subject about the complement situation. This conjecture may be a firm one, as in the case of the '*know* x *to be*' construction, or a good deal weaker, as in the case of the '*guess* x *to be*' construction in (54). Irrespective of the subject's degree of conviction, however, the complement situation is coded as one of several alternatives. It thus resembles the prepositional *to* tokens in (24)–(27). The subject may well be mistaken in his or her conjecture as is the case in both (55) and (56). Whether or not the judgment of the subject is correct in any given instance does not in any way affect the meaning of the two constructions in question. In all judgment

6. I should point out that the interpretation of the *to*-infinitive as coding the targeted of two alternatives was proposed for the infinitive as syntactic subject by Chuquet (1986: 115).

constructions the focus of the subject is on one of several possible situations, the alternative considered to be the correct one.

The second class of *to*-infinitive complements, exemplified in (57)–(59), codes general validity predications.

(57) When I am hungry I *love to eat* a piece of bread. (BNC HS7 258)

(58) The two men *ceased for a time even to acknowledge* one another in the street; and though they later resumed formal courtesies, close friendship was dead. (BNC B0R 458)

(59) Several informants in my study articulated the view that their parents *preferred them to speak* British English: Mom – mom likes me to speak mostly English, she said when I go out into, you know, upper class society, and I start speakin' Patois dey might not understand, and take me as an idiot. (BNC HXY 1076)

Constructions like (57)–(59) profile situations as likely to be realized on all suitable occasions. These occasions may be of more or less regular occurrence. Indeed instantiations of general validity constructions often make concrete reference to the occasions on which one can expect the situation to be realized (or not realized in the case of negative constructions such as 'loathe *to*-infinitive' or 'cease *to*-infinitive'). These references commonly take the form of adverbials, such as *When I am hungry* in (57) and *in the street* in (58). More often, the locus of realization of the complement must be adduced from the context, as in (59), where it is implied that the desire on the part of the parents that their children speak English obtains on all occasions of their speaking.

The third and largest class of *to*-infinitive complements codes goals in the projected future. These may be profiled as realized, as in (60), unrealized, as in (63) or as uncertain with respect to realization as in (61) and (62).

(60) By the time Madeleine *remembered to go* and check the box it was nearly lunch-time and she was making hors d'oeuvres with one hand and pouring apéritifs with the other. (BNC GUK 2851)

(61) Last time I wrote for Contact I finished by saying that we *hoped to go* and see Miss Saigon. Well, 25 of us went to see it on the 13th of February, and it's a good show. (BNC EEL 679)

(62) She thought someone was coming to fetch her in a boat to take her away. No one ever knew where it was she *hoped to go*. (BNC FEM 172)

(63) 'Daddy apparently *forgot to go* and see Mr Simms in Woodborough General.' (BNC CMJ 178)

We have seen in tokens (41)–(44) that prepositional *to* allows for the possibility that the trajector has not (yet) reached his or her goal. Indeed there is no guarantee that he or she will ever reach it. Verspoor makes a similar point about the *to*-infinitive: "We may conclude that the *to* infinitive expresses that the subject, figuratively speaking, moves towards the state of being expressed, is not there yet, but is projected towards it" (Verspoor 1998: 511). Note however, that whereas *to* itself may just mean 'towards/in the direction of', it can be combined with matrix verbs such as *remember* in (60) which show that the target in question has actually been reached. More common are tokens where the possible future realization of the complement situation is left open, as in (61) and (62). The 'hope *to*-infinitive' construction instantiated in these two tokens shares with the 'remember *to*-infinitive' construction in (60) the semantic component that the *going* in question was still only a potential future occurrence at the precise moment of *remembering* and *hoping*. In all three tokens the *to*-infinitive codes the *focused* or *targeted* of several possible alternative situations, the alternative with the spotlight on it, so to speak. In many cases it is to be construed as a probable rather than a possible candidate for realization. How may this interpretation of the *to*-infinitive be reconciled with a matrix verb, such as *forget* in (63) which explicitly excludes the realization of the complement situation? (63) does not merely code the non-realization of a potential situation. It actually codes the non-realization of an *expected* situation, of what, prior to its non-realization, one might have described as a likely outcome. Thus all four tokens (60)–(63) code what is profiled as the targeted alternative in the future vis-à-vis the time of the matrix verb.

The schematic definition of the *to*-infinitive as coding the targeted of several alternatives has been shown to account for its use in all three types of complement, in forward-looking constructions, general validity constructions and judgment constructions. The interpretation of the '*see* x *to be* y' constructions advanced in the Section 4 can now be seen to follow naturally from this schematic sense. It is a semantic blend of the conceptual construction illustrated in (1) and (2) and the perceptual construction illustrated in (3) and (4). In the blend the latter construction contributes either the semantic component of vision or that of understanding, and the former the semantic component of a targeted alternative. The blend of vision and targeted alternative yields in (24)–(26) a reading in terms of revised construal, and in (31)–(34) a reading in terms of false perception.

6. Conclusion

In this chapter I have reconsidered Bolinger's interpretation of the '*see* x *to be* y' construction in the light of evidence from large corpora. This evidence turns out to be converging in that it provides support for Bolinger's analysis. I have also related the semantics of the construction to a general schematic interpretation of the meaning of the *to*-infinitive form. This interpretation is in turn also based on corpus evidence. Having considered objections raised to Bolinger's thesis by Noël, who maintained that tokens from the BNC represented diverging evidence, I conclude that Bolinger is basically correct when he states that when followed by a *to*-infinitive complement, perceptual verbs are being used in a conceptual sense. Of a total of 503 tokens with active voice matrix verbs (see Table 1), only three, cited as (38)–(40), can plausibly be argued to code a predication of perception pure and simple. However, Bolinger's contention that this usage is roughly equivalent to the same verbs with a *that* clause such that *I saw it to be true* = *I saw that it was true* only applies to some half of the tokens in the corpora. In the other half, the speaker undermines the perception of the subject, such that *He saw it to be true* = *It appeared to him to be true, but was actually false.* In the first sense we can reduce the "roughness" of the equivalence by adding the adverb *actually* to Bolinger's formulation: *I saw it to be true* = *I saw that it was* actually *true.* My definition of the second sense also contains the adverbial *actually*. This is no accident. The adverbial *actually* points to the targeted of several conceivable alternative situations. The implication of latent alternatives is also part of the maximally schematic sense of the *to*-infinitive form.

References

Corpora:

British National Corpus. 2001. Oxford: Oxford University Computing Services.
Davies, Mark. *Corpus of Contemporary American English.* http://www.americancorpus.org/
WebCorp. 1999–2009. Birmingham City University. http://www.WebCorp.org.uk/

Secondary:

Bolinger, Dwight L. 1968. Entailment and the meaning of structures. *Glossa* 2(2): 119–127.
Bolinger, Dwight. 1974. Concept and percept: Two infinitive constructions and their vicissitudes. In *World Papers in Phonetics: Festschrift for Dr. Onish's Kizyu* 65–91. Tokyo: Phonetic Society of Japan.
Chuquet, Jean. 1986. *To et l'infinitif anglais: dètermination et opérations énonciatives.* Paris: Ophrys.
Duffley, Patrick J. 1992. *The English Infinitive.* London: Longman.
Egan, Thomas. 2008. *Non-finite Complementation: A Usage-based Study of Infinitive and* -ing *Clauses in English.* Amsterdam: Rodopi.

Fischer, Olga. 2003. Principles of grammaticalization and linguistic reality. In G. Rohdenburg & B. Mondorf, eds., *Determinants of Grammatical Variation in English*, 445–478. Berlin: Mouton de Gruyter.

Langacker, Ronald W. 1995. Raising and transparency. *Language*, 71(1), 1–62.

Noël, Dirk. 2003. Is there semantics in all syntax? The case of accusative and infinitive constructions vs. *that*-clauses. In G. Rohdenburg & B. Mondorf, eds., *Determinants of Grammatical Variation in English*, 347–377. Berlin: Mouton de Gruyter.

Popper, Karl R. 1972. *Objective Knowledge: An Evolutionary Approach*. Oxford: Clarendon Press.

Smith, Michael B. & Joyce Escobedo. 2001. The semantics of *to*-infinitival vs. *-ing* complement constructions in English. In M. Andronis, C. Ball, H. Elston, & S. Neuvel, eds., *Proceedings from the Thirty-seventh Meeting of the Chicago Linguistic Society: The Main Session*, Vol. 1. 549–563. Chicago, IL: The Society.

Tyler, Andrea & Vyvyan Evans. 2003. *The Semantics of English Prepositions: Spatial Scenes, Embodied Meaning and Cognition*. Cambridge: Cambridge University Press.

Verspoor, Marjolijn. 1990. *Semantic Criteria in English Complement Selection*. University of Leiden.

Verspoor, Marjolijn. 1998. *To* infinitives. In L. De Stadler & C. Eyrich, eds., *Issues in Cognitive Linguistics: 1993 Proceedings of the International Cognitive Linguistics Conference*, 505–526. Berlin: Mouton de Gruyter.

Wierzbicka, Anna. 1988. *The Semantics of Grammar*. Amsterdam & Philadelphia: John Benjamins.

Explaining diverging evidence

The case of clause-initial *I think**

Gunther Kaltenböck
University of Vienna

The syntactic status of clause-initial complement-taking predicates has been controversially discussed in the literature with analyses ranging from main clause to parenthetical. This chapter sheds light on the question by providing a usage-based account of 200 occurrences of initial *I think* in a corpus of spoken English. It investigates to what extent the two formal cues (i) presence or absence of the *that*-complementizer and (ii) prosodic prominence provide evidence for the relative prominence of *I think*. The data present diverging evidence, which can be reconciled however by (i) adopting a dynamic model of grammar and (ii) reassessing the function of the *that*-complementizer in spoken language, viz. as a filler used for rhythmic purposes or to give weight to the initial clause.

Keywords: initial clause, main clause, parenthetical, prosodic prominence, *that*-complementizer

1. Introduction

This chapter investigates the syntactic status of clause-initial *I think* followed by a so-called complement clause and in doing so illustrates how quantitative and qualitative corpus analysis can be used to gain insights into syntactic structure. The methodology adopted is thus an empirical one, based on the observation of

* I would like to thank the two anonymous reviewers for their detailed and constructive comments, Doris Schönefeld for her help in the editing process, and Bryan Jenner for his invaluable assistance in the prosodic analysis. I am also indebted to numerous colleagues in my department, especially the VIEWS team, for their useful feedback on a previous version of the chapter as well as to the organisers of the workshop on 'Prototypicality, Gradience and Fuzziness in Cognitive Linguistics' at the 3rd *International Conference of the German Cognitive Linguistics Association* in 2008, Alexander Bergs, Lena Heine, and Rolf Kreyer, and the workshop participants. Any remaining insufficiencies are of course my own.

naturally occurring data. In terms of the empirical cycle outlined by Schönefeld (this volume) the present study highlights particularly the phases of hypothesis testing and evaluation, while at the same time also providing a detailed descriptive account of the data. More precisely, it examines syntactic and prosodic aspects of the construction in question and shows that they yield evidence which at first glance appears to be incompatible: prosodic and syntactic evidence each seem to support different analyses of the syntactic status of initial *I think*. A closer investigation, however, reveals that it is possible to reconcile these apparent differences by modifying the original hypotheses and adopting a grammar model that allows for a dynamic relationship between usage and structure and incorporates a diachronic dimension.

As a highly formulaic phrase *I think* is a typical example of the larger syntactic category of complement-taking predicates (CTPs for short) especially the semantic subclass of grammaticalized complement-taking mental predicates, such as *I believe, I suppose, I guess*. CTPs such as these have been controversially discussed in the literature because of their unclear syntactic status. Are they main clauses, which syntactically govern a complement clause, or comment clauses, which are in a syntactically supplementary (i.e. parenthetical) relationship to the following clause? In the latter case the *that*-clause would no longer be subordinate, but a main clause. A complicating factor for the analysis of such CTPs is the fact that the *that*-complementizer can be omitted, as in (1).

(1) *I think* (that) Mary lives in Reading.

Various views have been expressed on the status of such clause-initial epistemic phrases with and without *that*. They have been analyzed as matrix clauses (e.g. Peterson 1999: 236, Stenström 1995: e.g. 293, 296; Svensson 1976: 375), parentheticals (e.g. Kärkkäinen 2003, Kruisinga 1932: 486, Ross 1973, Thompson 2002, Thompson and Mulac 1991), or ambiguous in status allowing both analyses depending on context and type of 'matrix' predicate (e.g. Aijmer 1972: 46, Biber et al. 1999: 197, Huddleston and Pullum 2002: 896, Quirk et al. 1985: 1113, Urmson 1952: 481).

The present chapter tries to shed some light on this question by providing a usage-based account of 200 occurrences of initial *I think* in a corpus of spoken English. More precisely, it investigates to what extent the corpus data provide evidence for the relative prominence of *I think*, which in a cognitive-functional perspective is the underlying principle for distinguishing between main and subordinate clause status (e.g. Langacker 1991, Thompson 2002). In spoken language there are two formal cues for signaling prominence of *I think* and hence a possible hierarchical difference between the two clauses: (i) the presence or absence of the *that*-complementizer as an explicit marker of syntactic subordination and

(ii) prosodic prominence, which in turn reflects communicative salience. The present study takes a close look at the syntax-prosody interface by comparing the two types of data and investigating to what extent they can provide evidence for a particular syntactic analysis of initial *I think* and, as a consequence, for the assessment of the role of the *that*-complementizer.

The corpus used for the study is the spoken section of ICE-GB, the British component of the *International Corpus of English* (Nelson et al. 2002). It comprises roughly 600,000 words and yields a total of 1,138 instances of clause-initial *I think*, 9 percent (102 instances) of which occur with a *that*-complementizer.

The chapter is structured in the following way. Section 2 briefly discusses how the use of the *that*-complementizer has been interpreted in previous studies as syntactic evidence for main clause status of the CTP-phrase. Section 3 then investigates cognitive-functional evidence, which suggests that CTPs are generally backgrounded, although the contextual factors responsible for this are far from clear. Section 4 turns to prosodic prominence as a formal signal for functional prominence of the CTP in spoken language. It identifies three different prosodic patterns and shows that there is little difference between the two constructional types *I think* +zero and *I think* +*that*. Section 5 compares the data for the two formal cues, syntax and prosody, and discusses how the diverging evidence can be accounted for. Section 5.1 discusses the role of the two potential cues for foregrounding, prosody and syntax, in a dynamic model of grammar that incorporates the complex interrelationship between the levels of usage and structure. Section 5.2 reassesses the role of the *that*-complementizer in the light of the corpus data. Section 6 provides a brief conclusion.

2. Syntactic evidence

One argument for identifying initial *I think* as a main clause is the fact that it may be followed by an explicit marker of subordination, viz. a *that*-complementizer. However, the *that* need not be present. In fact, corpus evidence clearly shows that the use of an explicit subordinator represents, with an average of nine percent, the marked option (cf. Givón's 1995 criteria of markedness).[1] Compare the results in Table 1, which also illustrate the well-known increase of *that* insertion in more formal texts (e.g. Elsness 1984, Biber 1999, Kaltenböck 2006a).

1. Similar results have been found by other studies, e.g. Thompson and Mulac (1991) for *think* in spoken American English (91%), and Tagliamonte and Smith (2005) for *I think* in British dialects (91%).

Table 1. Clause-initial *I think* followed by *that* and zero in ICE-GB (raw figures in brackets)

Text type (no. of words)		*–that*	*+that*	Total
Private dialogue s1a	(205,627)	94.9% (466)	5.1% (25)	100% (491)
Public dialogue s1b	(171,062)	89.3% (434)	10.7% (52)	100% (486)
Public monologue s2a	(152,829)	87.9% (80)	12.1% (11)	100% (91)
Scripted speech s2b	(108,164)	81.4% (57)	18.6% (13)	100% (70)
Total		91.0% (1,036)	9.0% (102)	100% (1,138)

Corpus evidence such as this has led Thompson and Mulac (1991) to propose a fairly strict division between main- and comment clause uses of *I think*. They suggest that certain combinations of main clause subjects and verbs (such as *I think*) 'are being reanalyzed as unitary epistemic phrases. As this happens, the distinction between 'main' and 'complement' clause is being eroded ... with the omission of *that* a strong concomitant' (Thompson and Mulac 1991: 249). This view of a syntactic reanalysis of *I think* has been criticized by Kearns (2007), who proposes a pragmatic explanation in terms of informational prominence for the presence or absence of an overt subordinator, but maintains the traditional matrix clause analysis of *I think* for all cases. Thompson (2002) herself, in a more recent publication, has moved in the opposite direction, suggesting that all CTP-phrases in conversation are best analyzed as epistemic formulaic fragments rather than superordinate matrix clauses irrespective of presence or absence of a *that*-complementizer. This view is largely based on functional evidence and is discussed in more detail in the following section.

In an attempt to provide evidence for a difference in status between CTPs taking a *that*-complementizer and those taking zero, various syntactic tests have been proposed. These are intended to demonstrate that the former are proper main clauses and the latter are not. I briefly discuss three such tests and show that the evidence they allegedly present is far from conclusive.

One test is the **tag-question test** (e.g. Aijmer 1972: 52, 1997: 8; Hand 1993: 501, Knowles 1980: 405). The argument is that the 'subordinate' clause in (2) has lost some of its subordinate status since it allows various 'main clause phenomena' (cf. Hooper and Thompson 1973, Green 1976), such as the tag question.

(2) *I think* Ø John is in Paris, isn't he?

However, the same seems to be true for sentences with *that*, as in (3) (cf. Aijmer 1997: 8), although Hand (1993: 501) marks it as questionable.

(3) *I think* that John is in Paris, isn't he?

Conversely, the 'matrix clause' in a sentence without *that*, as in (4a), does not seem to allow questioning in this way (cf. Aijmer 1997: 8, Knowles 1980: 405). This is equivalent to the behavior of 'real' parentheticals, as in (4b), and can be taken as an indication that the clause lacks illocutionary force.

(4) a. *I think* Ø John is in Paris, *don't I?
    b. John is in Paris, *I think*, *don't I?

The validity of this test, however, is questionable, as the unacceptability of the tags in (4) could also be attributed to a pragmatic restriction, viz. the inappropriateness of a speaker questioning (doubting) his/her own statement. Indeed, if we substitute a pragmatically more likely tag, as in (5), the result is acceptable to me in both cases.

(5) a. *I think* John is in Paris, don't you?
    b. John is in Paris, *I think*, don't you?

Another form of **question test** is intended to show that questioning of the CTP works with an explicit complementizer, as in (6a), but is problematic without a complementizer, as in (6b) (cf. Huddleston and Pullum 2002: 896, Asher 2000: 33).

(6) a. A: *I believe* that John is in Paris.
       B: Really. Do you?
    b. A: *I believe* John is in Paris.
       B: ?Really. Do you?

Similar results can be obtained from the **negation test** (adapted from Erteschik-Shir and Lappin 1979: 46):

(7) a. *I believe* that John is in Paris.
       – No, that's a lie. I don't actually.
       – No, that's a lie. He isn't actually.
    b. *I believe* John is in Paris.
       – No, that's a lie. ?I don't, actually.
       – No, that's a lie. He isn't, actually.

The results of these tests, however, depend on the type of predicate used. Unlike *believe*, which is well-known for its semantic ambivalence (cf. Hooper, 1975: 100–101, Quirk et al. 1985: 1113, Huddleston and Pullum 2002: 896), more fully grammaticalized predicates such as *I think* yield different results. Moreover, acceptability depends to a large extent on context and prosodic delivery. The above tests therefore have to be interpreted with caution and cannot be seen as providing conclusive evidence for a different status of CTP phrases with and without *that*. I return to the role of the *that*-complementizer in Section 5.2, which presents corpus evidence suggesting that in spoken texts *that* is no longer used as a marker of subordination.

3. Cognitive-functional evidence

Cognitive-functional perspectives generally support a parenthetical or comment clause analysis of *I think* (and similar CTP-phrases) irrespective of whether they are followed by a complementizer or not. Kärkkäinen (2003: 41, 2010), for instance, notes that epistemic phrases (such as *I think*) with *that* are functionally equivalent to those without. A similar view is expressed in Diessel and Tomasello's (1999) study of early child language, which explains the absence of the complementizer after *I think, I guess, I know*, etc. by their function as evidential markers. They argue that '[c]hildren don't use a *that*-complementizer because constructions that appear to be early complement clauses are really independent sentences accompanied by parenthetical matrix clauses (e.g. *I think*) that do not make an independent assertion' (Diessel and Tomasello 1999: 87). Another functional investigation is Thompson (2002), who challenges the standard analysis of CTP-phrases as matrix clauses and argues that finite indicative complement clauses (with and without complementizer) are generally not subordinate but override the 'main clause' (CTP). The CTP should therefore not be analyzed as superordinate matrix clause but as epistemic/evidential/evaluative fragment that simply expresses 'speaker stance towards the assessments, claims, counterclaims, and proposals' (Thompson 2002: 134).

In the following I take a closer look at Thompson's (2002) analysis, as the most fully argued functional account of CTPs, and critically review her approach to identifying discourse salience. In her argumentation Thompson refers to Langacker's (1991: 436ff) definition of a subordinate clause as 'one whose profile is overridden by that of the main clause ... *I know* ***she left*** designates the process of knowing, not of leaving', where 'profile' refers to the 'relative prominence accorded to various substructures' (Langacker 1991: 4). Thompson (2002: 131) interprets the notions of 'profile' and 'relative prominence' in terms of the interactional actions that an utterance is performing in a particular context (cf. Goodwin and Goodwin 1992, Linell 1998, Pomerantz and Fehr 1997, Schegloff 1990). From the analysis of her corpus examples she concludes that 'the talk doing the actions that the participants are jointly engaged in doing is either in a main clause turn or in a finite indicative complement' (Thompson 2002: 134), while 'the CTP-phrases do not constitute the speakers' interactional agenda' (Thompson 2002: 134). The 'action' or 'interactional agenda' is thus roughly equivalent with the ''issue' around which the talk centers' (Thompson 2002: 133) or, presumably, the discourse topic. Example (8) illustrates her point with the CTP *I don't care* and an *if*-clause complement, which in her view is functionally equivalent to a *that*-clause (= Thompson's ex. 13; boldface indicates the talk accomplishing the action).

(8) [Frank and his young son Brett have noticed that Brett's sister Melissa appears to be about to mark on Brett's art project]

1 MELISSA: are you gonna add like the little lines that jut out of [these]?
2 FRANK: [get your pen] back from that
3 BRETT: yeah
4 MELISSA: **it's erasable,**
5 **and I am not marking on it.**
6 BRETT: <u>I don't care **if it's erasable**.</u>
7 **don't touch it.**
8 MELISSA: **(HI I didn't HI)**
9 BRETT: **...I know**
10 **...don't**

Although Thompson's analysis is a compelling one, her identification of discourse prominence does not provide a satisfactory explanation for all data. A case in point is Example (8) above, where prominence could also be analyzed in terms of information structure. This would yield an entirely different result for the construction in question: the complement clause, which is entirely retrievable from the preceding co-text, has to be seen as informationally backgrounded, while the CTP represents the communicatively salient, i.e. new (irretrievable) bit of information, which contributes to the further development of the communication (cf. e.g. Firbas' 1992 notion of communicative dynamism). In contrast to Thompson it is therefore the assertion of the CTP *I don't care* that is the main point of the utterance. This problem has also been noted by Boye and Harder (2007: 576f), who conclude that epistemic stance cannot automatically be equated with secondary discourse function. In their model they consequently distinguish between 'stance-marking as an aspect of lexical meaning and stance-marking as an inherently secondary, 'parenthetical' discourse or usage function' (Boye and Harder 2007: 577) (see Section 5.1 for further discussion).

However, information structure cannot always provide a clear-cut answer either. Compare, for instance, the following example from Thompson (2002: 132), which contradicts a simple equation of informational retrievability and non-assertion.[2]

(9) [at a birthday party, after Kevin was discovered to have lettuce on his tooth, everyone has jokingly commented on it, and Kendra has asked for a toothpick]

WENDY: ...everybody's getting uh, tooth obsessed
KEN: <u>I guess we a=re.</u>

2. Although Boye and Harder seem to argue for a view of prominence in terms of newness (cf. Boye and Harder 2007: 576) in contradistinction to Thompson, they, somewhat surprisingly, fully accept Thompson's analysis of this example.

Here the complement *we are* represents given (retrievable) information, which is clearly reflected in its elliptical form. Nonetheless, the main point of the utterance is not the CTP *I guess* but the complement. The reason is that what is at issue here (the 'action' in Thompson's terms) is the act of agreeing or affirming the previous utterance, for which the CTP, owing to its semantic vagueness, is not a suitable candidate. This example illustrates that establishing the communicatively salient part of the construction is not always a simple straightforward matter of equating givenness with backgrounding but has to take into account a variety of factors: 'interactional action', information structure, and the semantic content of the predicate.

In spoken language, however, there is an additional means available to the speaker to signal prominence: prosody. As an iconic reflection of prominence (cf. Bolinger 1985), prosody helps us in Example (9) to identify the complement as the main point of the utterance rather than the CTP *I guess*. As noted for instance by Halliday (1985: 277), new or 'newsworthy' information is information that is presented by the speaker as such. Prosodic prominence is such a means of presentation.

4. Prosodic evidence

This section investigates the prosodic prominence of *I think* as a cue for functional prominence. It compares the two formal signals available for foregrounding the CTP, viz. the use of an explicit subordinator and prosodic highlighting, and investigates to what extent syntactic and prosodic evidence correspond. Section 4.1 first analyses the prosody of *I think* with *that* omission, which is compared in Section 4.2 with the results for *I think* followed by *that* insertion. The implications of this comparison are further discussed in Section 5.

4.1 *That* omission

In spoken language, prosody is a prime indicator of functional prominence, with prosodic prominence iconically reflecting the communicative salience of a linguistic element. Prosodic prominence is, however, not simply a matter of 'high' or 'low' but a gradual phenomenon. In a previous study I distinguished between 'prosodically independent' and 'right-bound' comment clauses. For initial position it is possible to further distinguish between two forms of 'right-bound', viz.

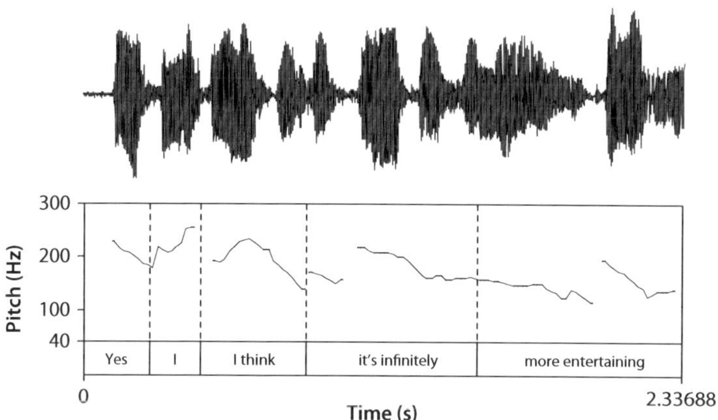

Figure 1. *I think* forming an independent tone unit

realization as head or pre-head, which leaves us with the following three degrees of prosodic prominence: (i) separate tone unit, (ii) part of the head, or (iii) part of the pre-head (Kaltenböck 2008, cf. also Kaltenböck 2009a).[3] Each of these types is illustrated below for *I think*.

i. *I think* with an independent tone unit is exemplified in (10) (see Figure 1), which has a nuclear accent on *I* and is followed by a tone unit boundary after *think*, indicated by a change in pitch level (cf. Cruttenden 1997: 35 on boundary markers).[4] As a possible alternative the nucleus may also be on the predicate *think* rather than on the pronoun *I* (cf. Simon-Vandenbergen 2000: 50, Kaltenböck 2010 for the specific function of early nuclear placement uses).

(10) Yes *I I think* it's infinitely more entertaining (s1b-024-12)

ii. An example of *I think* integrated into the head is given in (11) (see Figure 2), where *think* represents the first accented syllable in the tone unit, the so-called onset

3. The terminology of head, pre-head, nucleus (or tonic) and tone unit used here is that of the British tradition of intonational analysis, as discussed for instance in Couper-Kuhlen (1986: 78–109), Cruttenden (1997), Crystal (1969), Wichmann (2000). In a tone unit the nucleus is the only obligatory element. It carries a nuclear tone, which begins on the nuclear syllable and may stretch out over the tail, if there is one. The optional elements of a tone unit include a head (from the first accented syllable up to but not including the nucleus), a pre-head (any stressed syllables preceding the head), and a tail (any stressed syllables following the nucleus).

4. Dehé (2007: 267) refers to parentheticals such as these, where prosodic and syntactic criteria match, as "prototypical parentheticals".

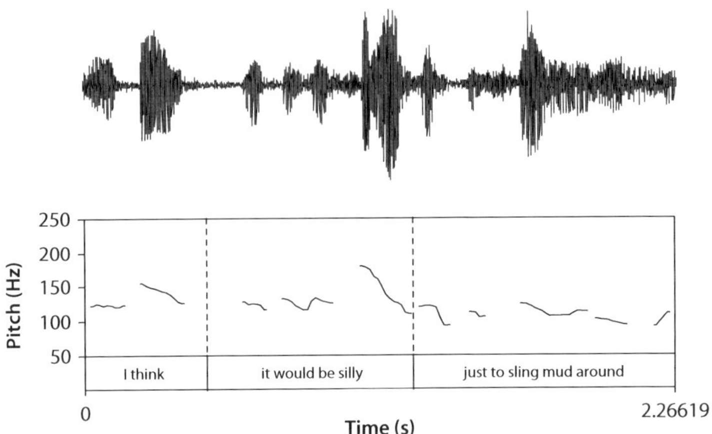

Figure 2. *I think* integrated into the head

(e.g. Wells 2006: 207) but is less prominent than the nuclear accent on *silly* (cf. Cruttenden 1997: 54 for a definition of head).[5]

(11) *I think* it would be silly just to sling mud around (s1b–022–19)

Typically in such cases the accent is on the predicate *think* as in Example (11). As unstressed element, *I* represents the pre-head but may be suppressed altogether as in (12) (where 〈,〉 indicates a short pause (see Figure 3).

(12) *Think* the tutorials are helpful (s1b–015–4)

Occasionally, the accent may occur on the *I* (rather than on *think*), which then starts the head, as in Example (13) (see Figure 4).

(13) *I think* it's all jolly good fun (s1b–024–28)

5. To distinguish between heads and nuclei the following criteria were applied:
   a. Onset syllables are generally on a higher pitch level than the nucleus owing to declination within a tone unit, i.e. the fact that pitch tends to be lower at the end of a tone unit than at the beginning (e.g. Couper-Kuhlen 1986: 82–83, Wichmann 2000: 103–105).
   b. If at the beginning of a tone unit, i.e. not preceded by a pre-head, the onset is often anacrustic, i.e. produced with greater speed (cf. Cruttenden 1997: 32).
   c. Only in case of a separate nucleus is *I think* followed by a tone unit boundary, as indicated by features such as anacrusis, final syllable lengthening, change of pitch level or pitch direction of unaccented syllables (cf. Cruttenden 1997: 35).
   d. Onsets are less prominent than nuclear accents, which is reflected phonetically in a smaller range of pitch movement and/or weaker energy pulses.

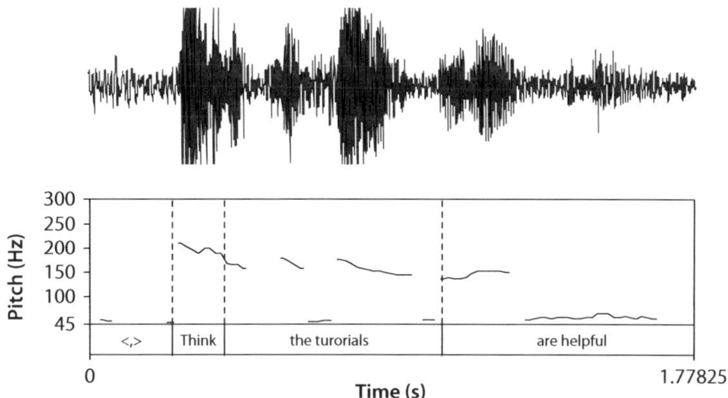

Figure 3. *I think* with *I*

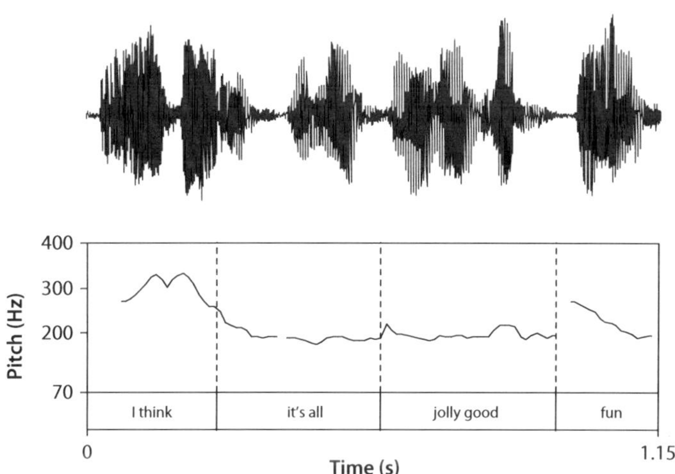

Figure 4. *I think* with accented *I*

iii. The third prosodic pattern is that of integration in the form of a pre-head, i.e. an unaccented (typically unstressed and anacrustic) syllable preceding the head (cf. Wells 2006: 214–215).[6] This pattern is exemplified in (14), where the string *I think it's* forms the pre-head, followed by an accented syllable *some*, which starts the head, and the nucleus on *quarter* (see Figure 5).

(14) *I think* it's something like a quarter (s1b-030-29)

6. The term 'stress' is used here as rhythmically stressed, while 'accent' refers to a syllable made prominent by rhythmic stress and pitch prominence, i.e. by a change in pitch, movement in pitch, or the start of a pitch movement (cf. Wells 2006: 93).

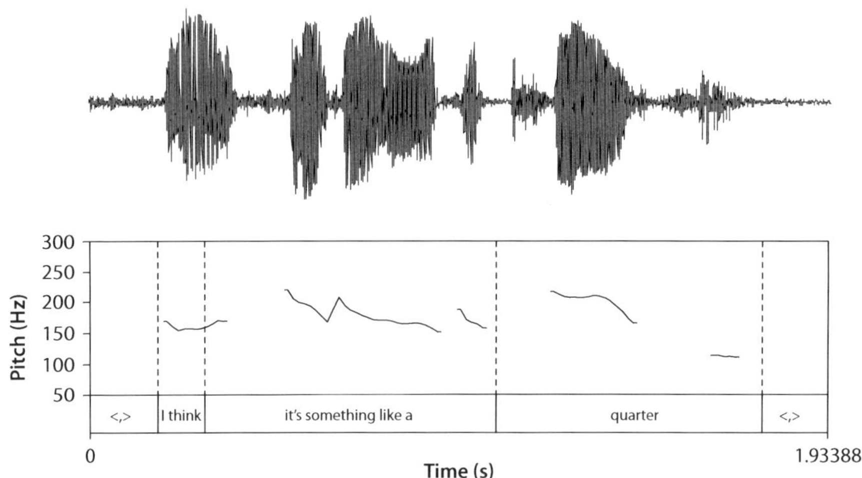

Figure 5. *I think* as part of the pre-head

For the corpus analysis, only subsection Public dialogue (s1b) in ICE-GB was taken into account, which is the only text category that has a sufficiently large number of *that*-clauses (viz. 52, cf. Table 1 above).[7] The prosodic analysis of *I think* +zero is based on 148 random instances (of a total of 434 in Public dialogue), which were analyzed both auditorily and instrumentally with the help of the acoustical analysis program PRAAT (Boersma and Weenink 2008). The results are summarized in Table 2.

We can see that the dominant pattern is that of *I think* being realized as part of the head (75.7%), followed by its realization as pre-head (19.6%). An independent tone unit for *I think* is extremely rare (4.7%). This lack of nuclear prominence is, however, not really surprising, as *I think* is clearly the most grammaticalized

Table 2. Prosodic patterns of initial *I think* in Public dialogue followed by a zero *that*-clause

	n	%
Independent tone unit	7 (of which nucleus on *I*: 3)	4.7%
Part of head	112 (of which accent on *I*: 9)	75.7%
Part of pre-head	29	19.6%
Total	148	100%

7. The reason for basing the prosodic analysis on one text type only, viz. Public dialogue, was to exclude text type/register as a potential conditioning factor and thus increase the homogeneity of the sample.

(pragmaticalized) of all comment clauses and has therefore been subject to a high degree of semantic bleaching (e.g. Mindt 2003). This semantic reduction makes *I think* an unlikely candidate for nuclear highlighting.[8]

4.2 *That* insertion

In contrast to *I think* +zero, insertion of the subordinator could be interpreted as an indication of main clause status of *I think*. The prosodic analysis, however, suggests otherwise. The analysis of all 52 instances of *I think* +*that* in Public dialogue (s1b) shows, first of all, that the same three patterns can be identified as for zero clauses above, viz. (i) nuclear accent, (ii) accented syllable in the head, and (iii) pre-head. These three patterns are illustrated by the examples in (15), (16), and (17) respectively (see Figures 6–8).

(15) *I think* that/any woman who wanted to join the MCC (s1b–021–26)
(16) And *I think* that they must be encouraged (s1b–036–72)
(17) I mean *I think* that if you take as it were a theological attitude (s1b–039–93)

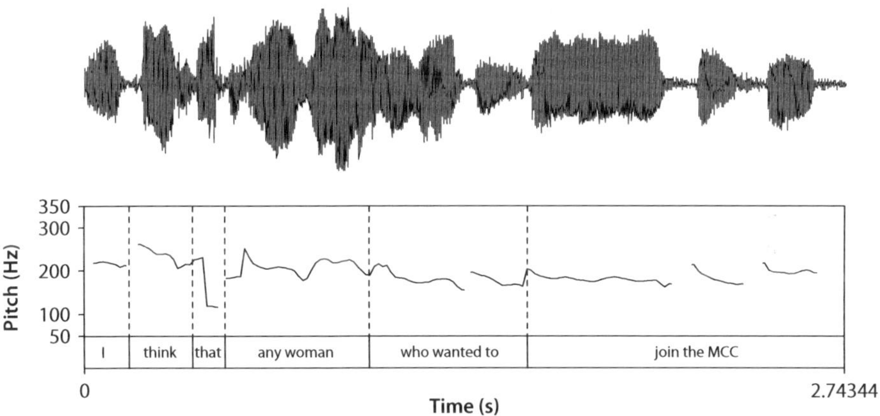

Figure 6. *I think* with nuclear accent

8. Previous studies have identified various functions of comment clauses and *I think* in particular. They show that comment clauses can be further grammaticalized from epistemic markers into pleonastic structuring devices, which are phonetically reduced and lack prosodic prominence (Kaltenböck 2008, 2009b, 2010). Initial *I think* realized as pre-head can be equated with such structural uses.

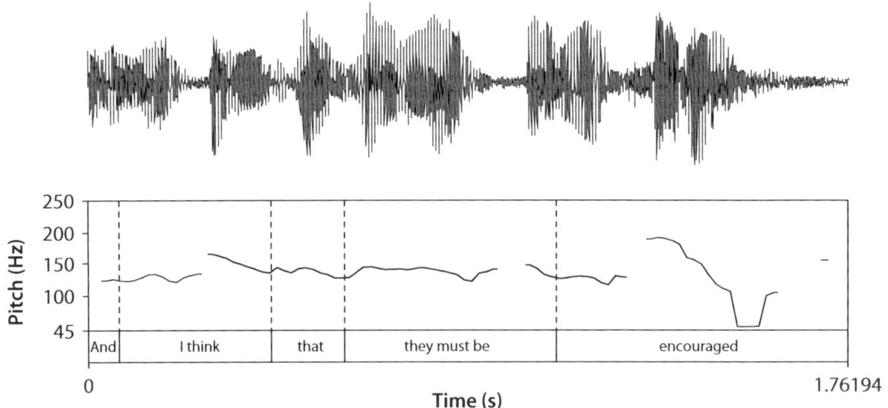

Figure 7. *I think* as part of the head

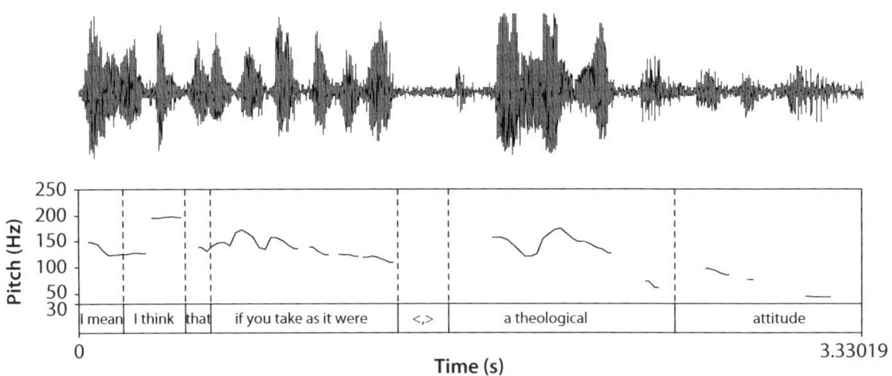

Figure 8. *I think* as part of the pre-head

In Example (15) *think* takes a **nuclear tone** with a tone unit boundary after the complementizer, as indicated by the pitch change on *any*. In Example (16), on the other hand, *think* represents the **onset of the head**, which leads up to (and includes) the initial syllable of *encouraged*. *Think* is preceded by the unstressed syllables *and* + *I*, which represent the pre-head. In Example (17) the **pre-head** includes both *I mean* and *I think*, with the head starting on *that*. As noted for zero *that*-clauses, the accent (both nuclear and non-nuclear) may shift away from *think* to the pronoun *I*.

Table 3. Prosodic patterns of initial *I think* in Public dialogue followed by a *that*-clause

	n	%
Independent tone unit	6 (of which nucleus on *I*: 2)	11.5%
Part of head	39 (of which accent on *I*: 5)	75.0%
Part of pre-head	7	13.5%
Total	52	100%

If we compare, as a next step, the results for *I think* +*that*-clause with those for *I think* +zero, we find a parallel distribution of the three prosodic patterns.[9] Table 3 shows that the most frequent pattern by far is again that of heads (75%), followed by pre-heads (13.5%) and independent tone units (11.5%).

In Section 5 I discuss the implications of this parallel distribution pattern for both constructional types.

5. Explaining diverging evidence

A comparison of the two types of data analyzed in the previous sections, viz. structural (*that* vs. zero) and prosodic realization, allows us to make the following two closely related observations. First, there is a discrepancy between structural and prosodic signals of prominence for *I think* +*that*. Second, different structural realization (viz. *I think* vs. *I think* +*that*) does not correspond with different prosodic behavior. I discuss possible implications of these two points in Section 5.1 and Section 5.2 respectively.

5.1 Relating syntactic structure and use

As noted in Section 2, the use of a *that*-complementizer is seen by some linguists as a clear indication of subordination of the second clause and hence as a sign of

9. Although the size of the database does not allow for firm conclusions in statistical terms, the results clearly show that realisation as part of the head accounts for a similar proportion of the data for both constructional variants.
Moreover, the general distributional pattern for each structural type has been confirmed by the analysis of a second rater, which showed a fairly consistent interrater agreement for both types: 86.5 percent for *I think* +*that* and 83.8 percent for *I think* +zero. Despite disagreement on the exact analysis of some individual cases, the overall pattern of distribution, viz. heads as preferred realisation followed by pre-heads and nuclei, as well as the parallel distribution pattern was confirmed by the second analyst. Cohen's kappa for *I think* +*that* is 0.68 and for *I think* +zero 0.61, which can be interpreted as 'substantial agreement' according to Landis and Koch (1977).

matrix clause status of the first. A typical representative of this view is the study by Thompson and Mulac (1991), which draws a sharp line between cases of *I think* (and similar CTPs) with complementizer and those without: the former are taken as clear instances of a matrix clause whereas the latter are interpreted as unitary epistemic fragments in supplementary (parenthetical) relationship to the second clause. The use of the *that*-complementizer in Thomspon and Mulac's view is thus linked to the syntactic reanalysis of the initial clause. Such a view, however, is in conflict with the prosodic results for *I think +that*, which show a clear preference for reduced prominence of the CTP-phrase. In other words, the two formal signals available for indicating relative prominence of the CTP, prosody and marker of subordination, do not correlate. This raises the question which of the two formal indicators is to be taken as decisive for the syntactic analysis. This question, in turn, is linked to the form of relationship assumed between the level of use and that of syntactic structure. I take up this point first before turning to the relative 'weight' of the two formal signals.

The question how the presumed syntactic structure and patterns of use are related is, of course, informed by one's view of grammar. In a cognitive-functional perspective, which subscribes to a usage-based, emergent view of grammar, linguistic structure is seen as arising from actual language use as conventionalization of recurrent usage patterns (e.g. Langacker 1987, 2000; Hopper 1987, 1988; Haiman 1994, Bybee and Hopper 2001: 12). As Du Bois (1985: 359–360) puts it 'recurrent patterns in discourse tokens exert pressure on linguistic types'. At the same time, however, it is important to acknowledge that the usage – structure relationship is not just a one-way street. While it is clear that structure is distilled out of usage, it seems necessary to accept that structure itself may exert some influence on usage. This has been discussed, for instance, by Boye and Harder (2007), who note that 'semantic choices are structured by the code, also if one believes that linguistic categories are usage-based' (Boye and Harder 2007: 572). In other words, structure, which manifests itself in linguistic code, crystallizes out of actual language use but at the same time exerts an influence on language use in the form of a 'structured potential' (Boye and Harder 2007: 572).

Of course this potential may no longer reflect current language use. This is the case where language use has changed over time with structural change lagging behind. With *I think* this is precisely the scenario we get. Although there are different views on the exact development of such CTPs (cf. Thompson and Mulac 1991, Brinton 1996, Fischer 2007a, b), there is agreement that they must have started out as some form of fully lexical main clauses (independent or matrix clause), expressing primary rather than secondary information (in Boye and Harder's terms). This is still reflected in the linguistic code, viz. the morphosyntactic form of a lexical clause and typical matrix clause features such as initial position and the (occasional) use of a subordinator. Such linguistic coding, however, no longer corresponds with the typical current use of *I think*, which is that of conveying secondary information.

While it is natural to expect linguistic structure to lag behind possible changes in usage, there are also factors that seem to favor a persistence of the original coding as primary information in Boye and Harder's sense. Thus it has been shown by Van Bogaert (2009: 424–428) that *I think* is part of a larger constructional network which involves other complement-taking mental predicates such as *I believe, I expect, I imagine*. These less grammaticalized complement-taking mental predicates together with other CTPs which only occur with their fully lexical meaning as clear instances of matrix clauses (e.g. *I am surprised, I don't give a damn*) can be assumed to exert considerable 'pulling power' (owing to their overall higher frequency), which slows down changes in the code of the more grammaticalized CTPs. The process at work seems to be one of analogization (cf. Van Bogaert 2009: 433) and could possibly be extended to include other non-CTP uses such as *I think about you, I'm thinking*.

Persistence of the original matrix clause code has also been made responsible for the use of the *that*-complementizer with highly formulaic (i.e. grammaticalized) uses of CTPs such as *I think*. In a recent study Torres Cacoullos and Walker (2009) have shown that fixed units such as *I think* and *I guess* are not completely autonomous from other forms of *that*-complementation. They therefore suggest that the notion of persistence or retention should be extended from semantics to syntax since 'grammatical properties also persist in the development of discourse formulas' (Torres Cacoullos and Walker 2009: 34). Structural coding in the form of a *that*-complementizer may therefore be a remnant of the function it previously had and not reflect the function it serves now. Compared to the 'rigid' structural form, which is more resistant to change, prosodic marking is a more flexible and therefore a more direct indication of current functions, which makes it a more reliable indicator for actual use, even more so since spoken language is typically at the forefront of new developments.

From the above it also becomes clear that in order to account for the diverging evidence identified in the previous sections, we need a dynamic model of language which captures the complex interrelationship between structure and use and allows for degrees of structural change, i.e. the change in the linguistic code, from a fully lexical clause (matrix clause)[10] to a grammatical element (comment clause). Such a model is offered by Boye and Harder (2007), who propose a scale of three

10. The term 'lexical clause' (cf. Boye and Harder 2007: 591) is used here to refer to the structural (i.e. morphosyntactic) properties of a typical clause, such as containing a VP and the ability to take dependents in the form of a subordinate clause. In Boye and Harder's framework 'lexical' contrasts with 'grammatical', which is equated with secondary discourse function.

categories for CTPs: (1) primary lexical CTPs, (2) secondary lexical CTPs, and (3) secondary grammatical CTPs. These different categories are also seen as different stages in the diachronic development of CTPs. As the terms already suggest, the classification takes into account both the structural and the usage status, each of which is described by a binary set of values: lexical vs. grammatical *structural status* and primary vs. secondary *usage status*. While the first stage is easily identifiable as matrix clause and the last stage as (clause internal and final) comment clause, the second stage is a hybrid category that is marked by a discrepancy between usage status and structural status and as such is descriptively ambiguous (cf. Boye and Harder 2007: 586). *I think* in clause-initial position seems to qualify for such an intermediate, potentially ambiguous stage. On the structural level its morphosyntactic form is that of a lexical clause (Boye and Harder 2007: 591) and its syntactic position that of a prototypical matrix clause, which, in turn, is reinforced by the use of the subordinator. In terms of its discourse function, however, initial *I think* is typically secondary.[11]

Let me elaborate this view in a more detailed interpretive model. From a cognitive perspective the expression of epistemic comment represents an interesting case of inherent ambiguity or indeterminacy. Much like an ambiguous or reversible image, such as Rubin's well-known face/vase illusion in Figure 9, the notion of 'comment' allows for two possible but complementary gestalts: as figure and as ground.

Figure 9. Rubin's ambiguous image depicting both a vase and two faces in profile (source: http://www.mi.sanu.ac.yu/vismath/jadrbookhtml/921.jpg)

11. Cases where the epistemic qualification of *I think* is the main point of the utterance are possible but extremely rare. Cf.

A: So you're telling me John is in Paris

B: I THINK John is in Paris (but I'm not sure)

In one reading a comment defines its existence by presupposing a state of affairs that is commented on, a so-called commentatum (Posner 1972). Such a commentatum typically represents given information as it is only natural to comment on a state of affairs the interlocutors are already familiar with. Such a reading is equivalent to foregrounding the comment and making it the figure against the ground of a given state of affairs or proposition. The alternative cognitive interpretation of a comment is as information of secondary value. Compared to asserting a state of affairs or proposition, evaluating or qualifying the proposition by providing an epistemic comment is generally of reduced communicative salience. Such a reading favors backgrounding of the comment and presenting it as ground against which the figure of the proposition can take shape.[12]

A similar view is expressed by Nuyts (2000: 122ff), who sees epistemic modal expressions as a 'battleground' where two conflicting functional forces are at work: an information structural force and an iconic (or conceptual-semantic) force. From the perspective of iconicity the status of the epistemic evaluation is that of an operator (i.e. a meta-representational element) over a state of affairs, which suggests main clause status for the epistemic expression 'since it directly reflects the meta-status of the qualification relative to the state of affairs' (Nuyts 2000: 123). In terms of information structure, on the other hand, the epistemic qualification is backgrounded and the state of affairs foregrounded, i.e. it carries the focal information. The information-structural force therefore works against a main clause interpretation for the epistemic expression, since main clauses prototypically carry foregrounded information and embedded clauses backgrounded information (cf. Brandt 1984, Givón 1984, Mackenzie 1984, Sadock 1984, Tomlin 1985).

Taking up Nuyts' metaphor, we can think of clause-initial epistemic markers such as *I think* as 'undecided battles' where the different forces outbalance each other and allow for two different interpretations of the status of *I think*. In other words, the result of these conflicting forces is one of ambivalence and indeterminacy (cf. Boye and Harder's hybrid category 'stage 2'). Which of the two possible readings of the CTP-phrase is activated depends on the actual realization of the construction in a given context. Factors that favor a foregrounded reading of the CTP are: (i) its morphosyntactic form as lexical clause, (ii) typical matrix clause (i.e. initial) position, (iii) use of an explicit subordinator. Factors which favor a backgrounded reading of the CTP are: (i) reduced semantic content of the predicate (e.g. *think*), (ii) formulaic nature of the CTP (e.g. *I* + *think*), (iii) secondary information status in its prototypical use (i.e. a statistical tendency to be used with non-salient discourse function). With initial *I think* these opposing factors balance each other out. In spoken language, however, there is an additional indicator that can

12. Compare a similar function of scene-setting adverbials.

help in identifying the status of initial *I think*, viz. prosody. For the reasons outlined above, prosodic signals can be taken as a more accurate reflection of actual usage status and can therefore be given more weight in interpreting the gestalt of a CTP construction than the use of *that*. In addition, the discussion in the following section presents further evidence for the assumption that, in spoken language, the use of a *that*-complementizer is far from a reliable indicator of subordination.

5.2 Reassessing the role of *that*

I now turn to the observation that structural variation (with and without *that*) does not correspond with different prosodic realization. As noted in Section 4.2, the two constructional types, *I think* +zero and *I think* +*that*, exhibit a similar distribution of the three prosodic patterns identified: they are both most frequently realized as heads, less frequently as pre-heads, and only rarely with a separate nuclear accent. This parallel distribution suggests that there is no fundamental difference in discourse function between the two constructional variants and confirms an assumption made, for instance, by Kärkkäinen (2003, 2010) or Nuyts (2000: 129 note 13).[13] Overt marking of subordination by a *that*-complementizer, in other words, does not have a noticeable impact on the prosodic foregrounding of *I think*, which raises the question whether *that* still functions as a marker of hierarchical difference between the two clauses. I pursue this point by taking a closer look at (i) the prosodic realization of *that*, (ii) the type of complement clause subject, (iii) adverbials between the two clauses, and (iv) co-occurrence with disfluency features.

5.2.1 *Prosodic realization of* that

Prosodic analysis of the *that*-complementizer shows that it can be intonationally grouped either with *I think* or the following clause. This difference in association is most obvious in cases where *I think* carries its own nuclear tone and is therefore followed by a tone unit boundary.[14] This boundary may either associate *that* with *I think*, as in Example (15) above, or associate it with the following clause, as in (18) (see Figure 10).

(18) *I think*/that he is the most neglected of that uh number of composers around the turn of the century (s1b-032-103)

13. This view is also implied, although not overtly expressed, in Thompson (2002) and Boye and Harder (2007).

14. In head and pre-head realisations of *I think* the complementizer is typically integrated into a larger pitch contour but may occasionally also show signs of association or dissociation with *I think*, albeit less markedly so.

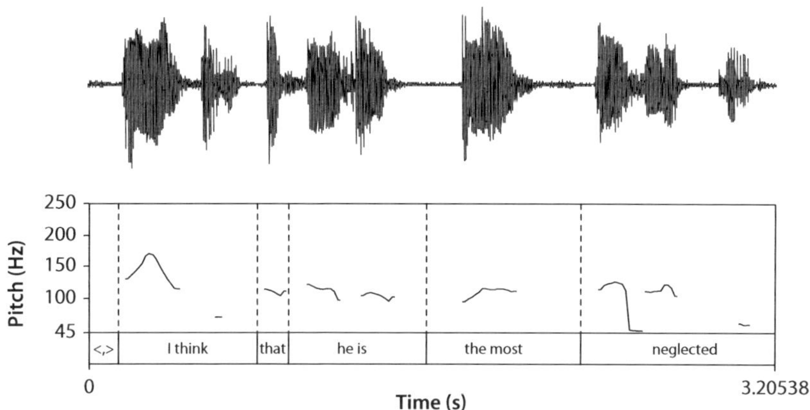

Figure 10. *That* associated with subsequent clause

The prosodic realization of *that* therefore does not necessarily reflect the syntactic analysis of the construction, which identifies the complementizer as part of the subordinate clause.[15] Such a mismatch between syntax and prosody is hardly surprising and has been noted before for various other constructions (e.g. Brazil 1997, Wichmann 2001, Dehé 2009). It is interesting, however, that there is a tendency for *that* to be prosodically grouped with *I think* rather than the following clause.[16]

How can we explain this lack of correspondence between syntax and prosody? Associating the complementizer on the usage level with *I think* (and indeed inserting it in the first place) seems to result from the speaker wanting to add weight to the CTP in the form of an extra syllable.[17] The reason for this may be twofold:

First, adding an extra syllable to the initial clause makes it longer and therefore more effective as clause-initial staller used for bridging a hesitation phase, which is one of the main functions of initial *I think* (e.g. Stenström 1994, 1995). Compare, for instance, the following example where *that* has a staller function similar to that of *uhm* and *and.*

15. Cf. however the semantic analyses by Davidson (2001), Lepore and Loewer (1989) and Hand (1993) for a different view.

16. This is also reflected in the fact that in the corpus *I think* and *that* are never separated by intervening material (e.g. hesitation sound, filler), whereas *that* is frequently separated from the clause of which it is the head. The level of performance therefore seems to suggest a closer association of *that* with the main clause rather than the subordinate clause.

17. With two syllables *I think* is one of the shortest of all comment clauses (cf. Kaltenböck 2006b, 2008), which incidentally also seems to have contributed to its advanced status of grammaticalization.

(19) Uhm *I I think* that uhm once you've spent your money on that the thing to spend your money on is a subscription to the local horticultural society (s1b–025–133)

Second, prosodic association or dissociation of *that* with *I think* can be motivated by rhythmic considerations. This is illustrated by Example (20), where chunking *that* with material following it rather than material preceding it results in two rhythmic chunks of roughly equal length: *then I think* and *that we* (see Figure 11).

(20) Then *I think* that we ought to ask Rabbi Sacks t uh uh to uh uh to say more because of course he has said two important things (s1b–028–63)

The underlying principle for rhythmic chunking seems to be that of rhythmic harmony, viz. a tendency towards rhythmic chunks of roughly equal size (principle of isochrony). This is illustrated in Example (21) (see Figure 12), where association of *that* with *I think* brings the first rhythmic unit in line with the average length of the following ones, i.e. roughly 1 second (note incidentally the same length of the second hesitation phase: *that* + *uh* + ⟨,⟩).

(21) *I think* that in the Labour Party we believe that uh ⟨,⟩ one year of sanctions would be preferable to one day of war (s1b–035–29)

While it is clear that the principle of rhythmic harmony cannot be pressed too far, it seems that the text type of public conversation is particularly susceptible to it, especially the text categories 'broadcast discussions' and 'broadcast interviews', which typically involve highly experienced public speakers and incidentally have the highest proportion of *that* in the corpus (6.6 and 3.2 occurrences per 10,000 words respectively as opposed to 1.2 occurrences for Private dialogue).

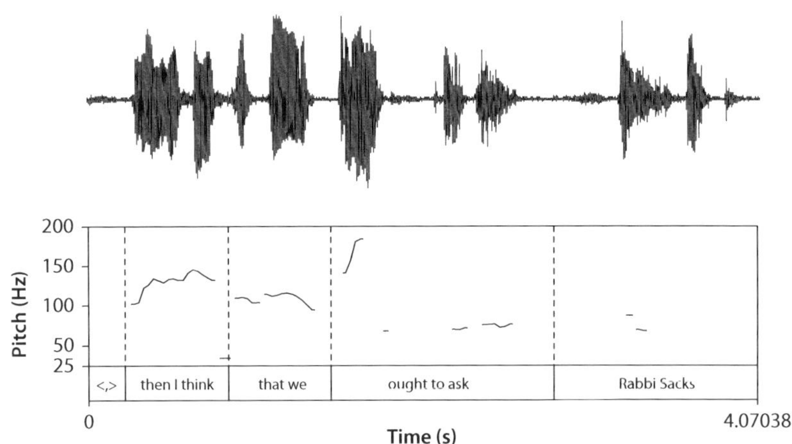

Figure 11. *That* chunked with subsequent material resulting in two rhythmic chunks

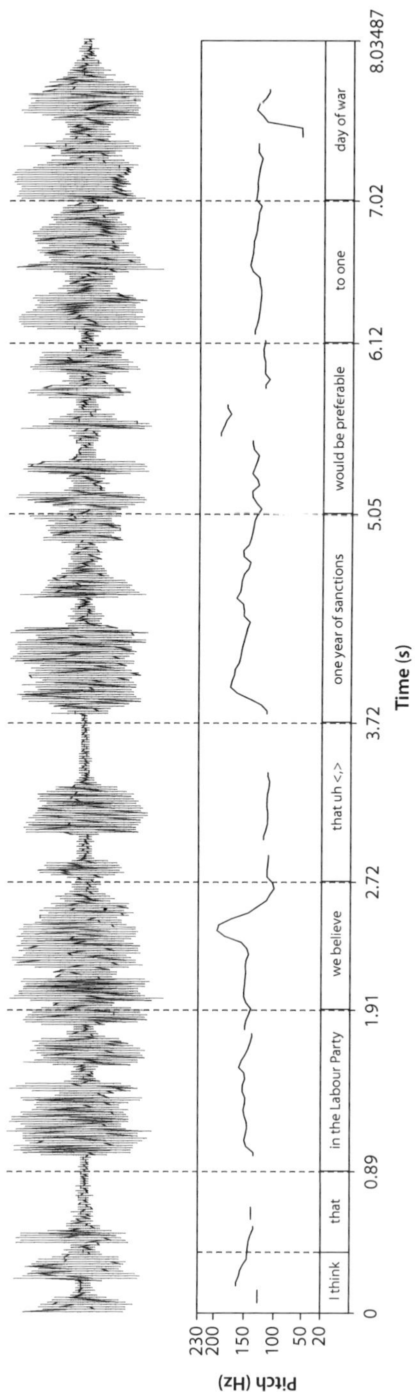

Figure 12. Rhythmic chunking of *that* with *I think*

5.2.2 *Type of complement clause subject*

The rhythm of the construction as a conditioning factor for the use or omission of *that* can also be linked to the type of subject in the *that*-clause. Consider, for instance, Example (22), where the subject of the second clause consists of an unstressed syllable (*there*), which is followed by two further unstressed syllables (*is a*). The resulting rhythmic pattern of the entire construction *I think there is a certain arrogance* (which has an accent on *I*) is the following sequence of strong and weak syllables: s s w w w s w s w w (see Figure 13). Note that a *that*-complementizer would add an extra unstressed syllable to the row of three unstressed syllables, which is not desirable for rhythmical reasons (cf. Schlüter 2005 on the role of rhythmic alternation for grammatical variation).

(22) *I think* there is a certain arrogance on the part particularly of the extreme left in Britain on this matter (s1b-027-136)

Closer inspection of the corpus data in Public dialogue reveals that unstressed subjects strongly favor *that* omission. A statistical analysis which takes into account all pronouns that are typically unstressed, i.e. existential *there*, anticipatory *it*, and all personal pronouns, i.e. disregarding all other types of subject such as full NPs, clauses, stressed pronouns (e.g. *this, that, mine*) and pronouns preceded by adverbials or hesitation markers (i.e. pronouns not immediately following *I think (that)*) shows that a preference for *that* is highly significantly affected by the presence of these unstressed subjects (cf. Table 4).

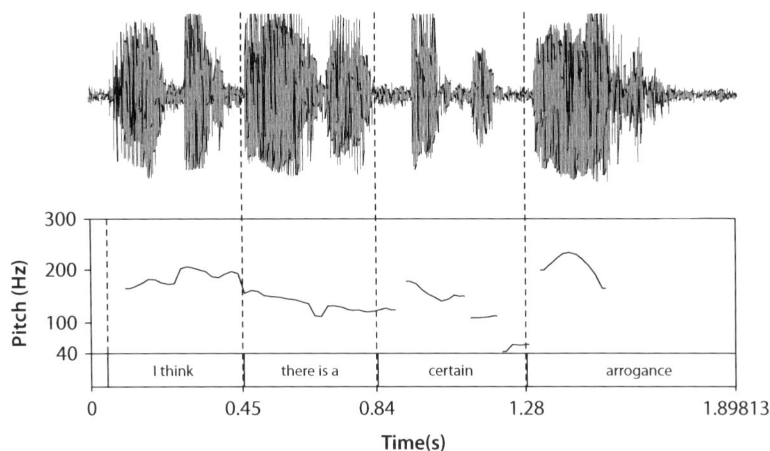

Figure 13. Unstressed complement clause subject

Table 4. Occurrence of *that* with unstressed pronominal subjects in the 'complement' clause

	–*that*	+*that*	Total
Unstressed pronominal subjects (personal pronoun, existential *there*, anticipatory *it*)	211 (94.2%)	13 (5.8%)	224 (100%)
Other subjects (full NP, clause, stressed pronoun, pronoun preceded by adverbial)	223 (85.1%)	39 (14.9%)	262 (100%)
Total	434	52	486
$\chi 2 = 9.095 >$ crit (df = 1, p = 0.01)			

This finding ties in with Elsness' (1984) observation that complex subjects correlate with *that*-retention. As a possible explanation for this he notes that '[a]lthough there is no risk of ambiguity in such constructions, one may see the selection of *that* connective as a contribution to greater syntactic clarity' (Elsness 1984: 532). This may be true for written texts. For spoken language, however, it is necessary to take into account rhythmic considerations, viz. unstressed subjects favoring *that* omission and, closely associated with this, memory constraints in online production: production of a syntactically complex subject, which can also be expected to have high informational value, will normally require extra 'thinking time' (cf. Rohdenburg's 1998 complexity principle), which is provided for by the *that*-complementizer.[18] This view is also in line with Ferreira and Dell's (2000) finding that the use of optional words such as *that* is sensitive to the availability of the embedded subject.

5.2.3 *Adverbials between the two clauses*

Elsness (1984) also mentions adverbials occurring at the boundary between matrix verb and object clause subject as a factor favoring *that* insertion. He attributes this to 'a (conscious or unconscious) desire on the part of the writer to avert ambiguity' (Elsness 1984: 532). In other words, *that* insertion identifies the adverbial as belonging to either the matrix- or the object clause. In the case of spoken *I think* (in Public dialogue), however, there are no instances where *that* is used to indicate association of an adverbial with the CTP. *That* always immediately follows *I think*. With *that* omission, on the other hand, all adverbials in pre-subject position (adverbs, PPs, clauses) are unambiguously identifiable as part of the 'complement' clause on semantic (and grammatical) grounds, as in (23).

18. Elsness (1984) notes coreferentiality of the pronominal object clause subject with the matrix clause subject as a further conditioning factor for *that* omission in written texts. For spoken *I think*, however, coreference of the two subjects does not play a major role: only 4.6 percent (20/434) of all zero *that*-clauses in Public dialogue have *I* as their subject, compared to 1.9 percent (1/52) of *Is* in *that*-clauses.

Table 5. Occurrence of *that* with adverbials preceding the 'complement' clause subject

	–that	*+that*	Total
Adverbials preceding 'object' clause subject	55 (80.9%)	13 (19.1%)	68 (100%)
No preceding adverbials	379 (90.7%)	39 (9.3%)	418 (100%)
Total	434	52	486
$\chi 2 = 5.13 >$ crit (df = 1, p = 0.05)			

(23) And *I think* [as an institution] uh we suffer (s1b-041-46)

Disambiguation can therefore be excluded as a conditioning factor for *that* insertion with spoken *I think*. The high proportion of *that* omission (80.9%) with pre-subject adverbials also attests to this. Nonetheless, *that* insertion is still significantly affected by adverbials preceding the 'complement' clause subject (cf. Table 5). Compare, for instance, Example (24).

(24) And *I think* that that [perhaps in the lectures] there was there wasn't really a a a an appreciation of the positive benefit to religious traditions of the cultural engagements which took place (s1b-028-37)

The reason why pre-subject adverbials favor *that* insertion again seems to lie in the greater syntactic complexity of the 'complement' clause. Just like complex subjects, adverbials in pre-subject position increase the syntactic weight of the 'complement' clause in unusual, i.e. initial, position, making it 'nose-heavy', as it were (cf. end-weight principle). This, in turn, increases production effort and favors the insertion of a filler in the form of *that*.

5.2.4 *Co-occurrence with disfluency features*

The *that*-complementizer, in other words, has an important filler function that allows the speaker to 'buy time'. This, in turn, can help alleviate production difficulties, as noted for instance by Jaeger (2005) (cf. also Clark 2004). Close analysis of the corpus data shows that there is indeed a trade-off between the use of *that* and production difficulties, with insertion of *that* correlating with fewer instances of repetition and/or restarts immediately preceding or following *I think that*. More precisely, with *that* omission we find such disfluencies in 16.7 percent (27 instances) of all cases, such as Example (25). With *that* insertion, on the other hand, such disfluencies occur in only 3.4 percent (1 instance) of all cases.

(25) *I I I think* there wh some of us are in great difficulty here (s1b-028-101)

From the evidence presented in this section we can conclude that the *that*-complementizer following initial *I think* no longer functions like a genuine subordinator.

Its function in spoken language is primarily a linear one, i.e. on the temporal plane, like a typical filler, not so much a hierarchical one, i.e. marking syntactic subordination and backgrounding.

6. Conclusion

This chapter has tried to cast light on the question of the syntactic status of initial complement-taking predicates (CTPs) by looking at clause-initial *I think* as a typical representative of a highly grammaticalized CTP. In doing so the study has adopted an empirical usage-based approach that incorporates the dimension of prosodic realization. The results of the corpus analysis have shown that the two formal cues for signaling prominence of *I think* present diverging evidence. While the occurrence of the *that*-subordinator seems to suggest foregrounding and superordinate status of *I think*, prosodic data indicate reduced prominence and hence secondary discourse function. In addition, the two constructional types, *I think* +zero and *I think* +*that*, exhibit parallel prosodic patterns, which shows that structural variation does not correspond with different prosodic behavior.

It is possible, however, to reconcile this divergence of evidence by evaluating and revising some of the original assumptions, as suggested by the 'empirical cycle' (see Schönefeld, this volume). More precisely, it is necessary to (i) reconsider currently held assumptions about the role of syntactic markers such as subordinators and (ii) adopt a dynamic model of grammar which accepts that structure emerges out of usage but at the same time may also exert a 'structuring' influence on usage (cf. Boye and Harder 2007) and is more 'conservative' in the sense that it typically lags behind changes in usage. In such a view prosody is a more immediate reflection of actual use than structural variation such as the use of the *that*-complementizer. This is confirmed by a closer investigation of usage data, which casts further doubt on the subordination function of *that* in spoken texts. The corpus analysis shows that it is no longer used to indicate syntactic hierarchy but as a filler (i.e. functioning on the linear plane), which is inserted for rhythmical purposes or to alleviate production difficulties.

An analysis of *that* as a filler rather than a genuine marker of subordination is of course much more compatible with the typical pragmatic use and information structure of grammaticalized CTP constructions, where the *that*-clause presents the main point of the message. Highly grammaticalized CTPs such as *I think* have been subject to considerable semantic bleaching and typically have only a secondary, qualifying function which consists in reducing the speaker's commitment to the proposition of the *that*-clause. In fact, it is precisely this hedging or 'distancing' function of *I think* that makes the use of *that* as a marker of subordination redundant. As argued elsewhere (Kaltenböck 2006a), the (hierarchical) function of a *that*-subordinator (which is more prominent with CTPs of more specific semantic content) is essentially also one of distancing the speaker from the proposition it introduces. With initial *I think*, however, this distancing function is already taken care of and makes the use of *that* redundant. If the *that* is still occasionally inserted, it is only for linear purposes, i.e. as a filler. In these uses the *that* is a pleonastic element whose grammatical meaning of subordination has been lost or 'bleached'. It is thus possible to establish a link between the semantic erosion (grammaticalization) of the CTP *I think* and the erosion of grammatical meaning of *that*, with the former entailing the latter. The reason why *that* is used as a filling device rather than some other filler can be attributed to the process of grammatical retention or persistence (as identified by Torres Cacoullos and Walker 2009). It seems plausible to assume that even highly formulaic units such as *I think* are not completely autonomous from less grammaticalized, more productive CTPs, but that there is a link in the form of some 'memory structure' (cf. e.g. Traugott's 2007 notion of a highly schematic macro-construction) which may reactivate a previously used grammatical element. As illustrated for *that*, this element is then used devoid of its previous grammatical properties, viz. as a fully bleached pleonastic item. Just as the notion of semantic retention or persistence can be extended to the domain of grammar in the form of grammatical persistence (as suggested by Torres Cacoullos and Walker 2009) the notion of semantic bleaching needs to be extended to include grammatical meaning.

References

Aijmer, Karin. 1972. *Some Aspects of Psychological Predicates in English.* Stockholm: Almqvist & Wiksell.

Aijmer, Karin. 1997. *I think* – an English modal particle. In T. Swan & O. J. Westvik, eds., *Modality in Germanic Languages. Historical and Comparative Perspectives,* 1–47. Berlin: Mouton de Gruyter.

Asher, Nicholas. 2000. Truth conditional discourse semantics for parentheticals. *Journal of Semantics* 17 (1): 31–50.

Biber, Douglas. 1999. A register perspective on grammar and discourse: variability in the form and use of English complement clauses. *Discourse Studies* 1 (2): 131–150.

Biber, Douglas, Stig Johansson, Geoffrey Leech, Susan Conrad, & Edward Finnegan. 1999. *Longman Grammar of Spoken and Written English.* Harlow: Longman.

Boersma, Paul & David Weenink. 2008. Praat: doing phonetics by computer (Version 4.4.33) [Computer program]. Retrieved December 2005, from http://www.praat.org

Bolinger, Dwight. 1985. The inherent iconism of intonation. In J. Haiman, ed., *Iconicity in Syntax,* 97–108. Amsterdam & Philadelphia: Benjamins.

Boye, Casper & Peter Harder. 2007. Complement-taking predicates: usage and linguistic structure. *Studies in Language* 31 (3): 569–606.

Brandt, Margareta. 1984. Subordination und Parenthese als Mittel der Informationsstrukturierung in Texten. *Sprache und Pragmatik* 1994: 1–37.

Brazil, David. 1997. *The Communicative Value of Intonation in English*. Cambridge: Cambridge University Press.

Brinton, Laurel. J. 1996. *Pragmatic Markers in English. Grammaticalization and Discourse Functions*. Berlin: Mouton de Gruyter.

Bybee, Joan L. & Paul J. Hopper. 2001. Introduction to frequency and the emergence of linguistic structure. In J. L. Bybee & P. J. Hopper, eds., *Frequency and the Emergence of Linguistic Structure,* 1–26. Amsterdam & Philadelphia: Benjamins.

Clark, H. 2004. Pragmatics of language performance. In L. R. Horn & G. Ward, eds., *Handbook of Pragmatics,* 365–382. Oxford: Blackwell.

Couper-Kuhlen, Elizabeth. 1986. *An Introduction to English Prosody*. London: Edward Arnold.

Cruttenden, Alan. 1997. *Intonation* (2nd ed.). Cambridge: Cambridge University Press.

Crystal, David. 1969. *Prosodic Systems and Intonation in English*. Cambridge: Cambridge University Press.

Davidson, Donald 2001. *Inquiries into Truth and Interpretation* (2nd ed.). Oxford: Clarendon.

Dehé, Nicole. 2007. The relation between syntactic and prosodic parenthesis. In N. Dehé & Y. Kavalova, eds., *Parenthetials*, 261–284. Amsterdam & Philadelphia: Benjamins.

Dehé, Nicole. 2009. Clausal parentheticals, intonational phrasing, and prosodic theory. *Journal of Linguistics* 45: 569–615.

Diessel, Holger & Michael Tomasello. 1999. Why complement clauses do not include a *that*-complementizer in early child language. *Proceedings of the 25*th *Annual Meeting, Berkeley Linguistics Society*: 86–97.

Du Bois, John W. 1985. Competing motivations. In J. Haiman, ed., *Iconicity in syntax,* 343–365. Amsterdam & Philadelphia: Benjamins.

Elsness, Johan. 1984. That or zero? A look at the choice of object clause connective in a corpus of American English. *English Studies* 65: 519–33.

Erteschik-Shir, Nomi & Shalom Lappin. 1979. Dominance and the functional explanation of island phenomena. *Theoretical Linguistics* 6 (1): 41–86.

Ferreira, Victor S. & Gary S. Dell. 2000. Effect of ambiguity and lexical availability on syntactic and lexical production. *Cognitive Psychology* 40: 296–340.

Firbas, Jan. 1992. *Functional Sentence Perspective in Written and Spoken Communication.* Cambridge: Cambridge University Press.

Fischer, Olga. 2007a. *Morphosyntactic Change. Functional and Formal Perspectives.* Oxford: Oxford University Press.

Fischer, Olga. 2007b. The development of English parentheticals: A case of grammaticalization? In U. Smit et al., eds., *Tracing English Through Time,* 99–114. Wien: Braumüller.

Givón, Talmy. 1984. *Syntax: a Functional-Typological Introduction.* Vol. 1. Amsterdam & Philadelphia: Benjamins.

Givón, Talmy. 1995. *Functionalism and Grammar*. Amsterdam & Philadelphia: Benjamins.

Goodwin, Charles & Marjorie Harness Goodwin. 1992. Assessments and the construction of context. In Ch. Goodwin & A. Duranti, eds., *Rethinking Context,* 147–189. Cambridge: Cambridge University Press.

Green, Georgia M. 1976. Main clause phenomena in subordinate clauses. *Language* 52: 382–397.

Haiman, John. 1994. Ritualization and the development of language. In W. Pagliuca, ed., *Perspectives on Grammaticalization,* 3–28. Amsterdam & Philadelphia: Benjamins.

Halliday, M. A. K. 1985. *An Introduction to Functional Grammar.* London: Edward Arnold.

Hand, Michael. 1993. Parataxis and parentheticals. *Linguistics and Philosophy* 16: 495–507.

Hooper, Joan B. & Sandra Thompson. 1973. On the applicability of root transformations. *Linguistic Inquiry* 4 (4): 465–497.

Hooper, Joan B. 1975. On assertive predicates. In J. P. Kimball, ed., *Syntax and Semantics.* Vol 4. 91–124. New York: Academic Press.

Hopper, Paul J. 1987. Emergent grammar. *Berkeley Linguistic Society* 13: 139–157.

Hopper, Paul J. 1988. Emergent grammar and the a priori Grammar postulate. In D. Tannen, ed., *Linguistics in Context: Connecting Observation and Understanding,* 117–136. Norwood, NJ: Ablex.

Huddleston, Rodney & Geoffrey K. Pullum. 2002. *The Cambridge Grammar of the English Language.* Cambridge: Cambridge University Press.

Jaeger, Florian T. 2005. Optional *that* indicates production difficulty: evidence from disfluencies. *Proceedings of DiSS'05 Disfluency in Spontaneous Speech Workshop.* 10–12 September 2005, Aix-en-Provence, France, 103–109.

Kaltenböck, Gunther. 2006a. '...*That* is the question': complementizer omission in extraposed *that*-clauses. *English Language and Linguistics* 10 (2): 371–396.

Kaltenböck, Gunther. 2006b. Some comments on comment clauses: a semantic classification. In R. Povolná & O. Dontcheva-Navratilova, eds., *Discourse and Interaction,* 71–87. Brno: Masarykova Univserszita.

Kaltenböck, Gunther. 2008. Prosody and function of English comment clauses. *Folia Linguistica* 42 (1): 83–134.

Kaltenböck, Gunther. 2009a. Initial *I think*: Main or comment clause? *Discourse and Interaction* 2 (1): 49–70. http://anglistic.univie.ac.at/staff/kaltenboeck/

Kaltenböck, Gunther. 2009b. English comment clauses: Position, prosody, and scope. *Arbeiten aus Anglistik und Amerikanistik* 34 (1): 49–75.

Kaltenböck, Gunther. 2010. Pragmatic functions of parenthetical *I think*. In G. Kaltenböck, W. Mihatsch, & S. Schneider, eds., *New Approaches to Hedging,* 237–266. Bingley: Emerald.

Kärkkäinen, Elise. 2003. *Epistemic Stance in English Conversation.* Amsterdam & Philadelphia: Benjamins.

Kärkkäinen, Elise. 2010. Position and scope of epistemic phrases in planned and unplanned American English. In G. Kaltenböck, W. Mihatsch, & S. Schneider, eds., *New Approaches to Hedging,* 203–236. Bingley: Emerald.

Kearns, Kate. 2007. Epistemic verbs and zero complementizer. *English Language and Linguistics* 11 (3): 475–505.

Knowles, John. 1980. The tag as a parenthetical. *Studies in Language* 4: 370–409.

Kruisinga, E. 1932. *A Handbook of Present-Day English.* Part II. Groningen: Noordhoff.

Landis, J. & G. G. Koch. 1977. The measurement of observer agreement for categorical data. *Biometrics* 33: 159–174.

Langacker, Ronald W. 1987. *Foundations of Cognitive Grammar.* Vol I: *Theoretical Prerequisites.* Stanford, CA: Stanford University Press.

Langacker, Ronald W. 1991. *Foundations of Cognitive Grammar.* Vol II: *Descriptive Applications.* Stanford, CA: Stanford University Press.

Langacker, Ronald W. 2000. A dynamic usage-based model. In M. Barlow & S. Kemmer, eds., *Usage-Based Models of Language,* 1–63. Stanford: CSLI Publications.

Lepore, Ernest & Barry Loewer. 1989. You can say *that* again. In P. French et al., eds., *Midwest Studies in Philosophy*. Vol XIV, 338–56. Notre Dame, Ind.: University of Notre Dame Press.

Linell, Per. 1998. *Approaching Dialogue: Talk, Interaction and Contexts in Dialogical Perspectives*. Amsterdam & Philadelphia: Benjamins.

Mackenzie, J. Lachlan. 1984. Communicative functions of subordination. In J. L. Mackenzie & H. Wekker, eds., *English Language Research: the Dutch Contribution I*, 67–84. Amsterdam: Free University Press.

Mindt, Ilka. 2003. Is *I think* a discourse marker? In E. Mengel et al., eds., *Proceedings Anglistentag 2002 Bayreuth*, 473–483. Trier: WVT.

Nelson, Gerald, Sean Wallis, & Bas Aarts. 2002. *Exploring Natural Language. Working with the British Component of the International Corpus of English*. Amsterdam & Philadelphia: Benjamins.

Nuyts, Jan. 2000. Tensions between discourse structure and conceptual semantics: The syntax of epistemic modal expressions. *Studies in Language* 23 (1): 103–135.

Peterson, Peter. 1999. On the boundaries of syntax: non-syntagmatic relations. In P. Collins & D. Lee, eds., *The Clause in English*, 229–250. Amsterdam & Philadelphia: Benjamins.

Pomerantz, Anita & B. J. Fehr. 1997. Conversation analysis: an approach to the study of social action as sense making practices. In T. A. van Dijk, ed., *Discourse as Social Interaction*, 65–91. London: Sage.

Posner, Roland. 1972. Die Kommentierung – oder. Ein Weg von der Satzgrammatik zur Textlinguistik. *Zeitschrift für Literaturwissenschaft und Linguistik* 5: 9–30.

Quirk, Randolph, Sidney Greenbaum, Geoffrey Leech, & Jan Svartvik. 1985. *A Comprehensive Grammar of the English Language*. Harlow: Longman.

Rohdenburg, Günther. 1998. Clausal complementation and cognitive complexity in English. In F.-W. Neumann & S. Schülting, eds., *Anglistentag 1998 Erfurt Proceedings*, 101–111. Trier. Wissenschaftlicher Verlag.

Ross, John R. 1973. Slifting. In M. Gross, M. Halle & M.-P. Schützenberger, eds., *The Formal Analysis of Natural Languages*, 133–169. The Hague: Mouton.

Sadock, Jerrold M. 1984. The pragmatics of subordination. In W. de Geest & Y. Putseys, eds., *Sentential Complementation*, 205–213. Dordrecht: Foris.

Schegloff, Emanuel. 1990. On the organization of sequences as a source of 'coherence' in talk-in-interaction. In B. Dorval, ed., *Conversational Organization and its Development*, 51–77. Norwood, NJ: Ablex.

Schlüter, Julia. 2005. *Rhythmic Grammar: The Influence of Rhythm on Grammatical Variation and Change in English*. Berlin: Mouton de Gruyter.

Simon-Vandenbergen, Anne-Marie. 2000. The functions of *I think* in political discourse. *International Journal of Applied Linguistics* 10 (1): 41–63.

Stenström, Anna-Brita. 1994. *An Introduction to Spoken Interaction*. London: Longman.

Stenström, Anna-Brita. 1995. Some remarks on comment clauses. In B. Aarts & Ch. F. Meyer, eds., *The Verb in Contemporary English*, 290–299. Cambridge: Cambridge University Press.

Svensson, Jan. 1976. Report indicators and other parentheticals. In F. Karlsson, ed., *Papers from the Third Scandinavian Conference of Linguistics*, 369–380. Turku: Textlinguistics Research Group, Academy of Finland.

Tagliamonte, Sali & Jennifer Smith. 2005. No momentary fancy! The zero 'complementizer' in English dialects. *English Language and Linguistics* 9 (2): 289–309.

Thompson, Sandra A. 2002. 'Object complements' and conversation. Towards a realistic account. *Studies in Language* 26 (1): 125–164.

Thompson, Sandra A. & Anthony Mulac. 1991. The discourse conditions for the use of the complementizer that in conversational English. *Journal of Pragmatics* 15: 237–251.

Tomlin, Russell. 1985. Foreground-background information and the syntax of subordination. *Text* 5: 85–122.

Torres Cacoullos, Rena & James A. Walker. 2009. On the persistence of grammar in discourse formulas: A variationist study of *that*. *Linguistics* 47 (1): 1–43.

Traugott, Elizabeth Closs. 2007. The concepts of constructional mismatch and type-shifting from the perspective of grammaticalization. *Cognitive Linguistics* 18: 523–557.

Urmson, J. O. 1952. Parenthetical verbs. *Mind* 61: 480–496.

Van Bogaert, Julie. 2009. The Grammar of Complement-Taking Mental Predicate Constructions in Present-Day Spoken British English. Doctoral dissertation. University of Ghent.

Wells. John C. 2006. *English Intonation: An Introduction*. Cambridge: Cambridge University Press.

Wichmann, Anne. 2000. *Intonation in Text and Discourse: Beginnings, Middles and Ends*. Harlow: Longman.

Wichmann, Anne. 2001. Spoken parentheticals. In K. Aijmer, ed., *A Wealth of English. Studies in Honour of Göran Kjellmer*, 177–193. Göteborg: Acta Universitatis Gothoburgiensis.

1.2 Constructional alternatives

I am about to die vs. *I am going to die*

A usage-based comparison between two future-indicating constructions*

Silke Höche
Leibniz University Hanover

This study portrays *be about to* as a construction which, although frequently described as nearly synonymous to *be going to*, falls somewhere in between the categories of futurate forms and ingressive aspectualizers. Constructional properties that distinguish *be about to* from *be going to* are worked out on the basis of several sources: The Oxford English Dictionary serves as testimony to the **diachronic** stages the two constructions passed through. For a detailed comparison of **synchronic** semantico-functional characteristics, large sets of data retrieved from the BNC are subjected to collostructional analysis. The results of these procedures **converge** in indicating that *be about to* has moved closer to ingressive aspectualizers, profiling the lead-up section to the onset of an event.

Keywords: collostructional analysis, event onset, futurate forms, ingressive aspectualizers, profile

1. Introduction: Aims and methods

In his book *The Mother Tongue*, Bryson (1990) reports on the case of the 17th-century grammarian Dominique Bonhours, who, according to Bryson, "proved on his deathbed that a grammarian's work is never done", uttering the following 'famous last words': "I am about to – or I am going to – die, either expression is used" (ibid.: 146). Bonhours' remark on the usage of the two available constructions was (and still is) correct, and while the choice of either expression would certainly not have changed anything about his miserable physical condition, one has to ask whether it matters from a linguistic perspective. While there is an abundance of

* I would like to thank Doris Schönefeld and two anonymous reviewers for their insightful comments and constructive criticism. All remaining errors are my own.

studies comparing the English *will* and *be going to* future constructions, investigating differences in meaning, usage (e.g. Comrie 1976, Wekker 1976, Gries and Stefanowitsch 2004) and grammaticalization patterns (Bybee and Dahl 1989, Heine et al. 1991, Pertejo 1999, Hilpert 2008), little has been said about the semantic-pragmatic difference between *be going to* V and *be about to* V, which seemingly denote comparable temporal relations. The few studies which go beyond the brief descriptive entries found in reference grammars (Jirsa 1997, Wada 2000) have a very specific focus and are largely based on the authors' intuition and/or very small samples of authentic language.

Bonhours' rather intuitive statement of course invites a more extensive and empirical analysis of the assumed interchangeability of the two available constructions. This invitation is taken up in the present study, whose aim is a multifaceted depiction of the *be about to* V pattern and its comparison to *be going to* V against a cognitive-linguistic, usage-based background, incorporating several sources of insight. There exists a broad spectrum of methodologies for the exploration of linguistic-conceptual structure, such as (the traditional) introspection, computer-aided investigations of large language corpora, inferential statistical analyses and comparison of the data obtained from such corpus investigations, psycholinguistic experiments such as eye-movement measures or lexical decision tasks, cross-linguistic comparison of linguistic phenomena – to name just a few (see Janssen and Redeker 1999, González-Marquez et al. 2007). And although there are widely recognized efforts among the cognitive linguists community to combine several of these methods in order to obtain **converging evidence**, a considerable part of the studies done in the field still lacks such a comprehensive foundation, presenting results arrived at by 'isolated' methodological procedures.

In accordance with the tenor and intent of the present book to discuss and promote the striving for converging evidence, my comparative investigation of *be about to* V vs. *be going to* V is to demonstrate the successful integration of at least two sources of evidence: **intuition/introspection** in conjunction with prior attempts at spelling out formal and functional features of the constructions, and **corpus investigation** in conjunction with **inferential statistical analysis**. The study aims to demonstrate the fruitful interaction between intuition/introspection, opening the door to the empirical cycle (see Schönefeld, this volume) by providing input for the formulation of first hypotheses on the subject, and large sets of authentic, statistically evaluated language data, the sensitive interpretation of which will test, refine, and, if necessary, modify these hypotheses. In order to provide a multidimensional discussion, both strands include considerations from a diachronic and synchronic perspective. To justify my methodological set-up, I comment briefly on some of the procedures.

The application of purely introspective methods has been criticized vehemently by some cognitive linguists (see Cuyckens et al. 1997, Geeraerts 2006, Gibbs

2007, inter alia). However, one cannot neglect or even deny the importance of introspection or intuition for the **analysis of conceptual/semantic** structure, which, as Talmy (2007: xiii) notes, is especially useful for the investigation of concrete word and sentence meaning. For more abstract representations, such as semantic components, lexical categories or **abstract constructional meaning**, being less easily accessible, introspective analysis at least serves the first formulation of hypotheses, and hence as a starting point for further empirical work. That the latter is indispensable is demonstrated by an increasing body of literature, proving that (even) native speakers are no reliable source when asked to make judgments about the meaning, variability or acceptability of expressions (Boberg 2002: 12, Sampson and McCarthy 2004: 3). Moreover, complementing introspective investigation with corpus-linguistic procedures has the advantage of making observations and results measurable: Not only can the recorded speech samples illustrate the particular linguistic forms under investigation, but also can careful statistical analyses of these data bring to light subtle patterns of usage. Furthermore, as is shown in this study, inferential statistic methodology (e.g. [distinctive] collexeme analysis, Stefanowitsch and Gries 2003, Gries and Stefanowitsch 2004) can be successfully applied for the detection of semantic differences between similar constructions, and possibly detect constructional characteristics which cannot be read off from raw frequency data, let alone be arrived at by pure intuition. Before presenting the 'statistically processed' results of a synchronic corpus study, however, the chapter first summarizes the sparse descriptions found for *be about to* V and its comparison with *be going to* V, and then exposes introspective and corpus-based considerations on the diachronic and functional motivation of the two constructions.

2. The state of the art: Consulting the grammar(ian)s

This section is to give a short overview of the information common descriptive/reference grammars provide on the semantics and use of *be about to* V and *be going to* V. The vagueness of the statements and the sometimes confusing terminology applied for the description of their constructional characteristics demonstrate the need for a more explicit and usage-based analysis, as attempted in this study. Nevertheless, the information provided by these descriptions serve as a reference point against which corpus data are to be tested in the course of this investigation for either converging or diverging tendencies.

In the few available comparative descriptions of *be about to* V and *be going to* V (e.g. Royster and Steadman 1923, Jespersen 1931, Wada 2000, Collins 2009), both forms are rendered as aspectual/tense constructions which locate the described event in the near future:

(1) a. *He was about to/going to jump off the bridge.*
b. *She is about to/going to leave home for drama school.*

Semantic features commonly assigned to both forms are **immediacy**, **prospectiveness**, **prediction**, or **intention** with regard to a particular event. There is, however, disagreement and inconsistency in the ascription of these features to either of the constructions when they are contrasted (cf. the quotations of Royster and Steadman [1923] and Poutsma [1929], given below). Quirk et al. (1985: 217) present *be about to* as a "quasi-auxiliary" denoting near future, which might be paraphrased by *be (just) going to*; and Pertejo (1999: 137) mentions the common treatment of periphrastic expressions such as *be about to* (and also *be upon* V*ing*) as real synonyms of *be going to*.[1] Although she adds that, unlike *be going to*, "in most cases [...] they are not capable of expressing other shades of future connotation as they usually have a rather fixed meaning", the nature thereof is left unexplained.

Few authors address the **non-synonymy** of the constructions, some of the explications being, again, rather vague:

> Limitation of future action to the **immediate** or **very near future** is indeed a function of the *going-to* future, but in actual usage it is comparatively rare that *going to* and *about to* are almost identical in meaning or interchangeable. *About to* has a fixed meaning (colorless incipient action), while *going to* is used most frequently with other shades of **future** signification [i.e. intention, earnest purpose, inevitability, S.H]. (Royster and Steadman 1923: 394f., my emphasis)
>
> [They] denote 'prospectiveness' with **various degrees of proximity**.[2]
> (Jespersen 1931/1954: 362, my emphasis)
>
> [...] the sense of **immediacy** carried by *be about to* is even **stronger** than it is with *be going to*. (Collins 2009: 155, my emphasis)

That is, the primary semantic differences between the two constructions show up in the (non-)presence or type of secondary modal meanings (e.g. intention or prediction), and in the degree of immediacy they denote. Note, however, Huddleston and Pullum's (2002: 212) suggestion that the factor *immediacy* is not even a necessary one for the usage of *be going to*, citing the acceptability of *I'm going to retire in ten years*. Wada (2000: 388ff) argues along the same line, showing that *be going to* readily combines with temporal adverbials which do not at all relate to the immediate future, while *be about to* V does not (see Section 5.4 in this chapter).

1. Note that the authors vary as to whether the structure of the construction is "*be about* + *to*-infinitive", "*be about to* + infinitive" or even "*be* + *about to* V".

2. Jespersen has a particular understanding of a prospective construction, which, in fact, questions the status of both patterns as future-constructions: "The prospective present is a **variety of the present** which looks forward into the future: the present is viewed as preparing the future" (1931/1954: 362, my emphasis; cf. also Comrie 1976: 64–65, using the same classification).

An additional factor is brought in by Poutsma (1929), who, also acknowledging the different degrees of immediacy associated with each construction, comments on register differences between them: "*To be about* is to be distinguished from *be going to* in that it is **less colloquial** than the latter and is more distinctly used to express **near** or **immediate future** (1929: 245, my emphasis).

While register differences are neglected in my discussion, I clarify and refine the somewhat opaque and narrow presentations of the 'division of work' of *be about to* V and *be going to* V in their function as future-designating patterns in the following sections.

3. Historical motivation

Cognitive linguists adhere to the conception of all constructions being motivated. They are guided by the assumption that, being pairings of form and meaning, all linguistic units owe their existence and semantic and formal characteristics to language-/system internal (e.g. ecological niches) and external factors (speakers' communicative needs, cognitive processes etc.). As Goldberg succinctly summarizes,

> Cognitive Construction Grammar seeks to provide motivation for each construction that is posited. Motivation aims to explain why it is at least possible and at best natural that this particular form-meaning correspondence should exist in a given language. [...] **Functional** and **historical** generalizations count as explanations, but they are not predictive in the strict sense [...] (2006: 217, emphasis added, SH).

Investigating historical motivation, this section sketches out the diachronic development of *be about to* V, comparing it to the well-described diachronic path of *be going to* V and to generalizations which have been stated for the development of future constructions across languages. The description draws on and incorporates data from a compilation of more than 800 instances of *be about to* V which were extracted from the quotation base of the OED (computerized online version), complemented by instances found in several other diachronic corpora (e.g. Helsinki Corpus, Lampeter, ICAMET).[3]

Pertejo (1999) dates the emergence of the periphrastic future form *be about to* V to the last quarter of the 15th century, and the year of the first 'real' quote

3. See Mair (2004) for a discussion of the usefulness of the OED as a diachronic corpus. Due to the rather low frequency of instances of *be about to* and its orthographical variants (*abuten/a-boute/aboute (for) to*) in the other diachronic corpora I consulted, my discussion is based to a large extent on instances found in the OED. Since the sources of quotes in the OED are unbalanced, the data were normalized for their statistical analysis (instances/100,000 quotes). Information on the number of quotations per century/quarter century in the OED is provided in Mair (ibid.).

(see below) the OED offers for future *be about to* V is stated as 1486.[4] A consultation of the selected diachronic corpora listed above provides interesting insight, since the search string *be about (for) to* (and its variants) retrieves examples which show that this construction seems to have come into use much earlier, most notably in combination with the adverb *faste*:

(2) a. *Aure to feawe men bien abuten to habben ›ese hali mihte* (OED, 'about', 1225)
b. [...] *as ›ou woldeste ›at he esyd ›e in ›i dysese, so be aboute to esyn hym* (ICAMET, rollho2b.txt, ca. 1300)
c. *So ar tho Nykeres faste aboute to brynge schipmen ther hit ys...* (OED, 'steek v.', 1303)

However, according to the OED, this pattern is different from the future construction we are interested in, describing the state of being 'busied in preparation for, to be preparing or **intending**'. The emergence of this form is ascribed by Jirsa (1997: 28) to a metonymic change in meaning of the spatial preposition/adverb *about*, originally denoting a spatial relation of 'close neighborhood'. According to him, due to its frequent collocation with motion verbs, *about* itself assumed a sense of motion: "Thus, the spatial adverb *aboute* also encodes some unspecified movement, or more properly, **mobilization**" (ibid, emphasis added, SH). The latter notion is clearly retained in the 'busied in preparation' sense, which emerged in the first quarter of the 13th century. This construction is the direct source of the future construction, which started to accompany the 'busy/preparing/intending' pattern at some time between 1330–1486. The first two entries the OED provides for *be about to* V as a future form are the following examples:

(3) a. *Þe adder..Vpon þe cradel ȝhe fleiȝ anon, And* ***was aboute*** *þe child* ***to*** *sting.* (OED, 'about', 1330)
b. *And as he* ***was a-boute to*** *be gynne to sey oure lady matenes & as he was at the inuita-tory that is Aue maria.* (OED, 'about', 1486)

Note that the example given in (3a) is presented in the OED in brackets, which vividly demonstrates the difficulty of the task to pinpoint when exactly the future pattern appeared in Middle English for the first time: Many of the examples provided by the corpora and quoted in the OED are ambiguous with respect to a 'preparation/intention' vs. 'future' reading, especially since they do not differ in form or co-text:

4. This information relates to the updated version of the OED entry for *about*, released in March 2009. In the earlier version, the first entry of future *be about to* was dated to 1535.

(4) a. *He sayd the deuyl was to come to hym, and* **was about to put** *hym in disperacion.* (ICAMET, miracles.txt)

b. *flir husband sall hafe his actioun agaynes him before fle iusticez of fle land, alsfortherly as he* **had bene aboute for to slae** *him.* (OED, 'furtherly', 1400)

In this respect, *be about to* displays a phenomenon which has been described as typical in grammaticalization processes: In grammaticalization theories it is assumed that particular meanings of a form are associated with a particular situation, and that grammaticalization involves an extension or shift of the situations/contexts in which a construction can be used. Heine, Claudi and Hünnemeyer (1991: 69f.), who adopt a metaphor-based explanation for such extensions or shifts, argue that for any apparent leap between the situation types/meanings there exists a continuum of situation types that bridge the two stages along the grammaticalization path. In such intermediate stages, pragmatic inferencing (a type of metonymic extension) allows speakers/hearers to gradually extend the meaning from one type (e.g. intention) to another (e.g. future). Moreover, 'original' and extended meaning of a form may co-exist, which then is a possible source of ambiguity. The examples given in (4) undoubtedly exemplify such an intermediate stage, where a future time reference may have emerged from pragmatic inferencing in that some action/event prepared in the present is likely to take place in the near future.

There are, however, several features that clearly mark a shift in the function of the construction. A strong indicator of the change in the semantics of *be about to* V and hence, its successful grammaticalization towards a future construction, is the increasing number of cases where the pattern unifies with passive infinitives. According to the data provided by the OED, these variants occurred for the first time in the middle of the 17th century, and were increasingly used from the middle of the 19th century onwards. In such uses, the subject slot of the *be about to* unit is filled by the logical subject of the passive infinitive. Since the major effect of this type of raising construction is a shift in focus from AGENT to PATIENT, the notion of 'intention' can no longer be the dominant one:[5]

(5) a. *Grotius had a little before read a little discourse of the Præ-Adamites, undigested and* **about to be revis'd.** (OED, 'pre-Adamite', 1656)

b. *The turnwrist plough* **is about to be introduced** *in the country.* (OED, 'turnwrest', 1794)

5. In contrast to generative-transformational descriptions, where 'raising' is seen as a rule of **moving** deep structure subject nominals of complementary clauses into the object or subject position (surface structure) of the matrix clause, Cognitive Grammar postulates a meaningful raising **construction** (cf. Langacker 2008: 435ff.).

Moreover, the types of subject occurring in the construction come to be non-human, inanimate even:

(6) a. *Below are small mammary projections* ***about to be*** *the outlets to the cysts beneath them.* (OED, 'mammary', 1804)
b. *When a mischance is* ***about to befall*** *any of their neighbours within a certain time.* (OED, 'grow', 1860)

This change is accompanied by an increase in the number of combinations with so-called ergative verbs (which can take both an AGENT and a PATIENT as their subject, e.g. *weigh, break, sell, open*) with a PATIENT subject, and unaccusative verbs (e.g. *die, fall, sink, dissolve*), only taking PATIENT subjects:

(7) a. *The ship being* ***about to weigh,*** *comes over her anchor...* (OED, 'heave', 1727)
b. *The wounded soldier rests his head* ***About to die*** *upon the dead.* (OED, 'about', 1816)
c. *To ascertain what temporary statutes were* ***about to expire.*** (OED, 'expire', 1855)

Both of the latter phenomena, which start in the 18th century and increasingly surface in the beginning of the 19th century, are also indicative of a change from the 'preparing/intention' meaning to the future meaning of *be about to* V.[6]

Thus, it seems that although there are some early uses of future *be about to* V in the late 14th/early 15th century, the 'full' shift from the 'intention' meaning to a 'future' meaning was accomplished only in the 19th century, where the construction cumulatively accepted features which are much more characteristic of a future construction than of a modal pattern expressing intentionality (i.e. its ability to be combined with a passive constructions, and to occur with inanimate subjects).[7]

6. Collins (2009: 156) gives a somewhat different account of the status of *be about to* V as a fully grammaticalized form: "*Be about to* is less grammaticalized than *be going to* (whose auxiliarization is in evidence phonologically in the appearance of *gonna* and semantically in the development of its volitional sense). Nevertheless, there are several examples which suggest that *be about to* may have started to undergo a similar semantic development." To illustrate his observation, Collins quotes usages of *be about to* expressing intentionality and volitional refusal. That is, he considers the modal meanings of *be about to* much more as a recent development than as a relic preserved from earlier stages of the grammaticalization path the construction passed through.

7. Although, in the strict sense, there is "no precise end point to a grammaticalisation process" (Mair 2004: 127) (including phonological reduction, morphological incorporation), the grammaticalization of *be about to* from a phrase expressing busyness and intention to a future construction seems to have been completed at that time.

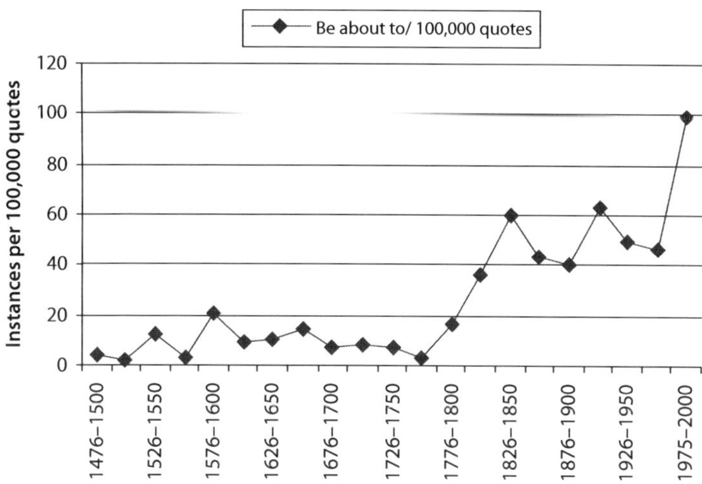

Figure 1. Diachronic usage frequencies of *be about to*

As shown in Figure 1, this is precisely the period that saw a tremendous increase in the usage of *be about to* V, starting in the last quarter of the 18th century.

While I cannot here answer the question whether the increase in frequency of use was a prerequisite for the full grammaticalization of the construction or whether its full grammaticalization led to a spread of the form to a wide range of contexts, it is noteworthy that *be going to* V developed in a similar fashion within roughly the same period: The grammaticalized, i.e. future-indicating use of *be going to* V set in towards the end of the 15th century (Danchev and Kytö 1994), a striking rise in frequency, however, did not occur until the end of the 18th century (Mair 2004). Also as regards the stages which both constructions passed through in their development, the similarities are obvious: *Be going to* V has been described at full length (Bybee and Dahl 1989, Traugott and König 1991, Danchev and Kytö 1994, inter alia) as following the same grammaticalization path identified for a wide range of future constructions of languages the world over, comprising the stages *allative* > *purposive* > *future* (or, alternatively, *motion* > *intention* > *future*) (Bybee and Dahl 1989, Bybee et al. 1994, Heine et al. 1991). Obviously, the same stages mark the grammaticalization path of *be about to* V. In its original meaning, *about* is a spatial preposition or adverb, describing a position of being "1. a. Around the outside, around; on every side. 2. Less definitely: on any side; near, in the neighbourhood" (OED, s.v. *about* [adv., prep.]). This originally **locative** meaning seems to have been extended from the notion of literally being in the neighborhood/around for some purposeful action to figuratively being mentally near (i.e. **intending**, planning) some action.[8,9] The shift towards the third stage, i.e. from **intention** to immediate **future**, has been explicated above as the result of pragmatic inferencing: Being busily involved in the preparation of some action or event is a likely indicator of the actual occurrence of these in the foreseeable future.

Note that speakers at the time of Early Modern English were well aware of the future meaning of both *be about to* V and *be going* V, even judging them as roughly synonymous, as the following explication suggests:

> About to, or going to, is the signe of the Participle of the future...: as my father when he was about to die, gave me this counsel. I am [about] or going [to] read. (Poole 1646: 26; square brackets in the source text; so quoted in Danchev and Kytö, 1994: 167)

What remains to be clarified then is why two constructions with roughly the same meaning emerged around the same time. As Danchev and Kytö (1994: 72) propose for *be going to*,

> the availability through language contact [i.e. with French, S.H.] of the andantive construction for the expression of future time filled a need for **further aspectual nuancing**. It may be claimed indeed that after the decay of the Proto-Germanic aspectual system [...], based mainly on morphological markers (prefixes), aspectuality began to be expressed by a variety of other means – new verbal paradigms of a mainly **periphrastic nature, lexically** and syntactically [...].[...] there can be no doubt that such specific aspectual meanings as DURATION, PRESENT RELEVANCE and INCHOATIVITY have played an important role in the nascence and further spread of the *go*-future in English (and other languages too). (emphasis added, S.H.)

Danchev and Kytö's suggestion readily lends itself to an explanation of the rise of future *be about to* V. Yet again, if there was a need for constructions expressing "further aspectual nuancing", one must, for the sake of economy, expect the two constructions to cover different such nuances or, in the course of their development, to have taken on different shades of meaning. This issue is discussed in the remainder of the study.

8. An allative component (i.e. a notion of 'towardness') is possibly added by the *to*-infinitive in the construction. See Fischer (2000), who points at the incomplete development of the English *to*-infinitive, never really losing its sense of 'towardness'.

9. In fact, the OED notes for some particular uses of prepositional about a meaning of '**near** so as to meddle with' (as in *This thinge the whiche ye ben aboute*, OED, 'about', 1385)

4. Conceptual motivation

As is assumed by several grammaticalization theorists, the development of constructions along their respective grammaticalization paths is driven by metaphor (Heine et al. 1991, Bybee 2007, inter alia).[10] In this light, I briefly consider the questions in how far conceptual metaphors might have motivated the diachronic development of *be about to* V and whether the assumed differences in meaning between *be about to* V and *be going to* V are the result of the difference in form, i.e. the particular lexical arrangement of the constructions and the metaphorical extension thereof.

Both *be about to* V and *be going to* V, containing lexemes with an originally spatial meaning (*about, go*), exemplify ubiquitous spatio-temporal metaphors, mapping a spatial path on a temporal path. More specifically, they exploit the MOVING EGO sub-model of the common metaphorical TIME IS SPACE mapping (see, e.g. Evans 2003), by means of which speakers conceptualize agents as moving across a temporal landscape, thereby approaching events, entering them, moving from one phase to the next, leaving them etc.[11] This model obviously comprises other metaphors, e.g. the ontological metaphor EVENTS ARE OBJECTS (depicting events as clearly delineated entities) and possibly PURPOSES ARE DESTINATIONS (cf. Lakoff's [1993] event structure metaphor), adding an intentional layer. However, if constructional meaning preserves facets of the original meaning of their lexical elements despite metaphorical extension and/or semantic bleaching (Bybee and Dahl 1989, Hilpert 2008), *be about to* V and *be going to* V should be expected to profile different elements of this metaphorical event model, which is a result of the different image schemas (assumed to structure metaphorical mappings) underlying their original spatial meanings: While *be about to* V most prominently builds on the CONTAINER ("around the **outside**", see p. 123) and the PROXIMITY/NEAR-FAR ("near, in the neighborhood") schemas, for *be going to* V it is the PATH schema which figures most saliently. These image-schematic differences may be a primary

10. Note that the role of conceptual metaphor in grammaticalization processes is subject to dispute. While most authors agree that both metaphorical extension and pragmatic inferencing are involved in grammaticalization, the weighting and role they give to these processes differ. Heine et al. (1991) see the role of metaphor as providing the macro-structure for grammaticalization paths, leaving the micro-structuring to inferencing/metonymy. Traugott and König (1991: 190) argue that metaphor and inferencing are at work in different grammatical domains, the development of tense and aspect categories being driven by metaphor. Croft (2000: 161) grants metaphor a minor role only in that it may "constrain the types of meta-analysis that constitute grammaticalization".

11. The complementary sub-model, the MOVING TIME model (alternative label: TIME IS MOTION [Lakoff 1993]) construes time as approaching, passing by and leaving behind the human experiencer.

source for the constructions' denoting "prospectiveness with various degrees of proximity" (Jespersen, see above). The different spatial positions of the AGENT with regard to the event and the presence or absence of motion obviously correlate with the different degrees of immediacy expressed by the patterns: *Be about* profiles a stative relation, depicting the AGENT in the near neighborhood, at the corners even, of the event, *be going to*, on the other hand, preserves a notion of motion and most prototypically construes the AGENT on a path towards some event. Quite naturally then, *be about to* V is associated with a **higher degree of immediacy**, possibly profiling the lead-up section to the initial phase of an event.[12] It then performs functions similar to those of an **aspectualizer** in highlighting a particular stage of an action, process or state, much more than assigning to the event a particular slot on a temporal axis relative to a reference point. Moreover, if the original lexical meaning is really retained (if only weakly) in the grammaticalized forms, *be going to*, containing a verb denoting 'self-propelled, volitional motion' should be expected to express 'intention' to a higher degree than *be about to*, lacking such an intentional component.

It was argued above that spatio-temporal metaphor possibly triggered the extension of the constructional meaning of *be about* from a purely locative sense to its temporal meaning of prospectiveness. The intentional/preparatory sense of *be about to* V, which for some time in the diachronic development of the pattern was its dominant meaning, can, however, not be explained on the basis of metaphorical mappings. It might be considered as that intermediate stage in the grammaticalization process which comes about through pragmatic inferencing (i.e. metonymic extensions, see above), bridging the otherwise leap-like development from spatial meaning to temporal/aspectual meaning.

The description offered here **converges** with those theoretical-descriptive accounts which ascribed to the semantics of *be about to* V a higher degree of prospectiveness (Jespersen, Poutsma, Wada) and possibly a lack of a secondary modal meaning (Royster and Steadman). The following corpus-based investigation is to shed empirical light on synchronic usage patterns of the two constructions and to fine-tune the partly intuition-based depiction presented and discussed so far.

12. It is assumed that events can be temporally segmented into different stages, i.e. onset (preparatory phase), nucleus (characteristic middle) and coda (definite close). Aspectualizing constructions such as *start to* V, *begin to* V, *cease to* V highlight these phases: While *start to* refers to the onset, *begin to* is said to profile the initial stage of the nucleus (Freed 1979, Brinton 1988). Thus, if *about to* V refers to the stage leading to the onset, it should be close in meaning to *start to* V, preceding it only slightly on a temporal scale. See Wada (2000) for a slightly different application of the notion 'onset' for the description of *be about to* V's temporal structure.

5. Measuring the difference: A corpus-based comparison of *be about to* V and *be going to* V

Having traced the possible historical and conceptual motivation of *be about to* V and *be going to* V as sources of their functional differences, we now turn to contemporary usage as recorded in large compilations of authentic speech, i.e. linguistic corpora, thereby entering the 'analytic research' phase of the empirical cycle (see Schönefeld, this volume). This major empirical part of the study provides and discusses results from a statistical analysis of data from the British National Corpus (BNC). Building on different types of frequency information, I describe subtle semantic differences of the two patterns which go far beyond the findings provided in Section 2, at the same type demonstrating the advantages of inferential statistic analyses, recently introduced into cognitive corpus linguistics by Gries and Stefanowitsch (see, for example Stefanowitsch and Gries 2003, or Gries and Stefanowitsch 2004).

5.1 Raw frequency

Concerning raw frequency, i.e. the absolute number of tokens of a form in a corpus, the following figures were obtained for the two constructions considered here: *Be going to* V (including *be gonna* V) has an overall frequency of 39,490 in the BNC, compared to 4,468 instances of *be about to* V. That is, *be going to* V is used almost ten times as frequently as *be about to* V, which might be indicative of a more specific use of the latter. Comparing the top 20 of the raw frequency data (given in Table 1), one can make the following three main observations:

1. 13 (in bold print) of these 20 verbs occur in both lists, a finding which suggests considerable semantic overlap of the two patterns.
2. Among these 13 verb, so called semantically light verbs such as *be, do, get, have, take, give, make* are most dominant, found in the top positions for both constructions, yet with different rankings.
3. The verbs which exclusively occur in the top 20 list of *be about to* V are verbs of initiation/inchoative verbs (*begin, embark, become, leave, launch*) or sudden change (*break, burst*), while those in the *going to* V construction are semantically highly heterogeneous, with no coherent grouping being possible (*have, put, see, work* etc.).

Although raw frequency data yield a first rough sketch of the characteristics of a construction, e.g. a preference of *be about to* V for verbs with incipient lexical aspect, one must acknowledge the disadvantages of linguistic descriptions based on

Table 1. Top 20 of most frequent verbs (raw frequency)

be about to V		*be going to/gonna* V	
1. **be**	491	1. **be**	7938
2. **go**	158	2. have	2668
3. **say**	156	3. **get**	2252
4. leave	131	4. **do**	2079
5. **start**	114	5. **say**	1201
6. **take**	106	6. **go**	1174
7. **make**	100	7. **take**	917
8. become	85	8. **make**	736
9. **do**	81	9. **happen**	656
10. begin	67	10. put	579
11. **happen**	58	11. **come**	540
12. **come**	56	12. **give**	532
13. **get**	56	13. see	436
14. enter	53	14. **tell**	385
15. **tell**	51	15. work	367
16. change	45	16. **ask**	364
17. **give**	45	17. look	290
18. turn	45	18. **start**	282
19. **ask**	43	19. need	278
20. embark	40	20. try	276

such data alone, as is discussed in great detail in Stefanowitsch and Gries (2003) and Gries, Hampe and Schönefeld (2005). One of the reasons why the interpretation of such data can be misleading is its leaving unconsidered the fact that verbs with a high frequency in the corpus in general are obviously more likely to occur in a particular constructions than less frequent verbs. In our case this applies to verbs such as *be, take, make, get, give* etc., which must be expected to be used highly frequently in all kinds of constructions and therefore do not reveal particular characteristics of a single construction. To remedy this and other drawbacks of linguistic analyses drawing on raw frequency, Gries and Stefanowitsch developed different types of methods (known under the umbrella term *collostructional analysis*) that incorporate additional kinds of frequency information, allowing for the detection of significant asymmetries in the distribution of lexemes in the investigated constructions. Two of these, *collexeme analysis* and *distinctive collexeme analysis*, are employed and exemplified in the following.

5.2 Collexeme analysis

Collexeme analysis (Stefanowitsch and Gries 2003) measures the attraction (or repulsion) between a construction and the lexemes that occur in a particular slot of this construction. The advantage of this procedure is that it takes into account the overall frequency of all verbs in *be about to* V (or *be going to* V) and in all other infinitive constructions in the corpus, the overall amount of infinitive constructions in the corpus and the ratio between these figures. It thereby yields a much more reliable list of those verbs which are the most characteristic representatives of the investigated patterns than can be obtained from raw frequency data. The statistical procedure of the analysis is based on the Fisher-Yates-Exact test, by means of which an index of collostructional strength is calculated.[13] This index provides information about the strength of the attraction or repulsion between lexeme and construction according to which the verbs are ranked as more or less typical instantiations of the pattern. Table 2 presents the 20 most strongly attracted lexemes of *be about to* and *be going to*, yielded by a collexeme analysis of the two constructions.

The information these data provide no doubt differs from that obtained from raw frequency figures: Neither *be about to* V nor *be going to* V are particularly drawn to semantically light verbs. Based on collostructional strength values, *be about to* V can be rendered as strongly attracting verbs denoting incipient action/initiation (*begin, start, leave, embark, launch*), all of them found among the ten most strongly attracted lexemes. Moreover, the collexeme analysis lends stronger support to the assumption (made on the basis of raw frequency) that the construction has a close affinity with verbs of sudden change of state: six of these, i.e. *burst, explode, break, collapse, die* and *plunge* appear among the top 20 collexemes. The verbs measured as significantly associated with *be going to* V, on the other hand, seemingly render the construction as highly flexible: The list contains stative verbs (*cost, sleep, miss*), highly transitive, dynamic verbs (*put, kill*), but also unaccusative verbs (*die, faint*), where the verbal subject undergoes a process instead of being actively involved therein. As in the case of raw frequency analysis (see above), a coherent semantic grouping of the items is next to impossible. Taken together, it is fair to say that these findings are symptomatic of a more specialized usage of *be*

13. All of the calculations discussed here were conducted with the program *Coll. analysis 3.2a. A program for R for Windows 2.x* (Gries 2007). The results are given in form of the negative logarithm to the base of 10 of the p-value, to be read as follows: Values bigger than 3 correspond to a p-value smaller than 0.001, values bigger than 2 correspond to a p-value lower than 0.01. Thus, collexemes with an index > 3 are subject to highly significant distributions.

Table 2. Top 20 of strongest collexemes of *be about to* V and *be going to* V

be about to V		*be going to* V	
verbs	coll. strength	verbs	coll. strength
1. begin	83.8403	1. get	Inf
2. leave	75.4033	2. happen	Inf
3. start	68.3808	3. do	240.9301
4. embark	65.3643	4. say	187.8841
5. happen	53.5298	5. die	126.4871
6. burst	43.9524	6. cost	95.7940
7. enter	36.9662	7. put	95.7343
8. launch	32.8658	8. go	69.9268
9. become	30.4966	9. ask	53.7349
10. say	29.4717	10. marry	52.5468
11. protest	21.2711	11. kill	48.2218
12. fall	19.8084	12. start	44.4293
13. explode	18.9475	13. take	39.0358
14. retire	18.3411	14. miss	38.2253
15. turn	15.3119	15. let	36.1748
16. go	15.2525	16. sleep	34.0071
17. break	15.1403	17. work	28.8126
18. die	14.1851	18. try	27.8504
19. collapse	13.6339	19. win	27.5150
20. plunge	13.6101	20. faint	27.5150

about to V, expressing incipient, sudden action, and they lend further support to the assumed aspectualizing function of the construction.[14]

The number of verbs being strongly associated with both constructions within the top 20 is now reduced to five (*start, happen, say, go, die*), which still points at some semantic overlap. However, though *collexeme analysis* is a powerful tool to identify constructional characteristics, it does so only for single, "isolated" constructions. For a **direct comparison** of roughly synonymous constructions, Gries and Stefanowitsch (2004) introduced *distinctive collexeme analysis*, which is most useful for the detection of subtle differences between semantically similar constructions. The following section discusses the results of such an analysis applied to *be about to* V vs. *be going to* V.

14. According to the data retrieved from the diachronic corpora, this particular development, i.e. the affinity between *be about to* and verbs denoting incipient action, first appeared between 1850–1900.

5.3 Distinctive collexeme analysis

Distinctive collexeme analysis (Gries and Stefanowitsch 2004) provides the means to discover asymmetries in the relative frequencies of collexemes which occur in the 'V' slot of both *be about to* V and *be going to* V. Similar to collexeme analysis, on the basis of the Fisher-Yates exact test a particular measure is determined which is indicative of the preference of a collexeme by either of the constructions. For the calculation of this so-called **index of distinctiveness**, four types of 'input frequency' are needed: the lemma frequency of the verb collexeme in *be about to* V, the lemma frequency of the verb collexeme in *be going to* V, and the frequencies of *be about to* V and *be going to* V with verbs other than the investigated collexeme. As an example, the frequencies which are necessary for the pair *be about to start/be going to start* are given in Table 3.

These data were collected for all the verbs occurring in either of the construction and fed into the program for the detection of statistically significant imbalances in the distribution of the verbs in the respective patterns. Table 4 provides the 20 most distinctive collexemes of each construction, all of them distinctively preferred by the respective construction at the significance level of $p < 0.001$ (i.e. IoD > 3).[15]

After the actual computation of distinctively attracted collexemes, a second step for the recognition of possible meaning differences between the constructions involves the grouping of the collexemes of each pattern on the basis of selected semantic features. Gries and Stefanowitsch (2004), who carried out a similar analysis for the comparison of the future constructions with *will* and *be going to*, considered factors such as *dynamicity*, *agentivity* and *semantic specificity* expressed by the distinctive collexemes as indicators of constructional meaning, in particular with respect to 'degrees of futurity'. For my purposes, I take a closer look at the factors *semantic class* and *aktionsart*. Especially the latter might be revealing with respect to the functional status of *be about to*, since the data so far, i.e. the strong association between this construction and verbs expressing initiation, point towards a distinct aspectual meaning of the pattern.

Table 3. Frequency information necessary for distinctive collexeme analysis

	Start	Start	Row totals
be about to X	**114**	4,354	4,468
be going to X	**282**	**39,208**	39,490
Column totals	396	43,562	43,958

15. Taken together, 86 of all verbs were measured to be distinctive for *be about to* at the significance level of $p < 0.001$, 31 verbs for *be going to*. These verbs form the basis for all further discussions presented here.

Table 4. Top 20 of most distinctive collexemes of *be about to* V vs. *be going to* V

	Verb	IoD *be about to*		Verb	IoD *be going to*
1.	begin	52.6306	1.	have	78.4595
2.	leave	45.6068	2.	be	55.3249
3.	enter	43.4963	3.	get	49.4898
4.	become	42.2149	4.	do	29.8754
5.	embark	35.7213	5.	work	17.2724
6.	launch	29.0049	6.	need	13.0697
7.	start	24.3748	7.	cost	9.2055
8.	burst	18.4844	8.	stay	7.6715
9.	protest	15.9719	9.	live	6.8530
10.	return	12.4221	10.	keep	6.5239
11.	retire	12.3802	11.	help	6.1708
12.	undergo	11.8884	12.	put	5.8419
13.	reply	10.9449	13.	look	5.2201
14.	break	10.9211	14.	miss	5.2080
15.	fall	10.3620	15.	talk	4.8716
16.	plunge	9.9061	16.	use	4.7633
17.	open	9.2099	17.	win	4.7303
18.	emerge	9.0904	18.	want	4.5503
19.	speak	9.0263	19.	try	3.9049
20.	explode	8.7836	20.	sleep	3.6380

5.3.1 *Semantic classes*

Table 5 gives an overview of the semantic verb classes that are particularly preferred by *be about to* V and *be going to* V according to the distinctive collexeme analysis (percentages relate to the total number of distinctive collexemes identified for each form). The distribution of the classes reveals the different semantic preferences of each construction:

Table 5. Semantic classes preferably attracted by *be about to* V and *be going to* V

be about to V		*be going to* V	
1. Begin	15.12%	1. Psych Verbs	15.63%
2. Motion	15.12%	2. Perception	12.50%
3. Change of state	12.34%	3. Functional verbs	9.47%
4. Communication	8.14%	4. Communication	6.26%
5. Completion	6.97%	5. Desire	6.26%

Be about to V most distinctively attracts so-called begin-verbs, i.e. verbs which have a notion of 'beginning' as part of their lexical meaning. These are *begin, start, launch, embark, enter, commence, resume* etc., exemplified by the following utterances:[16]

(8) a. *Stirling was told that the army was* **about to launch** *an attack.* (AR8: 1108)

b. [...] *the show was* **about to begin**, *and the audience were in their seats.* (C8E: 3062)

c. *He was* **about to embark** *on a new life in New York with the most boring woman in Britain.* (FB0: 806)

Of all the 86 verb types which were measured to be highly distinctive (i.e. IoD > 3) of *be about to* V, 13 (15.12%) belong to this semantic class. None of these were found to be distinctive of *be going to* V. These findings emphasize the aspectual characteristics of *be about to* V, i.e., its profiling the lead-up section to the initial stage of an event (as illustrated by the examples, the verbs used in *be about to* V frequently take an eventive noun as their object).

Equally frequently represented are verbs denoting motion, e.g. *fall, walk, cross, sail*, although their individual IoDs rank them lower than many of the begin-verbs. This particular preference may also be traced back to the higher degree of immediacy and the aspectual notion the construction is taken to express. If one assumes a strong correlation between the degree of immediacy of an event and the recognizability of markers pointing at its initiation, the high dominance of concrete motion verbs can be related to the visibility of the (expected) onset of the action. If, for example, something is *about to fall*, the chances are good that several signs (particular spatial constellations, instable position of the object etc.) point at the likeliness of the event to set in soon.

Finally, as could already be read off from the raw frequency data, it is the class of verbs denoting 'sudden change' which characterizes *be about to* V: 10 verbs of this class (e.g. *burst, break, explode, collapse*) appear on the list, whereas no such verbs were found in the list for *be going to* V.

(9) a. [...] *with every breath my own stomach was swelling and* **about to burst.** (CDM: 2870)

b. [...] *Felicity announced that her spine felt as though it were* **about to collapse.** (FSC: 253)

Here, too, the aspectual characteristics of the construction pointed at above can account for the preference for these verbs: Verbs of sudden change are punctual verbs, and using them in the *be about to* V construction results in the profiling of

16. Note that only in a few instances, *enter* is used in a spatial/motion sense.

the very last stage before the actual change of state sets in. In cases such as these the construction can be said to function as 'tension-increasing'.

With respect to *be going to* V, there are three semantic verb classes which stand out from the rest of the categories of highly distinctive verbs (31 types): First, most highly representative are psych verbs (*miss, like, try, think*) and verbs of perception (*look, see, feel, watch*) which are attracted by *be going to* V if compared to *be about to* V.

(10) a. *It was silly to have come at all if she was* ***going to feel*** *so shaky and helpless.* (G12: 1325)
b. *You mark my words, we're all* ***going to miss*** *the old doctor at Thrush Green.* (ASE: 1620)
c. *I don't know what the parents of some of my students* ***are going to think*** [...]. (H61: 18)

The preference of psych verbs can be attributed to the abstract nature (and thus the non-visibility) of the events these verbs designate – their usage in *be about to* V is less felicitous since visible markers which hint at an initiation of the actions are hard to spot for the speaker (unless the speaker reports on him/herself). Note that not only are these verbs distinctive of *be going to* V, but that of the class of psych-verbs no verb is even attested in *be about to* V in the BNC. The third group of verbs distinctively associated with *be going to* V is the class of functional (i.e. semantically light) verbs (*have, be, get, do*), which were calculated as those verbs which are most distinctive for the construction. All of these are highly flexible in their usage: *Have*, for example, can express possession, may be used as a light verb (*have a look*) or in the periphrastic perfect construction; *be* has a copular use, is part of the passive or progressive construction etc. Thus, in order to evaluate their contribution to the distinctiveness of *be going to* V, all of the examples containing these verbs would need to be (sub)categorized on a case-by-case basis, which would obviously lead to a different ranking. For reasons of space, a detailed discussion of these matters must be excluded here, but some remarks on *have* and *be* as the most distinctive collexeme of *be going to* V shall be given, based on the collocation lists of both patterns: In the majority of the instances of *be going to have*, the verb is used in periphrastic constructions, i.e. the modal construction, expressing obligation etc. (≈ 40%) (11a), the light verb construction, where it is complemented by a deverbal, eventive noun (15%) (11b), or a causative construction (≈ 5%) (11c).

(11) a. *And we are all* ***going to have to*** *deal with problems.* (AYK: 1793)
b. *I'm* ***going to have*** *a lie down in a minute.* (ACK: 1285)
c. [...] *we're* ***going to have*** *them build us one.* (KCH: 2484)

In about 40% of all hits *have* is used in its possessive (core or extended) sense, expressing a **stative** relation:

(12) a. *We're* ***going to have*** *a cottage, though, later on* [...]. (BMU: 1097)
b. *We're* ***going to have*** *a jolly good time after waiting so long for this.* (CH6: 300)

Of the 7,938 hits of *be going to be* in the BNC, only ≈ 6% are instances of the progressive form (e.g. *My primary task is* ***going to be trying*** *to make that work* [ECT: 1841]), and only ≈ 17% instantiate a passive variant (e.g. *Sooner or later someone is* ***going to be killed*** *in such an accident* [K1U: 2385]). The great majority, i.e. ≈ 77%, contains *be* as a copula complemented by a predicate nominal or adjective (13a), or by an adverbial (13b), and *be* in the existential construction (13c):[17]

(13) a. *Both are* ***going to be difficult.*** (J 97: 230)
b. *How long are you* ***going to be in*** *Barbados?* (FRS: 836)
c. ***There is going to be*** *a great deal of pain in the market place now.* (AL2: 256)

The uses of *be* as illustrated in (13) and those of *have* exemplified in (12) are predominantly of a stative nature, lacking dynamicity and agentivity, and, hence, possibly intention.[18] Thus, concerning the secondary modal meaning of *be going to*, it is a rather a notion of **prediction/probability** than of intention which surfaces in those uses.

5.3.2 *Aspectual classes*

As has been pointed out, *be about to* V should be considered an aspectual construction rather than a future construction. Thus, a second feature to be looked at is that of the lexical aspect of the verbs listed as distinctive collexemes in order to find out whether the aspectual characteristics already described for *be about to* V are concordant with those of the verbs distinctively attracted by it. The verbs were categorized into the four Vendlerian classes *achievement, accomplishment, activity, state*, to which I added a fifth class, viz. *inceptive/inchoative*, for the purpose of my study. The results of this analysis support and refine the observations on the quite different behavior of the two constructions.

The strong attraction of verbs which are of a very limited temporal extension, i.e. achievements, is one aspectual characteristic which clearly distinguishes *be about to* V from *be going to* V: 38.4% of all distinctive verbs listed for the former are of a punctual nature (e.g. *burst, break, explode*). Their combination with *be about to* V is in accordance with the "tension-increasing" nuance of the pattern.

17. In this respect, *be about to* V exhibits a completely different behavior: 97% of the instances containing *be* are passive forms.

18. The degree of intention expressed by X *be going to be* might hinge on the grammatical person of the subject X. Constructions with first person subjects (e.g. *I'm going to be there*) seem to rank higher in intentionality than second or third person subjects (e.g. *He is going to be there*).

The class of achievement verbs is followed closely by accomplishment verbs (e.g. *return, announce, invade*), which make up 32%. That is, more than 70% of the verbs measured distinctive for *be about to* V are telic verbs, which stands in stark contrast to the situational types denoted by the distinctive collexemes of *be going to* V: These are overwhelmingly of an atelic nature, i.e. activities (*work, talk, use*) (46.9%) and states (*stay, need, cost, know, like*) (34.4%). This finding is in line with observations made by Hilpert (2008: 119), who found that, while in its early stages, *be going to* V was predominantly used with telic and dynamic verbs, in later stages such preferences did no longer figure.

From another perspective, these results are novel or even unexpected – in two ways: Firstly, telicity is said to be connected with intention (cf. Hilpert 2008: 53f.), which would suggest that *be about to* V expresses intention to a higher degree than *be going to* V, and thus has preserved its 'former' meaning as a **secondary modal meaning** more strongly than *be going to* V. Secondly, these findings complement results obtained by Gries and Stefanowitsch (2004), who noticed that, compared to the *will* future, *be going to* V prefers highly dynamic verbs.[19] The authors interpreted this behavior as a possible indicator of a higher degree of premediation expressed by *be going to* V. Compared to *be about to* V, however, the pattern is characterized by a great number of collexemes which denote stative situations. This in turn would present *be about to* V as describing actions which are premeditated and hence, intended. That is, on the basis of these two criteria, i.e. the telicity and dynamicity of the distinctive collexemes, *be about to* V must be considered to express the modal notion of intention more strongly than *be going to* V, a result which **diverges** from the description offered by Royster and Steadman (1923) and my own hypothesis stated earlier (see Section 4), where I argued that the image-schematic structure underlying the original spatial meanings of the constructions points at a higher degree of intention expressed by *be going to* V. The higher degree of intention expressed by *be about to* V is likely to correlate with the short temporal distance between the time referred to by *be about* and the event expressed by the infinitive, which may evoke a stronger commitment to or involvement in the event or action on the part of the agent.

Finally, 10.3% of all the verbs measured distinctive of *be about to* V carry an inceptive lexical aspect e.g. *start, enter, leave, launch, depart*. These verbs highlight the beginning of an action or activity and thus strongly harmonize with the aspectual characteristics described so far for the construction. The virtual absence of

19. It should be noted here again that *distinctive collexeme analysis* highlights **the contrasts** between two constructions. Thus, some of the constructional characteristics read off from *distinctive collexeme analysis* are exaggerated and do not present absolute values of the patterns discussed with these means. The strong focus on contrasting constructional features also explains the seemingly ambivalent behavior of *be going to* V in different such analyses.

stative verbs in the construction is in accordance with Binnick's observation that "statives do not normally occur with **aspectual** auxiliary verbs such as **start**, stop, finish" (1991: 174, emphasis added, SH) and obviously supports the classification of *be about to* V as an aspectualizing form. Note that no single verb with inceptive lexical aspect was measured distinctive for *be going to* V, a finding which is in accordance with the more specific aspectual meaning ascribed here to *be about to* V.

Concerning the construction's status in the tense-aspect system of English, a note of caution is due here, however. While it seems that *be about to* V has moved into the neighborhood of *start to* V, it must be asked whether the former has developed into a genuine ingressive aspectualizer: It shares with *start to* V the concept of initiation and preparation, and both have in common that – in contrast to *begin to* V – the event they describe as being approached is not necessarily realized (cf. Freed 1979: 72, Duffley 2006: 105f.):[20]

(14) a. *He* ***started to protest, but*** *then he seemed to remember his promise and made a conscious effort to stop himself.* (GW0: 859)

b. *Rose was* ***about to protest, but*** *thought better of it.* (AEB: 343)

However, as a corpus analysis of *start to* V reveals, it hardly occurs in the company of begin-verbs or verbs with inceptive lexical aspect, since 'inception' is apparently a core feature of its constructional meaning. *Be about to* V still relies on such verbs to clearly express 'initiation', which is indicative of its not having this concept incorporated as a primary constructional meaning. Thus, *be about to* V can at best be described as having the potential to express ingressive aspect, and be placed somewhere between futurate-forms (*will, be going to*) and aspectualizers (*start to, begin to*) on a tense-aspect-continuum.

5.4 *I am just about to finish:* Temporal adverbials in the constructions

Having collected evidence for constructional idiosyncrasies of *be about to* V and *be going to* V on the basis of verb categories (i.e. semantic and aspectual), I shall now turn to a discussion of temporal adverbials the constructions attract, since these may provide further support for the different status the constructions have in the tense-aspect system of present-day English. Differing primarily with regard to the factor 'immediacy', the constructions must be expected to combine with different types of temporal adverbials, varying in degree of temporal proximity. As already noted in Section 2, Wada (2000) discusses in great detail why *be going to* V can go with future time adverbials, whereas the combination of *be about to* V with

20. As noted by Wada (2000: 408), *be about to*-sentences in the past tense "tend to occur with the following sentences which indicate or guarantee unfulfillment" of the intended action.

such adverbials is considered odd by native speakers. According to the author, *be going to/be about to* and the event denoted by the infinitive constitute two separate events with separate event times. *Be going to* is described as covering a bounded temporal span (indicated by *to*); the extension of this temporal span is variable and depends on the speaker's construal thereof. This variability goes in hand with a certain variety of temporal adverbs found in the construction. *Be about*, on the other hand, is said to incorporate the event expressed by the infinitive into the temporal area covered by the phrase, which leaves no option for adding future time adverbials. Thus, as Wada claims, one of the few adverbs frequently used in combination with *be about to* V is *now*. However, his discussion, which seemingly demonstrates a preference of *be about to* for the adverb *now*, is rather limited with respect to the size and range of the corpus (consisting of 5 novels) his examples are drawn from.

A search in the much larger BNC provides results which extend and refine Wada's somewhat impressionistic findings: An analysis of all temporal expressions accompanying the search strings *about to* V and *going to/gonna* V within a range of 4 slots to the left and to the right of these shows that the constructions do exhibit quite different preferences: The temporal adverb most frequently found in *be about to* V is *just*, occurring in 265 instances (i.e. in 5.9% of all constructional tokens, preferably in the past tense), followed by *now*, found in 40 instances (0.9%):

(15) a. *In the exercise you are* ***now about to*** *attempt you will begin to see a familiar place through unfamiliar eyes.* (CG 3: 561)
b. *When the call came I was* ***just about to*** *bite into his huge triple layer sandwich.* (ADR: 716)

Now is the most frequent adverb in *be going to* V with 740 occurrences (1.8%), followed by *just* (533 instances, 1.53%):

(16) a. *I think I know what you're going to ask me* ***now****, Inspector.* (HWM: 2281)
b. *I was* ***just*** *going to say I didn't believe a word of it but...* (CH8: 710)

Both *now* and *just* verbalize concepts of temporal closeness, with *just*, however, carrying a flavor of prospectiveness, as defined in the OED:

> 4. *absol.* of time: Exactly at the moment spoken of; precisely now (or then).[...] with **prospective reference**: Not after this (or that) moment; hence loosely, A very little after, 'directly', 'in a moment', very soon; also, of state or condition, On the point of being.., all but, very nearly (OED, s. v. *just* [adv.], emphasis added, SH)

Given the higher degree of immediacy proposed here for *be about to* V, the higher relative frequency of *just* in this construction should come as no surprise.

Now, which denotes a temporal relationship paraphrasable as 'at the present time or moment' (OED, s.v. *now* [adv.]), has also developed a more general temporal sense 'over or during the period under discussion' (ibid.), and senses where the temporal notion is weakened or even lost. All of these are possible in the two constructions considered here, so that the occurrence of *now* in either of the patterns cannot be interpreted as a reliable indicator of immediacy.

Much more revealing, however, is the spectrum of temporal adverbials found with the constructions: While *be about to* V hardly occurs with other adverbial phrases besides *just* and *now*, *be going to* V is not as 'picky', combining with lexemes/phrases which cover a wide range on the temporal scale of (non)-immediacy, including *in minutes, tomorrow, in years* and *in the distant future* even:[21]

(17) a. *He's gonna come over* ***in a minute*** *and get him!* (KP 9: 57)
b. *Do you know what you're going to be doing* ***in five years*** *time?* (FLK: 136)
c. *In any event it will be a vision of bow* [sic.] *the profit is going to be achieved* ***in the distant future.*** (EW5: 6)

Be going to V is readily used with adverbial phrases of the type *this* N (*time, year, morning* etc., 248 instances), where the demonstrative article still suggests temporal proximity, *next* N (*weekend, month, year* etc., 72), or *in a few/couple of* N (*minutes, days, weeks, years* etc., 37). These findings **substantiate empirically** Huddleston and Pullum's (2001) and Wada's (2000) claim that 'immediacy' is not necessarily a core feature of the construction's semantics. The fact that hardly any such examples could be found for *be about to* V in the BNC, and the marked preference which the construction displays for the adverb *just* are highly indicative of its strong sense of 'immediacy'/'prospectiveness'.

6. Summary and discussion

The main purpose of this chapter was to collect evidence **converging** on questions related to the constructional (non-)synonymy of two patterns which are often described as similar enough to paraphrase each other, viz. *be about to* V and *be going to* V.

Starting out with a sketch of the diachronic development of *be about to* V, which exhibits many parallels to that of *be going to* V concerning grammaticalization stages and early usage, I went on to consider possible distinguishing features of the constructional meanings of the two forms. These must be expected on the basis of

21. The following temporal adverbials were found most frequently in *be going to* V: 1. *now*: 710; 2. *just*: 533; 3. *never*: 350; 4. *tomorrow*: 230; 5. *always*: 184; 6. *today*: 170; 6. *next*: 97; 7. *soon*: 85; 8. *in a minute*: 68; 9. *this time*: 65; 10. *this year*: 47.

linguistic economy and the principle of isomorphism ('one form – one meaning'), which figures in any discussion of linguistic motivation.

The thread which runs through the analysis of *be about to* V is its development towards an aspectualizing construction, which is the major result of the construction's 'specialization', most probably triggered by the coexistence of and competition with *be going to* V. All of the statistical data adduced for the description and comparison of the two patterns, i.e. raw frequency, collostructional strength and distinctive collostructional strength, could, consulted in a step-by-step fashion, filter out their specific constructional characteristics: Most of the findings suggest that *be about to* V has developed aspectual characteristics, profiling the lead-up section to the onset of an action. This positions the construction much closer to aspectualizing expressions such as *begin to/start to* V than to forms expressing futurity. A look into diachronic corpora brings to light that this behavior of *be about to* V is a more recent development, verbs with inceptive lexical aspect being progressively more frequently used from the 1860s onwards. *Be going to* V, on the other hand, lacks the high degree of immediacy expressed by be *to be about to* V and is much more flexible both in regard to the semantic types of verbs it is associated with and the temporal adverbials it combines with.

A second, yet minor, point of discussion addressed the secondary modal meanings which are claimed to be conveyed by both constructions, most notably that of intention and prediction. Here, the evidence is slightly **diverging** or at least less conclusive: While both earlier descriptive accounts and the image-schematic structure of literal *be going to* V (SELF-PROPELLED MOTION) point at a higher degree of initiation, the great number of verbs characterized by low dynamicity and atelicity run counter to this assumption, instead suggesting the notion of prediction or probability as more prominent. In contrast, *be about to* V, strongly attracting telic, dynamic and semantically specific verbs, expresses intention and certainty to a higher degree. However, since, for example, aspectual notions do not only hinge on the *aktionsart* of the verb alone, but are also contributed by verbal particles and adverbial phrases embedded in the clause, a detailed analysis of each single instance of both constructions would be necessary then to further refine the results.

Taken together, the study has illustrated a kind of linguistic analysis which successfully combines elicitation and interpretation of data from different sources, where my own and other authors' intuition and introspection have triggered and guided particular lines of argumentation, which could be specified and modified by empirical investigation. This 'modus operandi' has yielded a multifaceted portray of the diachronic development and synchronic usage idiosyncrasies of *be going to* V and *be about to* V. It has provided **converging evidence** for the non-synonymy of the two constructions and invites a reconsideration of the status of *be about to* V in the tense-aspect system of English, which might be worked out further in future discussions by comparing it with the same means to similar forms such as *start to* V, *get to* V or *be on the verge of* V*ing*.

References

Binnick, Robert I. 1991. *Time and the Verb: A Guide to Tense and Aspect*. New York: Oxford University Press.

Boberg, Charles. 2002. Fact or opinion: A sociolinguistic view of native-speaker intuitions as evidence in linguistics. *LACUS FORUM XXVIII*: 3–13.

Brinton, Laurel J. 1988. *The Development of English Aspectual Systems: Aspectualizers and Post-verbal Particles*. Cambridge: Cambridge University Press.

Bryson, Bill. 1990. *The Mother Tongue*. New York: Perennial.

Bybee, Joan L. & Östen Dahl. 1989. The creation of tense and aspect systems in the languages of the world. *Studies in Language* 13: 51–103.

Bybee, Joan L., Revere D. Perkins & William Pagliuca. 1994. *The Evolution of Grammar: Tense, Aspect and Mood in the Languages of the World*. Chicago: The University of Chicago Press.

Bybee, Joan L. 2007. Diachronic linguistics. In D. Geeraerts & H. Cuyckens, eds., *The Oxford Handbook of Cognitive Linguistics*, 945–987. New York: Oxford University Press.

Collins, Peter. 2009. *Modals and Quasi-Modals in English*. Amsterdam: Rodopi.

Comrie, Bernard. 1976. *Aspect: An Introduction to the Study of Verbal Aspect and Related Problems*. Cambridge: Cambridge University Press.

Croft, William. 2000. *Explaining Language Change: An Evolutionary Approach*. Harlow: Longman.

Cuyckens, Hubert, Dominiek Sandra & Sally Rice. 1997. Towards an empirical semantics. In B. Smieja & M. Tasch, eds., *Human Contact through Language and Linguistics*, 35–54. Frankfurt: Peter Lang.

Danchev, Andrei & Merja Kytö. 1994. The construction *be going to* + infinitive in Early Modern English. In D. Kastovsky, ed., *Studies in Early Modern English*, 59–78. Berlin/New York.

Duffley, Patrick J. 2006. *The English Gerund Participle. A comparison with the infinitive*. New York: Peter Lang.

Evans, Vyvyan. 2003. *The Structure of Time*. Amsterdam & Philadelphia: Benjamins.

Fischer, Olga. 2000. Grammaticalisation: Unidirectional, non-reversible? The case of *to* before the infinitive in English. In O. Fischer, A. Rosenbach, & D. Stein, eds., *Pathways of Change: Grammaticalization in English*, 149–169. Amsterdam & Philadelphia: Benjamins.

Freed, Alice F. 1979. *The Semantics of English Aspectual Complementation*. Dordrecht, Boston, & London: D. Reidel.

Geeraerts, Dirk. 2006. Methodology in Cognitive Linguistics. In G. Kristiansen, M. Achard, R. Dirven, & F. J. Ruiz de Menodza Ibánez, eds., *Cognitive Linguistics: Current Applications and Future Perspectives*, 21–50. Berlin/New York: Mouton de Gruyter.

Gibbs, Raymond W. 2007. Why cognitive linguists should care more about empirical methods. In M. Gonzales-Marques et al., eds., *Methods in Cognitive Linguistics*, 2–18. Amsterdam & Philadelphia: Benjamins.

Goldberg, Adele. 2006. *Constructions at Work: the Nature of Generalization in Language*. Oxford: OUP.

González-Marquez, Monica, Irene Mittelberg, Seana Coulson & Michael J. Spivey, eds., 2007. *Methods in Cognitive Linguistics*. Amsterdam & Philadelphia: Benjamins.

Gries, Stefan Thomas. 2007. Coll. analysis 3.2a. A program for R for Windows 2.x.

Gries, Stefan Thomas & Anatol Stefanowitsch. 2004. Extending collostructional analysis: A corpus-based perspectives on 'alternations'. *International Journal of Corpus Linguistics* 9: 97–129.

Gries, Stefan Thomas, Beate Hampe, & Doris Schönefeld. 2005. Converging evidence: Bringing together experimental and corpus data on the association of verbs and constructions. *Cognitive Linguistics* 16–4: 635–676.

Heine, Bernd, Ulrike Claudi, & Friederike Hünnemeyer. 1991. *Grammaticalization: A Conceptual Framework*. Chicago: The University of Chicago Press.

Hilpert, Martin. 2008. *Germanic Future Constructions. A Usage-based Approach to Language Change*. Amsterdam & Philadelphia: Benjamins.

Huddleston, Rodney & Geoffrey K. Pullum. 2002. *The Cambridge Grammar of the English Language*. Cambridge: Cambridge University Press.

Janssen, Theo & Gisela Redeker (eds.). 1999. *Cognitive Linguistics: Foundations, Scope and Methodology*. Berlin & New York: Mouton de Gruyter.

Jespersen, Otto. 1954 [1931]. *A Modern English Grammar On Historical Principles. Part IV: Syntax*. London: George Allen and Unwin.

Jirsa, Bill. 1997. Synchronic applications for diachronic syntax: The grammaticalization of *to be about to* in English. *Colorado Research in Linguistics 15*: 25–31.

Lakoff, George. 1993. The contemporary theory of metaphor. In A. Ortony, ed., *Metaphor and Thought,* 202–251.Cambridge: Cambridge University Press.

Langacker, Ronald. 2008. *Cognitive Grammar: A Basic Introduction*. New York: OUP.

Mair, Christian. 2004. Corpus linguistics and grammaticalisation theory: Statistics, frequencies and beyond. In H. Lindquist and C. Mair, eds., *Corpus Approaches to Grammaticalization in English,* 121–150. Amsterdam & Philadelphia: Benjamins.

Oxford English Dictionary. Online version. http://www.oed.com.

Pertejo, Paloma Nunez. 1999. *Be going to+ i*nfinitive: Origin and development: Some relevant cases from the *Helsinki Corpus*. *Studia Neophilologica* 71: 135–142.

Poutsma, Hendrik. 1929. *A Grammar of Late Modern English. Part I. The Sentence: Second Half. The Composite Sentence*. 2nd ed. Groningen: Noordhoff.

Quirk, Randolph et al. 1985. *A Comprehensive Grammar of the English Language*. London: Longman.

Royster, J.F. & J. M. Steadman. 1923. The *going-to* future. *The Manly Anniversary Studies in Language and Literature*: 394–403.

Sampson, Geoffrey & Diane McCarthy. 2004. *Corpus Linguistics: Readings in a widening discipline*. London/New York: Continuum.

Stefanowitsch, Anatol & Stefan Thomas Gries. 2003. Collostructions: Investigating the interaction between words and constructions. *International Journal of Corpus Linguistics* 8.2: 209–43.

Talmy, Leonard. 2007. Foreword. In M. González-Marquez et al., eds., *Methods in Cognitive Linguistics*, xi–xxi. Amsterdam & Philadelphia: Benjamins.

Traugott, Elizabeth C. & Ekkehard König. 1991. The semantics and pragmatics of grammaticalization revisited. In E. C. Traugott & B. Heine, eds., *Approaches to Grammaticalization*. Vol. I, 189–218. Amsterdam & Philadelphia: Benjamins.

Wada, Naoki. 2000. *Be going to* and *be about to*: Just because Doc Brown was going to take us back to the future does not mean that he was about to do so. *English Linguistics: Journal of the English Linguistic Society of Japan* 17(2): 386–416.

Wekker, Herman C. 1976. *The Expression of Future Time in Contemporary British English*. Amsterdam: North-Holland Publishing Company.

Studying syntactic priming in corpora

Implications of different levels of granularity

Stefan Th. Gries
University of California, Santa Barbara

This chapter addresses syntactic priming (of the dative alternation) using corpus data from the ICE-GB corpus. Nearly 3,000 consecutive prime-target pairs were coded for their constructional choices as well as several other variables. The data are then analyzed on different levels of granularity: (i) cross-tabulation, (ii) with a binary logistic regression (including only fixed effects), and (iii) a generalized linear mixed-effects model (GLMEM) (including fixed and random effects). The GLMEM reduces the number of significant predictors most, but nevertheless yields the highest classification accuracy. Since contemporary cognitive linguistics assumes an item-based perspective on language acquisition, processing, and change, I argue that the GLMEM approach should be the method of choice for empirical cognitive linguistics.

Keywords: binary logistic regression models, corpus data, cross-tabulation, dative alternation, generalized linear mixed-effects models, item-specificity, empirical cognitive linguistics

1. Introduction

Syntactic priming/persistence, the tendency of speakers to re-use syntactic patterns they have recently comprehended or produced, is a phenomenon that has attracted considerable attention ever since Bock's pioneering work in the early 1980s. In a series of publications, Bock and colleagues showed that speakers who read (1a) are more likely to describe a transitive scenario with a passive sentence than speakers who read (1b).

(1) a. *The duckling was killed by the farmer.*
  b. *The farmer killed the duckling.*

Much initial work on this tendency focused on demonstrating that such priming effects are in fact a tendency to use identical syntactic constituent structures rather than, say, identical metrical structures or identical thematic role orderings. For example, Bock and Loebell (1990) showed that (2a) primes prepositional datives such as *John [sent [$_{NP}$ a book] [$_{PP}$ to [$_{NP}$ Mary]]]*, but (2b) does not even though it has the exact same metrical structure (but not the relevant syntactic structure):

(2) a. *Susan brought a book to Stella.*
b. *Susan brought a book to study.*

Bock (1989) showed both (3a) and (3b) prime passive such as *[$_{PAT}$ The duckling] was killed [$_{PP}$ by [$_{AGT}$ the farmer]]* even though only (3a) involves a *by*-passive:

(3) a. *The 747 was alerted by the airport's control tower.*
b. *The 747 was landing by the airport's control tower.*

Syntactic priming has turned out to be a very general and robust effect. It has been obtained

- from production to production (cf. Bock 1986);
- from comprehension to production (cf. Branigan et al. 2000, Bock et al. 2007);
- when the verb lemmas in primes and targets are the same or different (cf. Pickering and Branigan 1998);
- in L1 (cf. all studies quoted so far) and L2 (cf. Bock and Loebell 2003, Gries and Wulff 2003, 2009);
- across different languages (cf. Hartsuiker, Pickering, and Veltkamp 2004, Schoonbaert, Hartsuiker, and Pickering 2007, and Shin and Christianson 2009).

With very few exceptions, the work on syntactic priming has been experimental in nature, involving many different kinds of paradigms – studies involving corpus-based approaches are few and far between (cf. Estival 1985, Gries 2005, or Szmrecsanyi 2005). As a matter of fact, it is not uncommon to hear or read statements that question the utility of corpus data in the study of syntactic priming; the following is a case in point.

> [T]here are several nonsyntactic factors which could lead to repetition. [...] Corpora have proved useful as a means of hypothesis generation, but unequivocal demonstrations of syntactic priming effects can only come from controlled experiments (Branigan et al., 1995 492; cf. also Pickering and Branigan, 1999: 136).

In this study, I argue that, in spite of a degree of noisiness that exceeds that of experimental data, corpus data can not only coincide strikingly with experimental data – and, thus, provide converging evidence – but also have things to offer to priming researchers that are interesting and hard to obtain with the usual carefully-controlled experimental designs. More specifically, based on a reanalysis of data discussed in Gries (2005), I show that corpus data have a lot to add to the customary experimental approaches, in particular when it comes to (i) the analysis of the duration of priming and (ii) the issue of how priming effects are specific to the verbs involved and to (at least approximately) individual speakers/authors.

As for the duration of priming effects, there are conflicting findings. On the one hand, some studies show that the distance between prime and target has to be fairly small in order for priming effects to be obtained (cf. Levelt and Kelter 1982 or Branigan et al. 1999). On the other hand, other studies show that priming may well persist for longer times and across quite a bit of intervening material (cf. Bock and Griffin 2000, Pickering et al., 2000, Chang et al., 2000, and Bock et al. 2007). However, given the large number of distances and types of intervening material between primes and target, it is difficult to assess very many different distances between primes and targets in carefully controlled experimental settings. In addition, it is well-known by now that not all syntactic constructions are equally sensitive to priming effects, which brings us to the next topic, lexical specificity.

Previous studies have shown that different constructions are differently responsive to priming both 'between alternations' and 'within alternations'. As for the former, the dative alternation exhibits stronger priming effects than the voice alternation (cf. Bock 1986: Exp. 1); as for the latter, ditransitives are primed more strongly than prepositional datives (cf. Bock 1986; cf. Potter and Lombardi 1998 for the opposite result). But what about the lexical material – more precisely, the verb – that is involved in the clauses tested for priming? Not only is it well known that verbs have differently strong probabilistic preferences to occur with particular constructions, it is also well known that these preferences correlate with many other aspects of psycholinguistic processing such as ease and speed of lexical access or ambiguity resolution (cf. Garnsey et al. 1997, Stallings et al. 1998, Hare et al. 2003). It is therefore reasonable to assume that, if verbs 'prefer' to occur in constructions differently strongly, then they will be differently susceptible to priming effects. Surprisingly, this possibility has rarely been mentioned in experimental studies; see Potter and Lombardi (1998: 278) for an exception, and most studies have been content to provide F_1/F_2 and quasi-F statistics on the data to determine whether observed effects are significant across the ranges of verbs and speakers included in the experiment. However, as I already pointed out, not all studies chose their experimental stimuli such that they systematically and symmetrically exhaust the whole range of (strengths of) subcategorization preferences. And to some degree that is understandable:

- the number of verbs that participate in the usual suspects of alternations can be so large as to make it impossible to include a larger share of them into an experiment, especially when all other independent variables and the common experimental controls are not just included but systematically and exhaustively varied and crossed.
- operationalizing/measuring subcategorization preferences is not a straightforward matter. Most studies so far have used raw observed frequencies (cf., Connine et al. 1984 or Hare et al. 2003), but corpus-based research shows that it may be much more useful to use measures that control for verbs' and constructions' overall frequencies in a corpus (cf. Gries, under review).

More recently, in the study of alternation patterns, Gries and Stefanowitsch (2004) proposed the measure of distinctive collexeme strength to quantify a verb's preference for one out of several functionally similar constructions. This measure is typically based on computationally somewhat intensive Fisher-Yates exact tests of 2×2 co-occurrence tables and provides a kind of estimate of verbs' preferences to one of two constructions. Some experimental studies have now shown that this measure is a strong predictor of subjects' verb-specific construction preferences in priming tasks (Gries and Wulff 2003, 2009) and can even outperform the usual kind of raw frequencies in sentence completion and self-paced reading tasks (cf. Gries, Hampe, and Schönefeld 2005, 2010). A rigorous corpus-based approach thus not only provides a better operationalization of individual verbs' constructional preferences, but also the opportunity to include very many different verbs and their preferences into the analysis of structural priming effects; ultimately, this affords to the analyst a versatile and powerful tool with which to obtain (con- or diverging) evidence difficult to attain otherwise.

In the remainder of this chapter, I reanalyze corpus data on the dative alternation first studied in Gries (2005), but I go beyond that study by comparing three different ways to analyze the corpus data statistically. The first of these ways, the study of mere constructional frequencies, provides just a very simple lowest level of sophistication. The second of these ways – a binary logistic regression analysis – provides a much more precise set of results. Most importantly, however, the third way is the statistical approach of generalized linear mixed-effects modeling, a new technique which not only has several statistical advantages over more traditional methods but is also more compatible with the degree of importance attached to item-based patterns by usage-based linguists these days; these issues and their implications are discussed in more detail below.

The following section introduces in more detail the data that were investigated in this study and the analytical tools used.

2. Data and methods

In order to investigate syntactic priming corpus-linguistically, I first identified ditransitive constructions and prepositional datives with *to* and *for* in the British component of the International Corpus of English (ICE-GB).[1] These data were cleaned such that clauses that were the first or last construction either in one of the 500 corpus files or in a subtext of a corpus file were discarded (because they cannot function as targets or primes respectively) leaving 2,877 prime-target pairs (i.e. subsequent construction pairs of either type) for the analysis that could be coded for all intended variables.

The variables that are studied included both fixed and random effects. The dependent variable was CTARGET, the construction of the second of the two constructions constituting a prime-target pair: *ditransitive* vs. *prepositional dative* (automatically retrieved from the annotated parse trees within the corpus files). The fixed effects I included were the following:

- CPRIME: the construction of the first of the two constructions constituting a prime-target pair: *ditransitive* vs. *prepositional dative* (automatically retrieved from the annotated parse trees within the corpus files);
- MEDIUM: the medium in which prime and target occurred: *spoken* vs. *written* (automatically retrieved from the corpus files);
- LOGDISTANCE: the distance in parsing units between the occurrence of prime and target within each subtext of each file as determined from the annotation of the corpus, which was logged and centered;
- VFORMID and VLEMMAID: whether both constructions involved the same verb form and verb lemma: *yes* or *no* (cf. Pickering and Branigan 1998);
- SPEAKERID: whether in the spoken data both constructions were produced by the same speaker or not: *yes* or *no*.

In addition to these main effects, I also included the interactions of CPRIME with all other independent variables. This means, for example, that I checked whether the effect of the construction in the prime is differently strong in speaking and writing

1. The ICE-GB is a POS-tagged and fully parsed corpus of spoken and written British English of the 1990s; all annotation has been checked manually by several linguists (cf. http://www.ucl.ac.uk/english-usage/ice-gb/index.htm for details). The data discussed here differ slightly from those used in Gries (2005) because VPs with *to*/*for* were extracted using different fuzzy tree fragments and the distinctive collexeme strengths were updated accordingly.

(the first interaction), whether the effect of the construction in the prime varies as a function of the distance between prime and target (the second interaction), …[2]

The random effects, on the other hand, were as follows:

- VLemmaTarget: the exact verb lemma of each target;
- File: the name of the file in which the prime and target were observed.[3]

After all prime-target pairs were coded for all these variables, I performed the three statistical analyses briefly mentioned above. These analyses differ in terms of their level of granularity and statistical sophistication in the sense that they use successively finer degrees of resolution in their characterization of the situation that gives rise to a particular constructional choice.

First, at the coarsest possible level of granularity or precision, the only independent variable included is CPrime. That is, one just cross-tabulates the constructional frequencies in prime and target slots, which obviously provides only a very crude measure of whether priming can be observed and, if so, how strong the priming effect is.

Second, at a finer level of granularity, more information about the situation at the time of production is included. More specifically, one can include all

2. It is worth pointing out in this context how binary logistic regression goes beyond what a traditional variationist tool such as Varbrul can do: not only can such regressions handle continuous data, they can also include interactions of factors seamlessly; cf. <http://www.ling.upenn.edu/~johnson4/Rbrul_manual.html> for an R function that offers these kinds of functionality as well as the kind of random effects to be discussed below.

3. One reviewer raised the question of why verbs are not entered into the GLMEM analysis as a fixed effect, arguing that verb lemma effects can be considered "repeatable" (quoting Baayen 2008: 141) and that, therefore, modeling verb-specific effects as a random effect is more a matter of statistical convenience than theoretical conviction. I agree that modeling verb-specific effects as random effects is methodologically more convenient and that, in the spirit of Gries and Stefanowitsch's (2004) collostructional analysis, verb-specific effects can be seen as repeatable.

On the other hand, note that even the reference quoted by the reviewer – Baayen (2008), who refers to repeatability in his discussion of fixed and random effects – uses random effects to model item-specific effects in corpora, and this seems to be the (currently emerging) standard of how mixed-effects models are used in linguistics (cf. also Johnson's (2008: sect. 7.3–7.4) discussion). In addition, another criterion often referred to in this connection has to do with whether the levels of a factor in the sample that is being studied exhaust the full range of levels this factor has in the population. In the case of factors like sex of subject (in experiments) or CPrime (here), this is the case, and such factors are typically modeled as fixed effects. However, the verb lemmas studied in this paper's sample do not exhaust all possible verbs that can be used ditransitively in the population, which supports the inclusion of VLemmaTarget as a random effect. Finally, recall that GLMEM are better at taking different frequencies of factor levels and group-level variability into account than regular regression models (cf. Luke (2004: 6–7) as well as Gelman and Hill (2007: 245–246) for more discussion).

above-mentioned fixed effects and (some of) their interactions and perform a generalized linear model analysis on the data, in which the choice of construction in the target slot is predicted on the basis of these predictors. In Gries (2005), I performed an analysis of that kind, but used an ANOVA, which, with hindsight, was a sub-optimal methodological choice (cf. Jaeger 2008 for discussion of shortcomings of ANOVAs). In the second analysis of this study, I follow the exemplary study of Szmrecsanyi (2005) and use a binary logistic regression, which is the more appropriate measure since it does justice to the facts that the dependent variable is categorical and its distributional assumptions are more compatible with the data.

Finally, and most importantly for the present study, one can describe the situation at the time of production with an even higher degree of granularity. In this chapter, I am referring to the possibility of performing a generalized linear mixed-effects model (GLMEM), i.e. a binary logistic regression including not only the above fixed effects but also the random effects. That is, a part of the variation within the data is accounted for by including random effects for files (as a rough (!) approximation to distinguishing different speakers/writers, which in experimental studies is often captured by by-subjects analyses) and for verb lemmas in the target (as an operationalization of verb-specific preferences, which are often captured by by-items analyses). This approach has several advantages over more traditional methods.

First, GLMEM is geared towards including random effects such as, here, verb-specific effects and corpus file-specific overall patterns. While both of these kinds of random effects were in fact discussed in Gries (2005), verb-specific effects were only included by discussing a handful of verb preferences (experimental items used in Pickering and Branigan 1998), and corpus file-specific effects were only explored graphically using switch-rate plots. In this study, using GLMEM, I can include these two kinds of effects in a statistically more comprehensive way.[4] This has the advantage that, while these random effects are not predictors of the constructional choice *per se*, they make the estimation of the predictors more precise and more robust, and I compare binary logistic regression and GLMEM to show why this is important and revealing. Second, such mixed-effects models are better than traditional regression methods at handling the fact that, for example, different verbs will be differently frequent in the data and will, therefore, contribute different amounts of information to the model (cf. Gelman and Hill 2007: 246, 254). Finally, Baayen (2008: Section 7.2.1) shows how mixed-effects models outperform the current standard in psycholinguistics of reporting F_1/F_2 and quasi F statistics or ANOVAs on transformed data (cf. again Jaeger 2008).

4. The included random effects are only adjustment to intercepts, not also to slopes.

Before we turn to the discussion of the results in the following section, one final caveat is in order. Quite obviously, there are quite a few additional variables that could be included in the analyses to be discussed below. For example, Bresnan et al. (2007) include information-structural variables and constituent length differences in their study (and even verb sense as a random effect). Also, Jaeger and Snider (2007) include a different kind of verb-specificity effect called surprisal and show that, if a prime consists of a verb in a construction that the verb is not generally associated with, then the priming effect is stronger. It goes without saying that the inclusion of more independent variables and/or random effects will not only increase the overall classification accuracy but also increase the probability that what is studied are really priming effects of CPRIME and not other factors facilitating structural repetition. However, the classification of approximately 6,000 recipient and patients for, say, discourse accessibility is beyond the scope of the current chapter since the focus here is not on demonstrating that corpora can be used to study the psycholinguistic process of priming – some of the studies mentioned above have done that on a larger and more comprehensive scale than is possible here – but on showing that

- different quantitative approaches to corpus data differ substantially in terms of (i) the determinants of structural repetitions they identify, (ii) as a corollary, the quality of the results they yield, and (iii) their theoretical fit to the usage-based commitment of much of contemporary cognitive linguistics;
- the most appropriate statistical analysis of corpus data yields results supportive of, and complementary to, experimental data, which ultimately, supports the idea of converging evidence from methodological pluralism.

3. Results

3.1 Coarse granularity: Constructional frequencies

The first type of analysis at the coarsest level of granularity results in the observed frequencies in Table 1.

Table 1. Observed frequencies of both constructions in primes and targets

	CTARGET: prep. dative	**CTARGET: ditransitive**	**Totals**
CPRIME: prep. dative	746	549	1,295
CPRIME: ditransitive	514	1,068	1,582
Totals	1,260	1,617	2,877

Table 2. Expected frequencies of both constructions in primes and targets

	CTarget: prep. dative	CTarget: ditransitive	Totals
CPrime: prep. dative	607.7	687.3	1,295
CPrime: ditransitive	742.4	839.6	1,582

These observed frequencies must be compared to the frequencies expected by chance. These are computed here on the assumptions that (i) after each construction in CPrime, the speaker can produce either construction in the target, and (ii) the random, baseline probabilities to choose one construction in CTarget follows from the constructions' overall frequencies in the corpus:

Once this pattern is represented graphically (as in Figure 1), the result becomes clearer.

There is a marked priming effect: when the prime was a prepositional dative, then prepositional datives and ditransitives were more and less frequent than expected respectively, and when the prime was a ditransitive, then prepositional datives and ditransitives were less and more frequent than expected respectively. Note also that the strengths of the preferences for the two constructions are very similar to those reported in Bock's pioneering experimental study. Bock (1986: 364) found percentage ratios of prepositional dative and ditransitive preferences of 1.5 and 2.1 respectively (i.e. an 'odds ratio' of approximately 0.71), while I obtained 1.45 and 1.95 respectively (i.e. an 'odds ratio' of approximately 0.75). In spite of many potential additional predictors ignored in this study, this points to a large degree of convergence of the experimental and the corpus-based approaches.

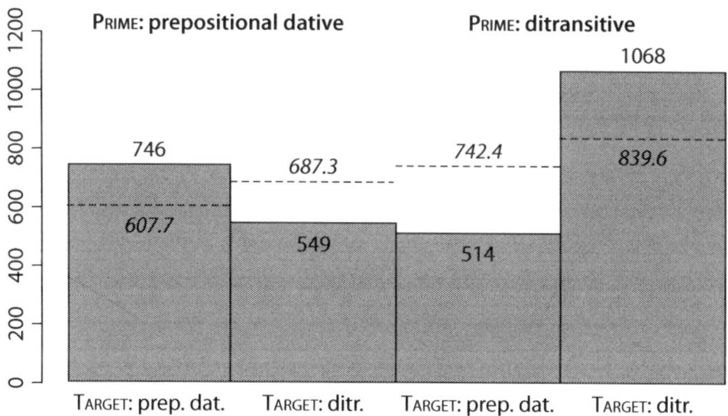

Figure 1. Bar plot with observed construction frequencies (with horizontal lines and italic numbers indicating expected frequencies)

While this result is straightforward to interpret, it is also not particularly informative since it does not provide any more detailed information. Here, clearly, a more refined method of analysis is required.

3.2 Intermediate granularity: Binary logistic regression

The statistical analysis on the intermediate level of granularity supports the much more shallow analysis of Section 3.1, but provides a wealth of additional information. Starting out from the maximal model that includes all above fixed effect predictors (main effects and interactions), I went through a model selection process that in a stepwise fashion (from interactions to main effects) eliminated all predictors that were not significant and did not participate in a higher-order significant interaction. The final, minimally adequate model shows that there is a highly significant correlation between the fixed-effect predictors that survived the model selection process and the construction chosen in the target (model L.R. $\chi^2 = 1340.76$; $df = 8$; $p < 0.001$). This final model has a reasonable degree of classificatory/predictive power ($C = 0.718$; Somer's $D_{xy} = 0.436$; Nagelkerke's $R^2 = 0.248$); cf. Table 3 for its classification matrix.

According to the chance expectation – always choosing the more frequent construction – one would get $^{1,617}/_{2,877} = 56.2\%$ correct classifications. The classification accuracy obtained in the model, however, is somewhat better: $^{1,833}/_{2,877} = 63.71\%$, and the difference between these percentages is highly significant ($p_{binomial\ test} < 0.0001$). It is worth briefly comparing the present classification accuracy to that of, say, Bresnan et al. (2007). On the one hand, the present classification accuracy is much worse because they achieved classification and prediction accuracies of 92%. On the other hand, this was to be expected, given that they included a much larger number of predictors in their model. Potentially more importantly, the performance can maybe be evaluated more accurately by considering the baseline accuracies of both studies. Bresnan et al.'s model improved the accuracy from the baseline of 79% to 92%, i.e. by approximately 16%, while the present model improved the accuracy from the baseline of 56.2% to 63.7%, i.e. by approximately 13%, which is much closer to Bresnan et al.'s improvement than a mere comparison of classification accuracies would suggest.

Table 3. Classification matrix of the binary logistic regression classifications (with italic numbers indicating correctly predicted constructions)

predicted/observed	CTarget: prep. dative	CTarget: ditransitive	Totals
CTarget: prep. dative	*720*	504	1,224
CTarget: ditransitive	540	*1,113*	1,653
Totals	1,260	1,617	2,877

The question remains, what are the predictors that made it into the final model and how strongly do they affect the constructional choice. Figure 2 represents the relevant predictors and how they influence CTarget. On the x-axis, I show all predictors plus the level whose coefficient is represented in the graph. Against the y-axis, I represent the coefficient size (with the "×") and its standard error (with the error bars). Positive and negative coefficients indicate preferences for the prepositional dative and the ditransitive respectively, and the more a coefficient deviates from zero, the stronger the effect; significance levels are indicated at the top of the graph.

As can be seen on the left of Figure 2, the main effect of CPrime is not significant (cf. the "ns" at the top and the fact that the standard error includes 0) and other main effects are significant but irrelevant for the study of priming (the fact that the proportion of ditransitives is larger in writing does not really mean much in this context). However, most main effects participate in interactions with CPrime; cf. Figure 3.

The first interaction shows that prepositional dative primes tend to yield prepositional dative targets, but that this effect is very much and highly significantly stronger when the verb form in the target is also exactly the same as in the prime. The second interaction shows that the same pattern holds with regard to whether the same verb lemma is used in both prime and target. The third interaction shows that prepositional dative primes tend to yield prepositional dative targets significantly more strongly when the speaker/writer is the same across both and target.

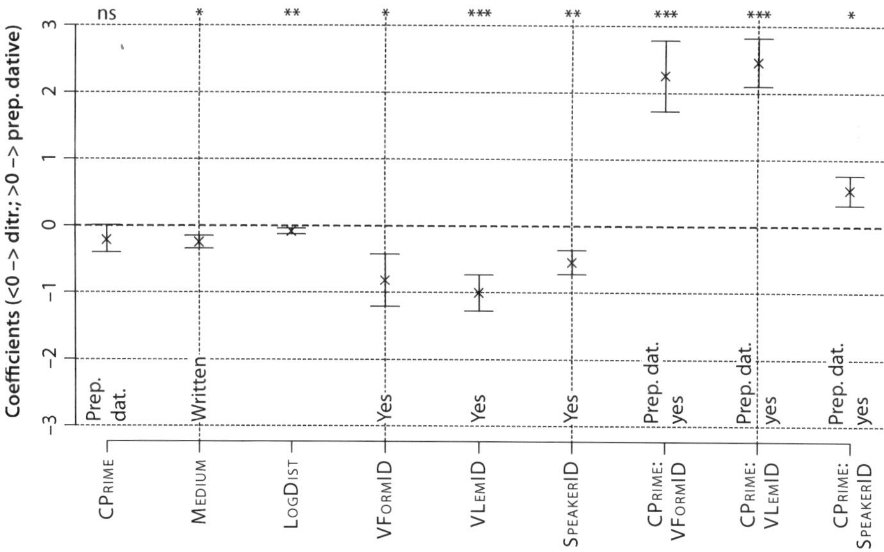

Figure 2. Coefficients of the independent variables in the minimal adequate model of the binary logistic regression (with their standard errors)

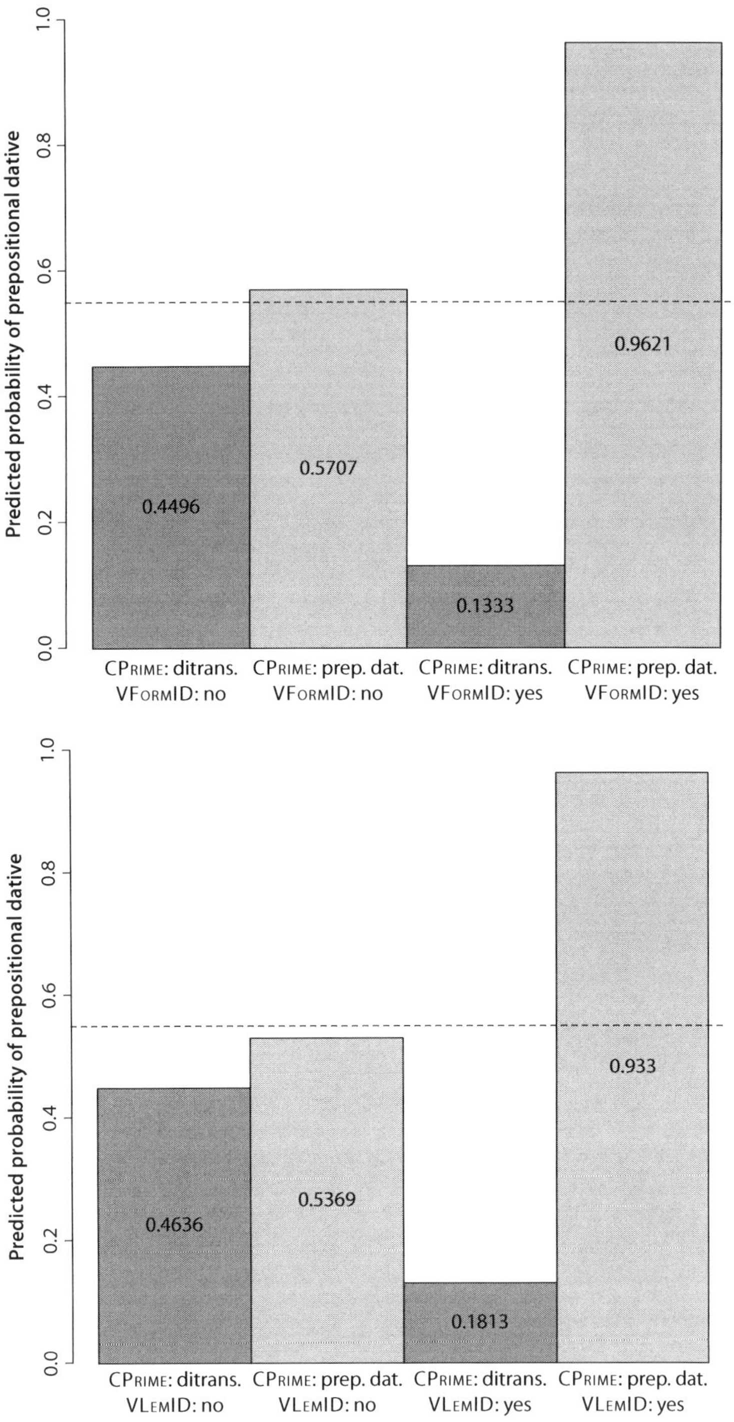
Predicted probability of prepositional dative
0.0
0.2
0.4
0.6
0.8
1.0
0.4496
0.5707
0.1333
0.9621
CPRIME: ditrans. VFORMID: no
CPRIME: prep. dat. VFORMID: no
CPRIME: ditrans. VFORMID: yes
CPRIME: prep. dat. VFORMID: yes
Predicted probability of prepositional dative
0.0
0.2
0.4
0.6
0.8
1.0
0.4636
0.5369
0.1813
0.933
CPRIME: ditrans. VLEMID: no
CPRIME: prep. dat. VLEMID: no
CPRIME: ditrans. VLEMID: yes
CPRIME: prep. dat. VLEMID: yes

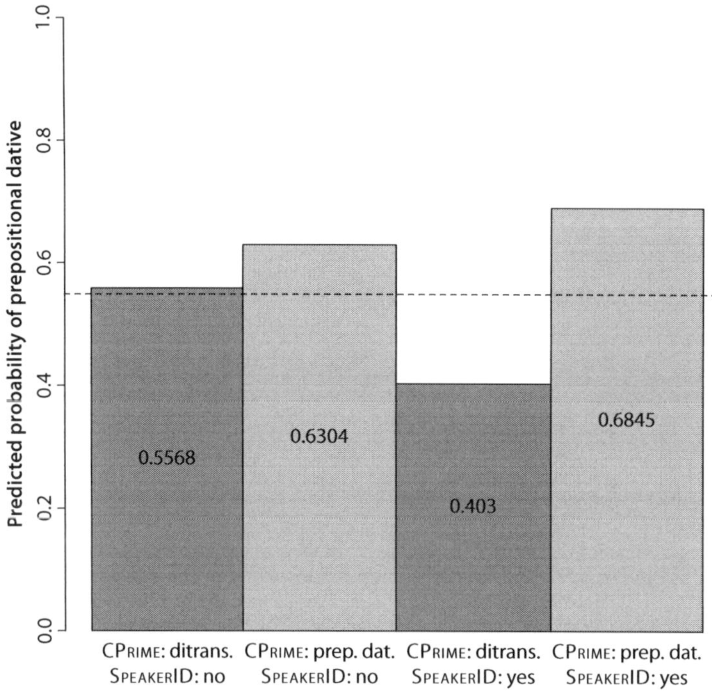

Figure 3. Interactions of VFORMID, VLEMMAID, and SPEAKERID with CPRIME (with the predicted probability of prepositional datives on the y-axis)

In sum, the data in general confirm some previous work cited above: syntactic priming exists and it is stronger the more prime and target are similar to each other otherwise, be it the verb form, the verb lemma, and/or the speaker. In the following section, the corpus data are explored even more precisely.

3.3 High granularity: Generalized linear mixed-effects model

The final analysis in this section is somewhat more complex and I can discuss neither all technicalities here (cf. Gelman and Hill 2007, Baayen 2008: Ch. 7, Johnson 2008: Sect 7.3–7.4) nor devote much time on the conceptual implications – instead, the focus is on exemplifying how the results that a GLMEM approach provides go beyond the standard binary logistic regression; the GLMEM was computed with the function lmer in the R environment (cf. R Development Core Team 2009).

Again, I started out from the maximal model that includes all fixed effect predictors (main effects and interactions) from above plus, now, two random effects as adjustments to the intercept. Then I first went through the same kind of model selection process, eliminating in a stepwise fashion (from interactions to main

Table 4. Classification matrix of the GLMEM regression classifications (with italic numbers indicating correctly predicted constructions)

predicted/observed	CTarget: prep. dative	CTarget: ditransitive	Totals
CTarget: prep. dative	*1,084*	117	1,201
CTarget: ditransitive	176	*1,500*	1,676
Totals	1,260	1,617	2,877

effects) all predictors that were not significant and did not participate in a higher-order significant interaction. In a second step, I tested whether each random effect could be removed with a significant loss of information, which was not the case.

The final, minimal adequate model shows that there is again a strong correlation between the fixed-effect predictors that survived the model selection process and the construction chosen in the target. This final model has a very high degree of classificatory/predictive power, as is indicated in its classification matrix in Table 4.

According to the chance expectation – always choosing the more frequent construction – one would again get $^{1,617}/_{2,877}$ = 56.2% correct classifications. The classification accuracy obtained in the random effects model, however, is extremely high, given that we are looking at noisy observational data in the behavioral sciences: $^{2,584}/_{2,877}$ = 89.82%. This classification accuracy is of course significantly better than the chance expectation – after all, the binary logistic regression was already better – but also highly significantly better than the traditional binary logistic regression (both $p_{binomial\ test} < 0.0001$) and remarkably close to the 92% and 94% accuracies that Bresnan et al. (2007) obtain on the basis of about three times as many predictors.

Again, what are the predictors that made it into the final model and how strongly do they affect the constructional choice? Figure 4 represents the relevant predictors and how they influence CTarget in a similar way as in Figure 2.

In some sense, the result is striking because the excellent classification accuracy is arrived at with only three fixed-effect predictors: CPrime, VFormID, and, crucially, their interaction plus the two random effects. In this model, prepositional datives in the primes already increase the chance of prepositional primes in the target (the main effect), but again the interaction CPrime:VFormID shows that this effect is particularly strong; the corresponding barplot looks very much like the left panel of Figure 3. None of the other predictors from the previous section reaches standard levels of significance (not even LogDistance, which is compatible with Bock et al. 2007: experiment 1). The question, thus, arises where the drastic 25% improvement of the classification accuracy comes from.

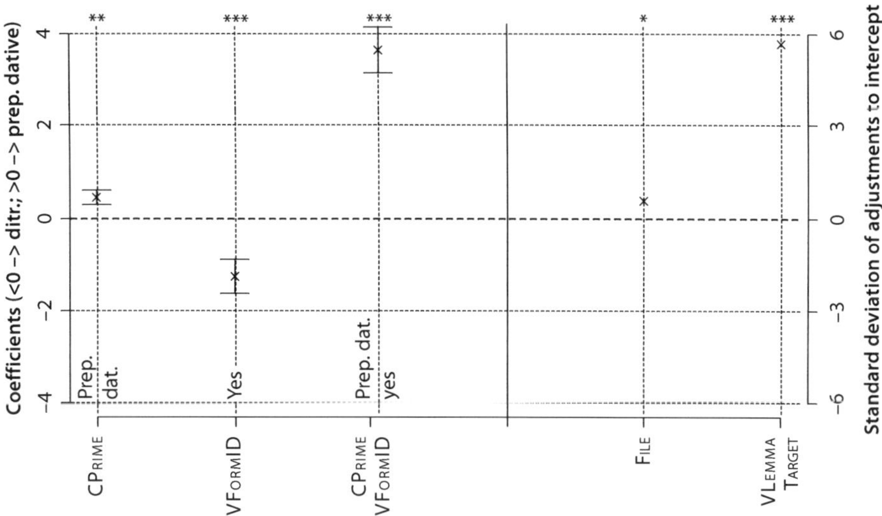

Figure 4. Fixed and random effects in the minimal adequate model of the GLMEM (left y-axis: fixed effects with standard errors; right y-axis: random effect standard deviations)

On the one hand, the improvement results from the fact that the coefficients of the regression are slightly different because the model fitting process took the different frequencies of verb lemmas and files into consideration and adjusted the coefficients accordingly. On the other hand and more importantly, the improvement results from the fact that every file and every verb lemma in the target now have their own regression intercept, which of course also affects – i.e. improves – the classifications. The most dramatic impact of these file/verb-specific intercepts is that they change the probability of the predicted construction – the prepositional dative – and when that predicted probability was below 0.5 in the binary logistic regression but increased to over 0.5 in the GLMEM, then the models make different classifications, and apparently the GLMEM is much more successful.

For example, there were 888 cases where the GLMEM made the right classification, but the binary logistic regression did not. Of these cases, 38 involved the verb lemma *send*, which was the lemma in a target construction 151 times. In other words, with the GLMEM, $^{38}/_{151} \approx 0.25 = 25\%$ of the verb lemma *send* are predicted better than with the logistic regression. Similar computations can be done for each verb, which can then be represented summarily as in Figure 5.

Overplotting of verbs notwithstanding, it becomes obvious immediately why a verb-specific account is so important: the verb lemmas differ drastically in terms of how much their classifications vary as a function of whether their idiosyncratic

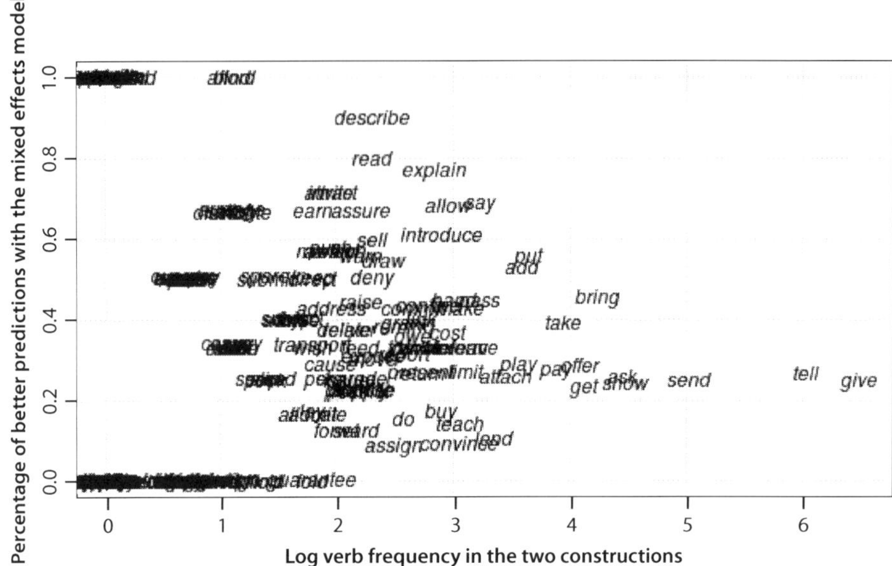

Figure 5. Percentage of improved classifications for each verb (on the y-axis) against each verb's logged frequency (on the x-axis)

preferences are included or not. Verbs such as *guarantee* do not benefit at all from a mixed-effects model approach; some of the higher-frequency verbs such as *give, tell, send, show, take*, and others benefit intermediately much, but some verbs cannot be handled by a regular logistic regression approach at all because (nearly) all their correct classifications only arise in the GLMEM model: *read, describe, afford, accord*, and others overplotted in the top left corner.

The same logic can of course be applied to the file-specific variation. I do not show the resulting plot here since the file names *per se* are not particularly revealing, but it is important to note in this connection how the inclusion of verb-/file-specific variation as random effects in a GLMEM goes beyond the kind of switch rate scatterplots proposed by Sankoff and Laberge (1978). Sankoff and Laberge plot the switch rates to a construction per file/speaker (on the *y*-axis) against the proportion of that same construction per file/speaker (on the *x*-axis), and when most dots are below the main diagonal, switches from one construction to the other (i.e. the absence of priming) are rarer across files/speakers than chance would predict (cf. Gries 2005: 395–6). While these plots are therefore a good visual diagnostic for problematic patterns in the data – e.g., files/speakers that exhibit priming effects or their absence that deviate from the norm considerably – the information they provide is not also used in the process of the statistical modeling. Put differently, if a particular file or speaker appears to be an outlier, then

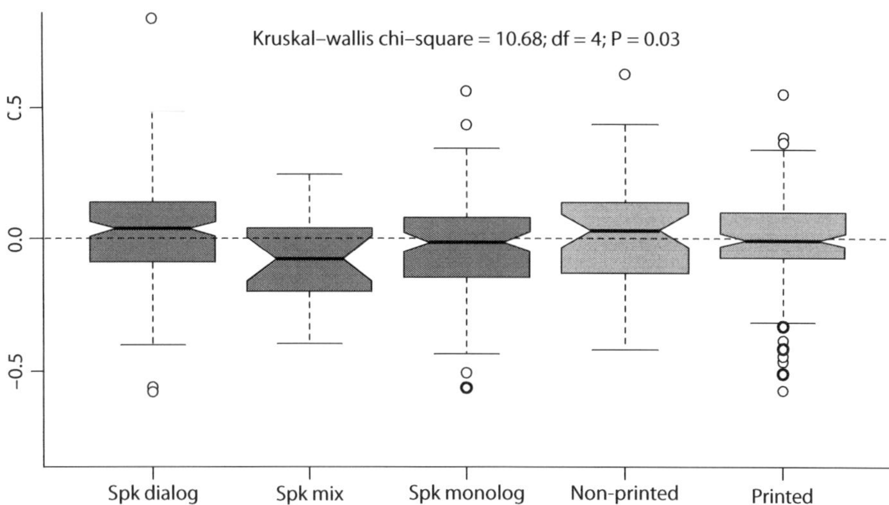

Figure 6. Percentage of improved classifications (on the y-axis) against each register (on the x-axis)

one can either exclude the file (to remove undesirable noise from the data) or one can include it nevertheless, but then the information about the (degree of) peculiarity of the data of this file/speaker is not used to make the subsequent modeling process any more precise. As mentioned above, the GLMEM approach, on the other hand, does exactly that and includes the information about particular files'/speakers' idiosyncrasies into the modeling process, which in turns makes the resulting coefficient estimates much more reliable and even allows for the interesting possibility of comparing groups of files (e.g., registers) or speakers (e.g., different sexes, different age groups, etc.). For instance, Figure 6 shows that the five registers of the ICE-GB differ significantly in terms of how much their files need to be adjusted to optimize the classification of the constructional choices: especially spoken dialog requires a lot of tweaking of the regression model whereas spoken monolog and written printed text does not.

4. Concluding remarks

So far, I have shown how – contrary to some opinions – the psycholinguistic phenomenon of syntactic priming can be studied fruitfully from a corpus-based perspective. In spite of the undisputed larger degree of noise that corpus data contain, the data provide converging evidence for several clear and significant trends attested in separate experimental studies: (i) the general strength of the repetition effect; (ii) the effect of VFormID that was found in both regression models; and (iii) the effect of VLemmaID that was found in the binary logistic regression and is compatible with the random effect of VLemmaTarget discussed in Section 3.3. In Gries (2005), I discussed how such findings can be straightforwardly related to, for example, Pickering and Branigan's account of priming based on combinatorial nodes, which is of course only one of several competing accounts. The more important point, however, is how the corpus-based data are best analyzed. Obviously, different statistical approaches are conceivable, ranging from the utterly simplistic cross-tabulation via binary logistic regression to generalized linear mixed-effects models. Just as obviously, however, the results are also quite varied.

Variationist tools like Varbrul notwithstanding, the binary logistic regression approach is probably the currently most widespread method for the kind of question studied here. However, while for the present data, the classification accuracy is significantly higher than the one obtained by chance, it is nevertheless not particularly high. More problematically, however, is the fact that the number of predictors reaching standard levels of significance – eight – is rather high and includes variables whose overall relevance to predicting one constructional choice priming is probably rather tenuous and whose effect is therefore weak (e.g., Medium, but cf. Szmrecsanyi (2006) for detailed discussion of register effects).

In some sense at least, the GLMEM approach behaves the opposite way: the number of predictors that turn out to be significant is very small – 3 – and the predictors are immediately and obviously key to priming, "obviously key" in the sense of having received support in many different studies and being integratable straightforwardly into a theoretical account based on psycholinguistic processing. At the same time, the classification accuracy is close to 90% and I have shown above, if only briefly, that this is due to the fact that the GLMEM approach includes a lot of item-specific information. This method should therefore be of interest to the population of empirical linguists – after all, it

- increases the classification accuracy;
- provides more precise coefficient estimates;
- in this case, does this with a smaller, and hence more parsimonious, set of predictors, which helps keep the analyst focus on what is really relevant once file/subject/item-specific variation is also accounted for.

It is this last part, however, that should also make this approach extremely interesting to cognitive linguists. These days, most cognitive linguists adopt a usage-based perspective in which item/exemplar-specific knowledge is essential to many aspects of language acquisition, processing, and change. With regard to language acquisition, studies by Tomasello, Lieven, Goldberg and others have illustrated that the acquisition of syntactic patterns is very much item-specific in the sense that, for instance, the acquisition of each argument structure construction is driven by one verb whose semantics match that of the construction and which, at an early stage, accounts for the vast majority of all instances of the construction (cf. Tomasello 2005 or Goldberg 2006: Ch. 4–5). With regard to processing, I have already mentioned a few examples above; recall how individual verbs' subcategorization preferences are correlated with the resolution of syntactic ambiguities and garden pathing, and Bybee and Scheibman (1999) have shown how phonological reduction processes (pointing to more automatic processing of elements having attained unit status) are correlated with individual verbs' frequency of occurrence in some syntactic pattern. With regard to language change, it is well known that, for example, grammaticalization processes are driven by the frequent co-occurrence of specific lexical items (cf. the evolution of *going to* V into a marker of futurity). In addition, we also know from, say, Dabrowska (submitted, and Dabrowska and Street 2006), that even native speakers exhibit large differences in linguistic competence. In other words, the random effects studied here target exactly and confirm the item/exemplar-specific and speaker-specific effects other work in cognitive/usage-based linguistics have uncovered.

In addition, priming studies that include more verb-specific effects than just the simple intercept adjustment I included in the GLMEM approach have even more to offer to cognitive/usage-based approaches. Snider (2008) studies prepositional dative/ditransitive as well as active/passive priming and finds that structural priming is sensitive to some of the same factors as lexical priming: high frequency structures prime less, and more similar prime and target structures prime more. Thus, these results not only support to some extent the position that syntax and lexis are not as different as many traditional (formal) approaches have assumed, but they also affect our choice of psycholinguistic models: Snider finds support for exemplar models that use clouds of exemplars represented in a feature space, but not for those that use construction-like representations. The importance of such findings for future work in cognitive linguistics can hardly be overestimated.

In sum, GLMEM approaches are not only statistically more successful, but provide also evidence converging with other contemporary cognitive-linguistic or exemplar-based approaches and are of vital importance in how they can fuel future theoretical developments. While I have so far mainly mentioned instances of converging evidence, it is worth recalling that GLMEM approaches can also offer interesting kinds of diverging evidence: since much of the item/speaker-specific variation is accounted for by the model's random effects, potentially relevant variables that are in fact more reducible to idiosyncratic variation will not be returned as significant; in other words, false positives are avoided and may speak against previous results from whatever type of (observational or experimental) approaches. Given all these advantages, I would therefore hope that this method becomes more and more widespread to improve the ways in which we as cognitive linguists look at our data.

References

Baayen, R. Harald. 2008. *Analyzing Linguistic Data: A Practical Introduction to Statistics Using R.* Cambridge: Cambridge University Press.

Bock, J. Kathryn. 1986. Syntactic persistence in language production. *Cognitive Psychology* 18: 355–387.

Bock, J. Kathryn. 1989. Closed-class immanence in sentence production. *Cognition* 31: 163–186.

Bock, J. Kathryn, Gary S. Dell, Franklin Chang, & Kristine H. Onishi. 2007. Persistent structural priming from language comprehension to language production. *Cognition* 104: 437–458.

Bock, J. Kathryn & Zenzi M. Griffin. 2000. The persistence of structural priming: transient activation or implicit learning. *Journal of Experimental Psychology: General* 129: 177–192.

Bock, J. Kathryn & Helga Loebell. 1990. Framing sentences. *Cognition* 35: 1–39.

Branigan, Holly P. Martin J. Pickering, & Alexandra A. Cleland. 1999. Syntactic priming in written production: evidence for rapid decay. *Psychonomic Bulletin and Review* 6: 635–640.

Branigan, Holly P., Martin J. Pickering, Simon P. Liversedge, Andrew J. Stewart, & Thomas P. Urbach. 1995. Syntactic priming: investigating the mental representation of language. *Journal of Psycholinguistic Research* 24: 489–506.

Branigan, Holly P., Martin J. Pickering, Andrew. J. Stewart, & Janet F. McLean. 2000. Syntactic priming in spoken production: linguistic and temporal interference. *Memory and Cognition* 28: 1297–1302.

Bresnan, Joan, Anna Cueni, Tatiana Nikitina, & R. Harald Baayen. 2007. Predicting the dative alternation. In G. Bouma, I. Krämer, and J. Zwarts, eds., *Cognitive Foundations of Interpretation*, 69–94. Amsterdam: Royal Netherlands Academy of Arts and Sciences.

Bybee, Joan & Joanne Scheibman. 1999. The effect of usage on degrees of constituency: The reduction of *don't* in English. *Linguistics* 37: 575–596.

Chang, Franklin, Gary S. Dell, J. Kathryn Bock, & Zenzi Griffin. 2000. Structural priming as implicit learning: a comparison of models of sentence production. *Journal of Psycholinguistic Research* 29: 217–229.

Connine, Cynthia, Fernanda Ferreira, Charlie Jones, Charles Clifton, & Lyn Frazier. 1984. Verb frame preferences: Descriptive norms. *Journal of Psycholinguistic Research* 13: 307–319.

Dabrowska, Ewa. submitted. Individual differences in native language attainment: A review article.

Dabrowska, Ewa & James Street. 2006. Individual differences in language attainment: Comprehension of passive sentences by native and non-native English speakers. *Language Sciences* 28: 604–615.

Estival, Dominique. 1985. Syntactic priming of the passive in English. *Text* 5: 7–22.

Garnsey, Susan M., Neal J. Pearlmutter, Elizabeth Myers, & Melanie A. Lotocky. 1997. The contributions of verb bias and plausibility to the comprehension of temporarily ambiguous sentences. *Journal of Memory and Language* 37: 58–93.

Gelman, Andrew & Jennifer Hill. 2007. *Data Analysis Using Regression and Multilevel/Hierarchical Models.* Cambridge & New York: Cambridge University Press.

Goldberg, Adele E. 2006. *Constructions at Work: The Nature of Generalization in Language.* Oxford: Oxford University Press.

Gries, Stefan Th. 2005. Syntactic priming: a corpus-based approach. *Journal of Psycholinguistic Research* 34: 365–399.

Gries, Stefan Th. under review. Frequencies, probabilities, association measures in usage-/exemplar-based linguistics: some necessary clarifications.

Gries, Stefan Th., Beate Hampe, & Doris Schönefeld. 2005. Converging evidence: bringing together experimental and corpus data on the association of verbs and constructions. *Cognitive Linguistics* 16: 635–676.

Gries, Stefan Th., Beate Hampe, & Doris Schönefeld. 2010. Converging evidence II: more on the association of verbs and constructions. In J. Newman & S. Rice eds., *Experimental and Empirical Methods in the Study of Conceptual Structure, Discourse, and Language*, 59–72. Stanford, CA: CSLI.

Gries, Stefan Th. & Anatol Stefanowitsch. 2004. Extending collostructional analysis: a corpus-based perspective on 'alternations'. *International Journal of Corpus Linguistics* 9: 97–129.

Gries, Stefan Th. & Stefanie Wulff. 2003. Do foreign language learners also have constructions? Evidence from priming, sorting, and corpora. *Annual Review of Cognitive Linguistics* 3: 182–200.

Gries, Stefan Th. & Stefanie Wulff. 2009. Psycholinguistic and corpus linguistic evidence for L2 constructions. *Annual Review of Cognitive Linguistics* 7: 164–187.

Hare, Mary L., Ken McRae, & Jeffrey L. Elman. 2003. Sense and structure: meaning as a determinant of verb subcategorization preferences. *Journal of Memory and Language* 48: 281–303.

Hartsuiker, Robert J., Martin J. Pickering, & Eline Veltkamp. 2004. Is syntax separate or shared between languages? Cross-linguistic syntactic priming in Spanish-English bilinguals. *Psychological Science* 15: 409–414.

Jaeger, T. Florian. 2008. Categorical data analysis: away from ANOVAs transformation or not and towards Logit Mixed Models. *Journal of Memory and Language* 59: 434–446.

Jaeger, T. Florian & Neal Snider. 2007. Implicit learning and syntactic persistence: surprisal and cumulativity. In L. Wolter & J. Thorson, eds., *University of Rochester working papers in the language sciences* 3: 26–44.

Johnson, Keith. 2008. *Quantitative Methods in Linguistics*. Malden, MA: Blackwell.

Levelt, Willem J. M. & Stephanie Kelter. 1982. Surface form and memory in question answering. *Cognitive Psychology* 14: 78–106.

Loebell, Helga & J. Kathryn Bock. 2003. Structural priming across languages. *Linguistics* 41: 791–824.

Luke, Douglas A. 2004. *Multilevel Modeling*. Thousand Oaks, CA and London: Sage Publications.

Pickering, Martin J. & Branigan, Holly P. 1998. The representation of verbs: evidence from syntactic priming in language production. *Journal of Memory and Language* 39: 633–651.

Pickering, Martin J. & Holly P. Branigan. 1999. Syntactic priming in language production. *Trends in Cognitive Sciences* 3: 136–141.

Pickering, Martin J., Holly P. Branigan, Alexandra A. Cleland, & Andrew J. Stewart. 2000. Activation of syntactic information during language production. *Journal of Psycholinguistic Research* 29: 205–216.

Potter, Mary C. & Linda Lombardi. 1998. Syntactic priming in immediate recall of sentences. *Journal of Memory and Language* 38: 265–282.

R Development Core Team. 2009. R: A Language and Environment for Statistical Computing. Vienna: R Foundation for Statistical Computing. <http://www.R-project.org>.

Sankoff, David & Suzanne Laberge. 1978. Statistical dependence among successive occurrences of a variable in discourse. In D. Sankoff & S. Laberge, eds., *Linguistic Variation: Methods and Models,* 119–126. New York: Academic Press.

Schoonbaert, Sofie, Robert J. Hartsuiker, & Martin J. Pickering. 2007. The representation of lexical and syntactic information in bilinguals: evidence from syntactic priming. *Journal of Memory and Language* 56: 153–171.

Shin, Jeong-Ah & Kiel Christianson. 2009. Syntactic processing in Korean-English bilingual production: evidence from cross-linguistic structural priming. *Cognition* 112: 175–180.

Snider, Neal. 2008 An exemplar model of syntactic priming. Unpublished Ph.D. Dissertation, Stanford University.

Stallings, Lynne M., Maryellen C. MacDonald, & Padraig G. O'Seaghdha. 1998. Phrasal ordering constraints in sentence production: Phrase length and verb disposition in Heavy-NP Shift. *Journal of Memory and Language* 39: 392–417.

Szmrecsanyi, Benedikt. 2005. Language users as creatures of habit: a corpus-based analysis of persistence in spoken English. *Corpus Linguistics and Linguistic Theory* 1: 113–150.

Szmrecsanyi, Benedikt. 2006. *Morphosyntactic Persistence in Spoken English: A Corpus Study at the Intersection of Variationist Sociolinguistics, Psycholinguistics, and Discourse Analysis.* Berlin & New York: Mouton de Gruyter.

Tomasello, Michael. 2005. *Constructing a Language: A Usage-based Theory of Language Acquisition.* Cambridge, MA: Harvard University Press.

Islands of (im)productivity in corpus data and acceptability judgments

Contrasting two potentiality constructions in Dutch*

Ad Backus and Maria Mos
Tilburg University

Dutch has a number of constructions for expressing that a particular event is likely or possible. Two of these, one using a derivational morpheme and the other a copula construction, are investigated to see whether they are both productive and to what degree their meanings overlap. Their distribution in a corpus showed some similarities and differences. In a follow-up magnitude estimation experiment, results showed that the judgments by native speakers of Dutch reflected these same similarities and differences. The consistent distinction in acceptability indicates that the corpus findings correspond to mental representations. We interpret this as converging evidence for the productivity and psychological reality of the constructions, and argue that corpus and experimental methods are complementary tools.

Keywords: constructional meaning, corpus evidence, magnitude estimation experiment, psychological reality

1. Introduction

This chapter investigates the central linguistic phenomenon of productivity. It does so against the background of the idea that one of the essential characteristics of language is that it is both conventional and creative: as speakers we constantly recruit chunks we have stored in memory, but we use them in novel ways and combine them in ever-changing variations in order to deal with the conceptual and communicative demands of everyday life. Seen that way, every utterance is the

* We wish to thank the two anonymous reviewers for their extensive and stimulating feedback on an earlier version of this chapter.

sum result of two complementary factors: conservatism and creativity. To what degree they balance each other out is unknown; this chapter aims to get us a bit closer to answering that question. Inspiration comes from a notion central to many of the theoretical proposals made in the usage-based tradition: that much more is stored in linguistic memory than just a list of words, including longer multiword chunks and syntactic patterns.

We investigate this issue through a contrastive analysis of two constructions in Dutch that can be considered roughly synonymous. Both convey potentiality, in the sense that they provide a comment on whether a certain action can be carried out or not. Languages seem to have a need for expressing this notion, but they vary as to the form constructions take to express it, ranging from morphological inflection of the verb (e.g. in Turkish) to syntactic constructions with modal auxiliaries ('can'). Two of the constructions Dutch makes use of, one morphological and one syntactic in nature, seem very close in meaning, and this has prompted our theoretical interest in them. Why would a language have two constructions for expressing virtually the same thing?

The first construction makes use of the derivational morpheme *-baar*, equivalent to English *-able*. It is added to verb stems to form adjectives that describe the property of some entity to undergo the action named by the verb (this definition is made much more explicit in Section 2.1.3), to yield words such as *eetbaar* (eat + *baar* = 'edible'), *onhoorbaar* (negative prefix 'un-' + hear + *baar* = 'inaudible') and *strafbaar* (punish + *baar* = 'punishable'). As adjectives, these words can be used attributively and predicatively; for reasons to be made clear below, we focus on their predicative use.

The other construction is a combination of a finite copula and an infinitive, and has the following template: [Subject $\text{Copula}_{\text{finite}}$ *te* ('to') Infinitive], to be referred to as the *is te* V construction. It does not have a direct equivalent in English, though it resembles idiosyncratic idioms such as *good examples are hard to find*. In Dutch, this pattern is productive and encountered frequently. The above English example is rendered as *goede voorbeelden zijn moeilijk te vinden*, an exact word-for-word match. More examples are provided later; for now, it is sufficient to note that the two constructions have very similar meanings.

Before going into any further details, let us suggest two possible answers to the question why two semantically similar constructions would exist in one language. First, there might still be some *semantic difference*: the constructions do not actually mean exactly the same thing. In that case, we should find differences in the constructional meanings, perhaps in the denotational meanings, perhaps in their stylistic values. Second, this may be a case of *competition*: the two constructions are rivals of each other and the language is changing its preference from one to the other. In that case, we expect to find differences in productivity.

We report on a corpus analysis of both constructions, and on the results of an experiment. Using evidence from these two sources, we argue, provides us with a sounder basis upon which to investigate productivity than if we used only one of them. If findings point in the same direction, they provide *converging* evidence for complementary aspects of linguistic knowledge, namely usage patterns and the cognitive representations they instantiate (cf. Gilquin and Gries 2009: 9, and the chapters by Gries, Brandt, and Kidd, Steinkraus, and Schönefeld in this volume).

In this chapter we test two hypotheses. First, based on our expectation that few verbs are excluded from occurring in the constructions, and that asserting potentiality is fairly often useful in conversation, we hypothesize both of them to be productive. Second, assuming that languages tend to avoid real synonyms (cf. Goldberg 1995: 67), we expect the two constructions to encode slightly different meanings. In order for the second hypothesis to make sense at all, the first hypothesis needs to be confirmed: if a construction is not productive, there is probably also no cognitively real (partially) schematic representation in the mind of the speaker, and thus no constructional meaning either.[1] In order to test these hypotheses, we ask the following questions for each of the two constructions:

- Is there *corpus evidence* for high type frequency (since high type frequency allows schematization, and therefore induces a schematic constructional representation rather than just a list of fully specific conventionalized chunks)?
- Based on usage data, what constructional meaning can be formulated for each construction, and are these meanings different?
- Can knowledge of this putative constructional meaning be shown through *experimental evidence* (since usage data cannot tell us whether a sequence is produced using a conventionalized chunk or by combining a schematic representation and a slot filler)?

The link between productivity and these research questions is that a construction perceived to exist by the analyst can only be shown to really exist in the minds of speakers if they demonstrably use the construction to construct novel combinations. If that cannot be shown, there is no proof for productivity as a cognitively real phenomenon for speakers of a language.

Productivity is of central concern to linguistics, we argue (based on, among others, Boas 2008: 130, Barðdal 2008, Wray 2008). It is clear that speakers do not communicate by repeating the same utterances all the time, so language is certainly

1. As was pointed out to us during the review process, it is, of course, possible for a speaker to analyze a stored exemplar of a complex construction, and recognize the contributions the various parts make to the composite meaning. Our expectation here is about productive use: the ability of some of us to identify the *n-* in *never* and *nothing* as contributing negation does not mean that we can use it as a productive prefix.

not organized in such a way that we store a huge number of utterances and then select the 'right' utterance for the present occasion. It is equally obvious that we use a great many stored chunks of language, not just single words but many multiword units and partially filled constructions. These are the two options speakers have in language production: ready-made chunks and novel creations, and both are used in virtually every utterance. How much is novel and how much stored, however, is as yet a largely unanswered question; a question that needs answering if we are to build a cognitively realistic model of linguistic competence, in particular of the abstract mental representations speakers may be realistically predicted to 'have'.

In derivational morphology, productivity is the term used to denote the degree to which a particular morpheme is used to form new words. Theoretical approaches such as Construction Grammar (e.g. Goldberg 2006, Boas 2003) remove any reason to limit this term to such a narrow domain. After all, grammatical constructions also differ from each other in the degree to which they are put to use by speakers in order to build new utterances, some being very 'productive', such as the Transitive Clause construction (e.g. *I read Dostoyevski over Christmas*); others being much more limited in use, e.g. the oft-discussed Time Away construction (e.g. *I idled my Christmas break away*, cf. Jackendoff 1997). Essentially the productivity of any construction, whether morphological or syntactic in nature, is its propensity to be used to form novel expressions. Here, we define a novel form as an instantiation of a construction formed by combining the schematic representation for the construction with one or more lexical items that fill the open slot(s). While direct evidence for whether an utterance is a novel creation or the production of a memorized form is not easy to obtain, a combination of corpus data regarding a construction's type frequency and experimental data regarding the acceptability of novel uses can yield useful and complementary information in this respect. In this chapter, we use *both* kinds of data.

The next section provides corpus data for the two constructions under analysis, first focusing on each construction individually and then contrasting them. Section 3 discusses a magnitude estimation experiment. The degree to which the two approaches provide converging evidence is discussed in Section 4.

2. Corpus evidence

This section provides the results of searches for instantiations of the two constructions in the Corpus of Spoken Dutch (Corpus Gesproken Nederlands; henceforth: CGN). For both constructions we first describe the search results, then report on a *collostructional analysis* (cf. Stefanowitsch and Gries 2003), carried out in order to find out which verbs are typically attracted to the respective constructions, and finally characterize the constructional semantics. The final subsection contrasts the two constructions, making use of a *distinctive collexeme analysis* (cf. Gries and Stefanowitsch 2004), in order to answer the question whether they are really synonyms or not.

CGN is a 10 million-word corpus consisting of spoken data from different genres, ranging from face-to-face conversations to official speeches. Around two thirds of the corpus are from speakers in the Netherlands; the other third is from the Dutch-speaking part of Belgium. All tokens are tagged in a number of ways, including the lemma and the word class they belong to.

2.1 A morphological potentiality construction: V-*baar*

2.1.1 *Main search results*

As the *is te* V construction occurs nearly always predicatively and we are interested in a direct comparison between the two constructions, we excluded from the analysis of V-*baar* those uses where the adjective was used attributively or adverbially.[2]

The search for all predicative tokens of -*baar* with a recognizable verbal stem resulted in 1282 tokens, of 171 different types. For this and all further analyses, forms of V-*baar* and *on*-V-*baar* with the same verbal stem (as in *betaalbaar* and *onbetaalbaar*, 'affordable' and 'unaffordable') were counted as belonging to the same type, leading to 171 different types. The ten most frequently occurring predicative forms are listed in Table 1. As is often the case with type-token distributions in language (cf. Zipf 1935), the ten most frequent types account for close to half of all the tokens (501/1282).

Table 1. Most frequent -*baar* types with verbal stem used predicatively

Type	Nr. of occurrences	Meaning
beschikbaar	141	available, reachable
(on)haalbaar	72	(un)feasible
(on)bereikbaar	68	(un)reachable
(on)voorstelbaar	52	(un)imaginable
(on)verstaanbaar	41	(un)intelligible
vergelijkbaar	38	comparable
(on)bruikbaar	37	(un)usable
(on)bespreekbaar	36	(not) discussable
(on)herkenbaar	34	(un)recognizable
kenbaar	28	knowable

2. An anonymous reviewer wondered about the frequency of the *is te* V construction in attributive position, as in *een te vermijden vergissing* 'a to avoid mistake', i.e. 'an avoidable mistake'. A search in the CGN turned up only 28 instances of this usage, so we feel justified in claiming that the construction is mostly used in predicative form.

From the translations it is clear that we are dealing with a homogeneous category in terms of the meanings of the instantiations: they all express potentiality. However, since frequent forms are stored as units, this does not necessarily mean that they contribute to the productivity of the construction, as speakers may just have these forms stored in their lexicon without linking them to each other (cf. Bybee 1995). In other words, that complex words have transparent meaning and structure does not mean that they are formed with a productive template. Another sign of productivity is the occurrence of many forms with low token frequency. In addition to the frequently used verbs listed in Table 1, there are many instantiations with low token frequencies in the corpus, including many hapaxes. This suggests that the pattern must have been productive at least at some time, but let us note straight away that only few of the low-frequency occurrences actually come across as 'unfamiliar'. We return to this issue at various points throughout the text.

2.1.2 *Collostructional analysis of V-*baar

In essence, our focus is on the fillers of the partially schematic construction (Subject V_{copula} V-*baar*), in particular on the slot for the verbal stem that precedes -*baar*. Raw type and token frequencies are not optimally informative in this case: the fact that a certain -*baar* form occurs predicatively five times in the corpus, as is the case for *betwistbaar* 'questionable', *brandbaar* 'inflammable' and *eetbaar* 'edible', may or may not be significant given the overall frequency of *betwisten, branden* and *eten*. One way to resolve this issue is to do a collostructional analysis.

This procedure was proposed by Stefanowitsch and Gries (2003) and measures whether a given lexical item, in this case a verb, is significantly attracted to (or repelled from) a certain construction, here, the V-*baar* construction, taking into account the frequencies of the lexical item elsewhere in the corpus and the total frequency of the construction. In other words, the list of collexemes provides an answer to the question which words are typically used with a particular construction, given their overall frequencies in the corpus. This method provides a useful tool for the description of partially schematic constructions. Knowing which verbs are attracted to the construction helps in establishing the characteristics of the open slot in the construction and the meaning of the construction in general. The analysis, however, does not tell us whether the construction is productive, though it does provide input for the formulation of hypotheses about which types of verbs can easily combine with the construction to form acceptable utterances. These can subsequently be tested experimentally.

Stefanowitsch and Gries chose the Fisher-exact test for their analyses, because this test does not make any distributional assumptions or require a particular sample size (Stefanowitsch and Gries 2003: 218). This is important, because often, as in this case, there is no normal distribution, and many types occur only a few times in the corpus. We used R and the script made available by Gries (2007) to compute the test.

For each verb, the required frequency counts were taken from the corpus, by searching for all occurrences of the lemma. The total number of predicates in the corpus (1076041) was chosen as the background number. Table 2 lists the 20 verbs (collexemes) most strongly attracted to the V-*baar* construction.

A comparison of Tables 1 and 2 reveals that most of the *frequent -baar* forms contain verbs that are *significantly attracted* to the construction as well, but the lists are certainly not identical: the infrequent verb *feilen* 'err' is one of the two most

Table 2. Collexemes of V-*baar*; values given for collostructional strength correspond to -log (p-valueFisher-Exact, 10)

	Translation		Collostructional strength
Collexeme (N)	**Verb**	***-baar* form**	
beschikken (141)	have at disposal	available	Infinite
feilen (2)	err	fallible	Infinite
bereiken (68)	achieve, reach	reachable	105.018
aanvaarden (38)	accept	acceptable	70.895
vertrouwen(37)*	trust	reliable	70.005
kwetsen (28)	hurt	vulnerable	69.965
verstaan (41)	hear, understand	audible	60.059
halen (72)	get	feasible	58.512
voorstellen (52)	suggest	imaginable	54.418
vergelijken (38)	compare	comparable	53.409
bespreken (36)	discuss	discussable	51.325
vatten (25)	get, catch	susceptible	49.135
herkennen (34)	recognize	recognizable	47.937
straffen (22)	punish	punishable	45.001
voorspellen (24)	predict	predictable	42.445
betalen (41)	pay	affordable	32.207
gebruiken (37)*	use	usable, useful	27.380
verkrijgen (12)	get, receive	available	22.986
afwenden (8)	avert	avoidable	18.306
besturen (9)	drive, operate	can be operated	16.782

*We analyzed *betrouwbaar* as containing the stem *vertrouwen* and *bruikbaar* as derived from *gebruiken*. The verbs *betrouwen* and *bruiken* do not exist, and the meanings of the *-baar* words link up reliably with these two verbs.

strongly attracted collexemes for this construction, even though *feilbaar* 'fallible' occurs only twice[3]. This is because there is only a single token of the verb outside the construction in the corpus. The example of *feilen* illustrates the added value of collostructional strength over raw frequency data. However, the advantage most important to us is that it allows a characterization of the degree to which various semantic subclasses are used in the construction.

2.1.3 *Meaning description*

Our analysis of the corpus data leads us to posit the following meaning:

> V-*baar* construction
> The most Patient-like argument of the verb has the property of being able to undergo the event described in the verb.

We discuss each aspect of this definition. Firstly, the V-*baar* instances describe a **property**; this meaning aspect is prototypically expressed in Dutch with an adjective. In its predicative use, the V-*baar* construction occurs mainly as Subject BE V-*baar*, and often the property ascribed to the subject is construed as objectively true, as in (1), where intelligibility is construed as an easily verifiable property of the dialect. Although it is not easy to put a finger on it, in quite a few instances, the construction seems to express that a Patient may easily – without any Agent's intention – be affected rather than that it is *possible* to affect the Patient (see Example (2)).

(1) *Maar jouw dialect moet wel verstaanbaar zijn voor anderen* (fn008312.245)
but your dialect must still intelligible be for others
'but other people still need to be able to understand your dialect'

(2) *Stress is een groot woord misschien maar ja iedereen is toch wel heel erg prikkelbaar denk ik.* (fn007487.73)
stress is a big word maybe but yes everyone is anyhow yet very badly irritable think I
'Stress is a big word maybe but yeah, everyone is extremely irritable, I think'

3. One anonymous reviewer correctly pointed out that *-baar* tokens are not included in the token counts for each verb, while for *is te* V (see Section 2.2.2) they are. While we agree that this causes a certain degree of imbalance, we see no better alternative: if *-baar* tokens were to be included in the count, other derivations should be too. It is far from clear, however, to what extent morphologically derived forms are really derived in speakers' constructicons, especially in the case of semantically and/or orthographically opaque derivations, diachronically motivated but synchronically uninterpretable forms, etc. In this particular case, the ranking would largely remain the same if *-baar* tokens were included in the verb token count. The verb *feilen* 'err', for instance, only occurs once outside the *-baar* construction.

The property is ascribed to an entity, which in the semantic frame of the verb fills **the most Patient-like role.** Very often, this corresponds with the direct object of the verb when it is used in an active sentence. It would not be accurate, however, to state that the property is always ascribed to the direct object, as Example (3) shows, in which the entity in question is a complement normally left implicit or marked obliquely. Still, though the topic of gossip is usually not expressed as an argument of the verb, it has to be retrievable in a discourse situation for the verb to make sense, unless there is a generic interpretation.

(3) *Dat circuit van Zon en Schild is natuurlijk ook uh zwaar roddelbaar.* (fn000979.299)
that circuit of Son and Shield is of-course also uh heavily gossipable
"'Son and Shield' as a workplace of course lends itself well to gossip'

While there are many types with low frequency, in going through our corpus results, we also found that many instances of the V-*baar* construction 'felt' familiar. In some cases, this can be substantiated with commonly accepted signs of storage, such as deviation in form and especially semantic specialization. For some words, a compositional analysis would not give the correct meaning. For example, *betaalbaar* (literally 'pay-able', 'affordable') does not just mean that something can be paid, but that it is reasonably cheap. This additional information may not be very surprising, as potentiality or the lack thereof is usually expressed when it is unexpected: in the case of 'payable' we may expect that services and goods can be paid for. However, it does mean that this form must be stored as a separate lexical item by speakers of Dutch.

This type-specific behavior (cf. Boas 2003) points at the storage of a large number of instances of the construction. This means that the corpus data, invaluable as they are for arriving at a refined notion of the meaning of the construction, are insufficient for determining whether the construction is productive or not, that is whether it indeed exists as an abstract representation in the minds of speakers. In Section 3, we discuss an experiment testing the psycholinguistic reality of the partially specific construction, but first we discuss the corpus results for the rival construction *is te* V.

2.2 A syntactic potentiality construction: *is te* V

This construction, also sometimes called the Modal Infinitive Potentiality Construction (Boogaart 2006) appears in many different forms, but it always contains a sequence of a subject noun phrase (often the simple inanimate pronoun 'it'), an inflected copula (usually 3rd person singular present tense *is*), the infinitival particle *te* ('to'), and a main verb infinitive. We posit the following meaning:

> *is te* V construction
> The action named by the verb can potentially be carried out on, with, or to the Patient-like argument named by the subject.

It has, therefore, both modal and passive ('can be done') semantics, while syntactically it is a copula construction. The subject noun phrase denotes what is semantically the patient of the main verb, explaining the passive meaning, cf. Example (4).

(4) *De expositie is nog te bezichtigen tot zeven mei* (fv600185.6)
the exposition is still to see until seven May
'The exposition runs until the 7th of May'

As we did for V-*baar*, we conducted a corpus analysis, in order to see what the range of verbs was that occurred in this construction, and to ascertain whether the construction really does mean the same thing as V-*baar* (see Diepeveen et al. (2006: 52–55) and Boogaart (2006) for earlier corpus analyses of this construction).

Ideally, the dataset should be the result of a search for all forms in the Corpus of Spoken Dutch (CGN) that make use of the template [Copula + *te* + Infinitive]. However, identifying all instances of the *is te* V construction in a corpus is not as simple as it is for V-*baar*. First of all, apart from *te*, none of the word forms in the construction is constant, so that searches cannot make use of a simple lexical query. Use can be made of Part-of-Speech tags, but this creates additional problems. As is typical for syntactic constructions, certainly ones that use common words like copular *is* and the infinitival particle *te*, there are many word sequences that look superficially like the *is te* V construction, but are really instantiations of other constructions. While a search for words with the *-baar* suffix yields very few false hits, there are many in the raw data one obtains after a search for all *is te* V sequences.

We searched the CGN for all occurrences of the sequence [*is* + *te* + Infinitive], with zero, one or two words intervening between *is* and *te* (searches with more than two words intervening yielded an unwieldy number of false hits) and other possible forms (past tense, non–3rd person singular, and subordinate clauses, in which Dutch has a word order that differs from main clauses), and manually weeded out the false hits. While certainly not all instances of the construction will have been found this way, we have good reason to think we did capture most of them.

2.2.1 *Main search results*

The corpus search in the CGN turned up 209 different verbs in the infinitive slot, producing a total of 1108 instances, figures that are not too different from those found for the predicative construction with V-*baar* (171 different verbs and 1282 tokens).

Table 3. Ten most frequent verbs in *is te* V construction found in CGN

Type	Frequency	Most common attested form	Meaning
doen 'do'	220	is niet te doen	is hard to do
zien 'see'	162	is te zien	can be seen (in)
hopen ' hope'	79	is te hopen	hopefully
zeggen 'say'	67	is te zeggen	that is, ...
vinden 'find'	44	is niet te vinden	cannot be found
geloven 'believe'	26	is niet te geloven	unbelievable
vergelijken 'compare'	25	is niet te vergelijken met	cannot be compared to
krijgen 'get'	20	is niet meer te krijgen	cannot be found anymore
merken 'notice'	17	is weinig van te merken	is hard to notice
spreken 'speak'	15	is niet te spreken	does not like it*

*Literally, this combination means 'cannot be spoken to'. Presumably through inferences such as 'he is so mad about this that you cannot speak to him about it', the collocation has become an idiom with the figurative meaning given in Table 3.

Table 3 lists the verbs most frequently found in the infinitive position of the construction in the CGN. In general, the distribution shows some similarities to the one observed for V-*baar*. First, there are a few clearly favored lexemes. Again, the ten most frequent verbs account for more than half of all tokens. As for V-*baar*, there is a clear frontrunner (*doen* 'do'), a clear number two (*zien* 'see'), and a small set of other verbs that occur frequently in the construction. Second, some semantic specialization is evident for the most frequent members, as the last column in Table 3 illustrates. The concept lexicalized by 'hopefully' is a few steps removed from 'can be hoped for', and the pragmatic force of 'unbelievable' is much stronger than a compositional 'cannot be believed' would convey. Third, many of the types tend to co-occur with the negation *niet*. Recall that words with -*baar* often also contain the negation prefix *on*-. Some verbs form collocations with other adverbial modifiers, as illustrated in the third column of Table 3. Finally, many verbs are used only once or twice in the construction in the corpus, suggesting the template is used productively.

The most commonly found verb, *doen* 'do', is, of course, also a very frequent verb overall. Presumably, the verbs that tell us most about the construction are those verbs that are most attracted to this construction. In order to find out for which verbs this holds, we performed a collostructional analysis.

2.2.2 *Collostructional analysis of* is te V

The collostructional analysis was carried out in exactly the same way as the one for V-*baar*, described in Section 2.1.2. Table 4 lists the 20 most strongly attracted verbs to the *is te* V construction.

Table 4. Collexemes of *is te* V; values given for collostructional strength correspond to -log (p-valueFisher-Exact, 10)

Collexeme (N)	Translation: Verb	Translation: in construction	Collostructional strength
stukkrijgen (1)	demolish	indestructible	Infinite
toerekenen (1)	ascribe	can be ascribed to	Infinite
hopen (79)	hope	hopefully	100.463
zien (162)	see	can be seen, found, visited, etc.	84.739
doen (192)	do	can be done	74.859
vergelijken (25)	compare	should be compared with	32.367
wijten (11)	blame	should be blamed on	21.822
achterhalen (9)	get a hold of	can be retrieved from	15.083
geloven (26)	believe	unbelievable	13.869
verklaren (11)	explain	can be explained	13.401
merken (17)	notice	be obvious	12.595
terugvinden (8)	retrieve	can be retrieved in	12.435
combineren (8)	combine	can be combined with	10.261
verstaan (10)	understand	be loud/clear enough	9.714
verwachten (13)	expect	is to be expected	8.992
herkennen (9)	recognize	can be recognized by	8.620
bereiken (8)	reach	can be reached	6.118
bekennen (4)	see	(nowhere) to be found	5.674
aanbevelen (3)	recommend	is to be recommended	5.364
aanmerken (2)	complain	can(not) be complained about	5.197

Recall that for V-*baar* we found that the list of most frequently occurring verbs in the construction and the list of verbs most attracted to it as revealed by collostructional analysis partially overlapped, but also showed some interesting differences. The same is true for *is te* V. Of the ten verbs most frequently found with *is te* V, four do not appear among the top twenty verbs attracted to the construction: *zeggen* 'say', *vinden* 'find', *spreken* 'talk to' and *krijgen* 'get'. Note that all of these are verbs with very basic meanings, which ensures a very high token frequency in any corpus. For high-frequency verbs, it is difficult to be highly attracted to *any* construction, simply because they occur frequently in many different constructions (cf. Gries, Hampe, and Schönefeld 2005: 650). Be that as it may, the list of verbs most attracted to the construction reveals some interesting characteristics.

First, native speakers of Dutch will recognize the familiar chunks that underlie the high position of some of these verbs, e.g. *is bijna niet stuk te krijgen*, literally 'almost cannot be broken', i.e. 'is still going strong'; *is te wijten aan X* 'X is to be blamed for'; or *is moeilijk te achterhalen*, literally 'is difficult to overtake', i.e. 'cannot be verified easily' (said in a figurative sense about a particular piece of information). In general, many combinations containing a particular verb and a particular degree adverb are lexicalized, in the sense that they recur in the corpus and may thus be considered conventional chunks.

However, what the verb ranking allows us to do most of all is get a good grasp of the constructional meaning (cf. Gries et al. 2005: 650–654). In order to do that, we examine the ranking and try to understand why these verbs are so attracted to the potentiality construction. What is it about *stukkrijgen* 'demolish', *toerekenen* 'ascribe', *vergelijken* 'compare', etc. that makes expression of their potentiality (or lack of it) so nameworthy?

2.2.3 *Constructional meaning*

The list of twenty most attracted verbs does not clearly form a natural category, which we take to reflect the wide semantic scope of potentiality constructions. However, some generalizations can be made on the basis of the list.

Perhaps the most striking feature of the construction is that it often encodes the speaker's **assessment** of potentiality. It is not potentiality as such that is conveyed, but whether the speaker thinks a certain event *is likely to* or *should* happen, cf. the examples below and their discussion. In the list of twenty, this holds for *stukkrijgen* 'demolish', *doen* 'do', *vergelijken* 'compare', *wijten* 'blame', *geloven* 'believe', *merken* 'notice', *combineren* 'combine', *verwachten* 'expect', *bekennen* 'see', *aanbevelen* 'recommend', and *aanmerken* 'complain'. That is not to say that every instantiation of these verbs in this construction has this semantic nuance, but often it is the case, as becomes clear once one starts investigating the actual instantiations in the corpus. While it is trivially true that most verbs refer to an event that can happen, and the assertion of this possibility is always a possible 'elaboration site' (in the sense of Langacker 2008: 198), the *is te* V construction makes this normally unimportant aspect salient. Given the vagueness of potentiality, saying that something could possibly happen implies making the assessment that it is worthwhile to even mention it. In other words, the existence of the construction reflects the fact that it makes sense to make a comment about something potentially happening if it is not obvious that it will. Presumably this is also the reason why the construction is often used in its negative form: saying that something is not possible will often be more noteworthy than just saying that it is. The construction, therefore, is often used as a stance marker: the speaker thinks that an activity is likely or unlikely to be carried out. In (5), the speaker does not just state that comparing Holland and Germany is something that cannot be done: the message is that as far as the speaker is concerned, they are incomparable. From there, it is a small step to necessity rather than mere potentiality, as in (6): it is not just that the event in (6), the act of blaming the illegal repairs, *can* take place: it *should* take place, and asserting this is the reason for constructing the utterance in the first place. The pragmatic impact of (6) is not that the illegal repairs were a possible cause of the fire, but that they most probably were (see also Boogaart 2006: 43)[4].

(5) *Maar Duitsland is niet te vergelijken met Nederland hoor, absoluut niet.* (fn007569.162) but Germany is not to compare with Holland really absolutely not
'But you cannot compare Germany with Holland, you know, absolutely not'

(6) *De brand in de skitreintunnel in Kaprun is vermoedelijk te wijten aan illegale reparaties.* (fn002178.1)
the fire in de ski.train.tunnel in Kaprun is probably to blame to illegal repairs
'The fire in the ski train tunnel at Kaprun should probably be blamed on illegal repairs'

It is, therefore, a personal judgment of the degree of potentiality rather than the assertion of absolute potentiality that is conveyed by the construction. This is often reinforced by adverbs of degree, which tend to form an essential part of the conventional chunk that frequent recurrence of the instantiation has forged[5]. Many examples seem to be motivated by a desire on the part of speakers to counter any expectations their interlocutors may have: the point is not to say that something is possible, but that it is more (or less) possible than the hearer might think:

(7) *Dat is niet te geloven* (fn000820.311)
that is not to believe
'That's hard to believe'

(8) *Ja 't is moeilijk te controleren natuurlijk hè* (fn000121.68)
yes it is difficult to check of.course isn't.it
'Yes, that's of course hard to check, isn't it'

A second feature, often overlapping with the previous one, is that the event denoted by the verb is carried out mentally rather than physically. Combined with

4. One anonymous reviewer points out that similar constructions exist in the Scandinavian languages, with similar semantic characteristics. The Scandinavian usage seems to involve a 'necessity' reading more than a 'potentiality' one, possibly suggesting a more advanced stage of grammaticalization in these languages.

5. Note that *moeilijk* 'difficult' in (8) as well as *vermoedelijk* 'probably' in (6), are such degree indicators, while *niet* 'not', the most frequently found adverb in the construction, encodes the limiting case of degree.

the stance character of the construction, and its tendency to be used to mark necessity rather than potentiality, it puts many examples in the domain of human interaction, particularly interaction involving persuasion. Among the 20 most attracted verbs, many name a type of mental activity, e.g. *toerekenen* 'ascribe', *hopen* 'hope', and *aanbevelen* 'recommend'. Again, it is certainly not the case that all these verbs are always used for mental activities, but most of the time they are. For instance, 'expect' and 'wish' in (9) reflect mental activity.

(9) *Dat bij deze koerswijziging zijn humor hem verlaten zal is noch te verwachten noch te wensen.* (fn001288.71)
that with this change.of.course his humor him leave shall is not to expect not to wish
'That with this change of course his sense of humor will leave him should neither be expected nor wished for'

Finally, it should be noted that virtually all verbs found in the construction are transitive, and those that are not make salient reference to some Patient-like element, such as a person spoken about (not marked as the direct object of the verb *spreken* 'speak' in an active sentence, but contained in a prepositional phrase with *over* 'about'). This suggests that the construction tends to be used to comment not so much on the potentiality of the event, but on the potentiality of the entity named by the (sometimes unexpressed) Patient argument of that verb to undergo the event. The *is te* V construction contains a copular predicate, used to comment on an entity that it 'can be V-ed', and, as in a passive, that entity surfaces as the subject of the construction.

To conclude, the meaning of the construction can be given as follows:

> *is te* V construction
> In the eyes of the speaker, the most Patient-like argument of the verb has the property of being able to undergo the event described by the verb. In particular, the construction is often used as a stance marker.

Now that both constructions have been described in some detail, they can be compared. Are V-*baar* and *is te* V synonyms? This question is dealt with in the final subsection.

2.3 Distinctive collexeme analysis

The distinctive collexeme analysis (Gries and Stefanowitsch 2004) was designed to compare distributional patterns for two constructions. We use this analytical procedure to identify which verbs have a strong preference for either the *is te* V or the V-*baar* construction. Since only the token counts for each verb in both constructions are incorporated in the analysis, and overall frequencies of the verbs are not considered, the list of preferred verbs for each construction is likely to differ from the results of the collostructional analysis of each construction. This is because the distinctive analysis serves a different purpose: while the collostructional analysis aids in developing a fine-grained semantic analysis for each construction, the distinctive analysis looks more directly for differences between them. The ten verbs that have the strongest preference for the *is te* V or the V-*baar* construction are listed in Table 5.

Looking at the characteristics of the verbs that significantly prefer one of the constructions over the other (44 for the V-*baar* construction, 25 for *is te* V), some interesting differences appear, but also a lot of similarities: all verbs listed have two (or three) lexical arguments, i.e., can be used in the transitive construction. Semantically, the Patient argument can be a physical object (*zien* 'see', *bereiken* 'reach') or a mental entity (*hopen* 'hope', *voorstellen* 'suggest') for both constructions. These observations illustrate that both *is te* V and V-*baar* occur with a broad range of verbs.

Table 5. Results distinctive collexeme analysis; values given for distinctiveness correspond to -log (p-valueFisher-Exact, 10)

Verb	Translation	V-*baar* (N)	*is te* V (N)	Preference	Distinctiveness
beschikken	have at disposal	141	1	-*baar*	37.937
bereiken	reach	68	8	-*baar*	11.005
aanvaarden	accept	38	0	-*baar*	10.391
halen	get	72	11	-*baar*	10.143
voorstellen	suggest	52	4	-*baar*	9.975
bespreken	discuss	36	0	-*baar*	9.839
denken	think	45	4	-*baar*	8.266
vertrouwen	trust	37	2	-*baar*	7.874
kennen	know	28	0	-*baar*	7.634
kwetsen	hurt	28	0	-*baar*	7.634
zien	see	0	162	*is te*	57.040
doen	do	18	192	*is te*	46.855
hopen	hope	0	79	*is te*	27.046
zeggen	say	0	67	*is te*	22.847
vinden	find, locate	3	44	*is te*	11.446
geloven	believe	0	26	*is te*	8.749
krijgen	get, receive	0	20	*is te*	6.717
spreken	speak	0	15	*is te*	5.030
verwachten	expect	0	13	*is te*	4.357
wijten	blame	0	11	*is te*	3.684

There are also a few interesting differences, one of which had escaped our analyses so far: a majority of the verbs that have a significant preference for the *is te* V construction can take a sentential complement as its Patient argument (from the top 10, no fewer than 7: *zien, doen, hopen, zeggen, vinden, geloven, verwachten*). Many mental activity verbs occur with such propositional complements. A sentential complement X is apparently easier to incorporate in the frame *het is te V dat X* 'it is to V that X'[6] than in the frame *het is V-baar dat X* 'it is V-able that X'. We have, at present, no clear idea about why this would be the case. Note that both frames are extrapositional variants of the constructions under focus here.

There are also some numerical differences: more verbs are significantly preferred by V-*baar* (44) than by *is te* V (25), where the overall number of verbs was slightly higher for *is te* V than V-*baar* (209 and 171 respectively). Verbs that prefer *is te* V tend not to occur at all with V-*baar*, but the reverse is not true. In total, 55 verbs occur in both constructions in our corpus, and only eleven of those at least five times in each construction. One possible interpretation of this difference is that *is te* V has a slightly broader range than V-*baar*. Note, however, that all attributively used forms of V-*baar* were excluded prior to the analyses. Had we not done that, the picture might have been different: CGN contains 3908 instantiations of V-*baar*, with some of the most frequent forms never occurring in predicative contexts.

In comparison with the lists given earlier for each construction separately, the results of the distinctive analysis resemble those of the raw frequency data more than those of the collostructional analysis. This is due to the fact that the overall frequencies of the verbs do not play a role in the distinctive collexeme analysis. As a result, the very general and frequent verbs that fell out of the collostructional analysis for *is te* V (e.g. *zeggen* 'say', *vinden* 'find') are included in the list of preferred verbs. It is interesting to see that these basic verbs are very rarely found with the V-*baar* construction.

Finally, a closer look at some of the verbs that are found with both constructions shows that these can be divided into two groups: for some verbs, the two constructions mean different things, whereas others seem synonymous. *Eten* 'eat' is an example of the former category: *eetbaar* means 'edible, not poisonous' and *is te eten* 'not bad, tasty'. This differentiation ties in well with the overall inclination of *assessed* potentiality for the *is te* V construction: it is the speaker's opinion about the flavor of the food that is transmitted. With *eetbaar*, we deal with factual potentiality: it is possible to eat X without getting sick. Not all verbs show such

6. Strictly speaking, this does not hold for *doen* 'do', as one anonymous reviewer points out: it does not occur with subordinate clauses introduced by *dat* 'that'; however, it does co-occur with subordinate clauses introduced by a different complementizer, *om te* 'to', as in *het is niet te doen om hier 's ochtends op tijd te zijn* (literally: it is not to do to here in.the.morning on time to be; 'it's virtually impossible to get here on time in the morning').

specialization: we see no difference in meaning between *vergelijkbaar* 'comparable' and *is te vergelijken*. The semantics of the verb already contains some degree of assessment: it is always the speaker who decides that two things can or cannot be compared. Possibly, for these verbs, it is the sentential context and other discourse-related factors, such as conversational priming or information structure, that determine which construction is actually used. Comparative conversational analyses of fragments containing instances of these verbs in the two constructions would probably tell us more about why speakers choose which construction at specific points in a conversation.

In sum, the verbs that show strong preferences to either of the constructions cover a broad range of transitive verbs for both constructions, with some aspects of the distribution pointing at a slightly smaller range for V-*baar*. Verbs that take a propositional complement tend to prefer *is te* V. When verbs do occur in both constructions, in some cases there is semantic specialization, i.e., the two instantiations do not mean the same thing.

3. Experiment

The corpus data discussed in the previous sections of this chapter provide ample evidence that the V-*baar* construction and the *is te* V construction occur frequently in present day Dutch. In addition to the clearly stored forms with high token frequency, there were many instantiations with low token frequency, which turn out to fit semantically with the generalized template. In other words, there are many forms that look as if they might be productively formed instantiations of the constructions rather than stored forms. The problem is, however, that it is impossible to determine whether these sequences were productively built from scratch, using the template, or 'lexicalized', despite their low token frequency. It is more than likely that speakers have many forms available as units in their mental lexicons, as was argued at various places in Section 2. That is, on the basis of natural language data, one cannot answer the question whether speakers of Dutch have a partially schematic representation or template for the constructions at hand, although the corpus data do make this a likely proposition.

In order to find out more about the knowledge Dutch speakers have concerning the types of verbs preferred in the constructions, we designed an experiment. In this experiment, the acceptability of various instantiations of the two constructions is tested. The experiment focuses on two aspects: the participant structure of the verbs and the notion of *assessment of potentiality*. With regard to the former, the CGN-data show that verbs with certain participant structures (i.e. transitive verbs, with Agent and Patient participant roles) are much more likely to occur in the constructions than other verbs. The *assessment* of potentiality especially came to the fore in the semantic analysis of the *is te* V construction.

If people make a consistent distinction in the acceptability of instantiations that can be traced back to the participant structure of the verb they contain, this indicates that they have a representation for these constructions that includes information about the types of verbs with which they can be combined. Earlier, we defined a construction's productivity as the existence of a (partially) abstract representation in speakers' constructicons, used to build and to interpret novel instantiations of that construction. In our operationalization of this mental representation, we now argue that a consistent distinction in acceptability of forms that corresponds to certain characteristics of these forms is evidence that the mental representation actually exists and is used by speakers. The next section describes the methodology and items used in the test, as well as the participants and the procedure.

3.1 Method

3.1.1 *Task*

The experiment conducted is a *magnitude estimation task* (Sorace 1996, Bard, Robertson, and Sorace 1996, Sorace and Keller 2005, Wulff 2009). This is a specific kind of judgment task, in which participants make up their own acceptability scale. In contrast to other grammaticality judgment tasks, participants are told to assign a random number to a first stimulus, and then grade subsequent stimuli relative to the previous one. This offers various advantages: participants are free to distinguish as many different categories or grades of acceptability as they like, whereas grammaticality judgment either limits these to two (yes-no) or a fixed number (when a Likert-scale is offered). When a Likert-scale is used, usually with a range of 5 or 7 options, responses in the middle of the scale are notoriously difficult to interpret: participants may be unsure about their response and therefore opt for the middle of the range, or they may be very certain that this stimulus belongs in the middle. Both problems are avoided with the magnitude estimation (ME) task.

ME was first applied to linguistic topics by Sorace (1996) though it had already been used successfully in physical domains, such as people's perceptions of the loudness of sound or the intensity of pain (Stevens 1957). Such stimuli can be measured along an objective scale intensity (decibel etc.), which does not exist for the acceptability of linguistic stimuli. The method can be used, however, to determine whether people consistently distinguish between types of stimuli theoretically postulated to be different, in our case between verbs with different thematic and grammatical role assignments, and instantiations that either do or do not reflect an *assessment* of potentiality (cf. Sprouse (in press) for an overview of linguistic experiments with ME and a discussion of its merits).

3.1.2 *Test items*

The experiment consisted of 84 items: 48 test items and 36 fillers. Test items contained either an instance of the *is te* V construction or V-*baar* (always used predicatively). Filler items were made up from other ways to express potentiality, such as 'it is possible that', or 'X can be V-ed'. In the test items, five categories of verbs were used, with four verbs in each category and all verbs occurring once with V-*baar* and once with *is te* V. For one category, an additional distinction was made between factual and assessed potentiality contexts (see below), resulting in eight additional test items, to bring the total to 48. Almost none of these verbs appeared with either of the constructions in the corpus data; the only exceptions are *combineren* 'combine' and *breken* 'break'. *Breken* only occurs with -*baar* (5 tokens in CGN); *combineren* is found twice with -*baar* and 8 times with *is te*. This, combined with the fact that we constructed all of the test sentences, makes it likely that the great majority of test items constituted novel combinations for the participants. In addition, for one category of verbs, test items were construed with either a clear *assessment* element or factual potentiality. Figure 1 reflects the distribution of test items.

The verb categories are described below, listing the verbs used and one example test item for each category.[7]

I. Prototypical transitive verbs, with Agent-Subject and Patient-Object.

These verbs are typically found with a human Agent in the subject position and a Patient affected by the action named by the verb (*schrijven* 'write', *schilderen* 'paint', *combineren* 'combine', *maaien* 'mow').

(10) *Deze gladde muur is eenvoudig schilderbaar met een roll*er
this smooth wall is easily paint-able with a roller
'It's easy to paint this smooth wall with a roller'

Construction type / Verb category		V-baar (N)	is te V(N)	Filler items (N)
1	Assessment	4	4	
	Factual	4	4	8
2		4	4	8
3		4	4	8
4		4	4	8
5		4	4	4
Total		24	24	36 / 84

Figure 1. Verb categories

7. A complete list of test items can be obtained from the authors.

II. Optionally transitive verbs with Agent-Subject and Patient-Object or Undergoer-Subject roles.

These verbs are found both in highly transitive utterances with an Agent and a strongly affected Patient (e.g. 'I melted the chocolate'), and in sentences with only one argument expressed: the Undergoer (*smelten* 'melt', *scheuren* 'tear', *breken* 'break', *drogen* 'dry').[8]

(11) *Chocolade is makkelijk te smelten in de magnetron*
chocolate is easy to melt in the microwave
'Melting chocolate is easy in the microwave'

III. Usually intransitive verbs with a (generally) implicit second argument.

These verbs usually occur with only one explicit argument: an Agent-Subject (*schreeuwen* 'yell', *wandelen* 'stroll', *zingen* 'sing', *roken* 'smoke'). They can only be understood, however, with reference to a semantic base which includes a second argument: a motion verb like *wandelen* 'stroll' always presupposes a path and a sound emission verb such as *schreeuwen* 'yell' implies a sound/message. Some of the verbs in this class may occur with a cognate object. The inclusion of this category allows us to differentiate between verbs that usually require expression of two arguments when used in an active declarative clause (in I, IV and V) and verbs that usually have only one explicit argument in such contexts (categories II and III).

(12) *Sigaren moeten eerst rijpen voordat ze rookbaar zijn*
cigars must first ripe before they smoke-able are
'Cigars must first ripen before they can be smoked'

IV. Non-prototypical transitive verbs, with Stimulus-Experiencer roles and BE-perfect

These verbs require two explicit participants, filling Subject and Object position, but they differ from the verbs in I in the sense that the participants do not have Agent and Patient roles, respectively: the subject is usually filled by a Stimulus, and the object position by an Experiencer (*lukken* 'succeed', *meevallen* 'turn out better than expected', *ontgaan* 'escape', 'fail to grasp', *ontschieten* 'elude').[9] The perfect tense

8. Compare transitive use *ik smelt chocolade altijd 'au bain marie'* 'I always melt chocolate in a water bath' and intransitive use *chocolade smelt op 36 graden* 'chocolate melts at 36 degrees'.

9. Although Dutch and English are related languages, the Dutch verbs in this category do not have a near equivalent in English with a similar argument structure. For example, the English equivalent of *lukken* is *to succeed*. While the Dutch verb prototypically occurs in the Stimulus-Experiencer construction '*het lukte me*' (literally: 'it succeeded me'), English construes it as an active clause with an Agent: '*I succeeded*'.

is formed with the auxiliary *zijn* 'be', which often involves a rather passive construal, downplaying any active involvement on the part of the subject (e.g. *het is me gelukt* it is me succeeded, 'I succeeded'). This is the only way in which this category differs from the next one.

(13) *Het is een ambitieus plan, maar als iedereen helpt is het zeker lukbaar.*
it is an ambitious plan, but if everyone helps is it surely succeed-able.
'It's an ambitious plan, but if everyone helps it should surely succeed'

V. Non-prototypical transitive verbs, with Stimulus-Experiencer roles and HAVE-perfect

Similar to category IV verbs, these occur with a Stimulus-Subject and an Experiencer-Object (*fascineren* 'fascinate', *verbazen* 'amaze', *afschrikken* 'deter', *verrassen* 'surprise'). The distinction between verbs in IV and V is that for category V different construals are available: in addition to perfect tense with the auxiliary *hebben* 'have' and its active construal, forms with the auxiliary *zijn* 'be' are also marginally acceptable, and these have a passive interpretation (*het heeft me gefascineerd* it has me fascinated 'It has fascinated me' versus *ik ben gefascineerd* 'I am fascinated').

(14) *Ongewenst bezoek is af te schrikken met een alarmsignaal*
unwanted visit is off to fright with an alarm-signal
'Unwanted visitors can be deterred with an alarm signal'

Based on our corpus data, our intuition is that the V-*baar* construction is used more to express 'factual' potentiality, whereas the *is te* V construction often reflects the speaker's stance or assessment of potentiality. In order to investigate whether these semantic nuances are part of the participants' mental representations of the constructions, we included sentences with either an explicit stance-marking element (e.g. *denk ik* 'I think') or where the potentiality was clearly determined externally (e.g. based on rules or laws). For practical reasons (the test could not be too long) this was only done for each of the four verbs in category I.

(15) *Pannenkoeken met stroop zijn goed te combineren met een glas koude melk, vind ik.* (Assessment)
pancakes with syrup are good to combine with a glass cold milk, find I
'Pancakes with syrup go well with a glass of cold milk, I think'

(16) *Deze korting is niet te combineren met andere aanbiedingen* (Factual)
this reduction is not to combine with other offers
'You cannot combine this discount with other special offers'

3.1.3 *Participants and procedure*

The participants were 72 adult native speakers of Dutch (aged between 18 and 82, mean age 43). All were born in the Netherlands and presently living there. They participated on a voluntary basis.

Participants received an email with a link to a website. Here they could log in and, after providing some personal information, participate in the experiment at a time convenient for them. A short introduction informed them that this experiment was set up to find out what kinds of sentences people rate as 'better' or 'worse', where 'bad' sentences were defined as unintelligible or ungrammatical – thus pointing at both form and meaning. The participants were then introduced to the experimental technique with a number of examples, first with non-linguistic stimuli (oddly-shaped objects whose size they had to grade relative to one another), then with sentences in which one or more word order restrictions were violated. Before starting they were told that the sentences in the experiment all contained information about something that was *possible*. They were instructed to read each sentence carefully, but not think too long about the number they filled in. Participants spent between 12 and 22 minutes online for the whole task (the software recorded this automatically). Test items appeared in a random order, different for each participant.

3.2 Results

For each participant, scores were recoded into Z-scores to make a direct comparison of individual scores possible. Although participants reported feeling unsure about being consistent in their grading, the test was found to be reliable (Cronbach's $\alpha = .85$). Each participant responded to all test items, making this a within-subject design.

3.2.1 *Effects of construction type and verb category*

We applied a GLM repeated measures analysis, with verb category (5 levels) and construction type (2 levels) as factors. The results of this test are represented visually in Figure 2, with mean Z-scores and standard deviation in Table 6. Since the sphericity assumption is not met (the Mauchly test is significant), Huynh-Feldt corrected F-values are reported.

The main effect of construction type is significant ($F_{(1, 71)} = 103.99$, $p < .001$) as is the effect of verb category ($F_{(2.63, 186.59)} = 189.07$, $p < .001$) and the interaction ($F_{(3.47, 246.52)} = 18.28$, $p < .001$). Pairwise comparisons show that for each pair of verb category both main effects and the interaction effect are significant.

The effect of construction type shows that the participants rated the tested instantiations of the *is te* V construction in general as more acceptable than the V-*baar* forms. Many of the test items contained instantiations that were very likely new to

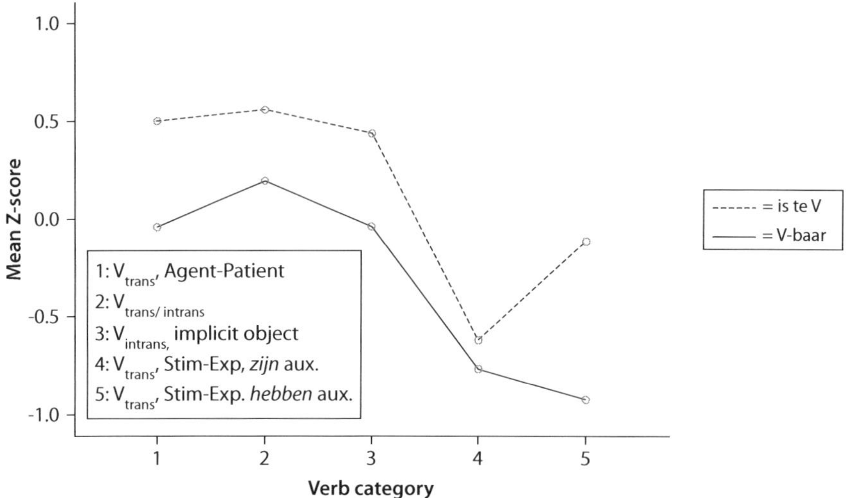

Figure 2. Mean scores per verb category, in both constructions

Table 6. Mean Z-score per verb category and construction type

Verb category	*is te* V (sd)	V-*baar* (sd)
I. V_{trans}, Agent-Patient	.500 (.343)	–.041 (.315)
II. $V_{trans/intrans}$	.557 (.416)	.196 (.392)
III. $V_{intrans,}$ implicit object	.438 (.406)	–.038 (.521)
IV. V_{trans}, Stim-Exp, *zijn*	–.620 (.385)	–.765 (.477)
V. V_{trans}, Stim-Exp, *hebben*	–.114 (.253)	–.925 (.489)

the participants. The overall difference in acceptability between the constructions may therefore be caused by the fact that the occurrence of novel words is a much rarer phenomenon than the creation of new combination of words. A novel instantiation of the V-*baar* construction leads to a new word, a word that the participants were unlikely to have encountered before. For the *is te* V items, the novel combination of a specific verb and the construction merely leads to a new clause. This means that the V-*baar* forms are more salient as novel instantiations, which might explain the overall lower degree of acceptability.[10]

With regard to the verb categories, two elements in the distribution of scores are particularly striking. The first of these is the clear distinction in acceptability between verb categories I, II and III on the one hand and IV and V on the other. For both constructions, this difference is at least 0.5 Z between any two-verb categories from

10. A number of participants made a remark about the occurrence of -*baar* in the test items after participating. No one mentioned *is te* V.

both groups. The first three verb categories have in common that they are regularly expressed with an Agent-Subject. They differ in that their usage in the constructions under focus here requires for the subject position a Patient that is obligatory in the corresponding active clause (category I), an Undergoer (II) or a Patient that is normally implicit in the corresponding active clause (III). It is likely that the easy acceptability of novel instantiations in these categories compared to the other two derives from the fact that the verbs involve a clear Agent-Patient asymmetry, while the Stimulus-Experiencer verbs in Categories IV and V lack this clear sense of agency.

The strongest interaction effect between verb category and construction type is visible in the pairwise comparison of verb categories IV and V (verb effect: $F_{(1,71)} = 21.77$, $p < .001$, construction effect: $F_{(1,71)} = 112.75$, $p < .001$, interaction effect: $F_{(1,71)} = 63.43$, $p < .001$). For V-*baar* items, it does not make much of a difference whether a Stimulus-Experiencer verb takes *hebben* 'have' or *zijn* 'be' as its auxiliary in the perfect tense. For *is te* V, on the other hand, those verbs that occur with *hebben* 'have' are judged to be considerably better than those that do not.

3.2.2 *Assessment of potentiality and factual potentiality*

For the analysis of factual potentiality versus assessment of potentiality, we only have 16 items, eight for each of the two constructions, divided over four verbs: each verb occurs in all four contexts. Again, we applied a GLM repeated measures analysis, this time over Z-scores for only the 16 relevant test items. Figure 3 shows

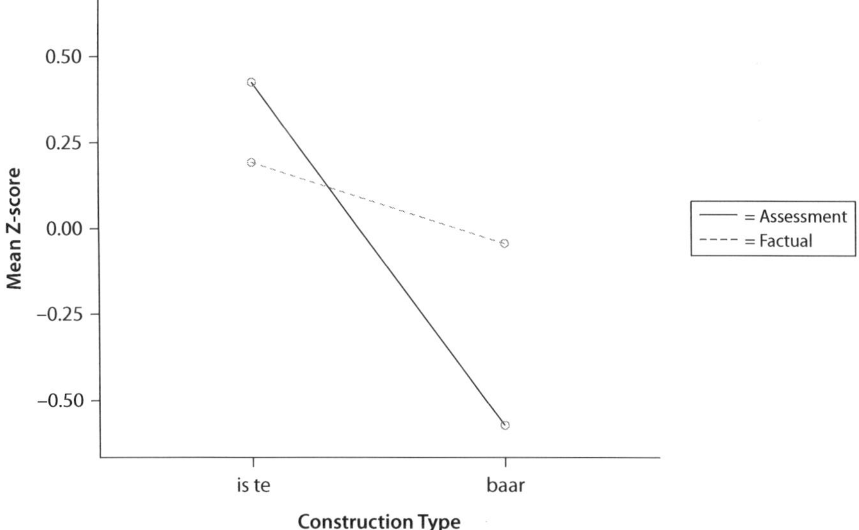

Figure 3. Acceptability of assessment and factuality readings in the two constructions

that the general preference for *is te* V is also present with these test items. More interestingly, *is te* V items with an assessment of potentiality, i.e. explicit stance markers like *denk ik* 'I think', score higher than factual potentiality. The reverse is true for V-*baar*, with an especially strong rejection of assessed potentiality (mean Z-score = –.574). The main effects and the interaction are significant (construction effect: $F_{(1,71)} = 85.51$, $p < .001$, potentiality type: $F_{(1,71)} = 8.00$, $p < .01$, interaction: $F_{(1,71)} = 67.92$, $p < .001$).

3.3 Summary and analysis

In sum, the acceptability of novel V-*baar* and *is te* V forms is much higher for verbs for which a Patient argument is interpretable than for other verbs with two arguments, at least for Stimulus-Experiencer verbs. Participants in the experiment give higher acceptability ratings to novel instantiations of *is te* V than of V-*baar*, possibly due to higher awareness of new words than of new multi-word combinations. In general, verbs with a Stimulus-Experiencer argument structure are rejected more strongly than other test items, but this tendency is weaker for *is te* V with those verbs that take *hebben* as their auxiliary in the perfect tense. Finally, it makes a difference whether what is expressed is factual potentiality or the speaker's assessment of potentiality: *is te* V is rated higher in contexts marked for stance, and V-*baar* for those expressing factual potentiality.[11]

Most of the results of the ME task correspond surprisingly well to the corpus data. The acceptability ratings for different verb types reflect frequency of occurrence in the corpus. For *is te* V, we found a slightly larger number of different verb types in the corpus than for V-*baar*, which ties in well with the overall higher acceptability ratings for *is te* V. The corpus analysis for *is te* V revealed that this construction is often used to express a speaker's assessment of potentiality rather than an objective fact. This is also replicated in participants' responses to test items, albeit in a slightly different way: here it seems more like assessment was rejected for V-*baar* items than that it was valued for *is te* V items. We interpret this as an indication that the subjective assessment of potentiality is not an available interpretation for the V-*baar* construction: this is an island of improductivity, at least in comparison with the *is te* V construction.

4. Conclusion

In this chapter we have investigated whether two seemingly synonymous potentiality constructions in Dutch, referred to here as V-*baar* and *is te* V, can be said to be

11. For a more extensive report on this experiment, including responses from children (grade 6, mean age 12;5), see Mos (2010).

productive. If a template can be shown to be used productively, in an experimentally controlled setting, this provides evidence for the cognitively real existence of a partially schematic pattern, i.e. a syntactic construction; otherwise we can only show with corpus data that there are various instantiations, which may well all be stored as (lexical) units that happen to instantiate the same underlying pattern.

A comparison of two constructions with allegedly the same meaning allowed us first of all to determine whether the two constructions are really synonymous. They turned out to differ in subtle ways, which suggests that the constructions do exist as independent templates, ready for use in novel ways, i.e. with new verbs in the open slot reserved for the verb stem (in the case of V-*baar)* or the infinitive (in *is te* V). These differences were revealed through collostructional analyses of the two constructions and a distinctive collexeme analysis, directly comparing them. While a few verbs occur frequently in both constructions, many were attracted to only one of them. This suggests that each construction has its own meaning, slightly different from the other one, which matches better with some verbs than with others. The main difference appears to be that *is te* V functions as a stance marker, enabling speakers to convey their subjective assessment of whether something is likely or not to happen, rather than objective possibility.

In order to verify the cognitive reality of the schemas, we conducted a magnitude estimation experiment, in which subjects judged the acceptability of various novel creations using the two constructions. The evidence this yielded converges with the corpus evidence, in at least two ways. First, the acceptability of novel instantiations of the two constructions is higher for some classes of verbs than for others, with classes for which the corpus turns up no examples scoring lowest in acceptability. Second, the preference for subjective expression of potentiality that the corpus analysis suggested for the *is te* V construction was confirmed by higher acceptability ratings for these contexts in the experiment. In addition, acceptability ratings for the constructions differ from each other, with *is te* V consistently rated higher. We tentatively interpret this to mean that *is te* V is more productive than V-*baar,* and that this is related to their character as multi-word phrase ('syntax') versus derived word ('morphology'), respectively. We conclude two things. First, both our hypotheses (about productivity and about non-synonymy) are supported by converging evidence from the corpus and experimental data. Second, the two sources of evidence complement each other: they demonstrate different aspects of the same phenomenon.

References

Bard, Ellen G., Dan Robertson, & Antonella Sorace. 1996. Magnitude estimation of linguistic acceptability. *Language* 72: 32–68.

Barðdal, Johanna. 2008. *Productivity; Evidence from Case and Argument Structure in Icelandic.* Amsterdam & Philadelphia: Benjamins.

Boas, Hans C. 2003. *A Constructional Approach to Resultatives.* Chicago: The University of Chicago Press.

Boas, Hans C. 2008. Determining the structure of lexical entries and grammatical constructions in Construction Grammar. *Annual Review of Cognitive Linguistics* 6: 113–144.

Boogaart, Ronny. 2006. "Het is te zien hoe dat je het ziet" De modale infinitief in Nederland en België. *Voortgang, Jaarboek voor de Neerlandistiek* 24: 37–50.

Bybee, Joan. 1995. Regular morphology and the lexicon. *Language and Cognitive Processes* 10 (5): 425–455.

Diepeveen, Janneke, Ronny Boogaart, Pieter Byloo, Theo Janssen, & Jan Nuyts. 2006. *Modale Uitdrukkingen in Belgisch-Nederlands en Nederlands-Nederlands: Corpusonderzoek en Enquête.* Münster: Nodus Publikationen.

Gilquin, Gaëtenelle & Stefan Th. Gries. 2009. Corpora and experimental methods: A state-of-the-art review. *Corpus Linguistics and Linguistic Theory* 5: 1–25.

Goldberg, Adele. 1995. *Constructions: A Construction Grammar Approach to Argument Structure.* Chicago: The University of Chicago Press.

Goldberg, Adele E. 2006. *Constructions at Wok: The Nature of Generalization in Language.* Oxford: Oxford University Press.

Gries, Stefan Th. & Anatol Stefanowitsch. 2004. Extending collostructional analysis; A corpus-based perspective on 'alternations'. *International Journal of Corpus Linguistics* 9: 97–129.

Gries, Stefan Th., Beate Hampe, & Doris Schönefeld. 2005. Converging evidence: Bringing together experimental and corpus data on the association of verbs and constructions. *Cognitive Linguistics* 16: 635–676.

Gries, Stefan Th. 2007. Coll.analysis 3.2. A program for R for Windows 2.x [Computer software].

Jackendoff, Ray. 1997. Twistin' the night away. *Language* 73: 534–559.

Langacker, Ronald W. 2008. *Cognitive Grammar: A Basic Introduction.* Oxford: Oxford University Press.

Mos, Maria. 2010. *Complex lexical items.* Doctoral dissertation, Tilburg University.

Sorace, Antonella. 1996. The use of acceptability judgments in second language acquisition research. In W. Ritchie & T. Bhatia, eds., *Handbook of Second Language Acquisition*, 375–409. San Diego: Academic Press.

Sorace, Antonella & Frank Keller. 2005. Gradience in linguistic data. *Lingua* 115: 1497–1524.

Sprouse, Jon. In press. A test of the cognitive assumptions of magnitude estimation: Commutativity does not hold for acceptability judgments. *Language.*

Stefanowitsch, Anatol & Stefan Th. Gries. 2003. Collostructions: investigating the interaction of words and constructions. *International Journal of Corpus Linguistics* 8: 209–243.

Stevens, Stanley S. 1957. On the psychophysical law. *Psychological Review* 64: 153–181.

Wray, Alison. 2008. *Formulaic Language: Pushing the Boundaries.* Oxford: Oxford University Press.

Wulff, Stephanie. 2009. Converging evidence from corpus and experimental data to capture idiomaticity. *Corpus Linguistics and Linguistic Theory* 54: 131–159.

Zipf, George K. 1935. *The Psycho-biology of Language: An Introduction to Dynamic Philology.* Cambridge: MIT Press.

1.3 Idioms and creative language use

Compositional and embodied meanings of somatisms

A corpus-based approach to phraseologisms*

Alexander Ziem and Sven Staffeldt
University of Düsseldorf and University of Würzburg

The chapter focuses on the problem of meaning determination of German idioms that consist of at least two words and contain a body part term as a constituent. Such so-called "somatisms" make up a considerable part of the phrasemes in German and English. What do these terms in idiomatic somatisms designate? Addressing this question, we examine two controversial issues in current cognitive linguistic research: (i) Are the meanings of bodily expressions in somatisms arbitrary? (ii) To what extent are the meanings of somatisms and of their somatic constituents grounded in human bodily experience? By analyzing selected examples of phrasemes containing *Finger* on the basis of substantial corpus data, answers to these questions are provided.

Keywords: conceptual metaphor and metonymy, embodiment, phraseological meaning

1. Introduction

It is well known that the meaning of a phraseologism cannot be fully captured by adding up the meanings of its lexical parts (see e.g. Kay and Fillmore 1999, Langlotz 2006: 16–25). Nevertheless, the lexical constituents are supposed to make an important contribution to the overall meaning.[1] In contemporary cognitive phraseology, however, the meaning of both whole phraseologisms and their parts is often described introspectively (cf. Langlotz 2006). There is still no reliable empirical method that allows for testing and falsifying intuitively plausible semantic

* We would like to thank two anonymous reviewers as well as Doris Schönefeld for many helpful comments on an earlier version of this chapter.

1. Dobrovol'skij (2000), cf. also the seminal work by Kay and Fillmore (1999).

descriptions; a corpus-based approach to phraseologisms is necessary to yield converging evidence, that is, evidence collected from different empirical sources by means of different methods.

In this chapter, using corpus data, we focus on the problem of meaning determination of a particular kind of phraseologisms that consist of at least two words and contain a body-part term as a constituent (e.g. *jm. auf die Finger schauen* ['to keep an eye on somebody'], *sich die Seele aus dem Hals schreien* ['to talk/shout until one is blue in the face'], etc.). Phraseologisms that contain at least one body-part term as a constituent are called somatisms. They make up a considerable part of the phraseologisms in German and English. However, there has not been much research on the semantic potential of the body-part terms in somatisms (Piirainen 2007: 212). What do these terms in idiomatic somatisms denote?

Addressing this question, our case study examines two controversial issues. The first issue concerns the compositionality of idiomatic expressions: Although somatisms are usually considered to be non-compositional (cf. Kövecses and Szabó 1996), it is still controversial according to which criteria a linguistic unit can be classified as a phraseologism (cf. e.g. Müller 2006). In the case of somatisms it is not arbitrary what the body-part terms denote, so that it is anything but trivial to ask in how far the meaning of a somatism is motivated by the semantic potential of the body-part term. The second issue addressed concerns embodied meaning: The entity being referred to is often not the body part itself but activities carried out with the help of the body part. Is the meaning of phraseologisms generally grounded in human bodily experience (in the sense of Gibbs 2006) and, if so, to what extent? Which cognitive mechanisms systematically motivate the meaning construction?

By analyzing selected examples of phraseologisms that contain the constituent *Finger*, our case study offers some answers to these questions. First, a corpus-based method is introduced to analyze recurrent somatisms in German; all somatisms containing *Finger* are identified and clustered in terms of meaning variation. Then, on the basis of both cognitive frames and conceptual metaphors/metonymies, systematic correlations between the functions of body parts and the figurative usage of body-part terms in somatisms are demonstrated.

Unlike the studies conducted by Gibbs, as well as Kövecses and Szabó, our study systematically consults corpus data. Following the assumption that converging evidence emerges when a phenomenon is investigated by means of at least two methodologies (cf. Schönefeld, this volume), it provides another source of empirical evidence, which may either converge or diverge on the conclusions drawn by Kövecses and Szabó, and Gibbs. Methodologically, we also aim at integrating frame semantics with corpus linguistic investigations in the field of phraseologisms. Collecting evidence from various sources, including results from psycholinguistic and neurolinguistic studies/experiments, frame theoretical modeling, introspective and corpus data, we ask whether the findings converge on the same conclusions or in what way conclusions drawn on the basis of one type of evidence are supported, complemented or falsified by other evidence. In this respect, the present investigation is a case study exemplifying what Steen (this volume) calls "methodological pluralism", that is, a study in converging evidence presented about the same phenomenon from different methodological perspectives.

2. Towards a definition of somatisms

Following Burger (2007), we define phraseologisms as relatively entrenched, polylexical, and idiomatic linguistic units. By definition, phraseologisms thus consist of more than one word. The psycholinguistically plausible assumption that a phraseological unit requires its own entry in our mental lexicon as well as the fact that the unit shares all properties of one-word-lexemes indicate a high level of entrenchment. Phraseologisms can thus be equated with complex linguistic signs or constructions that do not need to be construed all over again during language production and reception; rather, they are mentally accessible and reproducible as complex *units*. Verhagen (2009) describes this property of reproducibility as the entrenchment of a convention. In his usage-based conception of signs, entrenchment gives rise to the cognitive accessibility of symbolic signs. Phraseologisms are also symbolic units, that is, form-meaning pairings, in Langacker's technical sense of "unit" (cf. Langacker 1991: 16).[2] Due to their high degree of entrenchment, phraseologisms are considered to be stable. In line with these insights, we consider reproducibility and stability essential characteristics of phraseologisms. In our view, however, the most important property of phraseologisms is their cognitive status as lexemes. We adopt the most common definition (at least in the German speaking community) provided by Burger, Buhofer, and Sialm (1982: 1):[3]

> A connection of two or more lexical units is phraseological if (1) the lexical units cannot be fully explained by syntactic and semantic combinatorial regularities and if (2) in a linguistic community the multiple word unit is being used similar to a lexeme.

---

2. For that reason, Fleischer (1997) as well as Wotjak (1992) also use the term *phraseolexeme*.

3. The original text reads:

> Phraseologisch ist eine Verbindung von zwei oder mehr Wörtern dann, wenn (1) die Wörter eine durch die syntaktischen und semantischen Regularitäten der Verknüpfung nicht voll erklärbare Einheit bilden, und wenn (2) die Wortverbindung in der Sprachgemeinschaft, ähnlich wie ein Lexem gebräuchlich ist.

Furthermore, we assume that a phraseologism is idiomatic if its meaning cannot be entirely derived from the conventional meanings of its constituents. This is the case if the conventional referential domain of a linguistic unit does not coincide with the referential domain of the same expression when it functions as an integral part of a phraseologism.

In accordance with current cognitive-linguistic research in phraseology, we assume that the meanings of idioms can only be fully captured if they are considered to be conceptual in nature, that is, if they are objects of mental manipulation (Kövecses and Szabó 1996, Langlotz 2006). We also assume that metaphors and metonymies are conceptual entities in so far as elements of a source domain are selectively mapped on at least one target domain (cf. Croft and Cruse 2004: 193ff.). In their study on idioms Kövecses and Szabó (1996: 330) particularly stress that different cognitive mechanisms are involved in the process of constructing idiomatic meanings:

> The motivation for the occurrence of particular words in a large number of idioms can be thought of as a cognitive mechanism that links domains of knowledge to idiomatic meaning. The kinds of mechanisms that seem to be especially relevant in the case of many idioms are metaphor, metonymy, and conventional knowledge.

Against the background of these definitions and considerations, we are now in the position to characterize somatisms as phraseologisms that contain at least one body-part term as a constituent. The technical terms *somatism* and *somatic phraseologism* are thus synonymous.

In what follows, we analyze some somatisms in detail. We pay particular attention to the issue of compositionality, that is, whether or not the meaning of a phraseologism is in some way motivated by the conventional meaning of its body-part term. We argue that it is crucial to know to which epistemic domain the body-part term is linked metaphorically or metonymically. In this vein, it is thus argued that the cognitive motivation of idiomatic meaning is in most cases a metaphorical and/or metonymical extension. Hence, we are also interested in the kind of motivation that holds between the source and target domain.

3. Introspective and corpus-based investigations of phraseologisms

In (conceptual) metaphor theory, phraseologisms became objects of interest for epistemological reasons: They are prominent linguistic means to construe cognitive models, and they provide evidence for the underlying human conceptual system). In their seminal work on conceptual metaphors Lakoff and Johnson (1980), for example, analyze phraseologisms to illustrate that we employ cognitive mechanisms such as metaphor and metonymy in order to make the world 'comprehensible' and 'intelligible'. In the wake of Lakoff and Johnson, most researchers who have examined the conceptual underpinning of individual uses of metaphors or metonymies have followed roughly the same guideline. First, phraseologisms are identified in a (mostly arbitrarily collected) data set. In a second step, the non-figurative meaning of the phrases' lexical constituents is determined. Third, the meaning of the phraseologisms as such is figured out. Finally, the conventional non-figurative meaning is equated with the source domain while the target domain is supposed to be represented by the meaning of the whole phraseologism.

This procedure implies a number of tacit methodological assumptions. First, there is the assumption that the lexical meaning of a phraseologism's constituent is transparent and thus unproblematic. Second, it seems to be presupposed that phraseologisms are not polysemous (at least not in nature). Finally, it is a common view that any member of a linguistic community has roughly the same mental representation of the meaning of a phraseologism. In what follows, we challenge these assumptions.

The hypothesis that phraseologisms are considered to be lexical units has a considerable impact on the analysis of phraseologisms. Following this claim, the identification of the conceptual metaphor SEEING IS CONTROLLING would usually take three steps. First, one comes across a phraseologism like *jm. auf die Finger schauen* ['to keep an eye on someone'] that provides first evidence for the conceptual metaphor SEEING IS CONTROLLING. Second, to test this assumption, the conventional meaning of *schauen* ['to observe/watch'] as well as the meaning of the phraseologism as a whole are determined. Finally, the conventional meaning of *schauen* is considered as the source domain and the phraseological meaning 'to control' as the target domain. This third step is, in some way, the conclusion that has been drawn from the findings in the second step.

Although this procedure is not without problems, its application is usually not called into question. The use of this procedure often gives rise to claims that remain unverified. This is, for example, the case in Moon (1998). In a large-scale corpus study, Moon investigates so-called FEIs, that is, "fixed expressions including idioms", in contemporary British and American English. In her study, she takes account of both frequency of occurrences and semantic variations of FEIs. Addressing the latter, Moon (1998) analyzes FEIs in terms of (potential) ambiguity, polysemy, metaphor, and metonymy. With respect to metonymy she elaborates (194):

> Of database FEIs recorded as involving metonyms, many relate to parts of the body. The particular body part represents the whole person, as well as foregrounding the physical sense or ability that constitutes the central part of the FEI's meaning. For example, in *lend an ear*, *ear* indicates both the person and his/her attention; in *hard on someone's heels*, *heels* indicates a person and the part most (notionally) visible in running; and in *get one's head round something*, *head* indicates a person and his/her mind or understanding.

Undoubtedly, it is taken for granted here that phraseological constituents undergo specific metonymical meaning extensions. Even though, however, the assumption of these semantic shifts may be intuitively plausible, it requires validation by corpus investigations and/or experimental studies. This is because the postulated metonymical shifts are not results of systematic empirical investigations. They rather remain hypothetical, and need to be tested empirically, e.g. against corpus data in order to see in what way the latter converge on the conclusions drawn by Moon.

There is a second problem associated with the four-step procedure described above: As long as both the conventional meanings of each constituent and the meaning of the phraseologism are simple and transparent, there is not much to worry about. But how do we know whether the meanings are 'transparent'? Obviously, one needs intersubjectively reliable criteria to determine meaning, and these criteria must be applicable to single case studies. In the context of our study, such criteria yielding converging evidence (in the sense of "methodological pluralism", cf. Steen, this volume) could be (i) introspection and intuition respectively, (ii) hints given in dictionaries of phraseologisms, or (iii) authentic linguistic data (analyzed with the help of corpus linguistic methods). Introspective data provide first evidence, and it is undoubtedly a valuable albeit restrictive method to determine the meaning of any linguistic unit (cf. Talmy 2007, Schönefeld, this volume). Yet, considering that accepting intuitive linguistic judgments often implies the neglect of giving explications, the limits of introspection as a reliable method have become apparent (Gibbs 2007a: 5). In other words, the results of introspection are merely hypotheses that need to be validated and systematically tested by corpus or experimentally elicited data. In the case of phraseologisms, dictionaries as well as a collection of authentic data provide a good data basis for such a validation that relies on converging evidence in methodological terms.

To sum up, introspection may serve as a suitable method to set up hypotheses, and it may also provide provisional evidence for these hypotheses. For introspection to work well, however, it is essential that one is familiar with the object of investigation. If introspection is taken to be the one and only linguistic method that is applied in a case study, there is no opportunity to test hypotheses. Rather, the analyst herself becomes an integral part of the analyzed data. On the other hand, it is important to note that hypotheses usually emerge out of assumptions about 'the world' to which we have first and foremost introspective access. Even scholars working in the field of quantitative corpus linguistics stress the fact that introspection cannot – and should not – be avoided entirely before, during and after corpus investigations. Steyer (2002: 234), for example, emphasizes "that at no stage can linguistic competence be replaced by the computer. It is the analyst's job to decide how to interpret the corpus data and what to conclude from the data".[4] Turning back to the phraseologism *jm. auf die Finger schauen*: how is it possible to test the assumption that this phraseologism draws on the conceptual metaphor CONTROLLING IS SEEING? And how can we find out to what extent its lexical constituents motivate the phraseological meaning?

For the sake of simplicity and in order to avoid the notoriously complicated issue of determining the conventional meanings of lexical units, we suggest to take lexical meaning descriptions provided in dictionaries as a starting point. Meaning descriptions in monolingual dictionaries provide first evidence for entrenched meanings of lexical units. However, they are not conclusive. Additionally, dictionary entries may also cover meaning aspects that are of marginal interest for the analysis of phraseological meanings. To avoid semantic idiosyncrasies, it is thus necessary to compare meaning descriptions of at least three or four different monolingual dictionaries. By doing so, one receives a 'compiled' meaning description that we take as a first hypothesis about a possibly entrenched meaning of the lexical unit in question. In the case of *schauen* ['to look'], the result is indeed 'sehen' ['to see'], that is, 'to recognize something visually'.

With regard to phraseological meaning it is principally possible to proceed analogously. In dictionaries of phraseologisms, however, the meaning description of one and the same phraseological unit often varies considerably. Regarding *jm. auf die Finger schauen*, for example, it ranges from *jmdn. genau beaufsichtigen, kontrollieren* ['to look after someone carefully, to control someone'] (Duden 2008: 225) to *auf jn. gut/scharf aufpassen* ['to keep an eye on someone'] (Friederich 1976: 127 and Müller 2005: 136). Problems arise not only because three different verbs are mentioned but also because only seemingly synonymous verbs or verb phrases are given. What is missing is a semantic definition including a hyperonym and differentia specifica. Hence, the semantic descriptions presented would be appropriate only if the given verbs and verb phrases are synonymous, that is, if they can be used interchangeably without semantic variation. However, it is anything but obvious if this is really the case. Furthermore, one consequence resulting from such heterogeneous meaning description would be that we have to assume three different conceptual metaphors, namely LOOKING AFTER SOMEONE IS SEEING, CONTROLLING IS SEEING, and KEEPING AN EYE ON SOMEONE IS SEEING. There is neither a reasonable way to limit the possible numbers of conceptual metaphors nor to exhaustively distinguish metaphors on a linguistic level from those on a conceptual level (for a general critique cf. Steen, this volume). At this point the need for corpus-based investigations becomes apparent. The key question is: How is it possible to determine the meanings of phraseologisms from a usage-based perspective?

4. Original: "[...] dass linguistische Kompetenz in [...] keiner Phase durch den Computer zu ersetzen ist. Die Entscheidung, wie mit welcher Korpusinformation umzugehen ist und welche Schlussfolgerungen zu ziehen sind, bleibt dem Menschen vorbehalten" (Steyer 2002: 234).

4. Analyzing the meaning of somatisms: A corpus-based perspective

In what follows, we focus on two questions: What is the meaning of (a selected choice of) somatisms including *Finger* as a constituent? And what does the lexical unit *Finger* as a constituent of these somatisms denote? The first question is lexicographical in nature. Semantic descriptions of somatisms deriving from analyzed corpus-data of somatisms may serve as the foundational basis for dictionary entries. An answer to the second question, on the other hand, also involves a semantic analysis, but it has theoretical implications in that it needs to provide answers to the following questions: Do lexical constituents codetermine the overall phraseological meaning? Or is a phraseologism to be equated with a multi-word lexeme that cannot be decomposed into smaller units?

We show that there is converging evidence for the hypothesis that the meaning potentials (in the sense of Allwood: 2003) of central lexical constituents have indeed an impact on the overall meaning of the phraseologism. By analyzing phraseologisms containing *Finger* as a constituent it is additionally demonstrated that the conventional meaning of the body part term systematically motivates the figurative meaning, which the body-part term acquires as an integral part of a somatism.

4.1 Corpus data

In order to set up a corpus of somatisms, one first needs to decide which linguistic units should be investigated. Which somatisms containing *Finger* as a constituent do exist? And which of them are still being used in contemporary German? After having consulted eight German dictionaries of phraseologisms, 89 different *Finger* somatisms could be identified.[5] However, not all of these somatisms are still in use. To sort out those somatisms that are no longer common in contemporary German, we determined how often each of the somatisms occur in the corpus COSMAS II, the largest archive of written German texts covering approximately 5.5 million texts (cf. Scherer 2006: 81).

5. Schemann (1993) is the most extensive dictionary. Only self-constructed data are given, however, to illustrate usages of phraseologisms. Another disadvantage is that this dictionary generally does not provide meaning descriptions. Besides Schemann (1993) we included Duden (2008), Friederich (1976) as well as Müller (2005). In contrast to the other dictionaries, Müller (2005) also provides an onomasiological systematization. Additionally, we also consulted Röhrich (1991/94), a standard folkloristic dictionary, as well as Krüger-Lorenzen (2001). Zeit (2005) is less extensive, but nonetheless a useful data collection. Finally, we included a dictionary of phraseologisms published in 2007; the author/editor of this dictionary is not provided.

Table 1. Frequency of occurrence of the 13 most common finger phraseologisms in German[†]

Phraseologisms	Frequency
auf die Finger schauen/sehen/gucken ['to keep an eye on somebody']	67
die Finger davon lassen ['to keep away from somebody/something']	50
den/die Finger auf die Wunde/den wunden Punkt/etw. legen ['to criticize']	41
sich die Finger verbrennen ['to get one's fingers burnt over something']	30
keinen Finger krümmen/krumm machen/bewegen/rühren ['not to lift/raise a finger']	25
klamme Finger ['dump fingers']	25
mit dem Finger auf jn./etw. zeigen/weisen/deuten ['to point one's/a finger at somebody/something']	22
bei etw. seine Finger im Spiel haben ['to have a finger in every pie']	22
jm. in/zwischen/unter die Finger fallen/geraten/kommen ['to fall into somebody's hands']	19
sich die Finger wund wählen/schreiben/tippen ['to write one's fingers to the bone']	18
jm. auf die Finger klopfen ['to give somebody a rap across/on the knuckles']	17
(sich)/jn. um den Finger wickeln (lassen) ['to twist someone round one's little finger']	13
den (mahnenden) Finger (er)heben ['to wag (one's finger at somebody)']	11

[†] If possible, we added an English translation of the 13 phraseologisms included in this table. These translations cover, at best, the phraseological meaning; the lexical constituents making up a phraseologism, however, vary substantially.

Searching for constructions containing *Finger* one receives more than 22,000 hits. For the purpose of the present study, we randomly extracted 1000 instances (including two sentences before and two after the sentence in which *Finger* occurs). After having filtered out repeated and nonsensical, hence useless, instances, 921 occurrences eventually remain. On the basis of this relatively small corpus we are now in the position to check if each of the 89 finger phraseologisms is still used. The result is somewhat surprising: 46%, that is, 421 of all occurrences meet the defining criteria presented above for phraseologisms, while only 48%, that is, 446 occurrences of *Finger* are not phraseologically bound. The remaining part of 6% (54 occurrences) constitutes a special class because these instances deal with particular activities of fingers when playing a musical instrument. In this class, numerous metaphors are found, such as *seine Finger glitten über die Tasten* ['his fingers slid across the piano keys], *die Finger wirbelten über die Saiten* ['the fingers rolled across the strings] or *die Finger tanzten auf dem Klavier* [the 'finger danced on the piano']. Overall, one could thus say that every second of the 921 instances comprises a phraseologically bound usage of *Finger.*

Additionally, it turned out that out of the 89 finger somatisms that were identified in dictionaries only 31 occur in the corpus, and out of these 31 only 13 finger somatisms occur more often than ten times. Table 1 gives an overview of the 13 somatisms and their frequencies of occurrence. These 13 somatisms cover 360 instances, that is, 86% of the finger phraseologisms and 39% of all 921 occurrences. This quantitative dominance led us to the decision to restrict the fine-grained analysis to these 13 somatisms.

4.2 Analysis

For the purpose of a semantic analysis of phraseologisms, it is useful to have a closer look at the argument roles provided by the verbs of the phraseologisms listed in Table 1. Most of the identified phraseologisms express events, that is, they share all basic properties with verbs, including syntactic and semantic valency. Just like 'normal' verbs the phraseologisms in Table 1 have the capacity to combine with specific types of complements. The argument roles a verb and a verb-like phraseologism is associated with 'govern' the constituents of the sentence in which the verb and the verb-like phraseologism, respectively, is embedded. Constituents may be integral parts of phraseologisms, like *auf 'die Finger* ['at the fingers'] in the phraseologism *auf die Finger schauen*, but other constituents may also be provided by the sentence in which the phraseologism is realized. *Auf die Finger schauen*, for example, provides a slot but not a slot-filling element for the dative object.

Generally, a verb gives access to a cognitive "scene" containing information about the argument roles, such as "agentive", "patient", "instrument" (Fillmore 1971) etc., which the verb requires.[6] Such scenes resemble cognitive frames in many

6. Deviating from both Fillmore (1977) and Schank and Abelson (1977), Heringer (1999: 128–129, 233ff.) uses the notion *scene* to describe merely syntactical properties of verbs by means of evoked frames. Our usage of *scene*, however, encompasses all kinds of knowledge elements that are necessary to fully understand a verb's meaning. Our concept of "scene" thus follows Fillmore's (1977: 63) attempt to include all kinds of world knowledge in the semantic analysis. Fillmore later refrains from using *scene* as a technical term and uses the notion *frame* instead (cf. Ziem 2008: 221–237).

respects (Ziem 2008: 255–272). Both scenes and frames comprise slots. While slots in the case of verb scenes can be equated with syntactic roles attached to a verb, the slot structure of semantic frames is much richer. Following Minsky (1975: 2–46) and Fillmore (1977: 64–65), we assume that frame slots can be equated with questions about the object denoted by a linguistic expression. The frame evoked by the verb *schauen* ['to watch/observe'], for example provides a welter of questions, such as: Where does the activity *schauen* take place? What has motivated the activity? Why does someone observe something? Note also that syntactic roles attached to a verb scene resemble questions concerning the activity that the verb denotes. With regard to the phraseologism *auf die Finger schauen*, for instance, one could pose a question for each argument that the verb *auf die Finger schauen* takes: Who is keeping an eye on somebody? On whom is someone keeping an eye? We return to this point later.

From this illustration of semantic scenes and frames it follows that the semantic frame evoked by a verb makes much more information available than the information that the argument roles of the verb conveys. It is important to note, however, that argument roles are entirely covered by the evoked frame and that they can be investigated as such (Goldberg 2006: 39). Focusing on argument roles, which slots does the scene evoked by a verb provide? It is first and foremost necessary to distinguish so-called external valency from internal valency. In the case of *jm. auf die Finger schauen* the scene includes slots concerning an agentive ("Who is keeping an eye on someone?") and a dative ("On whom is someone keeping an eye?"). Both are instances of external valency, that is, they assign interchangeable values to those slots that the phraseologism provides. The range of arguments that may be realized here is limited due to lexical selection restrictions. Internal valency, by contrast, concerns invariable values that are already fixed by a constituent of a phraseologism, here for example the locative *auf die Finger* ['at the fingers'].[7] From a frame semantic point of view both internal and external valency correspond to highly salient slots of the frame evoked by the verb.[8]

In analyzing the 67 instances of the phraseologisms *jm. auf die Finger schauen* in our corpus it becomes evident, however, that the meanings of the phraseologism cannot be captured with the help of external valency alone. Particularly one slot lying beyond the scope of the verb's valency structure seems to be crucial: "*Why* is somebody keeping an eye on someone?" Considering the larger context as well as the immediate cotext in which the phraseologisms are embedded, many of

7. In the English phraseologism *to keep an eye on someone* the verb *to keep* does not require a syntactic argument for the locative.

8. Similarly, Fillmore and frame semantic researchers inspired by his work usually distinguish between so-called peripheral and core frame elements (cf. e.g. Boas 2008: 13).

the 67 instances provide an answer to this question: one has to keep an eye on somebody in order to control someone. Supporting evidence for this claim comes from lexicographic findings. In several studies it is maintained that the element 'controlling someone' is the most salient semantic property of the phraseologism *jm. auf die Finger schauen*. Consider, for example, the following semantic description (taken out of a German textbook for phraseologisms):

> E.4 TO CHECK – TO CONTROL
> to keep an eye on somebody
> *to supervise someone carefully; to pay attention to what somebody is doing, due to mistrust* (Hessky and Ettinger, 1997: 100)[9]

Yet, considering the wide range of different usages covered in the 67 instances in our corpus, the meaning aspect 'controlling someone' turned out to be neither a sufficient nor a necessary semantic property of the phraseologisms. Besides 'controlling someone', at least three other types of actions can be identified, namely 'to entertain somebody', 'to learn something' and 'to inform oneself/someone else'. To illustrate, consider the following corpus data:

(1) TO BE ENTERTAINED
Den begehrtesten Tisch im Restaurant haben wir [...] nicht gewählt – von dort aus kann man dem Koch bei der Pasta-Zubereitung ***buchstäblich*** *auf die Finger schauen.* (COSMAS II)
'We did not choose the most popular table in the restaurant [...] – from there you can **literally** keep an eye on the cook preparing the pasta'

(2) TO LEARN SOMETHING
[S]ie liessen sich nicht lumpen und schienen während der Vorbereitung Olivia Newton John und John Travolta, den beiden Stars aus «Grease», genau auf die Finger, ***beziehungsweise*** *auf die Füsse geschaut zu haben.* (COSMAS II)
'[T]hey did not splash out, and during the course of preparation they seemed to keep an eye on the fingers and the feet **respectively** of Olivia Newton John and John Travolta, the two stars of *Grease*'

(3) TO INFORM ONESELF/SOMEONE ELSE
Ist Frankreich anders?
Klaus Harpprecht schaut den Franzosen auf die Finger
*Endlich wieder ein Frankreich-Buch! Und erst noch ein aktuell-****informatives****, eines auch, das nicht bei den Clichés stehen bleibt – und ein Lesegenuss ist!* (COSMAS II)

9. Original in German: "E.4 PRÜFEN – KONTROLLIEREN – BEHERRSCHEN
jmdm. auf die Finger sehen/schauen/gucken (ugs.); jmdn. genau beaufsichtigen, kontrollieren; bei jmdm. aus Misstrauen genau darauf achten, was er tut" (Hessky and Ettinger 1997: 100).

'Is France different?
Klaus Harpprecht keeps an eye on Frenchmen
A new book about France, eventually! And an up-to-date and **informative** one, one that goes beyond the clichés – and one that is worth reading'

(4) TO CONTROL SOMEONE
Trotzdem soll es für den Bundesrat eine Signalwirkung sein, dass ihm vom ***wachsamen*** *Volk auf die Finger geschaut wird. Das Volk hat zum Glück immer noch das letzte Wort und* ***wird mit Bestimmtheit nicht zulassen,*** *dass unsere Freiheit, Unabhängigkeit und die Volksrechte durch einen EU-Beitritt verscherbelt werden.* (COSMAS II)
'Nevertheless, it ought to be a signal for the upper house of the German parliament that the people keep a **watchful** eye on it. Fortunately, the people have the final say and **will definitely not permit** that our freedom, independency and rights will be wasted by virtue of becoming a member of the EU'

The examples vary regarding their degree of idiomatization. In (1) the phraseologism is characterized by a low degree of idiomatization, indicated by the hedge *literally*. With the help of the adverb *respectively*, Example (2) alludes to a phraseological meaning, while in (3) and (4) a phraseological meaning clearly dominates.

To capture the different idiomatic meanings in these examples and to integrate them in the overall meaning of each phraseologism, we propose a two-step procedure. First, it is necessary to determine those meaning aspects that all usages have in common. In the case of *jm. auf die Finger schauen* these meaning aspects concern two syntactic arguments, namely an agentive and a dative, inherent in the scene evoked by the verb *to observe/to watch*. Secondly, the question "why is someone keeping an eye on somebody" (representing one frame slot) helps to determine those meaning aspects that cannot be captured by the syntactic arguments. Here, i.e. beyond the verb's valency structure, we find meaning variation: Depending on the context, the phraseologism *jm. auf die Finger schauen* could either mean 'to observe someone in order to control someone', 'to observe someone in order to inform oneself about something', 'to observe someone in order to learn something', or 'to observe someone in order to be entertained'.

From a frame semantic perspective one could say that the phraseologism *jm. auf die Finger schauen* behaves like a lexeme, and as such it evokes a frame with many slots. Although the phraseologism already assigns values to two slots, the value for another semantically crucial slot ("why does someone keep an eye on somebody?") is either provided by cotext data or needs to be inferred by the recipient. For this slot four default values are at hand. They cover all possible meanings, i.e. the meaning potential of the phraseologism.

But where do these default values come from? How do they emerge? It is worth noticing that the analyzed phraseologism *jm. auf die Finger schauen* is semantically linked to numerous other phraseologisms and phrases. The phraseologism is part of a network in that the source domain 'watching/observing somebody' supplies semantic information for many phraseologisms and phrases, such as *jn./etw. im Auge behalten* ['to keep somebody/something in mind'], *jm. bei etwas über die Schulter sehen* ['to look on something'], *sich etw. von jm. abgucken* ['to learn something from somebody'], *einen Einblick in etw. bekommen* ['to gain an insight into something'] and *nicht aus den Augen lassen* ['to not let somebody out of one's sight']. The possible meanings of these phraseologisms and phrases are instances of the semantic schema evoked by the verb 'to observe somebody' that, in turn, is an instance of the higher-level schema 'to see somebody'. In other words, 'to observe someone' as well as 'to see someone' are linked to the phraseologisms and phrases respectively by hyponymic relations. For this very reason the phraseologisms inherit two basic semantic properties from higher-level schemas evoked by the verbs *to observe* and *to see*: on the one hand the prevailing epistemological aspect motivated by the conceptual metaphor KNOWING IS SEEING (cf. Sweetser 1990, Lakoff and Johnson 1980), on the other hand the highly salient slot "for what purpose is someone keeping an eye on somebody?" that derives from the goal-oriented activity of observing. The latter addresses the relation of finality: someone observes/sees somebody or something *in order to* do something (e.g. to find something out). The relevant German interrogative pronoun is *wozu* ['what for'].

5. Embodied meaning: The meaning potential of somatic constituents

Having determined the phraseological meanings of *jm. auf die Finger schauen*, we are now in the position to analyze the semantic impact of the constituents on the phraseological meanings. To what degree does the somatic constituent contribute to the meanings of the phraseologism? More precisely, if the noun *Finger* in *jm. auf die Finger schauen* does not denote the body part finger, what does it denote instead? Answering this question means looking for and finding the semantic extensions (from the literal 'finger' sense) that motivate – via conceptual metaphor or metonymy – the occurrence of a particular body part term in a somatism.

The two-step procedure described above is not only a suitable device for analyzing phraseological meaning; it may also be applied to investigate the meaning of the constituents. First, it is striking that the conventional meaning 'to observe' is closely related to the constituent *schauen* ['looking at']. As a result, the conventional meaning of *schauen* – notwithstanding its metonymical usages – is reflected in the four different meanings of the phraseologisms analyzed in Section 4.2. Furthermore, in the phraseologism *jm. auf die Finger schauen*, the slot for the dative object *jemandem* ['someone'] is equivalent to the direct object demanded by the verb *to observe*. But where does the locative *auf die Finger* come from? This prepositional phrase functions as an argument of an internal valency slot. It functionally resembles the prepositional phrase *bei etwas* in *jn. bei etwas beobachten* ['to observe someone doing something']. The semantic impact of *Finger* on the meaning of the phraseologism can thus be specified by the question: what is someone observing?[10] An answer to this question elucidates the degree to which the body part term *Finger* semantically contributes to the overall meanings of the phraseologism.

To illustrate this, let us have a closer look at some corpus data, particularly at instance (4) presented in the last section. Here, the phraseologism *jm. auf die Finger schauen* is used in the sense of 'to control someone'. For convenience, we replicate the relevant part of (4):

(4) Trotzdem soll es für den Bundesrat eine Signalwirkung sein, dass ihm vom **wachsamen** Volk auf die Finger geschaut wird.
'Nevertheless, it ought to be a signal for the upper house of the German parliament that the people keep a **watchful** eye on it'

In order to understand what it is that is in control of the people, one needs to know what the noun phrase *die Finger* ['the fingers'] denotes. Needless to say that in (4) the noun phrase *die Finger* metonymically refers to the activities of the upper house of the German parliament. And it is also well known that the people are in control of these activities. To put it differently, in the given context, *schauen* evokes a frame with many slots. The most salient slot is 'what is someone observing?'[11] To this slot the value 'activities of the upper house of the German parliament' is assigned. Considering our corpus data, it turns out that all instances are similar in this respect: They are all about observing someone who is involved in an activity, either, as in (1), because it is her or his duty or profession to do so, or, as in (2), because someone is expected to do something, or, as in (3), because someone is used to doing something, here, since people living in France prefer a particular lifestyle. Hence, the noun phrase *die Finger* as a constituent of *jm. auf die Finger*

10. Since the argument roles triggered by the German verb *beobachten* differ from its English equivalent *to observe*, the corresponding interrogative pronoun differs too. For the German verb *beobachten* the relevant pronoun is *wobei* [lit. 'whereby'].

11. The German equivalent to this question is: "Wobei wird jemandem auf die Finger geschaut?"

schauen points to an activity (of the person whose fingers are observed) that is specified by the context in which the noun phrase is used.

The usage of *Finger* (and not of expressions denoting activities of fingers) is an instance of the conceptual metonymy FINGER FOR ACTIVITY (CONDUCTED BY THE USE OF FINGERS). It is a metonymy (and not a metaphor) since the source domain 'finger' and the target domain 'activity' are not distinct from one another. They are rather systematically correlated with each other. More precisely, they are contiguous in such a way that fingers are body parts with which numerous activities are carried out. In the phraseologisms analyzed the term *Finger* gives access to the activity carried out by fingers. In addition to this conceptual metonymy, a metaphorical mapping takes place if the concept coded by *Finger* does not imply a bodily action involving a finger (or fingers) in some respect. This is, for instance, the case in (3) and (4). Here *Finger* does not denote a bodily action but more abstract activities such as fulfilling a duty, keeping a promise, etc. In these cases both metonymical and metaphorical mappings are realized. (3) and (4) are thus "metaphtonymies" in the sense of Goossens (1995).

There is some evidence for the hypothesis that the occurrence of *Finger* is systematically motivated by the meaning of the somatism of which *Finger* forms an integral part. First, all usages of *jm. auf die Finger schauen* that our data set contains are instances of the conceptual metonymy FINGER FOR ACTIVITY. This finding gives rise to the assumption that metaphorical or metonymical mappings to other knowledge domains besides 'activities' are not employed, which may be due to the entrenched conceptual correlation between fingers and activities of fingers. Secondly, it is striking that knowledge concerning functional and motoric aspects of fingers – that is, knowledge involving possible activities and activities carried out with the help of fingers – is essential for the meaning of the somatisms. The results of the analysis confirm the hypothesis that the conceptual metonymy FINGER FOR ACTIVITY is also at work in many, if not all finger somatisms. In all instances analyzed so far the constituent *Finger* metonymically refers to activities carried out with the help of fingers.

We think that the conceptual metonymy FINGER FOR ACTIVITY (and supposedly any conceptual metonymy associated with a body part term in somatisms) is so productive because our bodily experience provides essential information for the conceptualization of other related phenomena.[12] Especially proprioceptive knowledge concerning functions as well as body perceptions of body parts are

12. We hypothesize thus that embodied experience is a crucial aspect of productivity in the field of somatisms. In investigating other phenomena, however, other aspects of productivity may be more prominent; see e.g. Backus and Mos, this volume.

important resources that motivate the meaning of somatisms.[13] In this context it is interesting to consider neuroscientific evidence for the essential role of fingers in daily life. A considerable part of the human primary somatosensoric cortex, which neuronally "represents" body parts, is responsible for the body part finger (Penfield and Rasmussen 1950, Enfield et al. 2006: 141). The fact that this neuronal area is much larger and denser than, for example, the area that "represents" a person's arms or back can be explained by acknowledging that tactility is closely related to (activities of) fingers. Moreover, with respect to motoric functions, fingers are more important than other body parts due to their fine motoric controllability.[14] With the help of fingers we can not only touch something, we can also use our fingers as tools and multifunctional communication devices. A pointing finger, for example, may help to identify an object or to draw somebody's attention to something or somebody (Cienki and Müller 2008). Besides pointing, many other deictic and iconic gestures help to establish joint attention. Think of a wagging or warning finger or an outstretched middle finger (as a gesture of insult). Given this multifunctionality of fingers, it is not surprising that most of such gestures have idiomatic equivalents (e.g. 'to wag one's finger at somebody', 'to point a finger at something').

6. Degrees of (de-) compositionality

Against the background of the empirical findings presented above, the question arises whether phraseologisms are decomposable. Given that the somatisms analyzed above (and supposedly phraseologisms in general) have the status of lexemes at least with regard to their mental accessibility, to what extent is the dichotomy compositionality/non-compositionality justifiable? So far, drawing on our empirical findings, we have tacitly assumed degrees of compositionality. However, we have not elaborated on this supposition nor have we generally called the dichotomy into question.

In current research the issue of (non-)compositionality of phraseologisms remains controversial. On the one hand psychologists like Cacciari and Tabossi (1988) argue in favor of radical compositionality. They hold the view that

13. See the general discussion in Enfield et al. (2006), Gibbs (2006) and also the helpful summarizing remarks on the relationship between body and language in Hampe (2005) and Ziemke and Frank (2007).

14. Elbert et al. (1995) have experimentally shown that the cortex area that "represents" the index finger enlarges similarly when someone learns to play the guitar and when someone learns Braille. This is due to the required fine motoric skills which are similar in both cases. In other words, the brain constantly adapts to recurring experiences and cognitive requirements.

constituents of phraseologisms are processed word-by-word until a constituent cannot be interpreted literally anymore. These words that resist literal interpretations are so-called "idiomatic keys". They trigger idiomatic readings. Cacciari and Tabossi's empirical findings provide evidence for the hypothesis that single constituents, i.e. idiomatic keys (in the case of somatisms, particularly body part terms), strongly motivate the emergence of phraseological meaning. Cacciari and Tabossi (1988) showed experimentally that as soon as nominal idiomatic keys are processed, literal meaning turns into idiomatic meaning. Recently, Rabanus et al. (2008) confirmed this finding for verbal idiomatic keys. Additional evidence for an idiomatic key model comes from Berghoff's (2005) neurolinguistic study of the processing of figurative language.

Along similar lines, though less radically, the psycholinguist Gibbs and his colleagues maintain that many phraseologisms may well be decomposed into different constituents. They postulate, for instance, that *pop the question* is literally anomalous, but that it is nevertheless reasonable to argue that this phraseologism is semantically decomposable (Gibbs 2007b: 706) since the constituent *pop* is used to refer to the act of uttering something while the constituent *question* gives access to the meaning 'marriage proposal' (cf. also Gibbs 1990: 422). In this view, compositionality is considered to be a gradual phenomenon. It is thus misleading to ask whether a phraseologism is decomposable or not. Compositionality is rather, as Gibbs (2007b: 706) emphasizes, a matter of entrenchment and, hence, a matter of degree:

> The analyzability of an idiom is really a matter of degree depending on the salience of its individual parts. For instance, many speakers view the phrase *fall off the wagon* as being less decomposable than *pop the question* because the meaning that *fall* contributes to *fall off the wagon* is not as salient as the meaning that *pop* contributes to *pop the question*.

Following this view, one could divide all phraseologisms into different subclasses depending on their degree of analyzability and decomposability.[15]

If compositionality is a gradual phenomenon, it should be possible to measure degrees of compositionality. Drawing on the computational approach of Berry-Rogghe (1974), Wulff (2008: 35–66) developed a persuasive, quantitatively oriented method for determining degrees of compositionality on the basis of large text corpora. She argues that the collocations of phraseological constituents have a

15. Dobrovol'skij makes also use of the term *analyzability/segmentability* (in German: 'Teilbarkeit') in this context. Using the terms *analyzability* and *decomposability* interchangeably, he notes that non-composable and non-analyzable phrases, respectively, equate with those idioms that cannot be segmented into smaller parts. In addition, Dobrovol'skij emphasizes that composable (i.e. analyzable) phrases equate with those idioms that can well be segmented into smaller parts (Dobrovol'skij 1997: 23, cf. also Dobrovol'skij 1982: 56, 1997: 91–95, 2000: 116.

considerable impact on the overall meaning(s) of a phraseologism. Following this assumption, she proposes a measurement process that basically encompasses two steps: First, the most frequent collocations of phraseological constituents are determined; second, these collocations are correlated with the collocations of the entire phraseologism. Broadly speaking, one could say the higher the number of collocations both have in common, the higher the degree of compositionality.

This method is particularly promising since it allows for measuring the degree of compositionality of a phraseologism as well as the semantic impact of each constituent:

> [T]he contribution made by each component word is not only weighted in terms of how much of *the construction's meaning* is accounted for by taking the component word into account, but also how much *of itself* each component word brings in. For instance, in *take the plunge*, *plunge* brings in nearly all of its semantics (in terms of the significant collocates it shares with the construction), whereas *take* only contributes a fraction of its meaning potential (*take* has many other significant collocates that are not associated with the construction *take the plunge* in particular) (Wulff 2008: 65).

However, as Wulff (2008: 65) critically remarks, the method does not always yield plausible findings. In measuring the degree of compositionality of verb-particle constructions, one result is that *give up* obtains the highest ranking of all. Even though such a finding "does not make any sense whatsoever" (Wulff 2008: 61), the method is still a suitable device to quantitatively determine the semantic impact of single constituents on the overall meanings of a phraseologism. However, this quantitative method cannot help to determine *in which way* each constituent contributes to phraseological meanings.

On the other hand, and in contrast to Wulff and Gibbs and his colleagues, Swinney and Cutler (1979) hypothesize that idiomatic phraseologisms should be generally considered as lexeme-like units. In the view of the so-called lexicalization hypothesis (or lexical representation hypothesis) it is thus unnecessary to derive the meaning of phraseologisms from single constituents. Idioms have therefore the status of long words stored in the mental lexicon.

Overall, it is important to note that many approaches tacitly assume that *either* compositionality *or* non-compositionality is a property of linguistic units in such a way that it systematically motivates the emergence of (phraseological) meanings. However, against the background of our empirical findings, we think that this view implies some misleading assumptions. First and foremost it implies that linguistic meaning necessarily emerges, to some extent, because of compositional *or* non-compositional processes. In other words, meaning is supposed to be ultimately based on compositionality *or* non-compositionality. This assumption ignores the possibility that meanings of phraseologisms may well be both non-compositional and motivated by single constituents. We are convinced that both factors need to be taken into account. Gibbs and his colleagues, Langlotz (2006), Taylor (2002), and Wulff (2008) seem to be the few to acknowledge this point.

Our analysis has shown that there is indeed little empirical evidence for the assumption that phraseological meanings can be fully reduced to the literal meanings of their constituents. There is thus converging evidence on the view held by Kövecses and Szabó (1996). Nevertheless, single constituents may crucially influence and motivate the emergence of phraseological meaning. Depending on the context, the phraseologism *jm. auf die Finger schauen*, for example, means either 'to observe someone in order to control someone', 'to observe someone in order to learn something', 'to observe someone in order to inform oneself about something', or 'to observe someone in order to be entertained'. Following the thesis of compositionality, *schauen* ['to look at'] but not necessarily *auf die Finger* ['at the fingers'] would be separately analyzable. Still, such a semantic decomposition would not capture the essential semantic property of control.[16] Considering the results of our analysis, it is evident though that the constituent *Finger* has a strong semantic impact: It is this constituent that gives access to the target domain of the metonymy FINGER FOR ACTIVITY. Table 2 summarizes the results of our analysis.

Table 2. Compositionality and embodied meaning of *jm. auf die Finger schauen*

	jm. auf die Finger schauen ['to keep an eye on s.b.]				
	meanings of the phraseologism				meaning of *Finger*
conventional meaning	to observe/watch s.o./sth				[finger frame]
slots	For what purpose (is s.o. observing/watching s.o.)?				What (is s.o. observing)?
	LEARNING	INFORMING	CONTROLLING	ENTERTAINING	
conceptual shift	['to observe s.o. in order to learn s.th.']	['to observe s.o. in order to inform oneself about s.th.']	['to observe s.o. in order to control s.o.']	['to observe s.o. in order to be entertained']	ACTIVITY
construal process	meaning of the phraseologism + metonymical shift of *Finger* (+ metaphorical shift of *Finger*)				conceptual metonymy

16. In this respect the example 'auf die Finger schauen' differs from Gibb's example 'pop the question'.

From the perspective of frame semantics, one could say that the lexical unit *Finger* evokes a frame with many slots. To some slots default values are already assigned. When recognizing the word *Finger*, we instantly activate knowledge about possible functions and sensomotoric capabilities of fingers. The meaning of *Finger* is embodied in that we have proprioceptive access to such knowledge, including knowledge about the activities that fingers are involved in. It is this tacit knowledge that substantially contributes to the meanings of somatisms containing *Finger* as a constituent. Hence, following Cacciari and Tabossi (1988), *Finger* serves indeed as an idiomatic key. Despite this convergence of evidence, however, it is reasonable to assume that meanings of phraseologisms (as complex units) are partially autonomous as well. Accepting the view that there are degrees of compositionality allows us to argue that both the idiomatic key word *Finger* and the whole phraseologism (as a quasi-lexeme) in which the idiomatic key is embedded evoke a frame. Both elements contribute to the phraseological meaning. One only need keep in mind that the key element *Finger* and its metonymical interpretation are so heavily entrenched that the conceptual metonymy FINGER FOR ACTIVITY is no longer transparent.

7. Conclusions

In this chapter, we have presented a method for analyzing phraseologisms on the basis of corpus data with the help of cognitive tools and mechanisms, such as semantic frames and conceptual metonymies. Additionally, we have discussed and incorporated research results from experimental studies in psycholinguistics and neurolinguistics in the field of phraseologisms, resulting in a more comprehensive theory of somatisms. Hence, the converging evidence presented here is an instance of "methodological pluralism" (Steen, this volume), that is, evidence relating to the same linguistic phenomenon by employing different methods.

Focusing particularly on somatisms containing *Finger* as a constituent, our case study presented investigated in detail the somatism *jm. auf die Finger schauen* and its constituent *Finger*. The somatism turned out to be polysemous or objects of contextual modulations. In order to capture its different idiomatic meanings we proposed a two-step procedure that could be applied to phraseologisms in general. First, prototypical meaning aspects that all usages share are determined. In the case of *jm. auf die Finger schauen* these meaning aspects concern two argument roles inherent in the scene evoked by the verb. The second step is to elucidate meaning variation. In general, one could say that polysemy and contextual modulation concern a particular slot of the frame evoked by the phraseologism. Assigning different default values to this slot gives rise to various meanings of the phraseologism in question. In the case of *jm. auf die Finger schauen*, for example, four default values come to light. Each of them addresses a particular knowledge domain, namely 'learning', 'informing', 'controlling', and 'entertaining' (cf. Table 2). The slot "for what purpose (is someone observing/watching someone)" is thus specified variably, which gives rise to meaning variation.

Also on the basis of corpus data, we sought converging evidence for the hypothesis that meanings of body-part terms in somatisms are systematically motivated by conceptual metaphors or metonymies. The empirical results of our case study confirm the finding of Kövecses and Szabó (1996: 330) that cognitive mechanisms (such as metaphor and metonymy) help establish the meaning of a phraseologically bound body-part term. In all instances of e.g. *jm. auf die Finger schauen* the body part term *Finger* metonymically refers to some kind of activity. Our study has shown that semantic analyses – even and particularly if they are intuitively plausible – need to be reevaluated by means of empirical methods on the basis of real-world data.

References

A. Dictionaries of German idioms

no author. 2007. *Lexikon der Redensarten. Bedeutung und Herkunft von A–Z.* Erftstadt: Area.

Duden ed. 2008. *Redewendungen. Wörterbuch der deutschen Idiomatik.* Third Edition. Mannheim et al.: Dudenverlag.

Friederich, W. 1976. *Moderne deutsche Idiomatik. Alphabetisches Wörterbuch mit Definitionen und Beispielen.* Third Edition. Ismaning: Hueber.

Hessky, R. & Ettinger, S. 1997. *Deutsche Redewendungen. Ein Wörter- und Übungsbuch für Fortgeschrittene.* Tübingen: Narr.

Krüger-Lorenzen, K. 2001. *Deutsche Redensarten und was dahinter steckt.* Third Edition. München: Heyne.

Müller, K., ed. 2005. *Lexikon der Redensarten. Herkunft und Bedeutung deutscher Redewendungen.* München: Bassermann.

Röhrich, L. 1991/94. *Lexikon der sprichwörtlichen Redensarten.* Fifth Edition. Freiburg, Basel, & Wien: Herder.

Schemann, H. 1993. *Deutsche Idiomatik. Die deutschen Redewendungen im Kontext.* Stuttgart and Dresden: Klett.

Zeit ed. 2005. *Zitate und Redewendungen. Redaktionsleitung Matthias Wermke.* Mannheim: Bibliographisches Institut.

B. Other publications

Allwood, J. 2003. Meaning potentials and contexts: some consequences for the analysis of variation in meaning. In H. Cuyckens, R. Dirven, & J. R. Taylor, eds., *Cognitive Approaches to Lexical Semantics,* 29–45. Berlin & New York: de Gruyter.

Berghoff, C. 2005. *Neuronale Kooperationsprozesse während der Verarbeitung figurativer Sprache. Eine EEG-Kohärenzanalyse.* Dissertation. University of Bielefeld. Retrieved on 12 September 2009 from http://deposit.ddb.de/cgi-bin/dokserv?idn=978742419&dok_var=d1&dok_ext=pdf&filename=978742419.pdf.

Berry-Rogghe, G. L. M. 1974. Automatic identification of phrasal verbs. In J. L. Mitchell, ed., *Computers in the Humanities,* 16–26. Edingburgh: Edinburgh University Press.

Boas, H. C. 2008. Resolving form-meaning discrepancies in Construction Grammar. In J. Leino, ed., *Constructional Reorganization,* 11–36. Amsterdam & Philadelphia: Benjamins.

Burger, H. 2007. *Phraseologie. Eine Einführung am Beispiel des Deutschen.* Third Edition. Berlin: Erich Schmidt.

Burger, H., A. Buhofer, & A. Sialm. 1982. *Handbuch der Phraseologie.* Berlin & New York: de Gruyter.

Cacciari, C. & P. Tabossi. 1988. The comprehension of idioms. *Journal of Memory and Language* 27: 668–683.

Cienki, A. & C. Müller. 2008. Metaphor, gesture, and thought. In R. W. Gibbs, ed., *The Cambridge Handbook of Metaphor and Thought,* 483–501. Cambridge: Cambridge University Press.

Croft, W. & D. A. Cruse. 2004. *Cognitive Linguistics.* Cambridge: Cambridge University Press.

Dobrovol'skij, D. 1982. Zum Problem der phraseologisch gebundenen Bedeutung. *Beiträge zur Erforschung der deutschen Sprache* 2: 52–67.

Dobrovol'skij, D. 1997. *Idiome im mentalen Lexikon. Ziele und Methoden der kognitivbasierten Phraseologieforschung.* Trier: Wissenschaftlicher Verlag.

Dobrovol'skij, D. 2000. Ist die Semantik von Idiomen nichtkompositionell? In S. Beckmann, P. König, & G. Wolf, eds., *Sprachspiel und Bedeutung. Festschrift für Franz Hundsnurscher zum 65. Geburtstag,* 113–124. Tübingen: Niemeyer.

Elbert, T., C. Pantev, C. Wienbruch, B. Rockstroh, & E. Taub. 1995. Increased cortical representation of the fingers of the left hand in string players. *Science* 270: 305–307.

Enfield, N. J., A. Majid, & M. van Staden. 2006. Cross-linguistic categorisation of the body: Introduction. *Language Sciences* 28: 137–147.

Fillmore, C. J. 1971. Types of Lexical Information. In D. D. Steinberg & L. A. Jakobovits, eds., *Semantics: An Interdisciplinary Reader in Philosophy, Linguistics and Psychology,* 370–392. Cambridge: Cambridge University Press.

Fillmore, C. J. 1977. Scenes-and-frames semantics. In A. Zampolli, ed., *Linguistic Structures Processing* 5: 55–81. Amsterdam, New York, & Oxford: North Holland.

Fleischer, W. 1997 *Phraseologie der deutschen Gegenwartssprache.* Second Edition. Tübingen: Niemeyer.

Gibbs, R. W. 1990. Psycholinguistic studies on the on the conceptual basis of idiomaticity. *Discourse Processes* 9: 17–30.

Gibbs, R. W. 2006. *Embodiment and Cognitive Science.* Cambridge: Cambridge University Press.

Gibbs, R. W. 2007a. Why cognitive linguists should care more about empirical methods. In M. González-Márquez, I. Mittelberg, S. Coulson, & M. J. Spivey, eds., *Empirical Methods in Cognitive Linguistics,* 2–18. Amsterdam & Philadelphia: Benjamins.

Gibbs, R. W. 2007b. Idioms and formulaic language. In D. Geeraerts & H. Cuyckens, eds., *The Oxford Handbook of Cognitive Linguistics*, 697–725. Oxford: Oxford University Press.

Goldberg, A. 2006. *Constructions at Work: The Nature of Generalization in Language*. Oxford: Oxford University Press.

Goossens, L. 1995. Metaphtonymy: The interaction of metaphor and metonymy in figurative expressions for linguistic action. In L. Goossens, P. Pauwels, B. Rudzka-Ostyn, A. Simon-Vanderbergen, & J. Vanparys, eds., *By Word of Mouth: Metaphor, Metonymy and Linguistic Action in a Cognitive Perspective*, 159–174. Amsterdam & Philadelphia: Benjamins.

Hampe, B. 2005. Image schemas in Cognitive Linguistics: Introduction. In B. Hampe, ed., *From Perception to Meaning*, 1–12. Berlin: de Gruyter.

Heringer, H. J. 1999. *Das höchste der Gefühle. Empirische Studien zur distributiven Semantik*. Tübingen: Stauffenberg.

Kay, P. & C. J. Fillmore. 1999. Grammatical constructions and linguistic generalizations: the What's X Doing Y? construction. *Language* 75(1): 1–33.

Kövecses, Z. & P. Szabó. 1996. Idioms: A view from Cognitive Semantics. *Applied Linguistics* 17 (3): 326–355.

Lakoff, G. & M. Johnson. 1980. *Metaphors We Live By*. Chicago: The University of Chicago Press.

Langacker, R. W. 1991. *Concept, Image and Symbol: The Cognitive Basis of Grammar*. Berlin & New York: de Gruyter.

Langlotz, A. 2006. *Idiomatic Creativity: A Cognitive-linguistic Model of Idiom-representation and Idiom-variation in English*. Amsterdam & Philadelphia: Benjamins.

Minsky, M. 1975. A framework for representing knowledge. In P. H. Winston, ed., *The Psychology of Computer Vision*, 211–277. New York: McGraw-Hill.

Moon, R. 1998. *Fixed Expressions and Idioms in English: A Corpus-based Approach*. Oxford: Clarendon:

Müller, S. 2006. Phrasal or lexical constructions? *Language* 82 (4): 850–883.

Penfield, W. & T. Rasmussen. 1950. *The Cerebral Cortex of Man: A Clinical Study of Localization of Function*. New York: Maxmillian.

Piirainen, E. 2007. Phrasemes from a cultural semiotic perspective. In H. Burger, D. Dobrovol'ski, P. Kühn, & N. R. Norrik, eds., *Phraseologie. Ein internationales Handbuch der zeitgenössischen Forschung* 1: 208–219. Berlin & New York: de Gruyter.

Rabanus, S., E. Smolka, J. Streb, & F. Rösler. 2008. Die mentale Verarbeitung von Verben in idiomatischen Konstruktionen. *Zeitschrift für Germanistische Linguistik* 36: 27–47.

Schank, R. C. & R. P. Abelson. 1977. *Scripts, Plans, Goals and Understanding: An Inquiry into Human Knowledge Systems*. Hillsdale: Erlbaum.

Scherer, C. 2006. *Korpuslinguistik*. Heidelberg: Winter.

Steyer, K. 2002. Wenn der Schwanz mit dem Hund wedelt. Zum linguistischen Erklärungspotential der korpusbasierten Kookkurrenzanalyse. In U. Haß-Zumkehr, W. Kallmeyer, & G. Zifonun, eds., *Ansichten der deutschen Sprache. Festschrift für Gerhard Stickel zum 65. Geburtstag*, 215–236. Tübingen: Narr.

Sweetser, E. 1990. *From Etymology to Pragmatics: Metaphorical and Cultural Aspects of Semantic Structure*. Cambridge: Cambridge University Press.

Swinney, D. A. & A. Cutler. 1979. The access and processing of idiomatic expressions. *Journal of Verbal Learning and Verbal Behavior* 18: 523–534.

Talmy, L. 2007. Foreword. In M. González-Márquez, I. Mittelberg, S. Coulson, & M.J. Spivey, eds., *Empirical Methods in Cognitive Linguistics* XI-XXI. Amsterdam & Philadelphia: Benjamins.

Taylor, John R. 2002. *Cognitive Grammar*. Oxford & New York: Oxford University Press.

Verhagen, A. 2009. The conception of constructions as complex signs: Emergence of structure and reduction to usage. *Frames and Constructions* 1 (1): 119–152.

Wotjak, B. 1992. *Verbale Phraseolexeme in System und Text*. Tübingen: Niemeyer.

Wulff, S. 2008. *Rethinking Idiomaticity: A Usage-based Approach*. London & New York: Continuum.

Ziem, A. 2008. *Frames und sprachliches Wissen. Kognitive Aspekte der semantischen Kompetenz*. Berlin & New York: de Gruyter.

Ziemke, T., & R. M. Frank. 2007. Introduction: The body eclectic. In T. Ziemke, J. Zlatev, & R. M. Frank, eds., *Body, Language, and Mind* 1 *Embodiment*, 1–13. Berlin & New York: Mouton de Gruyter.

Word-formation patterns in a cross-linguistic perspective

Testing predictions for novel object naming in Hungarian and German*

Susanne R. Borgwaldt and Réka Benczes
University of Braunschweig and Eötvös Loránd University

Previous research has shown that novel objects that are merged from two identifiable parts predominantly elicit noun – noun compounds in Germanic languages. However, it is unclear whether Hungarian allows shape/appearance modifiers in noun – noun compounds. Using a novel object naming task we compare language-specific preferences for labels for: (i) novel hybrid objects composed of two identifiable parts (such as an animal that is half fox and half chicken, i.e. *chicken fox*), and (ii) novel objects having a salient shape (such as a box shaped like a banana, i.e. *banana box*). The results are explored regarding the degree of semantic influence on word-formation patterns and interpreted within a cognitive-linguistic framework.

Keywords: compounding, cross-linguistic patterns, experimental evidence, word-formation

1. Introduction

When we encounter novel concepts for which we lack existing words in our vocabulary, languages allow for different possibilities to create new labels for them. Novel objects, for example, can be described by phrases that draw on salient

---

* We wish to thank our two anonymous reviewers and Doris Schönefeld, the editor of this volume, for their very helpful and constructive remarks. Needless to say, all remaining errors or inadequacies are our own responsibility. The order of names reflects that the original idea (and the materials used in the experiment) were developed by the first author. S. Borgwaldt provided the psycholinguistic background and collected and analyzed the German data, while R. Benczes provided the cognitive linguistic framework and collected and analyzed the Hungarian data.

features or the presumed function (e.g. a box that has a banana-like shape can be called *box in the shape of a banana*). Novel hybrid objects, i.e. objects that are merged of two identifiable parts, might also elicit novel compounds, that is, concatenations of labels denoting the two object parts in languages that employ compounding as a means of word formation (e.g. an animal that is part fox and part chicken can be called *chicken fox*).

Compounding, the concatenation of two or more lexical items to form a new lexical item, whose idiosyncratic meaning is typically influenced by the meaning of its parts, is a very productive word-formation process, found across a variety of languages (Holm 2000; Klein and Perdue 1997).[1] Thus, productive compounding enriches a language's vocabulary by enabling language users to readily create and comprehend new compounds (which, later on, can undergo lexicalization, as in the case of *breakfast* or *butterfly*).

The production and comprehension of novel compounds has been researched from different perspectives, for example in experimental investigations targeting the development of child language. In experiments focusing on novel compound production, children are typically presented with a set of pictures of hybrid objects, such as a house in the shape of a pumpkin. First the experimenter refers to a couple of hybrid objects by using a novel compound as a name (i.e. *pumpkin house*), after a training session the child is then asked to name a new set of hybrid objects by herself. In order to assess children's comprehension abilities for novel compounds, the child is shown sets of hybrid object pictures and asked to pick out the right ones that are referred to by the experimenter with novel compound names.

So far, researchers in the field of child language acquisition have shown that in languages with productive compounding (e.g. among others, English, Swedish, and Hebrew) children start to produce and understand novel noun-noun compounds when they are about two years of age (Mellenius 1997; Berman and Clark 1989; Nicoladis 2003; Grela, Snyder and Hiramatsu 2005). Gottfried (1997a, 1997b) showed that English-speaking children as young as three years of age also start to produce and understand metaphorical compounds. That is they are able to coin and to comprehend novel compounds in which one constituent expresses resemblance to another object, as, for example, in *egg ball*, referring to an oval ball, or *zebra shells*, referring to shells with black and white stripes.

1. According to Bickerton (1990) and Jackendoff (1999), compounds exist in protolanguage, i.e. in the first stage of language that is re-emerging in pidgins and language breakdown, as well as in Klein and Perdues' *basic variety*. What this means is that language users who are not able to cope with a complex fully-fledged modern language are able to form and understand compounds composed of two constituents.

Whereas in Germanic languages the relations licensed between the compounds' constituents include shape and resemblance, e.g. *starfish* or *Zwiebelturm*, "onion dome", the issue is less clear for Hungarian. Hiramatsu, Snyder, Roeper, Storrs, and Saccoman (2000) claim that Hungarian does not allow nouns as shape/appearance modifiers in compounds. The authors state that in both languages shape or appearance will instead be expressed by an adjective that is derived from the noun. Thus, a chair in the shape of a hand could only be called a "hand-shaped chair" in Hungarian and not "hand chair", like in English or German.

As there is little corpus data available to support or refute this hypothesis, we chose to investigate word formation patterns in Hungarian and German experimentally. We used a hybrid picture-naming paradigm (explained in detail in Section 2), to test Hiramatsu et al.'s (2000) hypothesis and to compare preferences employed by Hungarian and German participants. Specifically, we are interested in the following: (i) to what degree will the hybrid novel objects elicit novel noun-noun compounds; (ii) whether and to what extent will the Hungarian production patterns deviate from German production patterns; and (iii) will the semantic categories that the hybrid object parts belong to influence word formation patterns?

2. Experiment

In order to compare word formation strategies used in German and Hungarian, we elicited labels for hybrid novel objects from native speakers of the two languages.

2.1 Participants

Two groups participated in the study: 20 native speakers of German and 20 native speakers of Hungarian. The German participants were students of German at the University of Braunschweig, Braunschweig, Germany (mean age 25.8 years, range 21–36 years; 4 male). The Hungarian participants were students of English at Eötvös Loránd University, Budapest, Hungary (mean age 23.4 years, range 21–26 years; 2 male). The participants of both groups participated in this study voluntarily.

2.2 Materials

We selected 70 digitally manipulated pictures from a database of merged objects, collected from two online sources (Freaking News, Worth1000) for which copyright had been obtained. These pictures belonged to either of two categories:

Sixty pictures depicted hybrid objects that were composed of two identifiable parts, e.g. an animal that was half chicken, half fox (i.e. *fox chicken*, or *chicken fox*), or a pair of shoes made out of eggplants (i.e. *eggplant shoes*). The parts of these hybrid objects belonged to three different semantic domains: animals, plants, and artifacts (i.e. inanimate objects). This allowed for the creating of a stimulus set that contained 10 pictures for each of the six possible combinations: animal-animal, animal-plant, animal-inanimate, plant-plant, plant-inanimate, and inanimate-inanimate. Another ten pictures showed objects (both animate and inanimate) whose shape was manipulated, e.g. a lake shaped like a heart (i.e. *heart lake*), or a cloud in the shape of a horse (i.e. *horse cloud*).[2]

Hybrid entities, which can be described as "half X and half Y", are sometimes expressed by so-called "coordinating compounds". One might expect that "hybridity" is more plausible for components of the same category, i.e. animal-animal or inanimate-inanimate combinations, whereas other combinations do not really trigger that concept. We discuss this issue in detail in Section 2.8.

The names for the object parts were monomorphemic in both German and Hungarian. The pictures were randomized, and displayed in two differently ordered files to attenuate possible list effects.

2.3 Procedure

Participants were tested individually. They saw the pictures on a computer monitor, preceded by the following written instructions: "You will be seeing things that do not exist in reality. How would they be called in German/Hungarian, if they existed?" in their respective languages.

The 70 pictures were preceded by three practice trials to familiarize the participants with the task. Participants studied the pictures at their own pace, named each picture, and the experimenter recorded the first response they produced for each picture. Participants were not given any feedback during the experiment; if they asked the experimenter for further explanations, the experimenter merely repeated the initial instructions, in order not to influence the participants. The task took approximately 10 to 15 minutes.

2.4 Results

The pictures elicited labels with the following morphological structure.

2. For examples of the pictures used and a table with all stimuli and the semantic domains their parts belong to, see the Appendices

Table 1. Morphological structure of elicited labels

Labels (N = 1400)	German	Hungarian
[N N] compounds (2 objects)	1284 (92%)	841 (60%)
Metonymic [N N] (1 object and salient features/parts of 2nd object)[3]	53	21
[Adj N] compounds	2 (<1%)	389 (28%)
Metonymic [Adj N] (1 object and salient features or parts of 2nd object)[4]	2	139
Blends	75 (5%)	75 (5%)
Other	39 (3%)	95 (7%)
Descriptive phrases	12	26
N (only 1 object mentioned)	25	69
[V N]	2	0

A chi-square analysis confirmed that there were significant differences in the morphological structure of elicited labels between the two languages groups: $\chi^2(3) = 499$, $p < 0.0001$.

German participants showed an overwhelming preference for noun-noun compounding, whereas the Hungarian participants favored noun-noun compounds to a lesser degree. The Hungarian participants also produced adjective-noun compounds quite frequently, in contrast to the German participants. In the next sections we first separately analyze the German and the Hungarian data and then discuss and summarize the observed differences and similarities between the languages.

2.5 German data

2.5.1 *Noun-noun compounds*

Noun-noun compounds (with 92%) represent by far the majority of the German responses. This is in line with the dominance of this means of word formation

3. The rest of the compounds in the [N N] group were non-metonymical concatenations of the two objects visible in the images.

4. The rest of the compounds in the [Adj N] group were concatenations of a non-metonymical adjectival modifier and a noun, based on the two objects visible in the images. For a discussion, see Section 2.6.2.

often observed in German (e.g. Donalies 2004; Neef 2009; Olsen 1986).[5] Roughly 4% of the noun-noun compounds contained a metonymic component. In most of the cases the metonymy was expressed by the modifier, such as *Musikkuh*, "music cow" for 'accordion cow', a relationship, which, in the cognitive linguistic literature, is considered to be a manifestation of the PRODUCT FOR PRODUCER conceptual metonymy[6] (music being produced by the accordion); *Stachelfrosch*, "thorn frog" for 'cactus frog', a manifestation of the DEFINING PROPERTY FOR CATEGORY conceptual metonymy (the thorn as a defining property of cacti standing for the category itself); *Friedenswaffe*, "peace weapon" for 'feather sword', a manifestation of the EFFECT FOR CAUSE conceptual metonymy (a sword made out of feather can only result in peace); or *Liebessee*, "love lake" for 'heart lake', a manifestation of the EMOTION FOR THE SEAT OF EMOTION conceptual metonymy (the heart being viewed as the seat of the emotion of love).

When naming novel hybrid objects that contained an animal part, participants quite often referred to the depicted body parts of the animals, instead of the whole animal, as in *Affenkopfvioline* ("ape head violin") for 'ape violin', or *Giraffenhalsstrauß* ("giraffe neck ostrich") for 'giraffe ostrich'. Referring to a part of the whole instead of the whole can also be interpreted as a metonymical process; this relationship can be considered as the manifestation of the PART FOR WHOLE metonymy. On the other hand, participants could have also chosen this construction to accurately describe the salient feature of the hybrid novel object i.e. 'a violin with an ape head' or 'an ostrich with the neck of a giraffe', without resorting to conceptual metonymy.

2.5.2 *Adjective-noun compounds*

German participants produced only two adjective-noun compounds; both can be considered as being based upon a metonymical relationship: *Hotbanana* ("hot banana") for a 'pepper banana' hybrid, and *Sauerkiwi* ("sour kiwi") for a 'lemon

5. While the high percentage of noun-noun compounding is not surprising *per se* and in line with a study with German participants by Neef and Borgwaldt (in revision) that yielded similar percentages these results support the ecological validity of the child acquisition studies reported above, and studies with aphasic patients (Borgwaldt and Bose 2008), in which participants had to name the objects under constrained naming conditions as noun-noun compounds.

6. If metaphor and metonymy are part of our everyday thought processes, as Lakoff and Johnson (1980), for instance, claim to be the case, then it naturally follows that the compounds themselves that we form can also be of a metaphorical or metonymical nature. These processes can affect either or both of the constituents, or the semantic link between them (for a full discussion, see Benczes 2006).

We understand conceptual metonymy as a cognitive process in which one conceptual entity, the vehicle, provides mental access to another conceptual entity, the target, within the same frame or domain (for a discussion, see Kövecses and Radden 1998; Kövecses 2006). The types of conceptual metonymies mentioned in the chapter come from Kövecses and Radden (1998).

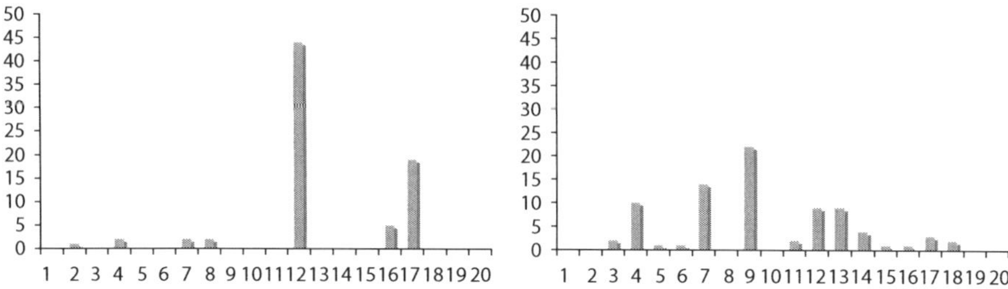

Figure 1. Number of blends elicited by German (left) and Hungarian (right) subjects. The *y* axis shows the number of blends per participant

kiwi' hybrid. These novel compounds can be regarded as manifestations of the DEFINING PROPERTY FOR CATEGORY conceptual metonymy (both 'hot' and 'sour' being a defining property of the category of peppers and lemons, respectively).

2.5.3 *Blends*

For German, only a very small number of blends was produced: 5%. This result is by no means surprising: as Kemmer (2003) notes, German still prefers compounding as the prime method of creating new words, which means that lexical blends are still rather rare in this language. As can be seen in Figure 1, the blends that were elicited from the German participants came predominantly from two participants (thus the production of blends can be considered as a reflection of individual preference or strategy).

2.6 Hungarian data

2.6.1 *Noun-noun compounds*

Table 1 shows that noun-noun [N N] compounds make up the vast majority of the Hungarian answers, covering 60% of the total responses. The large proportion of [N N] answers is not particularly surprising, as this type of word formation pattern is extremely productive in Hungarian and allows for a large variety of semantic relationships between the two constituents that participate in the compound (Kiefer 1998: 272). (The differences between the German and the Hungarian results are discussed in Section 2.7 in detail.)

With regard to the role of metonymy, only 2.5% of the [N N] answers were based on a metonymical modifying constituent. Examples include *nap virág* (literally, "sun flower", for 'light flower'), which can be considered as a manifestation of the PRODUCER FOR PRODUCT conceptual metonymy (the sun stands for the light that it gives); and, analogous to the German example, *tövis béka* (literally, "thorn frog", for 'cactus frog'), a representation of the DEFINING PROPERTY FOR CATEGORY conceptual metonymy.

2.6.2 *Adjective-noun compounds*

The large number of adjective-noun compounds in the Hungarian data also conforms to Hungarian word formation rules. Typically, a compound with a nominal head attracts another noun or an adjective as its modifying constituent (Kiefer 1998: 273). However, what is rather intriguing in the case of the adjectival answers is that here, as compared to the noun-noun compounds, we have a definite head constituent (the second, nominal element) that is modified by the adjective. Therefore, in these cases, the participants were perhaps more certain which entity in the hybrid image to choose as the semantic head. Altogether, adjective-noun compounds made up 28% of the Hungarian data (see Table 1), which is considerably different from the German data, where such constructions were produced only two times (less than 1%). This preponderance in the Hungarian answers can be attributed to the wide range of compound forming patterns in Hungarian (A. Jászó 1995; Kiefer 1998). In compounds where the first constituent describes, or qualifies the second constituent, Hungarian can have both an adjectival and a nominal modifier (the head of the compound is in most cases a noun). The answers that we have elicited from the subjects conform to these general rules of Hungarian word formation, irrespective of the semantic category of the entities.

The Hungarian data had a much larger proportion of metonymical compounds: 36% of the adjective-noun constructions were based on a metonymical modifying constituent.[7] In such cases typically a salient, defining property of one of the entities was used to stand for the entity as a whole (but see also Section 3.5 for more creative instantiations of metonymical usage). In other words, the DEFINING PROPERTY FOR CATEGORY conceptual metonymy can perhaps be claimed to be detected here, as in the case of *kinyújtható bika* ("extendable bull" for 'accordion bull') or *repülő ananász* ("flying pineapple" for 'pineapple birds'). According to Kövecses and Radden (1998), if categories are defined by a set of properties, then these properties are a part of the category. Categories can stand for one of their defining or salient properties, or vice versa: a defining or salient property may evoke the category itself. In both of the cited examples, one salient feature of the category – the extendibility of the accordion and the ability to fly – is used to stand for the category of accordion and bird, respectively. Sometimes the defining property that was selected as the metonymical vehicle to stand for the target (that is, the category as a whole) was a perception that was stimulated

7. As opposed to non-metonymical answers, where the modifying element literally described the way the entity in the image was altered. For example, zsiráf fejű strucc ("giraffe-headed ostrich" for 'ostrich giraffe').

by the image.[8] Accordingly, subjects produced *vicces bika* ("humorous bull" for 'accordion bull'), *félelmetes autó* ("frightening car" for 'lobster car'), *vicces bukósisak* ("funny helmet" for 'car helmet') among others. The relatively large proportion of metonymical adjective-noun constructions points to the ubiquity of conceptual metonymy: metonymy is a short-hand process by which we are able to mentally access a conceptually less salient entity via a more salient one, within the same semantic frame, domain or category. As Lakoff and Johnson (1980: 37) also noted, metonymy is "part of the ordinary, everyday way we think and act as well as talk".

Why did the Hungarian participants, however, select metonymical adjectival elements? The answer to this question is related to cognitive salience. As it has been emphasized above, metonymy is an integral part of our thought (and therefore, of our language), which is able to reconcile two conflicting factors: the need to be accurate and our natural inclination to think and talk about those entities that have the greatest communicative salience for us (Langacker 1993: 30). Langacker (ibid.; see also Kövecses and Radden 1998) explains that the main principles that govern our selection of an entity as being salient include both perception and function. The color, form, material, function and so forth of an entity are regarded as cognitively salient and therefore, in general, important to us, as these are exactly those features that we interact with (via vision, or taste, or touch, etc.). These salient features can often be expressed in the form of modifiers, that is, adjectives; as Taylor (2002: 450) points out, in an adjective-noun combination, the adjective "may evoke various kinds of relations and processes [...] putting an adjective alongside a noun can trigger a complex interaction between the semantic structures of the two items". Therefore, the selection of a metonymical property (such as *flying* to stand for the category of 'bird', as in the case of the above-cited example) can be considered as a highly natural process, which is "boosted" further by the very productive pattern of adjective-noun compounds in Hungarian.

2.6.3 *Blends*

Blends amounted to 5% of the Hungarian answers, a result that is definitely worthy of attention. Generally, Hungarian morphology relegates blending as a word formation process as a rare, atypical phenomenon, and probably, for this reason, some morphology texts do not even mention it (e.g. Kiefer 1998), or consider it as a feature of poetic language (e.g. Ladányi 2007), which is unusual in everyday

8. Kövecses and Radden (1998: 56) call this type of metonymy as perception for thing perceived, and consider it as an example for the part-and-part type: one entity within the same semantic domain is related to another part of the same domain (as opposed to part-and-whole metonymies, where the part can stand for the whole and vice versa). Here, however, it is reasonable to consider the perception felt by the participant to stand for the category (i.e., the whole).

speech. It is noteworthy that Hungarian linguistic terminology also uses the Latin form *contaminatio* for this process, which does carry a negative undertone within it – implying that blending somehow "corrupts" the meanings of the input (source) lexemes by creating a lexical blend of both. Yet out of our 20 Hungarian subjects, 15 produced lexical blends, as can be seen in Figure 1, which seems to indicate that this word formation process is considered by speakers as a viable method for creating new words in their language.[9]

Interestingly, the structure of the blends shows remarkable variety in the Hungarian data, though typologically they are in most cases so-called substitution blends (that is, a part of one source lexeme is blended with another whole lexeme – see Kemmer 2003). The whole lexeme can be preserved as the second constituent, as in *békutya* (answer provided for 'frog dog'; blend of *béka* ["frog"] and *kutya* ["dog"]), or as the first constituent, as in *karfiolfánt* (answer provided for 'cauliflower elephant'; blend of *karfiol* ["cauliflower"] and *elefánt* ["elephant"]). Overlap blends, in which neither source lexeme is fully preserved in the resulting blend, have also shown up in the answers, as in the case of *kukorinán* (answer provided for 'corn banana'; blend of *kukorica* ["corn"] and *banán* ["banana"]) or *krokogáj* (answer provided for 'crocodile parrot' and 'crocodile duck'; blend of *krokodil* ["crocodile"] and *papagáj* ["parrot"]). Variety in the structure of blends also showed up on the individual level: participants did not stick with one particular type of blend schema but were prone to use both substitution and overlap blends throughout the task.

2.7 Language comparison summary

In summary, the hybrid object-naming task produced different outcomes in the two languages:

In both Hungarian and German, the majority of the answers were noun-noun compounds, but in German there was a much stronger preference (92%) for noun-noun compounding than there was in Hungarian (60%).

Hungarian offered a morphological alternative to noun-noun compounding: adjective-noun compounding. This accounted for almost 28% of the Hungarian answers. In contrast, less than 1% of the German answers consisted of adjective-noun compounds.

9. In fact, examples for lexical blending do crop up nowadays relatively often in Hungarian journalism (see, for instance, Ladányi 2007). However, the appearance of blends in the responses of the majority of the Hungarian participants can perhaps be explained by the influence of their advanced knowledge of English, where blends account for about 5% of neologisms (Algeo 1991), and which are appearing in the English language at an ever-increasing rate (Kemmer 2003; Lehrer 2007).

In the Hungarian data there was a higher number of metonymic compounds (11%), than in the German data (4%). This, in turn, might be related to the Hungarian preference of adjective-noun compounding.

In both languages the percentage of blends was similar (5%), but in German the majority of the blends came from only two participants, while Hungarian blends were produced by 15 out of 20 participants.

And finally, there was a slightly greater tendency for Hungarians to just name one of the two parts (69 items) than for the German participants (25 items), when naming the hybrid object.

2.8 Compound type

At this point, we would like to add that it is not really clear what type of compound the Hungarian and German noun-noun compounds that were elicited belong to. Both Hungarian and German, analogous with English, follow the Right-Hand Head Rule, originally proposed by Williams (1981), which establishes that a compound word is syntactically and semantically right-headed (that is, the right-hand constituent defines the syntactic category and the semantic subcategorization of the compound as a whole).[10] However, some compounds have not one, but two semantic heads. Such constructions are described by Downing (1977) as "half-half", meaning that the meaning of the whole refers to an entity that is both [x] and [y] (where [x] and [y] are the two participating nouns in a construction [x y]). This relation has been pointed out in traditional grammars as well, and has been referred to by a number of names, including coordinating, copulative, dvandva, etc. (for a discussion, see Bauer 2008). Here we use the term "coordinating". In such compounds there is no clear modifier-head relationship between the two constituents of the compound, but rather both constituents can be considered as the semantic head of the construction. This type of relation is very typical in company names (e.g. *Hewlett-Packard*, *Sony Ericsson*, etc.) or geographical names (*Austria-Hungary*, *Alsace-Lorraine*, etc.). Coordinating compounds can and do show up in Hungarian, too, as exemplified by *adásvétel* ('trading', literally: *adás* = selling, *vétel* = buying; i.e. a transaction involving both buying and selling).[11]

As both Hungarian and German allow for coordinating compounds, it could be argued that noun-noun answers such as *róka madár* ("fox bird", as supplied for

10. Note that Williams (1981) defined the Right-Hand Head Rule for English. Kiefer (1998: 273) also proposes the same for Hungarian compounds. Not all languages conform to this rule, however: as pointed out by Selkirk (1982), languages such as French or Vietnamese abound in left-headed constructions.

11. However, suffixes can only be attached to the second constituent of the compound (i.e. the second constituent functions as the syntactic head).

the image of 'fox hen') or *kaktusz béka* ("cactus frog", as supplied for the image of 'cactus frog') are coordinating constructions, based on a "half-half" semantic relationship. At the same time, however, these compounds could also be considered as proper, right-headed constructions, i.e. descriptive compounds.

Three arguments can be raised in support of this latter hypothesis. First, both Hungarian and German participants often took first considerable time to decide in which order they should place the words in the eventual noun-noun construction (i.e. whether they should say *róka madár* or *madár róka*). Once they had decided on a specific construction, they seemed to be very certain, that the chosen construction expressed what they had wanted to verbalize. We interpreted this to indicate that the selection of the order of the words – and the eventual selection of the right-headed element – was deliberate. Second, there are plenty of noun-noun compounds denoting animals in Hungarian which are the simple concatenation of two species – such as *farkaskutya* ('Alsatian', from wolf [*farkas*] and dog [*kutya*]), *sárkánygyík* ('Komodo dragon', from dragon [*sárkány*] and lizard [*gyík*]) –, and in which the second constituent functions as the semantic head (i.e. provides the larger category to which the animal belongs), while the first constituent functions as a modifier and describes the entity to which the animal best resembles. This compound pattern might have influenced the answers provided by the participants. Third, some researchers (e.g. Becker 1992; Neef 2009) claim that dvandva compounds in German do not have linking elements (i.e. elements that are often inserted between the compound constituents, such as -s – in *Liebesbrief* [*love letter*], or -e – in *Hundehütte* [*dog house*]). In our study, the novel compounds that were produced by the German participants did contain linking elements, wherever appropriate (whether a compound contains a linking element, and which one, depends on the first constituent).

To us, the above observations seem to speak more in favor of an interpretation as descriptive compounds. Nevertheless, the current study does not allow us to draw strong conclusions with regard to the compound type; at this point both hypotheses – that the compounds are coordinating or that they are right-headed – seem to be viable.

3 Picture effects

We had selected pictures showing hybrid objects composed from different semantic domains in order to explore possible semantic influences on word formation patterns in the two languages.

3.1 Word formation preferences across semantic domains

The fact that not a single picture elicited only one particular word formation pattern in the Hungarian data sets points to the hypothesis that the answers provided by the Hungarians were not based on analogy. Rather, it seems that every single image allowed a large range of possible constructions, and the type of morphological structure that was eventually produced by the participant depended largely on personal preference. In comparison, the German answers showed overwhelming preferences for noun-noun compounding.

Table 2 shows the percentage of [N N] and [Adj N] compounds, lexical blends and other constructions with regard to the semantic domain that the entities in the image belong to.

The distributional pattern of morphological structures did not show any influence of semantic domains, except for the finding that lexical blends emerged most often in the plant-plant domain. Chi-square analyses showed that in both languages the proportion of blends for the plant-plant hybrids was significantly higher than the mean proportion of blends for the other hybrids (German: $\chi^2(1) = 8.88$, $p = 0.0029$, Hungarian: $\chi^2(1) = 3.85$, $p = 0.0497$).[12]

On the one hand, this could be due to analogy to preexisting lexemes both in Hungarian and German: *citrancs* in the case of the former (meaning 'grapefruit', a lexical blend of *citrom*, "lemon", and *narancs*, "orange"), and *Tomoffel* in the case of the latter (a lexical blend for a new plant, part *Tomate*, "tomato", and part *Kartoffel*, "potato").

Table 2. Percentage of preferred morphological structures, with regard to the semantic domain that the entities in the images belong to

		Animal Animal	Animal Plant	Animal Inanimate	Plant Plant	Plant Inanimate	Inanimate Inanimate	Shape
Hungarian	[N N]	59%	60%	60%	51%	69%	55%	66%
	[Adj N]	33%	30%	28%	31%	20%	32%	20%
	Blend	6%	6%	6%	9%	6%	3%	3%
	Other	2%	4%	6%	10%	5%	10%	11%
German	[N N]	90%	95%	96%	85%	95%	91%	92%
	[Adj N]	0%	0%	0%	1%	0%	0%	0%
	Blend	9%	5%	3%	10%	3%	4%	2%
	Other	1%	5%	1%	4%	2%	5%	4%

12. Chi square tests also revealed that in the German, but not in the Hungarian data, the proportion of blends for animal-animal hybrids was significantly higher than the mean proportion of blends for the other hybrids ($\chi^2(1) = 6.11$, $p = 0.0135$)

On the other hand, hybrid plants might also be considered to be more realistic than for example animal-inanimate hybrids, and therefore lexical blends might be considered as a viable, iconic label for them.

3.2 Shape images

Apart from the six categories combining objects from three semantic domains, our seventh category showed objects whose shape was manipulated. The low number of blends in the Hungarian data among the shape images contrasts with a large proportion of noun-noun compounds (66%). In fact, after the plant-inanimate hybrids, shape images prompted from speakers the highest proportion of nominal compounds in Hungarian. This result runs counter to Hiramatsu et al.'s (2000) claim, that Hungarian (along with Estonian) disallows shape/appearance modifiers in noun-noun compounds: according to Hiramatsu et al., shape or appearance modifiers are formalized in Hungarian as adjectival constituents; that is, a chair in the shape of a hand would be called a "hand-shaped chair" and not "hand chair". Nevertheless, in the Hungarian data noun-noun compounds based on shape/appearance abound: a kangaroo-shaped cloud was often called by subjects a *kenguru felhő* ("kangaroo cloud"), and a camel-shaped mountain was referred to as *teve hegy* ("camel mountain"). Based on our data it can in fact be stated that shape/appearance noun-noun compounding seems to be a productive word formation process in Hungarian. Actually, lexicalized and novel noun-noun examples of this type of conceptual relationship can be found in present-day Hungarian. An example for a lexicalized shape/appearance compound is *tűsarok* ('high-heeled shoes', literally: *tű* = needle, *sarok* = heel; i.e. 'heel that is like a needle') – though in this example it can be argued that there is a further metonymy involved in the compound (PART FOR WHOLE: heels for the shoe). As for a novel example, one can cite *vanília égbolt* ("vanilla sky"), meaning 'sky that has the appearance of vanilla'.[13]

Nevertheless, we do not wish to claim that the significance of adjectival compounds among the shape images should be underestimated. As Table 2 clearly shows, such constructions account for nearly one quarter of the answers; therefore, their proportion points to the fact that shape/appearance relations in Hungarian

13. The compound's status as a possible lexeme of Hungarian can, however, be questioned: the expression appeared as a mirror translation of the title of the Hollywood movie *Vanilla Sky*, and therefore the Hungarian compound might have been influenced by the structure of the English version. It also needs to be added here that according to Hungarian orthography, compounds are written without space between the two constituents – therefore it might be argued that the status of *vanília égbolt* as a compound is questionable. Nevertheless, in this chapter we will not take orthographical criteria into account, so that *vanília égbolt* will be considered as a compound word of Hungarian, too.

can *also* be formalized by adjective-noun compound expressions, although speaker preference – at least in our data – seems to be biased towards noun-noun constructions. In this respect, Hungarian follows German (see Ortner and Ortner 1984 for various types of German compound formation patterns) and English (see Downing 1977 and Warren 1978 for various types of English word formation patterns).

3.3 The "Other" category

The percentage of "other" constructions in the Hungarian data is 7%; in the German data, it is 3% (see Table 2). The types of constructions that we subsumed under this label were mostly phrases, e.g. prepositional constructions (e.g. *cigarette in the lock* for 'key cigarette') or single lexemes. It is noteworthy that out of the 95 Hungarian instances of responses belonging to the "Other" category, nearly three-quarters were simple nouns. However, the fact that one participant produced about half of these simple nouns does make the results one-sided. Nevertheless, single lexemes did occur in nearly every data set; therefore, we briefly discuss this category, too.

When Hungarian participants produced a single lexeme to describe the hybrid entity that they were shown, they often selected one of the entities in the image to stand for the whole image. In other words, 'heart apple' solicited *alma* ("apple"), and 'shark island' produced *sziget* ("island"). This can be considered as a case of a PART FOR WHOLE metonymy (more specifically A MEMBER OF A CATEGORY FOR THE WHOLE CATEGORY – see Kövecses and Radden 1998), where one member of the category ('apple') stands for the category itself ('heart apple'). Such answers were all basic-level terms. There was also one participant who denoted 'piano bench' as *harmónia* ("harmony"), which can be considered as a manifestation of the PRODUCER FOR PRODUCT metonymy: 'harmony' stands for the entity that produces it, that is, the piano (*harmónia* can also be analyzed as an EFFECT FOR CAUSE metonymy – i.e. the end result, harmony, standing for the cause, the piano). At the same time, it can also be argued that the other entity in the image, the bench, also motivated the selection of *harmónia*: in this case the object (the bench) stands for the action routinely associated with it (sitting down and taking a break). Interestingly, we were also provided with a couple of answers where participants gave a superordinate term for the hybrid image they were presented. An example that can be cited here is *játék* ("game") for 'guitar laptop', where obviously the participant tried to select a term that managed to somehow 'cover' both entities. However, as superordinate terms carry less cognitive information than basic or subordinate levels (Croft and Cruse 2004), it is not surprising that the number of superordinate-level answers was minimal in the data set.

3.4 Versatility across languages

One of the salient differences between the German and the Hungarian data is that the latter results show remarkable versatility. While the various images elicited relatively uniform answers from the German subjects, the answers of the Hungarian subjects were quite heterogeneous, irrespective of the semantic domains the images belonged to. This variety in the Hungarian answers showed up at both the semantic and the morphological levels as is shown in Table 3.

For every semantic domain, we selected a random image, and then examined the answers that were given for the respective images by randomly selected subjects. As it can be seen from Table 3, the Hungarian answers greatly varied from

Table 3. Comparison of Hungarian and German labels for randomly selected images

example	domain		Subject 1	Subject 2	Subject 3	Subject 4	Subject 5
apple tent	plant - inanimate	Hungarian	apple	tent apple	apple+tent (blend)	apple tent	tent
		German	apple tent	apple tent	apple tent	apple tent	tent apple
			Subject 3	**Subject 4**	**Subject 5**	**Subject 6**	**Subject 7**
giraffe ostrich	animal - animal	Hungarian	giraffe bird	bird giraffe	winged giraffe	giraffe ostrich	giraffe-patterned ostrich
		German	giraffe bird	giraffe ostrich	giraffe ostrich	giraffe ostrich	giraffe ostrich
			Subject 9	**Subject 10**	**Subject 11**	**Subject 12**	**Subject 13**
chameleon guitar	animal - inanimate	Hungarian	guitar+ chameleon (blend)	guitar-bodied lizard	frog guitar	chameleon guitar	bass chameleon
		German	guitar chameleon	guitar animal	chameleon guitar	lizard+ chameleon (blend)	guitar chameleon
			Subject 11	**Subject 12**	**Subject 13**	**Subject 14**	**Subject 15**
cigarette key	inanimate - inanimate	Hungarian	cigarette key	cigarette key	key to lung cancer	cigarette key	lighter key
		German	cigarette key	key+cigarette (blend)	cigarette key	roach key	cigarette key
			Subject 13	**Subject 14**	**Subject 15**	**Subject 16**	**Subject 17**
camel mountain	shape	Hungarian	camel hump	camel rock	camel	camel island	camel mountain
		German	rock camel	camel mountain	camel mountain	stone camel	camel rock

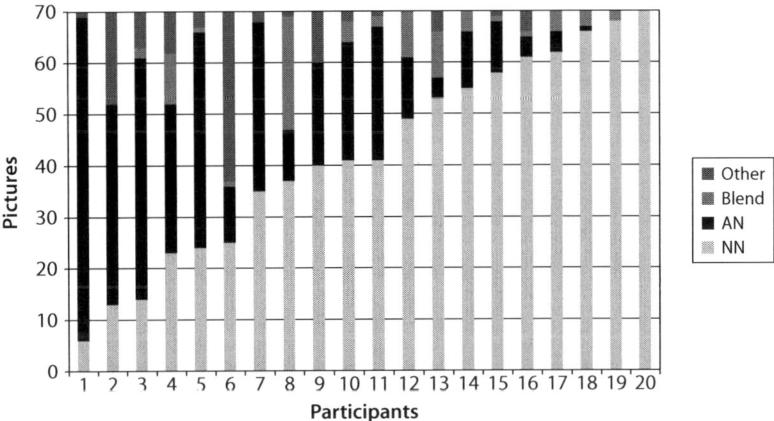

Figure 2. Variety of responses, by morphological structure, in the Hungarian data set

participant to participant. This variety can be observed in both the morphological structure of the elicited expressions: see for example the answers given for *apple tent*, where we can find a blend, two [N N] compounds and two single lexemes; and the semantics as well, as it can be noticed in the answers provided for *giraffe ostrich*, where two participants gave the superordinate term for *ostrich* (i.e. *bird*, instead of ostrich), one participant selected the winged feature of ostrich to stand metonymically for the bird itself, while another subject selected the pattern of the giraffe's skin to stand for the giraffe itself.

Compared to the Hungarian data, the German answers were rather consistent. Note, however, that compounding is a very common, even ubiquitous, process in German: nominal compounds account for two-thirds of German word formations (Duden 1998; cited in Onysko 2010).

It should be emphasized at this point that variety in the Hungarian answers was characteristic of every picture that was shown; Figure 2 shows the variety of the Hungarian responses.

Based on Figure 2 it can generally be claimed that [N N] and [Adj N] compounds are inversely proportional to each other – that is, participants who gave a high proportion of [N N] answers provided a low proportion of [Adj N] answers, and vice versa. Although lexical blends and 'other' types of constructions (such as nouns with prepositional phrases, as in the above mentioned *cigarette in the lock* example) make up only 12% of the total answers, they constitute a considerable proportion, especially if one considers that 15 out of the 20 Hungarian participants did come up with lexical blends (though the number of blends per subject ranged between 1 and 22). The German participants, in contrast, clearly favored noun-noun compounding, except for two participants, who produced a large percentage of blends, as can be seen in Figure 3.

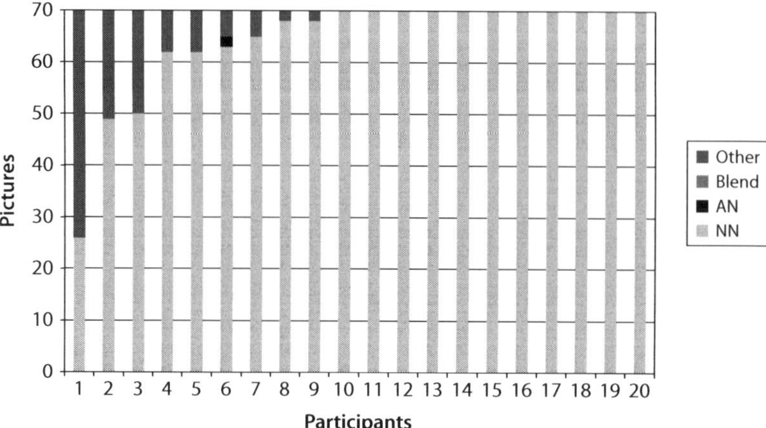

Figure 3. Variety of responses, by morphological structure, in the German data set

3.5 Creativity

One of the most intriguing aspects of the Hungarian data was the inclination of our participants to play with language and produce highly creative answers based on less conventional metonymical or metaphorical relationships and analogy to already existing words. Nine out of the twenty Hungarian participants came up with ingenious, often humorous expressions to describe the hybrid entities in the image. Interestingly, the participants who were more apt to play with language were also those who produced blends and who also had a relatively large number of adjective-noun answers in their data. At the same time, participants who came up with a vast majority of noun-noun constructions for the images did not elicit humorous, associative answers (and the same applies to the one Hungarian subject who produced *only* adjective-noun combinations). Therefore, it seems likely that morphological versatility in the Hungarian data goes hand in hand with linguistic creativity – and perhaps this correlation explains the smaller number of associations produced by our German participants, as the German data mostly constituted noun-noun combinations.[14]

German participants apparently had a hard time to escape from the easy all-encompassing noun-noun compounding way that the German language offers. Yet, in the German noun-noun compound data one pattern emerged that might

14. This is not to say that noun-noun compounds cannot be based on creative metaphorical, metonymical processes. As it has been argued in Benczes (2006), such compounds in English are often rooted in highly creative language use.

have been motivated by participants' desire to come up with more creative names: some participants selected relatively rare words to refer to the entities depicted, e.g. words belonging to a specific register, as in *Kippenschlüssel* ("fag key") for 'cigarette key' or *Auberginenlatscher* ("eggplant slippers") for 'eggplant shoes', thereby opting for a lexical and not a morphological strategy to avoid the otherwise predictable uniform German answer patterns.

It is difficult to pin down what factors motivate creative uses of language, as apparent in metaphorical and metonymical compounds. Benczes (2010) lists compactness, vividness, textual and socio-cultural context, memorability, analogy and remotivation among others as possible influencing factors. The role of context is exemplified by four creative constructions that we now present in detail. However, as the first analysis shows, the definition of Benczes's "context" needs to be slightly expanded by one further aspect: the context of "meaning", that is, the senses of the individual words.

The first creative construction that we wish to present is very special, as it showed up in not just one, but two data sets. Two of our Hungarian participants came up with *tök jó autó* (literally, "pumpkin good car") for 'courgette car'. The construction is based on the creative manipulation of *tök jó*: in Hungarian, *tök* has two meanings, a nominal and an adverbial one: it can either mean "pumpkin" or "very". Nevertheless, the adverbial meaning has got nothing to do with the nominal one: it has been created by the process of clipping from the adverb *tökéletesen* ("completely, utterly"). In the case of *tök jó autó*, however, the image of the courgette prompted speakers to conflate the homonymous meanings of *tök*. A further compound motivated by word meaning is *csirkefogó*, denoting "scoundrel", which one of our participants elicited for the image of 'fox hen'. The motivation behind this construction can be traced back to the etymology of the word. Literally, *csirkefogó* can be translated as "chicken grabber". It is a well-known characteristic of foxes that they do actually "grab" chickens from farms. The literal interpretation of *csirkefogó* is motivated by the image of the fox, via a SALIENT PROPERTY FOR CATEGORY metonymy. It should be emphasized that the expression *csirkefogó* is used only in conjunction with people (more specifically men), and not animals. The incongruity of the expression (as it is used in reference to an animal, and not a person) creates a humorous effect.

Another interesting case is represented by *néma dal* (literally, "mute song"), the answer one of the participants provided for 'trumpet fish'. The creativity lies in the incongruity of the compound – a song cannot, in principle, be mute. How does muteness come into play? The answer rests on the (DEFINING) PROPERTY FOR CATEGORY metonymy, by which muteness, as a property, stands for the category itself, the fish. As it has already been pointed out in Section 3.2, the DEFINING PROPERTY FOR CATEGORY metonymy often motivated the Hungarian adjective-noun compounds: However, in the example of "mute song", the reason for selecting the adjective was probably not communicative efficiency, but rather humor. Motivation for *mute* can be traced back to the context, though in this case the immediate context is not textual, but imagistic. It was probably the image of the trumpet (which, via a PRODUCER [trumpet] FOR PRODUCT [song] metonymy, can be accounted for *song* in the compound) that prompted the speaker to come up with *mute*, and not any other feature of fish, such as scaliness, having fins and so forth. According to Brône and Feyaerts (2003), one of the ways humorous effects can be reached in language is by the selection of a less-prototypical metonymical vehicle. Muteness can be considered as a less salient feature of fish. At the same time, muteness is incongruous with songs – and it is exactly this incongruity – or even absurdity – that creates a humorous effect.

Our last example, motivated by cultural context, is *magyar paradicsom* (literally, "Hungarian tomato", for 'lemon tomato'). The adjective, "Hungarian", metonymically stands for the lemon in the hybrid image; this relationship is motivated by cultural knowledge, rooted in one of the all-time classics of Hungarian film, *The Witness*. The satire, produced in 1969 but released more than ten years later, follows the life of an ordinary dike keeper during the Rákosi era of the 1950s (modeled after the Stalinist regime). In one of the scenes of the film, the then-leader of the country is presented with a lemon that is advertised as the new "Hungarian orange", along with the following commentary: "It may be a bit yellow, it may be a bit sour, but at least it is ours".[15]

4. Conclusion

This chapter explored language-specific preferences in German and Hungarian for labels given for (i) novel hybrid objects that are composed of two identifiable parts (such as a non-existing animal that is part chicken and part fox, i.e. *chicken fox*); and (ii) novel objects that have an identifiable, salient shape (such as a box that is in the shape of a banana, i.e. *banana box*). Using a novel object-naming task, we wished to compare German and Hungarian word formation patterns, and to explore a possible semantic influence on response patterns.

The research was motivated by the body of literature in child language acquisition that demonstrated that in Germanic and Semitic languages (e.g. among others, English, Swedish, and Hebrew) children from two years of age onwards were able to refer to these hybrid objects with novel noun-noun compounds labels (e.g. Gottfried 1997a, 1997b, Mellenius 1997; Berman and Clark 1989; Nicoladis

15. Source: http://hu.wikipedia.org/wiki/A_tanú (accessed: 19 June 2008).

2003; Grela et al. 2005). While we could assume that the response patterns from German participants would not differ that much from the data collected from the other Germanic participants, it was less clear which patterns would emerge in the Hungarian data. Hiramatsu et al. (2000) claimed that Hungarian and Estonian do not allow modifiers expressing shape or appearance in noun-noun compounds.

Contrary to this latter claim, our data show that in both Hungarian and German, the majority of the answers were noun-noun compounds (irrespective of the semantic category the object parts belonged to), but in German this preference was indeed much stronger than in Hungarian, where, after all, almost a third of the answers followed an adjective-noun pattern.

Interestingly, blends hardly surfaced in German, while nearly every Hungarian participant elicited at least one blend. We have also pointed out that the Hungarian participants were more inclined towards morphological versatility, and this versatility has been shown to go hand in hand with linguistic creativity.

Regarding the influence of semantics with regard to compound formation patterns, it turns out that in both languages lexical blends were found most often in the plant-plant domain, which might be explained by the fact that hybrid plants might be considered by speakers to be more realistic than for example animal-inanimate hybrids, and therefore lexical blends are seen as a viable, iconic label for them.

In sum, the above data provide converging evidence that in both Hungarian and German hybrid objects might be referred to with novel compound labels, failing to provide support for Hiramatsu et al.'s (2000) hypothesis. Nevertheless, the choice of constructions seems to be language- and possibly culture-specific, with German speakers preferring descriptive noun-noun compounds, and Hungarian speakers coining more creative constructions.

References

A. Jászó, Anna, ed., 1995. *A magyar nyelv könyve*. Budapest: Trezor Kiadó.

Algeo, John, ed., 1991. *Fifty Years Among the New Words: A Dictionary of Neologisms, 1941–1991*. Cambridge: Cambridge University Press.

Bauer, Laurie. 2008. Dvandva. *Word Structure* 1: 1–20.

Becker, Thomas. 1992. Compounding in German. *Rivista di Linguistica* 4: 5–36.

Benczes, Réka. 2010. Setting limits on creativity in the production and use of metaphorical and metonymical compounds. In S. Michel & A. Onysko, eds., *Cognitive Approaches to Word Formation*, 219–242. Berlin & New York: Mouton de Gruyter.

Benczes, Réka. 2006. *Creative Compounding in English: The Semantics of Metaphorical and Metonymical Noun-noun Combinations*. Amsterdam & Philadelphia: Benjamins.

Berman, Ruth & Eve Clark. 1989. Learning to use compounds for contrast: data from Hebrew. *First Language* 9: 247–270.

Bickerton, Derek. 1990. *Language and Species*. Chicago: The University of Chicago Press.

Borgwaldt, Susanne & Arpita Bose. 2008. Novel compound production and comprehension in aphasia. Poster presented at the 46th Annual Meeting of the Academy of Aphasia, Turku, Finland.

Brône, Geert & Kurt Feyaerts. 2003. *The cognitive linguistics of incongruity resolution: Marked reference point structures in humor*. Leuven: Katholieke Universiteit Leuven.

Croft, William & Alan Cruse. 2004. *Cognitive Linguistics*. Cambridge: Cambridge University Press.

Donalies, Elke. 2004. *Grammatik des Deutschen im europäischen Vergleich: Kombinatorische Begriffsbildung. Teil 1: Substantivkomposition*. Mannheim: Institut für deutsche Sprache.

Downing, Pamela. 1977. On the creation and use of English compound nouns. *Language* 53 (4): 810–842.

Duden. 1998. *Grammatik der deutschen Gegenwartssprache*. 6th edition. Mannheim: Dudenverlag.

FreakingNews home page. 2003–2009. http://www.freakingnews.com

Gottfried, Gail. 1997a. Comprehending compounds: evidence for metaphoric skill? *Journal of Child Language* 24: 163–186.

Gottfried, Gail. 1997b. Using metaphors as modifiers: children's production of metaphoric compounds. *Journal of Child Language* 24: 567–601.

Grela, Bernard, William Snyder, & Kazuko Hiramatsu. 2005. The production of novel root compounds in children with specific language impairment. *Clinical Linguistics* & *Phonetics* 19: 701–715.

Hiramatsu, Kazuko, William Snyder, Thomas Roeper, Stephanie Storrs, & Matthew Saccoman. 2000. Of musical hand chairs and linguistic swing. In C. Howell, S. Fish, & T. Keith-Lucas, eds., *BUCLD 24: Proceedings of the 24*th *annual Boston University Conference on Language Development*, 409–417. Somerville, MA: Cascadilla Press.

Holm, John. 2000. *An Introduction to Pidgins and Creoles*. Cambridge: Cambridge University Press.

Jackendoff, Ray. 1999. Possible stages in the evolution of the language capacity. *Trends in Cognitive Sciences* 3 (7): 272–279.

Kemmer, Suzanne. 2003. Schemas and lexical blends. In H. Cuyckens, H. Berg, R. Dirven, & K. Panther, eds., *Motivation in Language: Studies in Honor of Günter Radden*, 69–97, Amsterdam & Philadelphia: Benjamins.

Kiefer, Ferenc. 1998. Alaktan. In É. Kiss K., F. Kiefer, & P. Siptár, eds., *Új Magyar nyelvtan*, 187–289. Budapest: Osiris.

Klein, Wolfgang & Clive Perdue. 1997. The basic variety, or: Couldn't language be much simpler? *Second Language Research* 13: 301–347.

Kövecses, Zoltan. 2006. *Language, Mind, and Culture*. Oxford: Oxford University Press.

Kövecses, Zoltan & Günter Radden. 1998. Metonymy: Developing a cognitive linguistic view. *Cognitive Linguistics* 9 (1): 37–77.

Ladányi, Mária. 2007. *Produktivitás és analógia a szóképzésben: elvek és esetek* [Segédkönyvek a nyelvészet tanulmányozásához 76]. Budapest: Tinta Könyvkiadó.

Lakoff, George & Mark Johnson. 1980. *Metaphors We Live By*. Chicago: The University of Chicago Press.

Langacker, Ronald. 1993. Reference-point constructions. *Cognitive Linguistics* 4 (1): 1–38.

Lehrer, Adrienne. 2007. Blendalicious. In J. Munat, ed., *Lexical Creativity, Texts and Contexts*, 115–133. Amsterdam & Philadelphia: Benjamins.

Mellenius, Ingmarie. 1997. *The acquisition of nominal compounding in Swedish*. Lund: Lund University Press.

Neef, Martin. 2009. I-E Germanic: German. In R. Lieber & P. Stekauer, eds., *The Oxford Handbook of Compounding*, 386–399. Oxford: Oxford University Press.
Neef, Martin & Susanne Borgwaldt. In print. Fugenelemente in neugebildeten Nominalkomposita. In Barbara Schlücker & Livio Gaeta, eds., *Das Deutsche als kompositionsfreudige Sprache*. Berlin & New York: Mouton de Gruyter.
Nicoladis, Elena. 2003. What compound nouns mean to preschool children. *Brain and Language* 84: 38–49.
Olsen, Susan. 1986. *Wortbildung im Deutschen. Eine Einführung in die Theorie der Wortstruktur.* Stuttgart: Kröner.
Onysko, Alexander. 2010. Casting the conceptual spotlight: Hybrid compounding in German as an example of head-frame internal specifier selection. In S. Michel & A. Onysko, eds., *Cognitive Approaches to Word Formation*, 243–300. Berlin & New York: Mouton de Gruyter.
Ortner, Hanspeter & Lorelies Ortner. 1984. *Zur Theorie und Praxis der Kompositaforschung.* Tübingen: Narr.
Selkirk, Elizabeth. 1982. *The Syntax of Words* [Linguistic Inquiry Monograph 7]. Cambridge, MA: MIT Press.
Taylor, John. 2002. *Cognitive Grammar*. Oxford: Oxford University Press.
Warren, Beatrice. 1978. *Semantic Patterns of Noun-noun Compounds*. Gothenburg: Gothenburg University Press.
Williams, Edwin. 1981. On the notions 'lexically related' and 'head of a word'. *Linguistic Inquiry* 12: 245–274.
Worth1000 home page (2002–2009). http://www.worth1000.com

Appendix 1

Example pictures used in the study

Figure 4. Apple orange

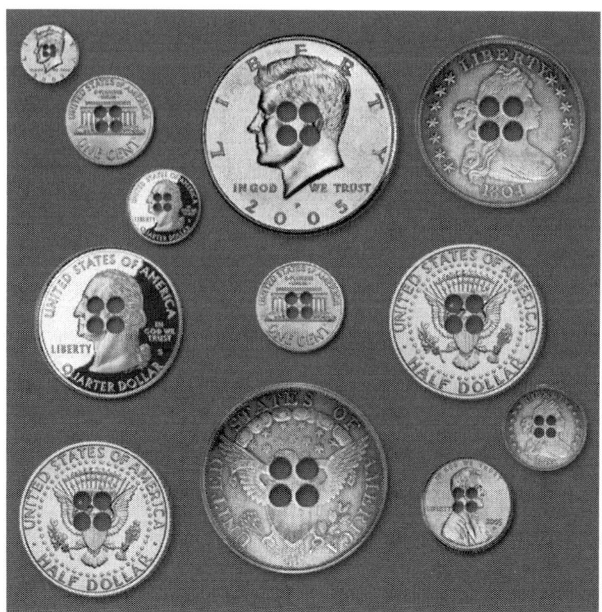

Figure 5. Coin buttons

Figure 6. Flower clock

These pictures were retrieved from http://www.freakingnews.com

Appendix 2

List of pictures used in the study

image	semantic domains	image	semantic domains
fox bird	animal – animal	*eggplant penguin*	plant – animal
penguin cat	animal – animal	*rose flamingo*	plant – animal
jaguar owl	animal – animal	*banana fish*	plant – animal
fox chicken	animal – animal	*cabbage elephant*	plant – animal
crocodile penguin	animal – animal	*cactus frog*	plant – animal
frog dog	animal – animal	*flower clock*	plant – inanimate
crocodile duck	animal – animal	*cucumber car*	plant – inanimate
giraffe ostrich	animal – animal	*violin cactus*	plant – inanimate
gorilla ant	animal – animal	*banana gun*	plant – inanimate
parrot crocodile	animal – animal	*eggplant shoes*	plant – inanimate
ape violin	animal – inanimate	*light flower*	plant – inanimate
bear hat	animal – inanimate	*cactus microphone*	plant – inanimate
fish gun	animal – inanimate	*pumpkin cabin*	plant – inanimate
chameleon guitar	animal – inanimate	*pear bus*	plant – inanimate
fish trumpet	animal – inanimate	*apple tent*	plant – inanimate
lobster car	animal – inanimate	*apple orange*	plant – plant
goose dice	animal – inanimate	*pineapple orange*	plant – plant
fish candle	animal – inanimate	*orange mushroom*	plant – plant
cow accordion	animal – inanimate	*banana corn*	plant – plant
hamster icecream	animal – inanimate	*tomato lemon*	plant – plant
shoe house	inanimate – inanimate	*cucumber tomato*	plant – plant
house train	inanimate – inanimate	*pepper banana*	plant – plant
coin buttons	inanimate – inanimate	*corn peas*	plant – plant
car helmet	inanimate – inanimate	*kiwi onion*	plant – plant
feather sword	inanimate – inanimate	*orange kiwi*	plant – plant
laptop guitar	inanimate – inanimate	*heart lake*	shape
cigarette key	inanimate – inanimate	*dolphin island*	shape
piano bench	inanimate – inanimate	*key lemon*	shape
guitar hammer	inanimate – inanimate	*shark lake*	shape
tank shoe	inanimate – inanimate	*horse cloud*	shape
flower parrot	plant – animal	*shark island*	shape
corn snake	plant – animal	*camel rock*	shape
mushroom toads	plant – animal	*heart apples*	shape
pineapple birds	plant – animal	*snail island*	shape
tree crocodile	plant – animal	*kangaroo cloud*	shape

PART 2

Multi-methodological approaches to language acquisition

The interaction of function and input frequency in L1-acquisition

The case of *was...für* 'what kind of...' questions in German

Rasmus Steinkrauss
University of Groningen

The study reported in this chapter investigates the L1 acquisition of a group of wh-questions by a German-learning boy. It is assumed their acquisition will generally follow input frequency, but also interact with functional factors and previous linguistic knowledge. The input frequencies of the target structures are assessed and an order of acquisition predicted. This order is then compared to the actual course of acquisition and the deviations investigated. Results show that the acquisition of wh-questions is influenced by their input frequency as well as their communicative use and the knowledge of related constructions. The study argues for a combination of quantitative and qualitative methods in language acquisition research and recommends the consideration of several factors at once.

Keywords: communicative use of constructions, language acquisition, quantitative methods, qualitative methods, wh-questions

1. Introduction

The order of acquisition of linguistic items is a long-standing issue in acquisition studies. Particularly the acquisition order of wh-questions has been studied widely. The reason for this interest was mainly the idea that a wh-pronoun is fairly directly based on a primary cognitive concept such as time or place, and that the acquisition order of wh-questions would therefore provide a direct insight into a child's cognitive development. In these studies, the cognitive complexity of the question was seen as the main factor influencing order of acquisition (e.g. Felix 1976; Ingram 1971; Smith 1933; Stern and Stern 1928; Tyack and Ingram 1977;

Wode 1983). In the more recent usage-based research however, the frequency of a structure in the ambient speech is emphasized as a central factor for acquisition (e.g. Tomasello 2003). At the same time, it is commonly acknowledged that additional factors must play a role as well. Only a few studies however relate the investigation of input frequency and acquisition order to other factors. Especially, the pragmatic function of a structure in face-to-face interaction is sometimes disregarded in more quantitatively oriented studies. This chapter therefore presents the results of a study combining input frequency measurements with a close look at interactional functions to provide converging evidence on what might be influencing the order of acquisition of a group of wh-question constructions.

1.1 Theoretical background

In cognitive linguistics, language acquisition is seen as the construction of a grammar from the ambient language (e.g. Tomasello 2003). Grammar is thought of as a structured inventory of symbolic units (Langacker 1987), i.e. pairings of a linguistic form with a meaning. These symbolic units are learnt in a process that is different for every language learner, depending on the language she or he experiences. Through observing the linguistic behavior of people around them, children will over time come to detect patterns in other people's use of language. Some linguistic forms frequently recur with certain meanings, and these pairings of form with function will eventually be remembered and stored as symbolic units, often called schemas. Schemas are thus the mental representations of linguistic patterns that a speaker has formed. They may vary in their level of abstractness ranging from fully specific (consisting of specific lexical material) to fully abstract (consisting of open slots that specify what specific lexical material may be inserted). Eventually, children can use the schemas they have built up in their own language production.

An effect of this is that children's speech is initially limited in form and function. In the beginning, the meaning of the linguistic constructions that a child uses is still very much tied to the situations from which the child has learnt them, and the form of the constructions consists of lexically specific material which is taken directly from the input and shows little flexibility (e.g. Lieven, Pine, and Baldwin 1997; Peters 1983; Pine and Lieven 1997; Pine, Lieven, and Rowland 1998; Tomasello 1992). Therefore, children's early productions are often very formulaic. An area for which this is particularly well documented is English wh-questions. Children initially produce only a few fixed phrases such as *what's that* or specific WH+V combinations such as *where is...* as wh-questions (Dabrowska 2000; Dabrowska and Lieven 2005; Klima and Bellugi 1966). The WH+V combinations that children use are taken directly from the input language, and there are fewer errors in questions constructed with these combinations than in questions that involve other WH+V combinations for which the child has not yet built up a specific schema (Rowland 2007; Rowland and Pine 2000; Rowland and Pine 2003). This suggests that specific WH+V combinations do not just describe the children's production adequately but also have explanatory power in that they play a real role in the children's grammar.

Which schemas a given child will construct from the input and use in his or her own production depends to a large degree on the frequency of the linguistic pattern that the schema represents. The distinction between type and token frequency (Bybee 1995) plays a crucial role in this respect. A high token frequency means that a linguistic structure occurs frequently in the same form. The structure is therefore more likely to be learnt as a whole, as a lexically specific schema. For example, *what's that* often occurs in the input in the same form and is thus often acquired as a fully specific question schema. In contrast, the last part of *where is...* questions shows a high type frequency: many different instances of the same type (a noun phrase) occur in that position. The resulting schema will therefore probably incorporate an open slot for noun phrases (Lieven and Tomasello 2008).

Frequency also influences the point of acquisition for a construction. All things being equal, patterns that occur in the input frequently should be easier to detect than infrequent patterns, and should thus be acquired earlier. Some of the studies cited above already provide indirect evidence for this (Rowland 2007; Rowland and Pine 2000; Rowland and Pine 2003). Other studies have investigated the correlation between the input frequency of single words or longer constructions and their point of acquisition in a child more specifically. A particularly detailed study, again on wh-questions, was conducted by Rowland et al. (2003). They studied the acquisition order of WH+V combinations for twelve English-learning children. For each child, they determined the number of the transcript at which a child used a WH+V combination for the first time and correlated it with the combination's frequency in the speech of the child's mother. For ten of the twelve children, the resulting correlation was significant. The point at which a child acquired a WH+V combination hence correlated with input frequency. The authors also looked at semantic and syntactic complexity as alternative explanations for acquisition order, but found that input frequency was a more powerful predictor than either complexity of the wh-pronoun, complexity of the verb, or complexity of pronoun and verb combined. Further evidence for the influence of frequency on acquisition order in the area of wh-questions comes from several studies looking at the acquisition of wh-pronouns (Clancy 1989; Forner 1979; Rowland et al. 2003 in a reanalysis of Savic 1975), and still other studies report a correlation between input frequency and order of acquisition also in other areas of acquisition

(Theakston et al. 2002 for different forms and meanings of the verb *go;* Theakston et al. 2001 for transitive and intransitive verb constructions).

These results are consistent with the important role that usage-based linguistics attributes to frequency for language development more generally (e.g. Bybee 2006; Croft 2001). At the same time, it is recognized that other factors must also influence language acquisition. However, of the studies cited above, only Rowland et al. (2003) have actually looked at factors beyond frequency. They specifically investigated whether complexity played a role in cases where input frequency and point of acquisition did not correlate. They did not find that this was the case however. For example, some WH+V combinations were acquired late although they were highly frequent. However, their late acquisition turned out not to be due to complexity.

One aspect that has been suggested to influence a child's acquisition and production of a linguistic structure is functional factors such as a construction's pragmatics (Cameron-Faulkner, Lieven and Tomasello 2003: 864) and a child's communicative interest (Tyack and Ingram 1977). Empirical support for this idea is provided by Clancy (1989) who compared the wh-question acquisition of two children. She found that one child primarily used wh-questions to accompany her own play, while the other used wh-questions to elicit information from the parents. While both children clearly understood the frequent and simple *what is* questions from early on, only the second child (who used wh-questions to elicit information) produced *what is* early. That child even used less frequent wh-question structures that were functionally equivalent to *what is*, apparently because these forms met her communicative interest. In contrast, the first child who used wh-questions to accompany her own play did not produce the frequent *what is* from early on, so that functional aspects (communicative interest and the meaning of a construction) can be assumed to have interacted with input frequency in this case.

Another factor potentially interacting with input frequency is the knowledge of other, syntactically and/or semantically related constructions. In a connectionist simulation, Morris et al.'s (2000) model on wh-question acquisition could only generalize to a target construction when it had first learnt a group of related constructions. On the basis of this, Abbot-Smith and Behrens (2006) predicted that children learn a construction faster (i.e. in a shorter period of time) when simpler, related constructions are already acquired, and slower when no such supporting constructions are acquired, or when constructions are present that are even hindering the acquisition. They tested this prediction for two German passive and one future construction, using the same case study data as the present study. Their prediction was confirmed: one type of passive was learnt quickly because the child had already acquired some supporting constructions, that is, constructions that were lexically or morphologically related to the passive construction. In contrast, the other type of passive was learnt only slowly because there were no supporting constructions. The future construction in turn was learnt slowly in spite of potentially supporting constructions because the child had already acquired another construction that was semantically highly similar to the future construction. The similar construction hindered the acquisition of the future construction. The study shows that the previous knowledge of other constructions potentially interacts with input frequency.

There is thus some evidence that not only input frequency but also the function of a construction and previously learnt constructions may influence the course of acquisition. But studies that actually assess input frequency, derive predictions for the course of acquisition and then investigate additional factors that might interact with input frequency are scarce. The present study wants to take a first step in filling this gap. The results reported here are taken from a larger study on the wh-question acquisition of a German-learning boy that investigates the impact of input frequency and its interaction with functional factors (Steinkrauss 2009).

1.2 Aim of the study

The aim of the current study is to examine the interplay between input frequency, the function of a construction, and previous knowledge of other related constructions for the acquisition order of a group of wh-question constructions.

To achieve this, the input frequency of all *was... für* 'what kind of...' questions in a very dense corpus of a German-learning boy is assessed. Based on input frequency, a prediction for the order of acquisition of the different types of *was... für* questions is derived. Then, the prediction is tested on the boy's production data. In a third step, reasons for deviations from the predicted order of acquisition are identified by closely investigating the structures' forms and their functions in discourse, as well as the boy's previous constructional knowledge.

The present study thereby attempts to take seriously the tenet of cognitive linguistics that usage is a determining factor in language development, and that learning a language does not consist in the acquisition of a structure that is separate from meaning but the construction and use of symbolic units where form and function are paired.

1.3 The role of converging evidence

With its design and the methodology applied, the current study is a direct exemplification of how the "order of the day" (Schönefeld, this volume) to provide converging evidence may be implemented in a challenging situation: when just one corpus of one speaker is analyzed – a classical case study – and when neither other corpora nor another methodology may be used to gain further evidence.

Such is the case in the current study. Departing from the fundamental assumption of cognitive linguistics that the language development of each speaker is based on individual personal linguistic experience, this study investigates how a specific speaker builds up his linguistic knowledge. The use of a corpus of another speaker therefore naturally forbids itself.[1] And while experimental evidence from the same speaker might complement the results of the corpus study in theory, this is not possible in practice when the corpus data have already been collected.

The solution to this dilemma is to investigate the same phenomenon – in this case, the representational status of a construction for a specific speaker – from different angles, that is by investigating frequency, which is essentially an analysis based on the (occurrence of a) form of a construction, and by investigating the function of a construction in discourse. The study thus pairs a quantitative with a qualitative approach to provide converging evidence, and it thereby also builds on a foundational assumption of cognitive linguistics: learning a language consists in the acquisition of linguistic forms that are inseparable from their meanings – in other words, symbolic pairings of form and function.

With regard to the empirical cycle outlined in the introduction of this volume, the current study is a classic example of running through the circle once – but in its own way. The null hypothesis, namely that the production of a construction fairly strictly follows its input frequency, is rejected after a comparison of input and production data. The alternative hypothesis that other factors also play a role in acquisition is then refined and immediately explored with the help of the corpus data. In the end, the study will have provided converging evidence from different levels of analysis to arrive at a new hypothesis that may again be put to the test in future investigations.

2. Method

2.1 Corpus

The participant of the current study is a monolingual German boy, Leo, growing up in Germany. The recordings were collected by the Max-Planck-Institute for Evolutionary Anthropology under the supervision of H. Behrens. They include

1. Of course, this is not to say that other studies should not use other corpora to carry out analyses on other individual speakers and look for more evidence. Quite the contrary, this study hopes to provide the ground for this. At present, this possibility is still hampered by the limited availability of corpora possessing the density needed for such an investigation.

the child's speech and the ambient speech, which consists of utterances mainly of his parents. Both parents have higher education and speak dialect-free, clearly articulated standard High German. The boy's language development was recorded from 1;11.15, the onset of multiword speech, up to 5;0.[2] Before 2;0, several sampling recordings of various lengths were carried out. From 2;0 to 3;0, five one-hour recordings per week were made. In addition, the parents kept a daily diary in which they noted all new and complex syntactic structures that had not been captured by the audio recordings. From 3;0 to 5;0, five one-hour recordings were made every four weeks, and the diary was discontinued. The corpus provides thus extraordinarily dense data of the child's development, especially for the period between Leo's second and third birthday.

The present study draws on the densest sampling period between 2;0 and 3;0. During this time, the mother was the primary caretaker of the child, and was paid for taking the diary notes and making the audio recordings. In some sessions, either the father or a research assistant took over the recording. These three adults were Leo's main caretakers. Leo did not attend kindergarten during this period so the dataset offers a representative sample of what the child heard.

Each recording was digitized and transcribed in SONIC-Chat (MacWhinney 2000) with transcription guidelines developed for German by Behrens (cf. Behrens 2006 for a description of the data). The data were coded morphosyntactically for the citation form of the word form and information such as part-of-speech, inflectional class, gender, case and agreement. Half of the information was coded automatically using the mor-program of CLAN. Disambiguation and further coding was carried out manually by Heike Behrens and two trained research assistants.

For the present study, all wh-questions in input and production were additionally coded for wh-type. To find all wh-questions, all utterances ending with a question mark, containing a wh-pronoun, or coded as containing an interrogative pronoun or determiner were extracted automatically and revised manually. All *was... für* questions were then extracted from all wh-questions.

2.2 Target structure

The target structure investigated in the current study is a *was...für* 'what kind of...' type of question. The selection of a wh-question is motivated by the fact that wh-question production and acquisition have repeatedly been shown to be quite formulaic and heavily influenced by input frequency, at least in English (see above). The *was...für* structure was chosen because it constitutes a clearly delineated group

2. Leo's age is given in Years;Months.Days or Years;Months. 1;11.15 is 1 year, 11 months and 15 days.

of specific variants. This means that the different *was... für* variants can easily be compared in terms of input frequency and point of acquisition, and since the variants are all of the same wh-question type, there are no obvious functional reasons why some variants should be learnt while others should not, as might be the case when comparing functionally very diverse wh-questions. Also, the structure shows a sufficient number of types and tokens in Leo's production to be regarded as an acquired construction rather than some odd one-off exception, and it is acquired so late that there is a sufficiently long period to study the prior input and production.

Commonly, *was...für* questions in German are used to ask for kinds or for a quality/characteristic (Götz and Haensch 2003; Kempcke and Seelig 2000; Kunkel-Razum and Auberle 2003):

(1) *Was fähr-st du für ein Auto?*
What ride-2SG you for a car
'What kind of car do you ride?'
Possible conventional answers:
'A 1975 Mercedes'/'A sedan'/'An old one'

Answers that pick out an individual exemplar such as "The white Mercedes over there."/"That sedan there." seem unconventional without any further situational context. They are however conventional answers to *welch* 'which' interrogatives, which are semantically similar to *was...für* interrogatives. It is usually assumed (Pafel 1996) that *was...für* asks for kinds or properties, while *welch* asks for individual exemplars (Helbig and Buscha 1992: 96). Compare Example (1) above with Example (2):

(2) *Welch-es Auto fähr-st du?*
Which-ACC.SG.M car[ACC.SG.M] ride-2SG you
'Which car do you ride?'
Possible conventional answers:
'The white Mercedes over there'/'That sedan there'

The *was...für* question asks for a kind of car, the *welch* question for a specific car from a set of cars. In natural language use however this theoretical differentiation is fuzzy and a strict functional separation, as argued for by Pafel (1996: 57–63), is not tenable. In the input to Leo, *was...für* questions mainly ask for kinds and *welch* questions for individual exemplars, but often the difference is unclear or the constructions are used interchangeably (see Steinkrauss 2009, for details).

The *was...für* construction can occur in two versions, a split version like (1) (*was fährst du für ein Auto*) where the finite verb *fährst* splits *was* from *für*, and a continuous version like (3) with no intervening material between *was* and *für*:

(3) *Was für ein Auto fähr-st du?*
What for a car ride-2SG you
'What kind of car do you ride?'

In most cases, the two versions appear to be semantically equivalent.[3] The current study focuses on Leo's acquisition of different instances of the split version, the reason being that Leo produces only a few continuous questions and only produces them late. The production data are therefore limited. Still, the continuous question type is discussed in Section 3.4 of the current study, where it turns out that continuous questions play the role of a hindering construction.

In *was...für* questions, *für* is always followed by an indefinite noun phrase such as in (1), where the singular noun *Auto* is preceded by the indefinite article *ein*. Plural nouns are either used without any article or preceded by a numeral (4). The number of the NP always determines the number of the *was...für NP* phrase as a whole, as the agreement between the verb *liegen* and the noun phrase shows:

(4) *Was liegen da für (zwei) Büch-er?*
What lie[3PL] there for two book-ACC.PL
'What kind of books are the (two) books lying there?'

There several conventional variants of the pronunciation of the question. For the data discussed in this chapter, it suffices to note the common reduction of the indefinite articles *ein* and *eine* in the noun phrase following *für* to /n/ or /ne/ and the reduction of the verb form *ist* (*is*) to /is/ or /s/.

3. Results

3.1 Input frequency and order of acquisition

Leo produces his first *was...für* question at 2;8.27. Up to that day, there are 457 *was...für* questions in the input. They can be divided into specific types based on the material occurring before *für*, that is, the wh-pronoun and the finite verb form (and possibly an adverb/modal particle and/or subject).

Most of these question types are infrequent and account for less than 2% of the total each, while some few types are very frequent in comparison. The most frequent type is *was ist das für...* 'what kind of... is that'. Table 1 lists the most frequent types in the input (token frequency > 10) together with their frequency.

3. Dekydtspotter et al. (2005) discuss an exception involving the use of quantifiers. This exception is of no importance to the current study however.

Table 1. The most frequent types of '*was...für*' questions in the input
PART stands for the modal particle *denn*

German question	English gloss	Input frequency
was ist das für...	what kind of... is that	56
was ist denn das für...	what kind of... is PART that	35
was denn für...	what kind of... PART	31
was ist das denn für...	what kind of... is that PART	20
was sind das für...	what kind of... are that	13
was war das für...	what kind of... was that	13
was war denn das für...	what kind of... was PART that	10

Assuming that the order of acquisition basically follows input frequency, the figures predict the following for Leo's acquisition of these types of *was...für* questions:

1. *was ist das für...* is the most frequent type in the input by far and should be acquired first
2. *was ist denn das für...* and *was denn für...* are nearly equally frequent and should be acquired after *was ist das für...*
3. *was ist das denn für ...* should be acquired even later. The remaining three constructions are comparatively infrequent and should be produced only infrequently, if at all, during the period under investigation, and later than all other constructions.

The top structure *was ist das für...* has two very frequent subtypes that only differ in the indefinite article after *für*. One of those in turn comprises the most frequent complete *was...für* question that Leo hears: *was ist das für eine Farbe?* 'what color is that?' (Table 2).

The additional figures allow us to refine our prior predictions. If Leo follows the input frequency in his productions,

4. Leo's *was ist das für...* questions should be both *was ist das für ein...* and *was ist das für eine...*questions, produced with about the same frequency

Table 2. Subtypes of '*was ist das für...*' questions in the input

German question	English gloss	Input frequency
was ist das für...	what kind of... is that	56
was ist das für ein...	what kind of $a_{masc/neut}$ ... is that	24
was ist das für eine...	what kind of a_{fem} ... is that	27
was ist das für eine Farbe?	what color is that?	20

5. *was ist das für eine Farbe?* is the top frequent complete *was...für* question in the input and can thus be extracted as a fully specific schema. It should therefore be produced by Leo frequently and occur among his first *was...für* questions

These predictions can now be tested on Leo's production. Between 2;0 and 3;0, Leo produces 43 *was...für* questions. His first question at 2;8.27 is a *was ist das für...* question, and that question type also makes up the largest part of his *was...für* questions. Other types follow only later.

The comparison between input and production in Table 3 shows that Leo only partially follows input frequency. The child's data confirm the predicted order of acquisition in that Leo produces *was ist das für...* questions first and most frequently, and that he produces the more infrequent *was sind das für...* and *was war das für...* questions only late, and infrequently. However, Leo never produces three *was...für* types that are much more frequent in the input. Importantly, this is not due to the fact that Leo produces only one type of *was...für* questions before 3;0. He does produce other types, but not those three that are frequent in the input. The first major deviation from the acquisition sequence predicted by input frequency is thus the non-production of *was ist denn das für...*, *was denn für...* and *was ist das denn für...* questions.

Also the additional predictions from input frequency are not confirmed. See Table 4 for details.

Contrary to the expectations, Leo does not produce about equally many *was ist das für ein...* and *was ist das für eine...*questions; rather, he nearly exclusively produces the first type. And Leo never produces the most frequent complete *was...für* question in the input, *was ist das für eine Farbe?*. These are two other major deviations from the predictions made on the basis of input frequency alone. These three deviations are analyzed in Sections 3.2–3.4 respectively.

Table 3. Leo's production of the most frequent types of '*was...für*' questions in the input PART stands for the modal particle *denn*

German question	Input frequency	Production frequency	Leo's age at 1st use
was ist das für...	56	31	2;8.27
was ist denn das für...	35	–	–
was denn für...	31	–	–
was ist das denn für...	20	–	–
was sind das für...	13	1	2;11.11
was war das für...	13	2	2;11.26
was war denn das für...	10	–	–

Table 4. Subtypes of '*was ist das für...*' questions in the input and in Leo's production

German question	Input frequency	Production frequency	Leo's age at 1st use
was ist das für...	56	31	2;8.27
was ist das für ein...	24	23	2;8.27
was ist das für eine...	27	5	2;10.3
was ist das für eine Farbe?	20	–	–

3.2 Why does Leo produce only '*was ist das für...*' questions in the beginning?

Why does Leo at first produce the most frequent type *was ist das für...* only, and never before 3;0 the next most frequent types *was ist denn das für...*, *was denn für...* and *was ist das denn für...*? Also in the period between 3;0 and 5;0, the latter types occur only very infrequently, and it takes until 3;2.12 before any of those questions is produced. Crucially, the non-production of these questions, which all contain the modal particle *denn*, cannot be accounted for by a non-acquisition of *denn*. In total, between 2;0 and 3;0, Leo uses *denn* as a modal particle 71 times in different constructions, not just in wh-questions (see Steinkrauss 2009 for details). This shows that he knows the word. Why, then, does Leo produce only one of the four most frequent *was...für* question types in the input?

One reason might relate to the structural properties of the four question types. All have in common that their structure consists of a simple *was* 'what' question to which a *für NP* phrase is added. For example, the structure of the question *was ist das für ein Auto* 'what kind of car is that?' can be divided into a *was ist das?* 'what's that?' question and the phrase *für ein Auto* (lit. 'for a car'). What differs for the four questions however is the extent to which Leo produces the four more basic *was* questions. Table 5 lists the production frequency of the four questions and their related *was* questions.

It is striking that Leo produces *was ist das für...* questions and very many of the related *was ist das?* questions, while he produces none of the other *was...für* questions and only very few of their related *was* questions. While we may assume that the more basic *was* and the longer *was...für* questions are related from a general linguistic, structural point of view, the question arises whether we may also assume that they are related in the child's individual grammar as well. If so, the *was* question type may function as a supporting construction for the *was...für* question type. The production data do not contradict this assumption, at least at this stage of the child's development: only when Leo knows the simpler *was* type does he produce the related *was...für* type.

Table 5. Production frequencies of the four most frequent types of 'was...für' questions in the input and their corresponding 'was' questions

was...für **questions**	**Production frequency**	*was* **questions**	**Production frequency**
was ist das für...	31	*was ist das?*	202
was ist denn das für...	–	*was ist denn das?*	3
was denn für...	–	*was denn?*	2
was ist das denn für...	–	*was ist das denn?*	3

If the *was ist das für...* 'what kind of... is that' construction is indeed linked to the *was ist das?* 'what is that?' construction in Leo's linguistic knowledge, this should be evident in the child's production. This is indeed the case. The data provide three different kinds of evidence converging on that same conclusion: (i) Leo's pause pattern in *was ist das für...*questions, (ii) the priming of an unconventional word order in a *was ist das für...*question by a *was ist das?* question, and (iii) expansions of *was ist das?* questions to *was ist das für...*questions. The three points are illustrated in the following.

Before Leo's first *was ist das für...*question at 2;8.27, Leo has already produced 70 *was ist das?* questions. They constitute the largest group of *was* questions by far. After some isolated *was ist das?* from 2;3.8 onwards, *was ist das?* is produced very frequently from 2;7 and can be seen as well-established at the onset of the *was ist das für...* questions. About 90% of the questions are produced with a very distinct intonation: fast, without a pause and with a single intonation contour, exhibiting a heavy main stress and a strong rising-falling pitch on *das*. The fluent pronunciation without pauses points to a deeply entrenched, initially possibly unanalyzed chunk (Hickey 1993; Peters 1983; Plunkett 1993).

In contrast, 13 of the *was ist das für...* questions before 3;0 are produced with one or more pauses. 10 of them show a pause after *das*, which makes this the main position for a pause in that construction. Just as a fluent intonation is regarded as an indication for a single chunk, pauses in child speech point to possible structural boundaries (Hickey 1993; Peters 1983; Plunkett 1993). In this case, the pause pattern suggests a boundary between *was ist das* and *für...*. This is exactly what we would expect if *was ist das?* is a supporting construction for *was ist das für...*. Two especially clear examples back up this interpretation: after a heavy stress on *das* which is uttered with a rising-falling intonation, Leo pauses for a while, and then continues with *für...*. The first part of the questions shows the intonation so characteristic of the *was ist das* questions, and the second part seems simply to have been added to the first. Leo's production thus suggests that there is a structural link between *was ist das?* and *was ist das für...* for Leo.

Another type of evidence for a structural connection comes from a *was ist das für...* question with an unconventional word order. Instead of after *was*, the finite verb *ist* is placed at the end of the question, just like in indirect questions or echo questions. In traditional grammars, this is referred to as non- or uninversion. The question occurs while Leo (*CHI) and his mother (*MUT) are trying out games they find in an old book that they browse through. At one point, Leo says *was* 'what' and trails off. The mother reacts with *was das ist?* 'what that is?' and goes on to explain that it is an old book with games. Leo then asks *was das für ein Spiel ist?* 'what kind of game that is?', probably referring to a game in the book:

Excerpt 1: Age 2;11.26

	*CHI:	was ...
		what...
	*MUT:	was das is(t)?
		what that is?
	*MUT:	das is(t) ein ganz altes Spielebuch, Leo
		that's a very old book with games, Leo
	*MUT:	das is(t) noch von der Oma
		that's still from grandma
	*MUT:	hm?
		see?
→	*CHI:	was das fuer ein Spiel is(t)?
		what kind of game that is?

Conventionally, the question should have been *was ist das für ein Spiel*. The unconventional word order clearly seems due to the mother's echo question *was das ist* a few turns before. A little later in the same recording, Leo utters two more *was ist das für ein Spiel* questions, both in the conventional word order. It seems that for the moment, Leo is syntactically primed by his mother. His knowledge of how to construct conventional *was ist das für...*questions is still too weak to overcome the priming effect (cf. Abbot-Smith and Tomasello 2006: 277).

Importantly, the priming syntactic structure is *was das ist*, thus a type of a simple *was (ist)* question, and not a type of *was...für* question. This shows that *was...für* questions are in some way related to *was (ist)* questions for Leo. Leo takes over the word order of the echo question and inserts a *für NP* to form a *was...für* question. This in turn suggests that the *für NP* seems to be some unit of speech available to Leo for the construction of *was...für* questions. Again, the evidence indicates a structural link between the two question types and that *was ist das?* is a supporting construction for *was ist das für...*.

While the first two types of evidence suggest a structural connection between *was ist das?* and *was ist das für...* in Leo's grammar, the third type of evidence indicates that there is also a semantic connection. At 2;9.9, Leo utters *was ist das für ein Buch?* 'what kind of book is that?' as part of the following exchange:

Excerpt 2: Age 2;9.9

	*CHI:	was ist das?
		what is that?
	*VAT:	ein Buch
		a book
→	*CHI:	was ist das fuer ein Buch?
		what kind of book is that?

After Leo asks *what is that?* and the father replies *a book*, Leo inquires further and specifies his question. A similar example is an exchange two weeks later, when a *was ist das?* question is not answered by the parents and Leo specifies his question twice by adding a *für NP* before he finally gets an answer. In both cases, the *was ist das für...* questions clearly build further on the earlier *was ist das?* question, not only structurally but also semantically.

To sum up, there are several types of evidence in Leo's production suggesting that there is a structural and semantic connection between *was ist das?* and *was ist das für...*for Leo, and that he knows that a *was ist das?* question can be expanded to a *was ist das für...* question. Importantly, the evidence stems from different domains of investigation (fluency, priming, and turn-taking) and still converges on the same conclusion. Because Leo produces many *was ist das?* and *was ist das für...* questions, but (virtually) none of the other three frequent *was...für* and their related *was* constructions, we may conclude that Leo's previous knowledge influences what kind of *was...für* questions he produces. This explains the first discrepancy between input frequency and production identified above. In this case, the effect of input frequency is mediated by Leo's previous knowledge of related linguistic constructions.

3.3 Why does Leo produce so few '*was ist das für eine...*' Questions?

The second discrepancy between input and production is that Leo does not produce about equally many *was ist das für ein...* ('what kind of $\text{a}_{\text{masc/neut}}$... is that') and *was ist das für eine...* ('what kind of a_{fem}... is that') questions. Instead, until 3;0, he produces 23 of the former and only 5 of the latter. The first *was ist das für ein...* question at 2;8.27 suggests a possible explanation for this discrepancy:

Excerpt 3: Age 2;8.27

*CHI:	was ist das für $\text{ein}_{\textit{masc/neut}}$ $\text{Wurst}_{\textit{fem}}$?
	what kind of $\textit{a}_{\textit{masc/neut}}$ $\textit{sausage}_{\textit{fem}}$ *is that?*

The question is ungrammatical because the indefinite article *ein*$_{masc/neut}$ 'a' does not agree in gender with the noun *Wurst*$_{fem}$ 'sausage'. This is Leo's only error of agreement with *Wurst* in the whole corpus (the noun occurs 34 times between 2;0 and 5;0). That means we can conclude that the error is not due to the noun used, but to the *was ist das für...* construction as a whole.

There are two possible explanations for this error. The first is that Leo only has a *was ist das für ein*+Noun schema at this stage and that he inserts any noun into the Noun slot. If the noun is feminine, this leads to an error of agreement, as in the *Wurst* example in excerpt 3 above. The second possible explanation is that Leo has a *was ist das für*+X schema at the time he produces the *Wurst* question, but he does not have the knowledge that the X slot may be instantiated with *eine* and a feminine noun. The data support the second explanation. If Leo initially only had a *was ist das für ein*+Noun schema, we would expect only *was ist das für ein...* questions in the beginning, and several errors of agreement with feminine nouns in that construction. Both expectations are not backed up. Already Leo's next question on the following day does not contain *ein* but *zwei*, and the *Wurst* question above is the only error of agreement until 3;0. All other questions with a feminine noun are produced with the conventional article *eine*.

This strongly suggests that Leo has a *was ist das für*+X schema at the time he utters the *Wurst* question. His next *was...für* question, *was ist das für zwei...*, shows that there is a slot after *für*, and the predominant production of *was ist das für ein...* questions, inclusive of the incorrect *ein Wurst* question, shows that *ein*+Noun is the prototypical material for Leo to instantiate that X slot. The knowledge that also *eine*+Noun can be inserted in the X slot develops only later; all five *was ist das für eine...* questions are produced only after 2;10.3.

But what may be the reason for the fact that in the beginning Leo only knows *ein*+Noun but not *eine*+Noun as an instantiation for the X slot? A possible cause are the type and token frequencies of the *was ist das für...* questions in the input. The 24 *was ist das für ein...* questions in the input before 2;8.27 are used with 15 different nouns, none of which used in more than five questions, thus 21% of all *was ist das für ein...* questions. Because many different nouns are used after *ein*, Leo can abstract an *ein*+Noun pattern easily. In contrast, the 27 *was ist das für eine...* questions are used with only 3 different nouns. In 20 questions, thus 74% of all questions, the noun is *Farbe* 'color'. Because there is little variation after *eine*, it is difficult to abstract an *eine*+Noun pattern. *Ein*+Noun thus becomes the prototypical instantiation of the X slot.

Leo's infrequent production of *was ist das für eine...* questions in spite of their high input frequency is thus due to the repetitiveness of identical input. Because the type frequency of nouns following *eine* is low, it is difficult to abstract a *was ist das für eine*+Noun schema. Hence, Leo produces few questions of that type. The effect of the overall high input frequency of *was ist das für eine...* questions is thus limited by the low type frequency of the slot after *eine*.

3.4 Why does Leo never produce '*was ist das für eine Farbe?*'

The previous section has shown that a high type frequency can support abstraction while a high token frequency leads to entrenchment. But why, then, did Leo not pick up the highly frequent question *was ist das für eine Farbe?* 'what color is that?' and produce it himself? The question occurs 20 times in the input in the same form and still Leo does not produce it a single time until 3;0 – in the whole corpus until 5;0, Leo utters that question only once, at 4;4.7. A close look at the function of the question reveals why Leo does not produce it.

There are several conventional ways in German to ask for the color of an object. Two basic types of question can be distinguished: *welch* 'which' questions, and *was für* questions. The latter split into two subtypes: continuous questions and split questions (see Section 2.2). All types occur in the input.

The general assumption in the literature presented in Section 2.2 is that the functions of *was für* and *welch* constructions differ. But as mentioned above *was für* and *welch* questions are often used interchangeably. This also applies to the *Farbe* questions. The input data show that the parents readily used both question types in the same contexts and also replace them with each other in cases where they repeat the question or where several *Farbe* questions are asked in a row. The high proportion of *Farbe* questions in all *was für* and *welch* questions in the input before 3;0 is an expression of that: for both question types, questions asking for a *Farbe* constitute the largest subtype (between 14% and 18%). *Farbe* questions are thus highly common for both question constructions. This suggests that the theoretical difference between the two construction types does not seem to play a decisive role for *Farbe* questions in actual discourse.

In spite of the virtually identical function of the different types of color questions, they are not used with the same absolute frequency in the input. Continuous *was für* and *welch* questions are most frequent by far (Table 6):

Table 6. Input frequencies of all questions asking for a 'Farbe' (color) before 3;0

	was für eine Farbe		
welche Farbe	**Continuous**	**Split**	**Other *Farbe* questions***
71	88	46	29

* Other *Farbe* questions include 28 *was...für* questions and one other question (*wie* 'how'). In 25 of the 28 *was...für* questions, *was für eine Farbe* is in oblique case, such as in *mit was für einer Farbe* (*with what kind of color*). Three questions are *das ist was für eine Farbe?* (*that is what kind of color?*).

The question that Leo does not produce although it is frequent in the input is *was ist das für eine Farbe*, a split question in which the copula verb *ist* 'is' is used. The question does not mention the object the color of which the question asks for. If one wants to ask a *was...für* color question and also name the object, a form of *haben* 'have' has to be used instead of the copula. The *haben* form agrees with the object in number. Again, there is both a continuous (5) and a split (6) version:

(5) *Was für eine Farbe hat das Auto?*
What for a color has the car

(6) *Was hat das Auto für eine Farbe?*
What has the car for a color
'Which color does the car have?'

Consequently, all *was...für* questions asking for a color can occur in a split and a continuous version, and each version contains either the copula *sein* 'be' and a pronoun like *das* 'that', or *haben* and the name of the object whose color the question is about. The two different verbs do not distribute equally over the split and continuous *was für* types, as Table 7 shows.

Whenever a *haben* form is used, the continuous version is strongly preferred. Conversely, the use of a *sein* 'be' form (including *ist*) is associated with the split version. This association is highly significant (Yates' $\chi^2 = 67.9$, $df = 1$, $p < 0.001$).

Thus, whenever one of Leo's caregivers asks a question about color, it is most likely to be a continuous *was für* question, because these are most frequent. Continuous *was für* color questions in turn are strongly associated with the *haben* + object construction. Continuous *was für* questions with a form of *haben* as the main verb are thus the typical, and most frequent type of questions asking for a color in the input (79 tokens), with *welch* 'which' questions being a close second (71 tokens). So although *was ist das für eine Farbe* is the most frequent *was ist das für* question in the input, it is not the typical question used to ask for a color, and it is therefore no surprise that Leo does not use that question to ask for a color himself.

Table 7. Input frequencies of all '*was...für*' color questions divided by verb and (pro)noun used before 3;0.
Five continuous questions do not contain any verb. The total input frequency of continuous color questions is thus 88 (as in Table 6)

	Continuous	**Split**
haben + object	79	11
sein + pronoun	4	35

The communicative goal of the question, to ask for a color, is fulfilled better by a different question construction. This shows again that it is not input frequency alone that determines which constructions Leo picks up and uses, but input frequency in interaction with function. In the case at hand, we have two different groups of questions: one more structurally defined group, and one more functionally defined group. The structural group comprises all *was...für* 'what kind of...' questions that share their structure and also the abstract function to ask for a kind. The functional group comprises all color questions that share the function to ask for a color but have different structures (*welch*, split *was...für*, and continuous *was für*). The commonalities of the questions in the structural group are not enough to establish a set of constructions across which frequency would be the main factor determining Leo's production. Instead, it is the common function to ask for a color that establishes a set of constructions where input frequency influences Leo's choice in production. Before 3;0, Leo produces six questions asking for a color. Five are *was...für* questions with *haben*, three of which are continuous questions, and one is a *welch* question, the second largest type of color questions in the input. So if Leo wants to ask a question about a color, he may use more typical and more frequent color question constructions than *was ist das für eine Farbe*, and that is what Leo does. Similar to Abbot-Smith and Behrens' (2006) study, the production of a frequent structure was suppressed because the child was already using other, functionally equivalent structures.

Another reason why Leo probably does not ask *was ist das für eine Farbe* questions, and so few color questions overall, seems to be the general function of color questions. In the input, the majority of all color questions are questions that do not seek information (192 of 232 questions). They rather try to elicit color terms from Leo on a number of different objects in order to test his knowledge and teach him the German names for colors. It thus makes little sense for Leo to ask this kind of questions to his parents; he does not know the color names yet and can neither teach nor test his parents. Real information-seeking color questions are asked by Leo's parents only after Leo starts to show a more stable knowledge of the color terms towards the end of his 3rd year of life. And only then does Leo start to ask color questions himself. His questions are all information-seeking, asking for the color of objects that Leo does not see. Presumably, this is the only useful function of color questions for Leo. Asking for colors of visible objects does not make sense because Leo now knows the color terms. Situations where Leo does not see an object and wants to know its color do however not arise very often. Color questions are therefore generally infrequent in Leo's production.

To conclude, Leo does not produce the question *was ist das für eine Farbe* because other color questions are more frequent in the input, and because color questions in general are only of limited use to Leo. Again, we find that input frequency influences acquisition. But the effect of frequency is mitigated by the lack of a general usefulness of the construction for the child. Also, the analysis shows that input frequency information might be misleading when input frequency is calculated for a group of predominantly structurally similar constructions and not for functionally similar constructions.

4. Discussion

The present study investigated the acquisition of a group of wh-questions to assess the influence of input frequency on order of acquisition. Several major discrepancies between the course of acquisition predicted by input frequency and the course of acquisition in the child's actual production could be observed. In all cases, the input frequency of the questions still played a role, but always in conjunction with other factors that have already been suggested in the literature.

In particular, the function of a linguistic structure, i.e. its meaning and its usefulness for the child, and the child's knowledge of other structures that are semantically and structurally related, were found to strongly influence the child's production and to mediate the influence of input frequency. When a structure's function is not immediately useful for the child (as in the case of the color questions), the child might not produce that structure in spite of a high input frequency. This supports the evidence provided by Clancy (1989) that a child would not use a frequent construction if that construction did not meet the child's communicative interests. Also, a structure might not be produced because another structure that fulfils (almost) the same function is more frequent, and therefore used instead. This was the case for the question *was ist das für eine Farbe?* 'what color is that?', where other, more frequent types of color questions were produced. The structure was thus not used because another structure with the same function was already available to the child (Abbot-Smith and Behrens 2006). Similarly, the use of two of the three next most frequent *was...für* types after *was ist das für...* ('what kind of... is that') which only differed from that type in the use of a modal particle might also have been delayed because their function was too similar to the *was ist das für...* question type already acquired. Findings on other wh-questions that differed only with regard to the presence or absence of a modal particle support this interpretation (Steinkrauss 2009). In the current study, the non-production of the three next most frequent *was...für* types after *was ist das für* was traced back to the almost complete absence of simpler *was* questions on which the *was...für* questions were based. Converging evidence for a structural as well as a semantic connection were found in Leo's production and confirm the idea that the presence of some constructions may support the acquisition of other constructions (Abbot-Smith and Behrens 2006). Finally, the present study also confirmed earlier findings that type and token frequency in the input lead to different outcomes in acquisition. Because one specific question (*was ist das für eine Farbe*) was used in the same form over and over again, no quick abstraction could take place for that question type and other *was ist das für eine...* questions were produced later than *was ist das für ein...* questions although the latter were even slightly less frequent in the input.

These findings suggest that input frequency should be used with care as a tool and an explanatory factor in language acquisition research. When measuring and comparing the frequency of different constructions, it seems important to take into account their function as well. Otherwise input frequency might be measured for a group of constructions which are only structurally related but not functionally related. In that case, the constructions might look comparable while in fact they are not, and comparing their frequencies can therefore be misleading. Also, if function is not taken into account, it might be overlooked that there are constructions which do not meet the communicative needs of the child and that can therefore not be expected to be produced, independently of their frequency in the input. And thirdly, it is important to investigate also whole constructions, not just the beginnings of utterances. Assessing only the frequency of the initial parts of a structure, such as here in the case of *was ist das für eine...* questions, can mask that the type frequency of that construction can be quite low which makes an abstraction difficult for the child. In these cases, a construction might not be acquired although it appears to be very frequent at first sight.

The study thus argues for a combination of quantitative and qualitative methods in language acquisition research and to consider several factors at once. Even when analyzing case study data, such an approach will result in evidence from different domains, opening the possibility to find converging support and providing a more complete picture of the mechanisms underlying language acquisition. In previous studies, frequency analyses have often been based on counting linguistic forms only. This disregards the fundamental characteristic of constructions to be form-function pairings. The results presented here show that the form of a construction and its frequency tell just half the story. Language acquisition is based on usage, and usage means the use of a form in a specific situation, to a specific end. The latter should therefore be taken into account as well.

References

Abbot-Smith, K. & H. Behrens. 2006. How known constructions influence the acquisition of other constructions: the German passive and future constructions. *Cognitive Science* 30 (6): 995–1026.

Abbot-Smith, K. & M. Tomasello. 2006. Exemplar-learning and schematization in a usage-based account of syntactic acquisition. *The Linguistic Review* 23: 275–290.

Behrens, H. 2006. The input-output relationship in first language acquisition. *Language and Cognitive Processes* 21 (1–3): 2–24.

Bybee, J. 1995. Regular morphology and the lexicon. *Language and Cognitive Processes* 10: 425–455.

Bybee, J. 2006. From usage to grammar: the mind's response to repetition. *Language* 82 (4): 711–733.

Cameron-Faulkner, T., E.V.M. Lieven, & M. Tomasello. 2003. A construction based analysis of child directed speech. *Cognitive Science* 27 (6): 843–873.

Clancy, P.M. 1989. Form and function in the acquisition of Korean Wh-questions. *Journal of Child Language* 16 (2): 323–347.

Croft, W. 2001. *Radical construction grammar: syntactic theory in typological perspective.* Oxford: Oxford University Press.

Dabrowska, E. 2000. From formula to schema: The acquisition of English questions. *Cognitive Linguistics* 11 (1–2): 83–102.

Dabrowska, E. & E.V.M. Lieven. 2005. Towards a lexically specific grammar of children's question constructions. *Cognitive Linguistics* 16: 437–474.

Dekydtspotter, L., R. A. Sprouse, & T. D. Meyer. 2005. Was für N interrogatives and quantifier scope in English-German interpretation. In L. Dekydtspotter, R. A. Sprouse, & A. Liljestrand, eds., *Proceedings of the 7th Generative Approaches to Second Language Acquisition Conference (GASLA 2004),* 86–95. Somerville: Cascadilla Proceedings Project.

Felix, S. 1976. WH-pronouns in first and second language acquisition. *Linguistische Berichte* 44: 52–64.

Forner, M. 1979. The mother as LAD: Interaction between order and frequency of parental input and child production. In F. R. Eckman & A. J. Hastings, eds., *Studies in First and Second Language Acquisition,* 17–44. Rowley: Newbury House Publishers.

Götz, D. & G. Haensch. 2003. *Langenscheidt Großwörterbuch Deutsch als Fremdsprache.* Berlin: Langenscheidt.

Helbig, G. & J. Buscha. 1992. *Leitfaden der deutschen Grammatik.* Leipzig: Langenscheidt.

Hickey, T. 1993. Identifying formulas in first language acquisition. *Journal of Child Language* 20: 27–41.

Ingram, D. 1971. The acquisition of questions and its relation to cognitive development in normal and linguistically deviant children: A pilot study. *Word: Journal of the Linguistic Circle of New York* 27 (1 (Apr)): 119–124.

Kempcke, G. & B. Seelig. 2000. *Wörterbuch Deutsch als Fremdsprache.* Berlin/New York: de Gruyter.

Klima, E. S. & U. Bellugi. 1966. Syntactic regularities in the speech of children. In J. Lyons & R. J. Wales, eds., *Psycholinguistics papers: Proceedings of the 1966 Edinburgh conference,* 183–219. Edinburgh: Edinburgh University Press.

Kunkel-Razum, K. & A. Auberle. 2003. *Duden deutsches Universalwörterbuch.* Mannheim: Dudenverlag.

Langacker, R. W. 1987. *Foundations of cognitive grammar, vol. 1: Theoretical prerequisites.* Stanford, CA: Stanford University Press.

Lieven, E.V.M., J.M. Pine, & G. Baldwin. 1997. Lexically-based learning and early grammatical development. *Journal of Child Language* 24 (1): 187–219.

Lieven, E. V. M. & M. Tomasello. 2008. Children's first language acquisition from a usage-based perspective. In P. Robinson & N. Ellis, eds., *Handbook of Cognitive Linguistics and Second Language Acquisition,* 168–196. New York: Routledge.

MacWhinney, B. 2000. *The CHILDES Project: Tools for Analyzing Talk.* Mahwah, NJ: Erlbaum.

Morris, W. C., G. W. Cottrell, & J. L. Elman. 2000. A connectionist simulation of the empirical acquisition of grammatical relations. In S. Wermter & R. Sun, eds., *Hybrid Neural Symbolic Integration,* 175–193. Berlin: Springer.

Pafel, J. 1996. Die syntaktische und semantische Struktur von was für-Phrasen. *Linguistische Berichte* 161: 37–67.

Peters, A. M. 1983. *The Units of Language Acquisition.* Cambridge: Cambridge University Press.

Pine, J.M. & E.V.M. Lieven. 1997. Slot and frame patterns and the development of the determiner category. *Applied Psycholinguistics* 18 (2): 123–138.

Pine, J.M., E.V.M. Lieven, & C.F. Rowland. 1998. Comparing different models of the development of the English verb category. *Linguistics* 36 (4): 807–830.

Plunkett, K. 1993. Lexical segmentation and vocabulary growth in early language acquisition. *Journal of Child Language* 20: 43–60.

Rowland, C.F. 2007. Explaining errors in children's questions. *Cognition* 104: 106–134.

Rowland, C.F. & J.M. Pine. 2003. The development of inversion in wh-questions: A reply to Van Valin. *Journal of Child Language* 30 (1): 197–212.

Rowland, C.F. & J.M. Pine. 2000. Subject-auxiliary inversion errors and wh-question acquisition: 'what children do know?'. *Journal of Child Language* 27 (1): 157–181.

Rowland, C.F. et al. 2003. Determinants of acquisition order in wh-questions: Re-evaluating the role of caregiver speech. *Journal of Child Language* 30 (3): 609–635.

Savic, S. 1975. Aspects of adult-child communication: The problem of question acquisition. *Journal of Child Language* 2 (2): 251–260.

Smith, M.E. 1933. The influence of age, sex, and situation on the frequency, form and function of questions asked by preschool children. *Child Development* 4 (3 (sep)): 201–213.

Steinkrauss, R. (2009). Frequency and Function in WH Question Acquisition: A Usage-based Case Study of German L1 Acquisition. Groningen Dissertations in Linguistics. University of Groningen.

Stern, C. & W. Stern. 1928. *Die Kindersprache: eine psychologische und sprachtheoretische Untersuchung.* Leipzig: Johann Ambrosius Barth.

Theakston, A.L. et al. 2001. The role of performance limitations in the acquisition of verb-argument structure: An alternative account. *Journal of Child Language* 28: 127–152.

Theakston, A.L. et al. 2002. Going, going, gone: The acquisition of the verb 'go'. *Journal of Child Language* 29: 783–811.

Tomasello, M. 1992. *First verbs: A case study of early grammatical development.* Cambridge: Cambridge University Press.

Tomasello, M. 2003. *Constructing a Language: A Usage-based Theory of Language Acquisition.* Cambridge, MA: Harvard University Press.

Tyack, D. & D. Ingram. 1977. Children's production and comprehension of questions. *Journal of Child Language* 4 (2): 211–224.

Wode, H. 1983. Some stages in the acquisition of the questions by monolingual children. In H. Wode, eds., *Papers on language learning, language acquisition and language teaching,* 47–93. Heidelberg: Julius Groos.

Relative clause acquisition and representation

Evidence from spontaneous speech, sentence repetition, and comprehension

Silke Brandt and Evan Kidd
University of Basel and University of Manchester

According to usage-based approaches, representations and processing of linguistic constructions emerge from usage events. We present corpus data, which show that object relative clauses are mostly attached to an inanimate head NP and contain a pronominal subject (***the ball** that **he** just threw*). In two experiments, English- and German-speaking children were best at processing object relatives identical in form and function to these frequent exemplars. In contrast to earlier studies, we did not find that subject relatives were always easier to process than object relatives. Our data provide further evidence suggesting that children and adults do fine-grained analyses of their linguistic input, and that linguists should do the same to derive hypotheses about the nature of linguistic representations and processing.

Keywords: empirical methods, language acquisition, syntactic representations, usage-based, relative clause

1. Introduction

Using both corpus and experimental data and choosing the correct experimental method or using a variety of experimental methods is crucial when it comes to analyzing and describing children's acquisition of linguistic constructions. First of all, when we look at data from children's spontaneous speech, we have to deal with sampling issues. That is, even dense databases, which are based on about five or more one-hour recordings of caretaker-child interaction per week, do not catch enough exemplars of infrequent complex structures or infrequent lexical items within specific constructions to allow for reliable calculations and conclusions (Rowland and Fletcher 2006, Tomasello and Stahl 2004). In addition, most corpus data come from a limited number of specific settings and contexts, such as playtime with the caretaker, which can further restrict the range of linguistic constructions used by the children (cf. Behrens 2008).

When we want to do a detailed analysis of children's representations of complex constructions that are quite infrequent in spontaneous speech, such as relative clauses (cf. Brandt, Diessel, and Tomasello 2008), we thus need to set up experiments to probe children's knowledge of these constructions. However, like data from spontaneous speech, data from experimental settings also have to be interpreted with some caution. Children have relatively short attention spans, limited working memory, limited cognitive control, etc., and these general cognitive limitations have an impact on children's behavior in language experiments as well as their language production in natural settings (e.g. Felser, Marinis, and Clahsen 2003, Hamburger and Crain 1984, Trueswell 2008, Valian 1991). For example, young children might not be able to act out or produce sentences such as '*the chicken that the cow kicks bites the pig*' or '*put the frog on the napkin in the box*' because they have limited cognitive control as well as limited working or short-term memory, which does not allow them to deal with such long sentences and complex scenes, and not because they lack a representation of embedded structures or (reduced) relative clauses.

Interestingly, studies that use different methodologies to test children's representations of linguistic structures sometimes diverge in their results and conclusions. For example, several preferential-looking studies suggest that children as young as 1;9 (i.e. one year; nine months) have an abstract, verb-general presentation of the transitive construction (e.g. Gertner, Fisher, and Eisengart 2006, Naigles 1990). However, studies where children were asked to act out or point to scenes described by transitive sentences with novel verbs, or where children were asked to produce transitives with novel verbs, suggest that children do not have a fully abstract, verb-general representation of the transitive construction before the age of 2;6 or 2;8 (e.g. Akhtar 1999, Tomasello, Brooks, and Stern 1998). These latter studies indicate that children start with verb-specific representations that gradually develop into abstract, verb-general representations of the transitive construction.

Abbot-Smith, Lieven, and Tomasello (2008) propose that children's varying behaviors across different methods is due to the fact that some methods, such as preferential looking, depend on weak representations of linguistic structures, whereas other, more active and complex methods like act-out or pointing require the coordination of various cognitive and sensory-motor processes and thus depend on stronger representations (see also Abbot-Smith and Tomasello 2006). Importantly, unlike nativist-generative accounts of language acquisition (e.g. Marcus 1998, Radford 1990), usage-based accounts such as that proposed by Abbot-Smith et al. (2008) do not assume that children either have or have not acquired specific constructions or categories at a certain point in development; rather, these accounts suggest that categories and constructions are gradually learned from and strengthened by exemplars in the input. Children are assumed to have an abstract – though weak – representation of the transitive, for example, as soon as they show some knowledge of transitive sentences with some verbs in their comprehension or production behavior. Each exemplar that, based on formal, functional, and/or relational similarities, can be categorized as an instance of a particular category or construction strengthens the representation of that category or construction (cf. Abbot-Smith and Tomasello 2006). Thus, the more transitives a child experiences and recognizes as instances of that construction, the stronger her representation of the transitive construction becomes. However, in order to really develop a strong item-general representation of the transitive, children have to hear and use this construction with a variety of verb types and noun or pronoun types (see also Bybee 1995, Goldberg 1995, Langacker 2000). At the same time, as children derive abstract linguistic categories and constructions from particular exemplars, they also build up item-specific representations that are connected to the more abstract representations. If, for example, children hear many transitives with the verb *push*, these exemplars will support the strengthening of both an abstract transitive SVO schema and a more item-specific S *push* O schema (Abbot-Smith and Tomasello 2006).

Since children at around age 2;0 have heard and produced a great number of transitives with familiar verbs such as *push* or *kick*, they presumably have strong item-specific representations of transitives with familiar verbs, such as S *push* O or S *kick* O. When they are asked to act out or produce a transitive with a novel verb, however, they have to work with a verb-general representation, such as SVO, which is not as strong as their item-specific representations (cf. Abbot-Smith et al. 2008).

The assumption that weak representations allow for positive results from looking-time measures, but not for positive results in more active paradigms, such as reaching or pointing, is supported by studies on the development of object permanence. For example, in a study by Baillargeon (1987), 3;5 month-olds witnessed how a box was hidden behind a screen. Then they either saw the screen rotating through a full 180° without the box reappearing (impossible event), or they saw the screen rotating only until reaching the hidden box (possible event). The infants looked longer at the impossible event than the possible event. However, Munakata, McClelland, Johnson, and Siegler (1997) demonstrated that 7 months olds are still more likely to reach for or release objects that were moved behind transparent barriers than objects that were moved behind opaque barriers. These results suggest that infants can represent objects even if they are out of sight, but initially these object representations are too weak to guide reaching or other active, more complex behaviors, which require the coordination of several cognitive and sensory-motor processes and thus need more processing capacity. Simulations with Parallel Distributed Processing models suggest that object representations become stronger with more experience with absent objects, and that these stronger representations potentially lead to positive results when measuring infants' object permanence with more active and complex tasks (Munakata et al. 1997).

Similarly, Chang, Dell, and Bock (2006) simulated the difference between looking-time and production measures in experiments on the acquisition of the transitive construction with a connectionist model. In summary, the graded representations account suggests that more complex or active tasks rely on stronger representations, and that the strengths of the representations, in turn, depend on the number of exemplars supporting the specific representations. Strong representations allow for some automatization, which, in turn, frees up some processing capacity to deal with the task demands (Case 1985, Munakata et al. 1997, Siegler 2000).

Experience with specific linguistic constructions also plays an important role in some accounts of adults' language processing. MacDonald and Christiansen (2002), for example, suggest that individual differences that are found in psycholinguistic experiments, and that are traditionally attributed to differences in working-memory capacity (e.g. Just and Carpenter 1992, King and Just 1991) are really an effect of the individuals' experience with specific linguistic structures, which in turn have an impact on their linguistic processing strategies and capacities (see also MacDonald 1999). For example, King and Just (1991) found an interaction between verbal working memory and relative-clause type: participants with lower working memories showed longer reading times and poor comprehension of object relatives (e.g. *the reporter that the senator attacked praised the judge*) in comparison to subject relatives (e.g. *the reporter that attacked the senator praised the judge*), but no such difference was found for high-span readers. Just and Carpenter (1992) take this as evidence for a separate verbal working memory, which influences sentence processing. This claim is based on the assumption that the processing of object relatives requires greater working memory because the distance between the filler or head NP and the gap is greater than in subject relatives (for similar approaches see Gibson 1998, Gordon, Hendrick, and Johnson 2004). However, MacDonald and Christiansen (2002) argue that these data can also be interpreted as evidence supporting the Frequency*Regularity Hypothesis (Seidenberg 1985). In English, subject relatives have more in common with frequently used canonical SVO sentences than do object relatives. In both subject relatives and canonical SVO sentences, the NP preceding the verb is the subject and the NP following verb is the object. For the interpretation of subject relatives, English-speaking subjects can thus use the same processing strategies as for the interpretation of simple sentences. The successful interpretation of object relatives, on the other hand, depends on direct exposure to irregular OSV structures (MacDonald and Christiansen, 2002: 40, for a similar approach to children's processing of relative clauses see Diessel and Tomasello 2005). To explain why people with higher verbal working memory are better at processing object relatives, it is argued that people with high verbal working memory have more experience with processing linguistic stimuli in general. And people who have more experience with sentence processing in general also have more experience with processing object relatives and other non-canonical structures. In support of this claim, Wells, Christiansen, Race, Acheson, and MacDonald (2009) showed that adult participants who were exposed to an equal amount of both subject and object relatives showed a decrease in reading time for object relatives relative to subject relatives, suggesting that exposure to infrequent forms results in an attenuation of processing difficulty traditionally explained by appeals to either working memory or syntactic derivation.

To summarize, the claims by Abbot-Smith et al. (2008; see also Abbot-Smith and Tomasello 2006) and MacDonald and Christiansen (2002) suggest that linguistic experience shapes linguistic processing. In MacDonald and Christiansen's connectionist approach, experience has a direct impact on sentence processing. In their Simple Recurrent Network model, they do not separate linguistic processing from linguistic representations. Linguistic knowledge is thought to 'emerge from the interaction of network architecture and experience' (Mac Donald and Christiansen 2002: 37) (see also Elman 1990, Seidenberg and McClelland 1989). In contrast, Abbot-Smith et al. (2008), like other usage-based approaches, suggest that linguistic experience shapes and strengthens linguistic representations, which, in turn, have an impact on language processing and the level of automatization in sentence parsing (see also Langacker 2000). Whether linguistic experience has a direct impact on language processing, or whether it is mediated by changes in linguistic representations, is hard to decide on empirical grounds.

In the following, we will present a corpus study that investigated the kinds of relative-clause representations German-speaking children might develop from the exemplars in their input. Furthermore, we will present results from a corpus study looking at German- and English-speaking children's own production of relative-clause constructions and two different experimental tasks (sentence repetition and referential selection) that tested German- and English-speaking children's representations of subject and object relative clauses.

As has been shown for adults (e.g. Gibson 1998, Just and Carpenter 1992), in the majority of past studies that tested comprehension or production of relative clauses, children performed better on subject relatives (e.g. *the dog that bites the cat*) than on object relatives (e.g. *the dog that the cat bites*). It has been suggested that this asymmetry is due to limited working memory (Booth, MacWhinney, and Harasaki 2000), perspective shifts (MacWhinney 1982), non-adult parsing strategies (e.g. Tavakolian 1981), difficulty with sentences that involve movement (e.g. Friedmann and Novogrodsky 2004, Goodluck, Guilfoyle, and Harrington 2006), and non-canonical word order in object relatives (e.g. Diessel and Tomasello 2005). However, all of these studies neglected some crucial formal and functional differences between subject and object relatives that might be encoded in children's (and adults') representations of relative-clause constructions. We detail these below.

2. Subject and object relatives in spoken corpora

Looking at more than 400 relative clauses in spoken English discourse, Fox and Thompson (1990) found that, while subject relatives are most often used to provide information about animate entities, object relatives are used to ground inanimate entities in discourse. Therefore, object relatives are much more likely to be attached to inanimate head NPs. The grounding is accomplished by linking the inanimate entities to given discourse participants, expressed by pronominal *I* or *you*, or other given referents in the immediate context, expressed by third person pronouns or proper names. By being explicitly related to given referents, the new inanimate entities are made relevant to the ongoing discourse (Fox and Thompson 1990: 300). The corpus study showed that object relatives are overwhelmingly used with inanimate head NPs (such as *the car* in (1)) and pronominal relative-clause subjects (such as *she* in (1)), as in the following example (Fox and Thompson 1990: 303):

(1) ***The car** that **she** borrowed had a low tire.*

This distribution can be derived from two more general linguistic patterns. First of all, subjects are topical; they refer to given referents, which are encoded by pronouns (cf. Du Bois 1987). Secondly, objects tend to be inanimate (cf. Mak, Vonk, and Schriefers 2002, 2006). Similar distributional patterns were recently reported by Roland, Dick, and Elman (2007) and Reali and Christiansen (2007a). Roland et al. (2007), for example, investigated a variety of written and spoken English corpora and found that the vast majority (e.g. 80% in the Switchboard data) of object relatives in the spoken corpora had pronominal subjects. They also report that animate head NPs are mainly used with subject relatives, whereas inanimate head NPs are most often used with object relatives.

Statistical regularities found in written corpora or adult-adult interaction do not necessarily have to show up in child-directed speech, but when we look at the input of a German-speaking child, we can see the same pattern. Within a sample of almost 150 object relatives, 85% contain pronominal subjects, and 78% are attached to inanimate head NPs (Brandt 2005). Looking at spoken corpora from four English children and one German child between the ages of 2;0 and 5;0, we found that both English- and German-speaking children use object relatives with inanimate heads 75% of the time. In addition, in both languages, at least 75% of the object relatives produced by the children had pronominal subjects (Kidd, Brandt, Lieven, and Tomasello 2007). Similarly, Diessel (2009) showed that, in spoken corpora,

English-speaking children almost exclusively use subject relatives with animate head NPs, and that the vast majority of non-subject relative clauses (i.e. object relatives or adverbial relatives) are used with inanimate head NPs and pronominal subjects. Thus, the same constraints that influence relative-clause production in adults seem to influence children's relative-clause production in spontaneous speech.

In the vast majority of previous studies on relative-clause acquisition children were tested on object relatives with animate head NPs and lexical relative-clause subjects, such as '***the chicken*** *that* ***the pig*** *pushed jumped over the sheep*' (Corrêa 1995). Children performed poorly on these sentences, without exception. There is evidence that children (and adults) perform fine-grained statistical analyses of their input (e.g. MacDonald 1999, Tomasello 2003). As described above, it has also been suggested that linguistic experience shapes children's and adults' representations of grammatical structures, which, in turn, have an impact on their processing capacities and strategies (cf. Abbot-Smith et al. 2008). Therefore, we suggest that the difficulties with object relatives observed in previous studies were, at least in part, due to the fact that the test sentences did not match the kinds of object relatives that children and adults had heard and produced before.

In fact, more recent studies in adult psycholinguistics have shown that high processing costs associated with object relatives can be reduced or eliminated when the clauses are attached to inanimate heads (Mak et al. 2002, 2006; Traxler, Morris, and Seely 2002, Traxler, Williams, Blozis, and Morris 2005), or when they contain pronominal subjects (Gordon, Hendrick, and Johnson 2001, Reali and Christiansen 2007a, 2007b; Warren and Gibson 2002, 2005). Our first experimental study (Kidd et al. 2007) was a sentence-repetition task that investigated whether children's difficulty with object relatives can also be reduced or eliminated once the test sentences are formed according to the constraints identified in the corpus studies.

3. Sentence repetition

We asked 3- and 4-year old English- and German-speaking children to imitate subject- and object relatives with animate and inanimate head NPs as well as object relatives with pronominal and full-NP subject. The children were tested on the following kinds of sentences:

(2) *This is* ***the boy*** *that* ***the girl*** *teased at school yesterday.* (obj_an_np)
(3) *That is* ***the dog*** *that* ***you*** *stroked in the park yesterday.* (obj_an_pro)
(4) *Here is* ***the food*** *that* ***the cat*** *ate in the kitchen today.* (obj_in_np)
(5) *There is* ***the book*** *that* ***you*** *read in the front room last night.* obj_in_pro)
(6) *Here is* ***the lady*** *that helped the girl at school today.* (subj_an)
(7) *Here is* ***the plant*** *that grew in the garden last summer.* (subj_in)

All test sentences were controlled for length in terms of words and syllables. In the German test sentences, all NPs were masculine singular and thus unambiguously marked for case. There were four test items in each condition and some less complex fillers, such as coordinate structures, which were presented to the children in randomized orders. The characters described in the sentences were present as small toys. The children were told that they played the parrot game, where they would have to say *exactly* the same as the experimenter.

Following expectations derived from the distributions found in the naturalistic data, children from both age groups and both languages made fewer errors when repeating object relatives with inanimate heads (examples (4) and (5)) and/or pronominal subjects (examples (3) and (5)) than object relatives with animate heads (examples (2) and (3)) and/or full-NP subjects (examples (2) and (4)) (see Figures 1 and 2). Conducting an ANOVA on children's performance on the object relatives, we found significant main effects for the animacy status of the head NP (English: $F_{(1,47)} = 6.44, p = .015$; German: $F_{(1,46)} = 9.07, p = .004$) and the form of the relative-clause subject (English: $F_{(1,47)} = 12.06, p = .001$; German: $F_{(1,46)} = 60.35, p < .001$). Both German- and English-speaking children performed best when they were tested on those kinds of object relatives that they most often say and hear in discourse. Moreover, children did not have more problems repeating object relatives that followed the constraints found in natural language than repeating subject relatives. The subject-object asymmetry reported in a great number of previous studies was thus eliminated with these prototypical object relatives. In contrast to those early accounts of syntactic acquisition that attributed children's difficulties with object relatives to poor syntactic knowledge, non-adult processing strategies, or limited working memory, we showed that their syntactic knowledge is closely tied to their linguistic experience. Furthermore, although the 4-year-olds performed better overall, none of the main effects showed an interaction with age. This suggests that, like adults, even the younger children are sensitive to these discourse constraints.

Focusing on the children's performance on subject relatives, Figures 1 and 2 show that the English-speaking children performed better on the subject relatives with animate head NPs, whereas the German-speaking children performed better on the subject relatives with inanimate head NPs. German- and English-speaking children regularly use subject relatives with both inanimate and animate head NPs (cf. Kidd et al. 2007). We can only speculate that the German-speaking children had fewer problems imitating subject relatives with inanimate head NPs because these test sentences were always intransitive, whereas the subject relatives with animate heads were all transitive (see examples above). The English-speaking children, on the other hand, might have had more difficulty with the subject relatives with inanimate head NPs because they were expecting an object relative after hearing a string such as INANIMATE – *that*. In English, only the material following

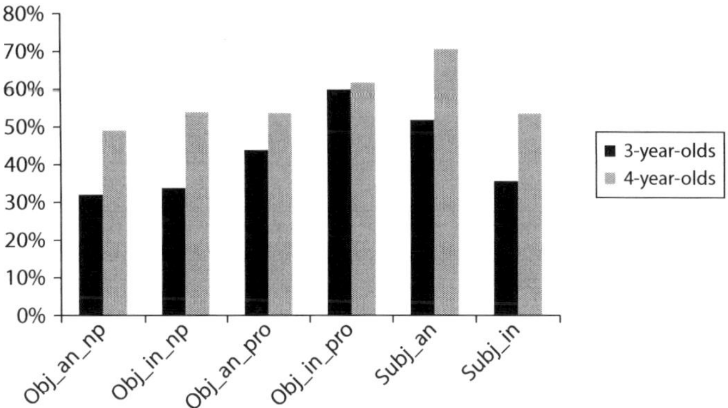

Figure 1. Percentage correct imitation by English-speaking children

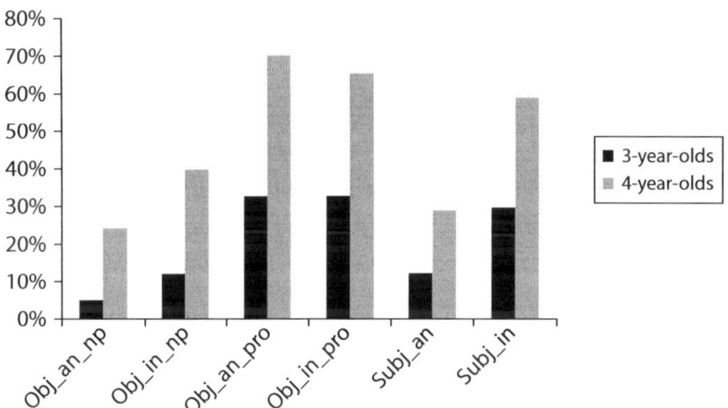

Figure 2. Percentage correct imitation by German-speaking children

the relativizer indicates whether the sentence is a subject or object relative. The German-speaking children only heard strings with case-marked relative pronouns, such as INANIMATE – *den* 'who-ACC' or INANIMATE – *der* 'who-NOM', where the relative pronoun already indicates whether the following clause is a subject or an object relative (cf. Kidd et al. 2007).

Given our sentence-repetition task, we cannot be completely sure that as well as testing production we were also testing relative-clause comprehension, as has been the case in most of the previous studies on relative-clause acquisition. Although there are studies suggesting that children's imitation behavior is good evidence for their grammatical competence (for an overview see Lust, Flynn, and Foley 1996), and that sentence imitation involves sentence comprehension

(Potter and Lombardi 1990, 1998; Sachs 1967), we cannot fully rule out that some of the children we tested were just mimicking the experimenter.

To our knowledge, there are two comprehension studies that looked at animacy or the form of the relative-clause subjects as factors influencing children's difficulty with object relatives.[1] Controlling the number of animate vs. inanimate entities in subject- and object-relative constructions, Corrêa (1995: 194) showed that 'object focus sentences (...) appeared to be particularly affected by animacy'. Portuguese-speaking children had fewer problems acting out object relatives with two animate referents and an inanimate head, such as (8), than object relatives with three animate referents including an animate head, such as (9):

(8) *The sheep pushed* ***the fence*** *that the horse knocked down.*
(9) *The pig pushes* ***the sheep*** *that the horse knocked down.*

In a study with Hebrew-speaking children involving production and comprehension, Arnon (2010) showed that children better understood object relatives containing pronominal subjects than object relatives with full-NP subjects. However, we are not aware of any study that systematically tested children's comprehension of object relatives controlling for both factors. Therefore, we designed a referential-choice task that tested children's understanding of subject- and object relatives, controlling for animacy of the head NP and the discourse status and form of the subject in object relatives and the object in subject relatives (Brandt, Kidd, Lieven, and Tomasello 2009). In contrast to the act-out method that has been used in most studies on children's relative-clause comprehension (e.g. Corrêa 1995, Eisenberg 2002, Goodluck and Tavakolian 1982, Kidd and Bavin 2002, Sheldon 1974), the referential-choice task places minimal demands on the children. We were thus able to show relative-clause comprehension in children much younger than in most previous studies, where successful comprehension is not typically evident until around 4 years or later.

4. Referential selection

In our second study we asked young 3-year-old German- and English-speaking children to select a referent that the experimenter described with either a subject- or an object relative clause. Subject relatives had pronominal or full-NP objects, while object relatives had pronominal or full-NP subjects. We always used third person singular and case-marked pronouns *he* (in German *er*) and *him*

1. Goodluck and Tavakolian (1982) also showed that the number of animate entities in subject relatives influences the ease of comprehension in children.

(in German *ihn*). The referent of the third person pronoun was always the same toy doll, *Peter*, who was introduced at the beginning of the experimental session and who kept reappearing for all sentences containing pronouns. Finally, object relatives had animate or inanimate head NPs. In order to only have plausible transitive relative clauses, subject relatives always had animate head NPs. These manipulations resulted in six conditions, as shown in Table 1. There were four test items in each condition, and the test sentences were controlled for length in terms of words and syllables. As in the previous study, the German sentences contained only masculine singular NPs, which are unambiguously marked for case.

All animals, inanimate entities, and humans that were referred to in the test sentences were present as small toys. The animals and inanimate entities served as referents for the relative-clause head NPs. We had two of each kind that could easily be distinguished by size, color, and/or shape. For example, we had a big lion and a small lion.

In order to set a context in which a relative clause could be used to identify a referent, the experimenter presented, for example, one of the two lions and a dog and said: *Look, the dog is chasing this lion*. Then she acted out this first background scene and put the first lion on one side of a disk that was fixated in front of the child. Then she presented the second lion with the same dog and said '*Look, the dog is pushing this lion*'. This scene was also acted out, and the second lion was put on the other side of the disk by the experimenter. These background scenes were followed by a distracter scene, where the dog did something else, and then the experimenter used a relative-clause construction, such as '*Can you give me the lion that the dog chased?*' to tell the child to pick one of the two lions.

This procedure is different from that of previous relative-clause comprehension studies (e.g. Corrêa 1995, Eisenberg 2002, Goodluck and Tavakolian 1982, Kidd and Bavin 2002, Sheldon 1974), where children were asked to act out relative-clause constructions containing two clauses, such as '*The chicken that the pig pushed jumped over the sheep*' (Corrêa 1995). In order to succeed in this

Table 1. Examples of test sentences for each condition

	subj	obj
an_np	*Can you give me* ***the dog*** *that chased* ***the lion****?*	*Can you give me* ***the monkey*** *that* ***the frog*** *combed?*
an_pro	*Can you give me* ***the donkey*** *that just tickled* ***him****?*	*Can you give me* ***the donkey*** *that* ***he*** *just fed?*
in_np		*Can you give me* ***the cake*** *that* ***the uncle*** *stole?*
in_pro		*Can you give me* ***the ball*** *that* ***he*** *just threw?*

act-out task, children have to understand agent-patient relations expressed in the sentence, i.e., they have to understand 'who is doing what to whom'. In the referential-selection task we used for the current study, the children have to match agents or patients with verbs or actions. For example, what distinguishes the small and the big lion is that one was chased by the dog, while the other one was pushed by the dog. Therefore, based on the link between a certain lion and a certain action the child can choose the correct referent after hearing *can you give me the lion that the dog chased?* without necessarily fully understanding 'who did what to whom'. However, in order to succeed in the task used here, the children still need to parse the relative clause as a restrictive noun modifier.

We used this task because it places minimal demands on the children. The act-out task had been criticized before for being too demanding and not showing children's full grammatical competence (e.g. Hirsh-Pasek and Golinkoff 1996). The referential-choice task allows us to test children who are quite young. Moreover, it allows us to use relative clauses in an experimental setting for the same purpose for which they are used in real life: to identify things (e.g. Givón 1993, Lehmann 1984) and link new entities to given entities (Fox and Thompson 1990). Relative-clause constructions like the ones that were used in the act-out tasks in previous studies mentioned above, on the other hand, are rarely used in real life (cf. Diessel 2004).

For the main analysis, we coded whether the children chose the correct referent described by the relative clause. In accordance with the results from the corpus studies and the sentence-repetition task (Kidd et al. 2007), German- and English-speaking 3-year old children showed better comprehension of object relatives with inanimate heads and/or pronominal subjects than object relatives with animate heads and full-NP subjects (see Figure 3 below). An ANOVA on children's performance on the object relatives showed that both factors, the animacy of the head NP and subject type within the relative clause, had a significant effect on the German children's performance (animacy: $F_{(1,23)} = 19.75$, $p < .001$; subject type: $F_{(1,23)} = 5.03$, $p = .035$). The English-speaking children performed significantly better on object relatives with pronominal relative-clause subjects ($F_{(1,19)} = 4.93$, $p = .039$). They also showed better performance on object relatives with inanimate heads, but the effect did not reach significance ($F_{(1,19)} = 2.86$, $p = .11$).

Importantly, what Figure 3 also shows is that neither the English-nor the German-speaking children always performed better on subject relatives than on object relatives. In fact, children from both languages performed better on object relative clauses with inanimate head NPs than on the subject relative clauses. Moreover, the English data and an ANOVA across languages showed an interaction between NP type and structure. Taken together, the German and English children showed better performance on object relatives with pronominal subjects than object relatives with full-NP subjects, but it did not matter whether the subject relatives contained

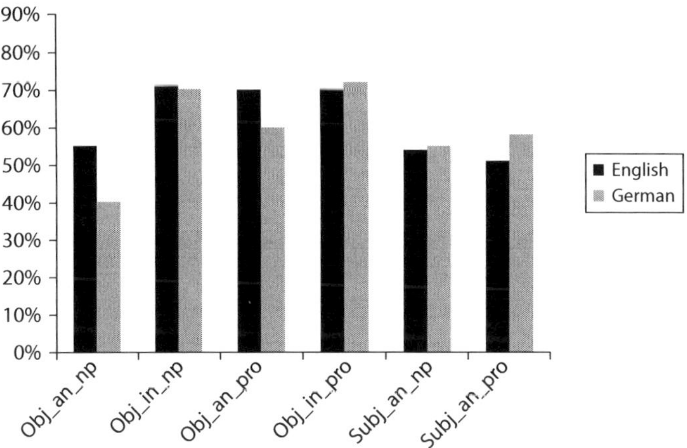

Figure 3. Percentage correct choice in referential-selection task

full-NP or pronominal objects ($F_{(1,42)} = 8.04$, $p = .007$). This is probably due to the fact that, in general, objects are expressed by both lexical NPs and pronouns, whereas subjects are most often expressed by pronouns or null forms (e.g. Du Bois 1987).

5. Discussion

We now have converging evidence from two corpus studies, two experimental tasks and two languages supporting the claim that linguistic experience shapes children's representations of relative-clause constructions, which in turn have an impact on their processing of these complex structures (or perhaps that sentence processing is directly influenced by linguistic experience, see MacDonald and Christiansen 2002 and discussion above). Our corpus studies showed that, like adults, German- and English-speaking children mainly use object relatives with inanimate head NPs and pronominal subjects. In the first experimental task, children had to imitate subject and object relative clauses (Kidd et al. 2007). In the second task, another group of German- and English-speaking children were asked to select a referent based on a description with a subject or object relative clause (Brandt et al. 2009). In both tasks, German- and English speaking children showed better comprehension and production of those object relative clauses that were formed according to the constraints found in the corpora.

In terms of methodology, we can conclude that, despite potential problems of sampling or limited contexts, a corpus analysis can be a good potential indicator of children's knowledge of linguistic constructions. The two experimental tasks presented here might be criticized since in order to succeed in these tasks, children need to have a good short-term memory. In the sentence-repetition study, children had to recall sentences with 11–13 words; in the referential-selection task, children had to remember two background scenes and also parse quite long sentences. However, within both studies, all test sentences were matched for length; they only differed in structure (object vs. subject relatives), semantics (animate vs. inanimate head NPs), and lexical items (full-NP subjects vs. pronominal subjects). And it turned out that the semantic and lexical differences that are born out of discourse pressures (cf. Fox and Thompson 1990) make the difference.

Unlike in most previous experimental studies on relative-clause acquisition and processing, the children in our experimental tasks did not always perform better on subject relatives than on object relatives. It is thus unlikely that only factors such as limited working memory, non-canonical word order, problems with perspective shifts, or problems with sentences involving movement were responsible for children's poor performance on object relatives in past studies, as has been suggested, for example, by Booth et al. (2000), Diessel and Tomasello (2005), MacWhinney (1982), and Friedman and Novogrodsky (2004). We do not want to make the strong claim here that none of these factors has an influence on children's processing of relative clauses or other linguistic constructions, but we suggest that there is an additional factor that can explain a big part of the variance observed in children's and adults' processing of object relative clauses with different formal and functional features: linguistic experience.

A number of studies have already demonstrated that children start with item-specific representations of various constructions, such as the transitive, complement clauses, or wh-questions (e.g. Kidd, Lieven, and Tomasello 2006, Rowland 2007, Tomasello 2000). What all of these studies have shown is that, especially early in development, children are best at comprehending or producing these various constructions when they contain the same lexical items with which they are most frequently used in the input. At the same time, there is evidence that children also start to build up some more item-general and abstract representations of linguistic constructions as soon as they start to use or comprehend some item-specific structures (e.g. Gertner et al. 2006). But these abstract representations seem to be weaker than the more frequent item-specific structures and often lead to positive results only in looking-time studies (cf. Abbot-Smith et al. 2008).

Evidence for some lexically specific representations of object relative clauses was provided by a study by Reali and Christiansen (2007b). Using *Google* counts, they found that there are some highly frequent, lexically specific pronoun-verb combinations in object relatives. For example, *the* X *who **I met*** is far more frequent than *the* X *who **I distrusted**.* In a complexity-rating and a self-paced reading task, English-speaking adults indicated that doubly-nested object relatives containing highly frequent pronoun-verb combinations were easier than object relatives with less frequent word combinations. Reali and Christiansen (2007b) take this as evidence that parts of object relatives are recognized and accessed as lexically specific strings or chunks.

In the studies that are presented in the current chapter, we did not control for lexically specific patterns in relative clauses. However, the test sentences that children had least problems with in comprehension and production can be categorized as prototypical object relatives. They contained inanimate head NPs and pronominal subjects, but not always the exact same pronominal forms that are most frequently found in object relatives in spontaneous speech. The prototypical object relatives in the referential-selection task contained third person singular pronouns, whereas object relatives in spontaneous speech most often contain first or second person singular pronouns (Kidd et al. 2007). The fact that children still performed better on these prototypical object relatives than on the less prototypical object relatives that contained full-NP subjects and animate head NPs suggests that even the younger children have already developed a semi-abstract representation of these structures, such as INANIMATE – PRO – VERB, which is strong enough to let them succeed in quite active tasks.

In the sentence-repetition study, we did not find any significant interactions with age, which indicates that the 3-year-olds are sensitive to the same factors (i.e. animacy of the head NP and type of relative-clause subject), and that they are operating with the same kinds of representations of object relatives as the 4-year-olds. The 4-year-olds just performed better overall. As indicated by results from other studies, even adults are operating with the same kinds of semi-abstract, prototype representations of these complex structures (e.g. Reali and Christiansen 2007a, Traxler et al. 2005). Moreover, we also found the same pattern of results in the referential-selection task and the sentence-repetition task. If we compare the 3-year-olds' performance across tasks, they performed better in the referential-selection task than in the sentence-repetition task overall, but we still found the same main effects in both tasks. As noted in the introduction, many studies testing children's comprehension of simple transitives showed effects of item specificity in young children and with relatively active and complex tasks as opposed to older children or looking-time paradigms (cf. Abbot-Smith et al. 2008, Tomasello 2000). The studies presented here as well as other studies on children's and adults' processing of object relative clauses, on the other hand, show prototype effects across development and various tasks. This might be due to the fact that transitives are used for a greater variety of functions, and that they are used with a greater variety of lexical items (e.g. Thompson and Hopper 2001). In addition, most studies on children's comprehension of transitives investigated whether children comprehend these structures with novel verbs (e.g. Tomasello 2000), whereas our studies investigated how or whether children produce and comprehend relative clauses with prototypical and less prototypical, but not unfamiliar, head NPs and subject types.

Future research will have to show whether children perform even better when they are tested on object relatives with highly frequent lexically specific patterns, as has been shown for adults (Reali and Christiansen 2007b), and whether they can develop an even more abstract and strong enough representation, such as NP – PRO – VERB, if they are trained on more varied input. At this point we are also unable to tell on which grounds children develop semi-abstract or prototype representations of object relatives. We will have to carry out training studies to investigate whether children make comparisons across several object relative exemplars when these exemplars are used in the same contexts, when they serve the same function (e.g. to ground inanimate entities in the ongoing discourse), and/or when they contain the same lexical items (e.g. pronominal *you* as the relative-clause subjects). In spontaneous speech, these factors are most often confounded. In our experiments, we found effects of formal and semantic properties, but future studies could also systematically control for effects of context and function.

References

Abbot-Smith, K., E. Lieven, & M. Tomasello. 2008. Graded representations in the acquisition of German and English transitive constructions. *Cognitive Development* 23: 48–66.

Abbot-Smith, K. & M. Tomasello. 2006. Exemplar-learning and schematization in a usage-based account of syntactic acquisition. *Linguistic Review* 23: 275–290.

Akhtar, N. 1999. Acquiring basic word order: Evidence for data-driven learning of syntactic structure. *Journal of Child Language* 26: 339–356.

Arnon, I. 2010. Rethinking child difficulty: The effect of NP type on children's processing of relative clauses in Hebrew. *Journal of Child Language* 37, 27–57.

Baillargeon, R. 1987. Object Permanence in 3 ½ and 4 ½ Month Old Infants. *Developmental Psychology* 23: 655–664.

Behrens, H. 2008. *Corpora in Language Acquisition Research*. Amsterdam & Philadelphia: Benjamins.

Booth, J. R., B. MacWhinney, & Y. Harasaki. 2000. Developmental differences in visual and auditory processing of complex sentences. *Child Development* 71: 981–1003.

Brandt, S. 2005. *The Acquisition of Relative Clauses in German and English: The very first steps.* Unpublished Master thesis. University of Leipzig: Leipzig.

Brandt, S., H. Diessel, & M. Tomasello. 2008. The acquisition of German relative clauses: A case study. *Journal of Child Language* 35: 325–348.

Brandt, S., E. Kidd, E. Lieven, & M. Tomasello. 2009. The discourse bases of relativization: An investigation of young German and English-speaking children's comprehension of relative clauses. *Cognitive Linguistics* 20: 539–570.

Bybee, J. 1995. Regular morphology and the lexicon. *Language and Cognitive Processes* 10: 425–455.

Case, R. 1985. *Intellectual Development. Birth to Adulthood.* New York: Academic Press.

Chang, F., G. S. Dell, & K. Bock. 2006. Becoming syntactic. *Psychological Review* 113: 234–272.

Corrêa, L. M. 1995. An alternative assessment of children's comprehension of relative clauses. *Journal of Psycholinguistic Research* 24: 183–203.

Diessel, H. 2004. *The Acquisition of Complex Sentences.* Cambridge, UK: Cambridge University Press.

Diessel, H. 2009. On the role of frequency and similarity in the acquisition of subject and non-subject relative clauses. In T. Givón & M. Shibatani, eds., *Syntactic Complexity*, 251–276. Amsterdam & Philadelphia: Benjamins.

Diessel, H. & Tomasello, M. 2005. A new look at the acquisition of relative clauses. *Language* 81: 882–906.

Du Bois, J. 1987. The discourse basis of ergativity. *Language* 63: 805–855.

Eisenberg, S. 2002. Interpretation of relative clauses by young children: Another look. *Journal of Child Language* 29: 177–188.

Elman, J. L. 1990. Finding structure in time. *Cognitive Science* 14: 179–211.

Felser, C., T. Marinis, & H. Clahsen. 2003. Children's processing of ambiguous sentences: A study of relative clause attachment. *Language Acquisition* 11: 127–163.

Fox, B. & S. A. Thompson. 1990. A Discourse explanation of the grammar of relative clauses in English conversation. *Language* 66: 297–317.

Friedmann, N. & R. Novogrodsky. 2004. The acquisition of relative clause comprehension in Hebrew: A study of SLI and normal development. *Journal of Child Language* 31: 661–681.

Gertner, Y., C. Fisher, & J. Eisengart. 2006. Learning words and rules: Abstract knowledge of word order in early sentence comprehension. *Psychological Science* 17: 684–691.

Gibson, E. 1998. Linguistic complexity: Locality of syntactic dependencies. *Cognition* 68: 1–76.

Givón, T. 1993. *English Grammar. A Function-Based Introduction.* Amsterdam & Philadelphia: Benjamins.

Goldberg, A. E. 1995. *Constructions. A Construction Grammar Approach to Argument Structure.* Chicago: The University of Chicago Press.

Goodluck, H., E. Guilfoyle, & S. Harrington. 2006. Merge and binding in child relative clauses: The case of Irish. *Journal of Linguistics* 42: 629–661.

Goodluck, H. & S. Tavakolian. 1982. Competence and processing in children's grammar of relative clauses. *Cognition* 11: 1–27.

Gordon, P. C., R. Hendrick, & M. Johnson. 2001. Effects of noun phrase type on sentence complexity. *Journal of Memory and Language* 51: 97–114.

Gordon, P. C., R. Hendrick, & M. Johnson. 2004. Memory interference during language processing. *Journal of Experimental Psychology: Learning, Memory, and Cognition* 27: 1411–1423.

Hamburger, H. & S. Crain. 1984. Acquisition of cognitive compiling. *Cognition* 17: 85–136.

Hirsh-Pasek, K. & R. M. Golinkoff. 1996. *The Origins of Grammar: Evidence from Comprehension.* Cambridge, MA: MIT Press.

Just, M. A. & P. A. Carpenter. 1992. A capacity theory of comprehension: Individual differences in working memory. *Psychological Review* 99: 122–149.

Kidd, E. & E. L. Bavin. 2002. English-speaking children's comprehension of relative clauses: Evidence for general-cognitive and language-specific constraints on development. *Journal of Psycholinguistic Research* 31: 599–617.

Kidd, E., S. Brandt, E. Lieven, & M. Tomasello. 2007. Object relatives made easy: A cross-linguistic comparison of the constraints influencing young children's processing of relative clauses. *Language and Cognitive Processes* 22: 860–897.

Kidd, E., E. Lieven, & M. Tomasello. 2006. Examining the role of lexical frequency in the acquisition and processing of sentential complements. *Cognitive Development* 21: 93–107.

King, J. & M. A. Just. 1991. Individual differences in syntactic processing: The role of working memory. *Journal of Memory and Language* 30: 580–602.

Langacker, R. W. 2000. A dynamic usage-based model. In M. Barlow & S. Kemmer, eds., *Usage-based Models of Language*, 1–63. Stanford, CA: CSLI Publications.

Lehmann, C. 1984. *Der Relativsatz*. Tuebingen: Gunter Narr Verlag.

Lust, B., S. Flynn, & C. Foley. 1996. What we know about what they say: Elicited imitation as a research method. In D. McDaniel, C. McKee & H. Cairns, eds., *Methods for Assessing Children's Syntax*, 55–76. Cambridge, MA: MIT Press.

MacDonald, M. C. 1999. Distributional information in language comprehension, production, and acquisition: three puzzles and a moral. In B. MacWhinney, ed., *The Emergence of Language*, 177–196. Mahwah, NJ: Lawrence Erlbaum.

MacDonald, M. C. & M. H. Christiansen. 2002. Reassessing working memory: Comment on Just and Carpenter (1992) and Waters and Caplan (1996). *Psychological Review* 109: 35–54.

MacWhinney, B. 1982. Basic syntactic processes. In S. Kuczaj, ed., *Language Development (Vol 1): Syntax and Semantics*, 71–136. Hillsdale, NJ: Lawrence Erlbaum.

Mak, W. M., W. Vonk, & H. Schriefers. 2002. The influence of animacy on relative clause processing. *Journal of Memory and Language* 47: 50–68.

Mak, W. M., W. Vonk, & H. Schriefers. 2006. Animacy in processing relative clauses: The hikers that rocks crush. *Journal of Memory and Language* 54: 466–490.

Marcus, G. F. 1998. Can connectionism save constructivism? *Cognition* 66: 153–182.

Munakata, Y., J. L. McClelland, M. H. Johnson, & R. S. Siegler. 1997. Rethinking infant knowledge: Toward an adaptive process account of successes and failures in object permanence tasks. *Psychological Review* 104: 686–713.

Naigles, L. 1990. Children use syntax to learn verb meanings. *Journal of Child Language* 17: 357–374.

Potter, M. C. & L. Lombardi. 1990. Regeneration in the short-term recall of sentences. *Journal of Memory and Language* 29: 633–654.

Potter, M. C. & L. Lombardi. 1998. Syntactic priming in immediate recall of sentences. *Journal of Memory and Language* 38: 265–282.

Radford, A. 1990. *Syntactic Theory and the Acquisition of English Syntax: The Nature of Early Child Grammars of English*. Oxford: Blackwell.

Reali, F. & M. H. Christiansen. 2007a. Processing of relative clauses is made easier by frequency of occurrence. *Journal of Memory and Language* 57: 1–23.

Reali, F. & M. H. Christiansen. 2007b. Word chunk frequencies affect the processing of pronominal object-relative clauses. *The Quarterly Journal of Experimental Psychology* 60: 161–170.

Roland, D., F. Dick, & J. L. Elman. 2007. Frequency of basic English grammatical structures: A corpus analysis. *Journal of Memory and Language* 57: 348–379.

Rowland, C. F. 2007. Explaining errors in children's questions. *Cognition* 104: 106–134.

Rowland, C. F. & S. L. Fletcher. 2006. The effect of sampling on estimates of lexical specificity and error rates. *Journal of Child Language* 33: 859–877.

Sachs, J. S. 1967. Recognition memory for syntactic and semantic aspects of connected discourse. *Perception and Psychophysics* 2: 437–442.

Seidenberg, M. S. 1985. The time course of phonological code activation in two writing systems. *Cognition* 19: 1–30.

Seidenberg, M. S. & J. L. McClelland. 1989. A Distributed, Developmental Model of Word Recognition and Naming. *Psychological Review* 96: 523–568.

Sheldon, A. 1974. The role of parallel function in the acquisition of relative clauses in English. *Journal of Verbal Learning and Verbal Behavior* 13: 272–281.

Siegler, R. S. 2000. The rebirth of children's learning. *Child Development* 71: 26–35.

Tavakolian, S. 1981. The conjoined clause analysis of relative clauses. In S. Tavakolian, ed., *Language Acquisition and Linguistic Theory*, 167–187. Cambridge, MA: MIT Press.

Thompson, S. A. & P. Hopper. 2001. Transitivity, clause structure, and argument structure: Evidence from conversation. In J. Bybee & P. Hopper, eds., *Frequency and the Emergence of Linguistic Structure*, 27–60. Amsterdam & Philadelphia: Benjamins.

Tomasello, M. 2000. Do young children have adult syntactic competence? *Cognition* 74: 209–253.

Tomasello, M. 2003. *Constructing a Language. A Usage-based Theory of Language Acquisition.* Cambridge, MA: Harvard University Press.

Tomasello, M., P. J. Brooks, & E. Stern. 1998. Learning to produce passive utterances through discourse. *First Language* 18: 223–237.

Tomasello, M. & D. Stahl. 2004. Sampling children's spontaneous speech: How much is enough? *Journal of Child Language* 31: 101–121.

Traxler, M. J., R. K. Morris, & R. E. Seely. 2002. Processing subject and object relative clauses: Evidence from eye movements. *Journal of Memory and Language* 47: 69–90.

Traxler, M. J., R. S. Williams, S. A. Blozis, & R. K. Morris. 2005. Working memory, animacy, and verb class in the processing of relative clauses. *Journal of Memory and Language* 53: 204–224.

Trueswell, J. C. 2008. Using eye movements as a developmental measure within psycholinguistics. In I. A. Sekerina, E. M. Fernandez & H. Clahsen, eds., *Developmental Psycholinguistics: On-line Methods in Children's Language Processing*, 73–96. Amsterdam & Philadelphia: Benjamins.

Valian, V. 1991. Syntactic subjects in the early speech of American and Italian children. *Cognition* 40: 21–81.

Warren, T. & E. Gibson. 2002. The influence of referential processing on sentence complexity. *Cognition* 85: 79–112.

Warren, T. & E. Gibson. 2005. Effects of NP type in reading cleft sentences in English. *Language and Cognitive Processes* 20: 751–767.

Wells, J. B., M. H. Christiansen, D. S. Race, D. J. Acheson, & M. C. MacDonald. 2009. Experience and sentence processing: Statistical learning and relative clause comprehension. *Cognitive Psychology* 58: 250–271.

Converging evidence in the typology of motion events

A corpus-based approach to interlanguage

Nina Reshöft
University of Bremen

This chapter investigates the influence of motion event typology on second language acquisition. Recent research on motion events (e.g. Slobin 1996a/b, 2000, 2004) has shown that speakers of typologically different languages (*verb-framed* vs. *satellite-framed*, cf. Talmy 1985, 1991, 2000) differ in where they code manner and path of motion. English, for example, codes manner in the verb and path in adjuncts. Romance languages typically code path in the verb, while manner expression is optional. The corpus analysis focuses on the way Romance learners of English express motion events in their written L2 production. The analysis provides converging evidence with previous research in that learners are likely to transfer the verb-framed patterns from their L1s to their English interlanguage.

Keywords: corpus analysis, satellite-framed, second language acquisition, verb-framed

1. Introduction

This chapter investigates the impact of motion event typology on L2 acquisition. The aim is to find out whether typologically different lexicalization patterns have an influence on second language production.

The typology of lexicalization of motion events (Talmy 1985, 1991, 2000) distinguishes two major types of languages. In Talmy's binary typology, *satellite-framed languages* (henceforth S-languages) and *verb-framed languages* (henceforth V-languages) differ typologically in their characteristic way of expressing the direction (path) and the manner of motion. English, along with other languages (e.g. other Germanic languages and Slavic languages) belongs to the S-language type. These languages typically code manner of motion in the main verb, leaving it to external elements (*satellites*) to code the path of motion (e.g. ***run** into the house*).

By contrast, Romance languages, which are verb-framed (along with Turkish, Hebrew, and Japanese, for example), prefer different lexicalization patterns. The preferred pattern is to code the path of motion in the main verb and to specify other aspects of the movement, e.g. the manner of motion, by adjunct phrases outside the main verb (e.g. French ***entrer** dans la maison **en courant*** '**enter** the house **running**'). On the whole, "the two types differ in where they indicate the 'core feature' of a motion event – the change of location" (Slobin 2000: 108).

For the analysis of lexicalization patterns for spatial expressions and the different semantic elements in a motion event, Talmy (1985: 61) describes the following semantic categories:

> The basic motion event consists of one object (the 'Figure') moving or located with respect to another object (the reference-object or 'Ground'). It is analyzed as having four components: besides 'Figure' and 'Ground', there are 'Path' and 'Motion'. The 'Path' (with a capital P) is the course followed or site occupied by the Figure object with respect to the Ground object. 'Motion' (with a capital M) refers to the presence *per se* in the event of motion or location (only these two motion states are structurally distinguished by language).

Talmy pays special attention to cases where more than one semantic element is *conflated* in a single morpheme. Thus, satellite-framed languages prefer lexicalization patterns in which the concept of 'Motion' is conflated with the concept of 'Manner', that is, the main verb expresses at once the fact of motion and its manner. By contrast, the conflation of 'Motion' with 'Path' is the preferred pattern in verb-framed languages.

Speakers of S-languages are provided with an easily codable way for expressing manner of a motion. According to Slobin (2000), speakers of S-languages "habitually" code manner in the finite verb, having a wide range of options to give more detailed descriptions of manner in addition to the manner verb. Speakers of verb-framed languages, when encoding path in the main verb, have alternative options such as additional manner expressions and adverbials. As a consequence, detailed descriptions of manner of motion are mostly omitted in verb-framed languages and only used "when manner is at issue" (Slobin 2000: 108).

It has been claimed that the difference lies in the options of a given language to specify certain features of an event and that languages that are similar in their grammatical constructions exhibit similar patterns of conceptualization of an event (Slobin 2000). The difference between the two types of languages is mainly based on grammatical constraints, which presuppose that speakers deal differently with the lexicalization of an event. An important distinction was described by Tesnière (1959), who emphasized the distinction between *mouvement* ('movement') and *déplacement* ('displacement'). This distinction is reflected in the use of certain verbs, which not only fall into two broad semantic categories, but also differ with regard to the grammatical constraints that exist in some languages. These have been formulated, for example, by Braun (1976), who discusses the difference between French and English constructions of motion and change of place and the acquisition problems that occur due to these constraints. In the cases where motion, manner and change of place are expressed at the same time, there is a considerable difference between French and English with regard to possible combinations of verbs and spatial PPs. Although combinations of manner verbs with spatial PPs are possible in French, these motion event descriptions do not usually express direction of movement. Thus, the sentence *Il court dans la maison* cannot be translated by the English 'He is running into the house'. In this case, the French preposition *dans* is static so that the English translation would be 'He is running in the house'.

Much cross-linguistic research in the last decades has looked at motion events and found convincing evidence in favor of Talmy's typology. Various methods have been applied that often converged on similar results. For example, converging evidence was found in picture-elicited oral narratives (e.g. Slobin 1996a/b, 2000, Navarro and Nicoladis 2005), creative fiction (e.g. Slobin 2000), and translation (Slobin 2004).

Most of the research on motion events led to the assumption that native speakers of English tend to provide more information about manner when speaking or writing about motion events. English has a large collection of motion verbs that convey manner, but not directionality, combinable with a large collection of satellites that can be added to the verb (Slobin 1996b), whereas Romance languages, as outlined above, are faced with grammatical constraints and therefore prefer verbs of inherently directed motion.

The purpose of this study is to find converging evidence from corpus data. The importance of analyzing a phenomenon from different methodological perspectives has been pointed out by Gries, Hampe, and Schönefeld (2005) and Schönefeld (this volume). However, an important aspect concerning evidence drawn from corpus data (in comparison with other methodologies) must not be neglected. It is questionable whether, due to their different nature, data drawn from corpora as well as findings from corpus analyses are comparable to results that arise from other approaches (Schönefeld, this volume). Evidence from different domains does not necessarily stand for the same phenomenon tested (ibid.; see also Steen, this volume). However, if the results from the present study converge on results that are similar to those found in previous research, we can give more weight to the phenomenon in question.

The corpus analysis carried out in the present study is based on the different lexicalization patterns for motion events in English and Romance languages. It investigates corpus data from the SLA perspective. When learning a foreign language, learners are faced with the difficulty of acquiring patterns that are different in their

L1s. It has been claimed that utterances produced by the majority of speakers learning a foreign language do not correspond to those that would have been typically produced by a native speaker. Such utterances are referred to as *interlanguage*, a linguistic system that has its own grammatical structures and lies somewhere between a learner's first language (L1) and the target language (L2). It constitutes a mental grammar that learners draw upon in L2 production (Selinker 1972).

The present study investigates whether L1 lexicalization patterns for describing motion events are *transferred* to the interlanguage when L1 and L2 are typologically different. Several terms have been proposed in SLA research to describe cross-linguistic influence (see Ellis 1994, Odlin 1989 for an overview). Odlin's (1989) definition of *transfer* seems to be adequate to describe cross-linguistic influence in a fairly neutral way: "Transfer is the influence resulting from similarities and differences between the target language and any other language that has been previously (and perhaps imperfectly) acquired" (Odlin 1989: 27).

Following Slobin's (1996a) *Thinking for Speaking* hypothesis, it can be assumed that patterns that are typical in speakers' L1s occur to a certain degree in L2 production. For the present study, the expectation was to find verb-framed language patterns in the interlanguage of the satellite-framed type, i.e. fewer manner verb types and fewer manner verb tokens than in the native speaker data. Furthermore, if we assume that even advanced learners of English have not fully acquired the typical English lexicalization patterns for descriptions of motion events, they were expected to use fewer path descriptions than native speakers of English, especially in combination with manner verbs.

2. Method and procedure

Previous research on motion events has looked at typologically different languages drawing on various methods and often resulting in converging evidence. As pointed out above, most research has been based on picture-elicited oral narratives, creative fiction, translation, and various experimental data. Some evidence for the transfer of these patterns was found by Cadierno (2004), who analyzed written elicitation data to find out whether Danish learners of Spanish express motion events differently from native speakers of Spanish. It was shown that to a certain degree learners used lexicalization patterns that were similar to their first language.

The method pursued here is restricted to written corpus data. That is, it is somewhat different from previous research in that it is not aimed at the elicitation of certain descriptions of movement but observes all instances of motion descriptions in corpora that include L2 essays written for a different purpose. The aim was to find out whether the results converge with the results retrieved from experimental data.

2.1 The corpora

The data discussed here are drawn from three subcorpora of the *International Corpus of Learner English* (henceforth ICLE), which provides a useful basis for the description of English interlanguage patterns and for their comparison with corresponding L1 patterns. The ICLE consists of EFL writing from learners representing many different L1 backgrounds. It contains literature examination papers as well as argumentative essays written by higher intermediate to advanced learners of English and dealing with topics such as the prison system, feminism, equality, the Gulf War, censorship, society, university degrees, and the military service.

In order to provide an analysis of the data in which we can observe linguistic patterns used by Romance learners of English for descriptions of motion events, three subcorpora were consulted, each consisting of about 200,000 words: the French subcorpus (henceforth ICLE-F), the Italian subcorpus (henceforth ICLE-I), and the Spanish subcorpus (henceforth ICLE-S). Although all three L1 backgrounds investigated here are said to belong to the V-language type, the three subcorpora were analyzed separately. This procedure allows us to find differences and similarities in the way that speakers from the three Romance L1 backgrounds lexicalize motion events in their written L2 production.

Comparable English native speaker data were drawn from a reference corpus that consists of subcorpora of the *British National Corpus* (henceforth BNC). The subcorpora selected for the present analysis consist of school and university essays on miscellaneous topics such as literature examination, travel reports, creative writing, the Spanish Civil War, trade, gender, communications theory, and linguistics. The set of subcorpora consists of a total of 209,171 words and is therefore comparable in size to each of the three learner corpora.

2.2 Motion verbs and verb categories

The present study focuses on self-movement expressed by intransitive motion verbs. However, some of the verbs can appear in transitive constructions with a locative object (e.g. *enter the room*) and were also included in the analysis. All types of "translational" motion descriptions were observed, where "an object's basic location shifts from one point to another in space" (Talmy 2000). The analysis comprises literal and non-literal descriptions of motion.

In order to investigate the actual frequencies of motion verb types and tokens used by Romance learners of English, the procedure was to collect a large number of English motion verbs that can potentially function to describe self-movement. (A complete list of all verbs is provided in the Appendix.) The motion verbs under discussion are different in their conceptual structure. Following Talmy's typology, the verbs were divided into three broad semantic categories: (i) manner verbs, (ii) path verbs, and (iii) simple (unspecific) motion verbs.[1]

The distinction between the three types is not absolute, that is, there are some features that are shared by the verbs allocated to these classes. Thus, the verbs were divided into classes according to the feature that is dominant. The category of manner verbs contains all verbs that express a manner or a means of motion (e.g. *run*, *drive*). Similarly, if the core feature of the verb is a medium (e.g. *fly*, *swim*), it falls into the category of manner verbs as well because a medium engenders a certain manner of motion. The category of path verbs comprises motion verbs that specify a certain reference point of the path (e.g. the source or goal, as in *come* and *arrive*) or a specific direction (e.g. forward as in *advance*). The category of simple motion verbs (e.g. *go*, *move*) is different from that of path verbs in that it includes verbs that do not imply a reference point or a specific direction.

A quantitative type and token analysis of the occurrences that were found in the corpora was carried out in order to compare the presence of manner and path features within the verbs. Since in English, motion verbs can be freely combined with many path particles, an analysis of the path descriptions that were used in combination with the motion verbs was carried out in order to find out whether typical English patterns can be found in the interlanguage data.

3. Analysis and results

The present chapter is concerned with the analysis of the data extracted from the two corpora and its comparison with regard to the main components of motion events, i.e. manner and path. The first part gives an overview of the verb types, the second part analyzes the tokens that were found for the three motion verb types, and in the third part, the results for the analysis of path descriptions are presented for all three motion verb types.

3.1 Verb types

The first part of the analysis is concerned with the lexical diversity of the motion verbs that were found in the ICLE and in the BNC. Table 1 displays the number of verb types for each category in the learner corpora and in the reference corpus.

1. Research on motion events has usually distinguished path verbs and manner verbs. The category of simple (unspecific) motion verbs was added in the present study to account for a more detailed analysis.

Table 1. Number of verb types in the ICLE and BNC corpora

	French learners (ICLE-F)	Italian learners (ICLE-I)	Spanish learners (ICLE-S)	Native English speakers (BNC)
manner verbs	29	23	21	84
path verbs	30	26	28	44
simple verbs	3	3	3	2

The number of path verb types in the learner corpora is quite similar (30 types in the ICLE-F, 26 types in the ICLE-I, and 28 types in the ICLE-S). The native speakers of English used more different types of path verbs, but the difference between the number of manner verb types used by the learners as compared to the native speakers is even more conspicuous. There is no significant difference between the three learner groups ($p = 0.97$, chi-square test). However, the number of verb types is significantly different from the number of types used by the native speakers (ICLE-F: $p = 0.04$, ICLE-I: $p = 0.02$, ICLE-S: $p < 0.01$). This reflects the fact that satellite-framed languages have "a whole series of verbs in common use that express *motion* occurring in various manners" (Talmy 1985: 62, emphasis in the original).

Table 2 shows the verbs that were found in the learner data only, those that were found in the native speaker data only, and those that occurred in both corpora. Most of the verbs that occurred in the ICLE were also found in the BNC. However, the difference between the learner corpora and the reference corpus is more obvious for manner verbs than for path verbs, indicating that there seem to be more difficulties with the acquisition of manner verb constructions than with path verb constructions. Note, too, that in this table, all three ICLE subcorpora are conflated and that many manner verbs were used in one of the subcorpora only, which does not count for the path verbs, most of which were used more frequently.

3.2 Verb tokens

This part of the analysis is concerned with the frequencies that verb tokens of the three types were used with in the learner corpora and in the native speaker data. Previous research (e.g. Slobin 2000) has shown that the domain of manner is more elaborated in S-languages than in V-languages. That is, manner-of-motion verbs are used more frequently in English than in Romance languages. Table 3 displays the results for verb tokens in the ICLE and in the BNC.

Table 2. Diversity of manner verbs, path verbs and simple motion verbs in the ICLE and BNC

	ICLE	ICLE and BNC	BNC
manner verbs	chase, circle, flap, flop, force oneself, roll, rotate, skim, strut, tread	burst, climb, crawl, cycle, dance, drift, drive, float, flow, fly, hurry, jump, launch, march, race, rattle, revolve, ride, run, rush, sail, skip, slip, spring, step, stride, sweep, swim, swing, throw oneself, travel, walk, wander	balance, bolt, bounce, brush, buzz, clamber, crash, creep, dive, flounder, glide, hop, leap, loiter, lunge, manoeuvre, meander, pace, paddle, pitch, plod, pop, pull, range, reel, scramble, shoot, shrink, shuffle, slide, spin, sprint, stagger, stamp, stomp, storm, stroll, stumble, sway, swirl, swoop, toss, trickle, trudge, tumble, twist, vault, wade, wallow, wind, work
path verbs	advance, desert, dip, plunge	access, approach, approximate, arrive, ascend, come, continue, cross, depart, descend, draw, drop, embark, emigrate, enter, escape, fall, flee, get, leave, pass, penetrate, proceed, progress, reach, retire, retreat, return, rise, set, shift, sink, turn, withdraw	abandon, back, cut, head, near, plummet, recede, slump, tip, topple
simple verbs	put oneself	go, move	

Table 3. Relative frequencies of verb tokens in the ICLE and BNC (number of tokens in parentheses)

	French learners (ICLE-F)	Italian learners (ICLE-I)	Spanish learners (ICLE-S)	Native English speakers (BNC)
manner verbs	11% (100)	11% (76)	9% (62)	22% (336)
path verbs	58% (512)	58% (404)	61% (439)	55% (849)
simple verbs	31% (273)	31% (218)	30% (217)	23% (357)

Although path verbs are used most frequently in both the learner and the reference corpora, the number of manner verbs is more than twice as high in the BNC data as compared to the ICLE data. However, the Romance learners used more simple motion verbs to describe motion events than native speakers of English. Again, there is no significant difference between the three learner groups ($p = 0.98$). Although the frequencies show a considerable difference between the learner data and the native speaker data, the difference is only significant between the ICLE-S and the BNC ($p = 0.035$), whereas it is not significant between the native speaker data and the other two learner corpora ($p = 0.08$ for both ICLE-F and ICLE-I, as compared to the BNC).

3.2.1 *Manner verbs*

In addition to the weak diversity of manner verbs in the ICLE subcorpora, the low frequency of manner verbs is even more conspicuous with regard to the total number of verb tokens for each verb. Many of the manner verbs that were found in the corpora occurred only once, twice, or three times. The following examples show that the manner verbs in the ICLE are not semantically rich. The verbs carry a quite neutral manner meaning, as in the following samples:

(1) *Thus the first chapter is the thesis: this thesis is understood by Mrs Ramsay, who tries to make the other characters realize it: sometimes they seem to come close to it, by very soon they* **step** *back.* (ICLE-F)

(2) *Dreams are important, we can* **fly** *away with fantasy but we must come back and make a distinction of what is real and what is not.* (ICLE-I)

(3) *One night when Dorian is* **wandering** *in East London, he comes across a little theatre, then, attracted by curiosity goes in, and sees a beautiful young actress playing Juliet.* (ICLE-I)

In examples (1)–(3), more than one motion verb is used to indicate motion, but in all cases, manner of motion is only indicated by one finite verb (*step*, *fly*, *wander*), while other descriptions of motion are lexicalized by a simple motion verb (*go*) or a path verb (*come*). All the manner verbs used in these examples do not convey much information about manner. In Example (2), no distinction of the manner verb *fly* is made; instead, an adjunct phrase (*with fantasy*) is added to provide more information. The second part of the sentence shows that the subsequent motion event, which describes the opposite direction, is expressed by means of a path verb (*come*). The same is true for the other examples. A manner verb seems to be used only when it is necessary to express manner. Thus, for such sentences, a minimum of information about the manner of motion is conveyed.

(4) *The only problem there, is that after one week, there is every chance that the guys would be fed up with* **crawling** *in the mud,* **marching** *for six hours in the middle of the night, or going on bivouac for three whole days!* (ICLE-F)

In Example (4), two manner-of-motion verbs are used (*crawl* and *march*). Note that in the overall set of learner corpora *crawl* is used only once, and *march* is used twice (once in the ICLE-F and once in the ICLE-S). *Crawl* is a manner verb that could not have been substituted by a verb of simple or directed motion, because the context requires the use of a manner verb here. *March* also conveys manner, and again the context requires the use of a manner verb. However, it is possible that in the example cited above it was not intended to express a distinctive manner of walking because the example comes from a native speaker of French, and the French manner-of-motion verb *marcher* is not semantically equivalent to the English manner-of-motion verb *march* because *marcher* can simply mean 'going on foot' or 'walk', while in English, *march* and *walk* have different meanings. The manner-of-motion verbs with five and more occurrences in the three learner corpora are listed below (sorted by number of verb tokens, total of verb tokens in parentheses):

ICLE-F: *travel* (26), *drive* (10), *walk* (9), *fly* (7), *run* (6), *rush* (6)
ICLE-I: *walk* (18), *drive* (11), *jump* (8), *run* (6), *travel* (5)
ICLE-S: *fly* (11), *run* (7), *travel* (9), *walk* (9)

Slobin (2000: 119) distinguishes manner-of-motion verbs with regard to more detailed descriptions of manner and divides the verbs into semantic fields:

- Rapid motion
- Leisurely motion
- Smooth motion
- Obstructed motion
- Furtive motion
- Manners of walking
- Manners of jumping

Dividing the verbs with more than five occurrences listed above into semantic fields as proposed by Slobin, two verbs of rapid motion (*run*, *rush*) can be found in the ICLE-F, whereas in the ICLE-I and the ICLE-S the only verb for rapid motion is *run*. There is only one verb indicating manner of jumping (*jump*), which only occurs more than five times in the ICLE-I, and one verb indicating manner of walking (*walk*) in all three subcorpora. The verbs *travel*, *drive*, and *fly*, which occur relatively frequently as compared to other manner verbs, refer to different mediums (e.g. car, boat etc.) that allow for the verbs to fall into the manner verb category.

By contrast, the native speaker data contain more fine-grained distinctions of manner. The manner verbs occurring at least five times in the BNC subcorpora are listed below (sorted by number of verb tokens, total of verb tokens in parentheses):

BNC: *run* (54), *walk* (40), *fly* (22), *travel* (20), *sail* (14), *jump* (10), *drift* (7), *drive* (7), *paddle* (7), *pull* (7), *ride* (7), *slip* (7), *climb* (6), *rush* (6), *step* (6), *swim* (6), *spring* (5)

Examples (5)–(8) illustrate the contexts in which manner verbs were used in the BNC:

(5) *Seagulls* **swooping** *crazily upwards, Unwanted pieces of the black night Sticking cruelly to their Feathers the sea carrying a Dark viscosity, which Did not reflect the Weak winter sky above.* [BNC_W_KAV]

(6) *Mr Trotter breathed heavily as he* **brushed** *past his wife and* **stomped** *heavily up the stairs.* [BNC_W_KA1]

(7) *The young boy was extremely embarrassed but soon swallowed his pride and* **climbed** *back into his canoe while we all fell about with laughter around him and it was then that I heard the bang.* [BNC_W_KA1]

(8) *I knew, as I watched the miserable small boy with large shadowed eyes* **clamber** *into the boat, that it would be a long afternoon.* [BNC_W_KA1]

These examples show far more differentiated descriptions of manner than the examples cited above from the ICLE data. All the motion events described in the above examples could have as well been expressed by semantically poorer manner-of-motion verbs. Moreover, English native speakers make such fine-grained distinctions as *climb* and *clamber*, which are semantically almost identical. Manner-of-motion verbs with almost equivalent meanings were not found in the ICLE data.

3.2.2 *Path verbs*

As Slobin (1997) notes, basic manner verbs seem to exist in most languages. English has a "rich" lexicon of manner-of-motion verbs including those that make finer distinctions of manner, as described by the semantic fields of manner-of-motion verbs (Slobin 2000). For path verbs, fewer distinctions are made than for manner verbs.

It has to be considered that learners of English do not have the same English vocabulary at their disposal as native speakers of English. But looking at the diversity and frequency of path verbs, we can see that the usage is quite different from that of manner verbs. Path verbs occur relatively frequently in descriptions of motion events in the learner corpora. The data suggest that Romance learners of English have easier access to path verbs than to manner verbs because many of the path verbs occurring in the learner corpora have close equivalents in the students' L1s because they are of Latin origin. Table 4 displays some of the English path verbs and their respective translations.

Table 4. Examples of English path verbs of Latin origin and their French, Spanish, and Italian translations

English	French	Spanish	Italian
ascend	*(monter)**	*ascender*	*ascendere*
descend	*descendre*	*descender*	*discendere*
advance	*avancer*	*avanzar*	*avanzare*
progress	*progresser*	*progresar*	*progedire*
pass	*passer*	*pasar*	*passare*
enter	*entrer*	*entrar*	*entrare*

* Note that in French, the translation of the English verb *ascend* would be 'monter'. Interestingly, the only occurrence of *ascend* comes from the French subcorpus of the ICLE. The use of *ascend* might have been motivated by the related noun *ascension*, which is common in French.

However, lexical transfer cannot be the only reason why the use of path verbs is not as infrequent in the learner data as the use of manner verbs. Other path verbs that do not have close equivalents in French, Italian, and Spanish were also used with high frequency in the learner corpora. For path verbs, more distinctions were made between verbs indicating the same direction or specifying the same aspects of a path. That is, a large amount of path verb types and tokens occur in the ICLE subcorpora. The following path verbs were used at least five times in the learner corpora (sorted by number of verb tokens, total of verb tokens in parentheses):

ICLE-F: *come* (149), *reach* (111), *escape* (52), *leave* (40), *enter* (31), *get* (19), *arrive* (16), *fall* (14), *turn* (14), *pass* (12), *rise* (12), *approach* (10), *return* (6), *progress* (5), *withdraw* (5)
ICLE-I: *come* (125), *reach* (74), *enter* (38), *pass* (28), *leave* (26), *escape* (19), *fall* (16), *arrive* (13), *rise* (12), *get* (11), *approach* (10), *cross* (7), *return* (5), *shift* (5)
ICLE-S: *come* (124), *reach* (47), *leave* (43), *arrive* (42), *get* (41), *fall* (24), *enter* (23), *escape* (23), *pass* (19), *advance* (12), *continue* (11), *return* (11), *turn* (8)

Examples (9)–(13) give an overview of the contexts that path verbs were used in to describe motion events in the learner corpora:

(9) *Dedalus and his son Icarius imagined to make wings out of wax to* ***come*** *out of the labyrinth, in which they had been cooped up. Icarius, identifying himself with a bird,* ***approached*** *the sun too near and* ***fell*** *into the water.* (ICLE-F)

(10) *To avoid the truth Pincher Martin has been preoccupied with his body during his whole life but now death* ***arrives*** *he can't* ***escape*** *to reality anymore.* (ICLE-F)

(11) *At the same time, Mr Ramsay and James* ***reach*** *the lighthouse, which the whole novel had been* ***approaching****.* (ICLE-F)

(12) *The 29th century takes from the failure of the Romantic Drama,* ***passes*** *through the Melodrama and* ***reaches*** *the Society Drama.* (ICLE-S)

(13) *Poor people* ***cross*** *borders to* ***escape*** *from poverty.* (ICLE-S)

The examples show that path verbs are used with high frequency, which is not the case for manner verbs. Nevertheless, a manner verb would convey more information in many of these motion descriptions, and in most of the contexts, manner would be necessary to convey the attitude or perspective towards the motion event. In Example (9), it would be very uncommon in native speakers' English to describe the default motion of a bird or of someone "identifying himself with a bird" with a different verb than *fly*, as described by Slobin (1997: 456):

> In an S-language, where the main verb is free to express manner in all simple clauses [...] the use of a manner verb *per se* does not make manner salient. It is normal, for example, to say things like *the bird flew in through the open door*. Indeed, the *absence* of a manner verb carries information, in that it violates a neutral expectation. If I tell you that the bird *came in through the open door* you might wonder if it entered in some noncanonical fashion – perhaps on foot. In a V language, by contrast, the default motion description is to use a neutral verb. In fact, in some such languages it is distinctly odd to speak of a bird as 'flying', rather than simply 'coming' or 'going'.

This has also been observed by Braun (1976: 390) who notes that "[i]t is assumed that the bird flew and the serpent crawled" a reason why manner is often left unexpressed in French.

As outlined above, the frequencies of path verbs in the learner corpora and in the native speaker corpora do not differ as much as the frequencies of manner verbs. In V-languages, the main verb typically expresses motion and the path of motion simultaneously. These languages have "a whole series of surface verbs that express motion along various paths" (Talmy 1985: 69). Although English belongs to the satellite-framed language type, it also has a large number of path verbs:

> English does have a certain number of verbs that genuinely incorporate Path, as in the Spanish conflation type [...]. And these verbs even call for a Spanish-type pattern for the rest of the sentence. Thus, Manner must be expressed in a separate constituent [...] by contrast with the usual English pattern [...]. But these verbs (and the sentence pattern they call for) are not the most characteristic of English. In fact, the majority [...] are not original English forms but rather borrowings from Romance, where they are the native type (72).

Our data confirm this assumption and, moreover, they suggest that path verbs are even used relatively frequently in the native speaker data. However, Talmy emphasizes that languages differ with regard to the pattern that is dominant, that is, in the frequency that manner verbs and path verbs are used with in the two types of languages. For V-languages, when expressing motion along various paths, the general pattern is to introduce each path segment by a path verb, which results in a "'compacting' of directional verbs into path expressions associated with a single verb" (Slobin 1997: 440). For S-languages, the general pattern is to express each path segment by a satellite or prepositional phrase that are combined with one motion verb.

3.2.3 *Simple motion verbs*

The percentages for verb tokens have shown that simple motion verbs are used quite frequently in the ICLE subcorpora to describe motion events. Instead of using a manner verb in order to leave space for additional information in the sentence structure, manner is either left unexpressed, or a phrase is added to the motion verb, indicating by which means or in what manner the movement was carried out. Examples (14) and (15) demonstrate how simple motion verbs were used in instances where a manner verb would have been more appropriate.

(14) *People have got used to walking less and less because they* ***use car*** *even to* ***go*** *to a place which is five hundred metres distant.* (ICLE-I)

(15) *My grandfather for example, used to* ***go*** *to work to Switzerland* ***by bicycle****.* (ICLE-I)

In these cases, motion could have been as well expressed by manner verbs (*drive, cycle/ride*). The sentence structure would then have left space for additional information. Simple motion verbs or other simple motion constructions are used frequently in the learner corpora, and they often occur along with additional simple motion verbs or path verbs within the same sentence.

Overall, motion events are described in a very simple and neutral way in the learner corpora. Most often, simple motion verbs or path verbs are used to introduce the fact that a movement is carried out, but manner seems to be avoided in descriptions of motion events, even when the use of a manner verb would result in a less complicated sentence structure and avoid a repetition of the same motion verb. On the whole, in the essays written by Romance learners of English, we can recognize a strong tendency to disprefer manner-of-motion verbs, even when the movement is carried out in a certain manner.

3.3 Path descriptions

According to Talmy's typology, *satellites*, i.e. directional verb particles that are used outside the main verb, express different types of directions, depending on what type of Ground they refer to. Satellites in Talmy's (1985: 102) analysis are defined as

> certain immediate constituents of a verb root other than inflections, auxiliaries, or nominal arguments. They relate to the verb root as periphery (or modifiers) to a head. A verb root together with its satellites forms a constituent in its own right, the 'verb complex', [...]. It is this constituent as a whole that relates to such other constituents as an inflectional affix-set, an auxiliary, or a direct object noun phrase.

Satellites can occur as free lexical items or as affixes in Talmy's definition (1985: 105). He makes a clear distinction between satellites and prepositions:

> First, it is only a preposition that disappears when the Ground nominal is omitted: a satellite remains. Next, the two classes of forms do not have identical memberships: there are forms with only one function or the other. For example, *together*, *apart*, and *forth* are satellites that never act as prepositions, while *from*, *at*, and *toward* are prepositions that never act as satellites.

However, there are other lexical items that can function as a satellite or a preposition (e.g. *past*). Talmy refers to these verb particles as "satellite-preposition" (Talmy 1985: 106). Both satellites and prepositions, as defined by Talmy, semantically describe the direction (path) of motion. For the present analysis, not only *satellites* in Talmy's sense are analyzed, but directional descriptions on the whole – that is, all sorts of directions coded outside the verb. All sorts of directions that are used in combination with motion verbs fall into the category of path descriptions for the present analysis. In addition, locative objects (e.g. *enter **the house***) are counted as path occurrences because they also convey information about the Ground (and the path). For the present analysis, all these lexical items are referred to as *path*, providing information about path and Ground information as a whole.

As Slobin (1996b: 205) notes, speakers of English add more detailed path descriptions to motion verbs than speakers of Romance languages:

> English-speakers may devote more narrative attention to the dynamics of movement because of the availability of verbs of motion (often conflated with manner) that can readily be associated with satellites and locative prepositional phrases to trace out detailed paths in relation to ground elements.

Table 5 shows the relative frequencies of paths that were used in combination with manner verbs in the learner and reference corpora. While in the learner corpora about half of the manner-of-motion verbs were used without any path (47% in the ICLE-F, 52% in the ICLE-I, and 43% in the ICLE-S), almost three quarters (74%) of the manner verbs in the native speaker data were combined with at least one path. Two or three paths were used about twice as often (16%) in the reference corpora as in the learner corpora (ICLE-F: 9%, ICLE-I: 8%, ICLE-S: 8%).

Table 5. Relative frequencies of manner verbs used with paths (number of tokens in parentheses)

	French learners (ICLE-F)	Italian learners (ICLE-I)	Spanish learners (ICLE-S)	Native English speakers (BNC)
0	47% (47)	52% (40)	43% (27)	26% (89)
1	44% (44)	40% (31)	49% (31)	58% (195)
2	9% (9)	8% (6)	6% (4)	14% (46)
3 or more	–	–	2% (1)	2% (8)

These results show that on the whole, paths are used more frequently in the BNC than in the ICLE corpora. Again, the difference between the three learner groups is not significant ($p = 0.38$). However, there is a significant difference between each of the learner corpora and the BNC (ICLE-F: $p = 0.01$, ICLE-I: $p = 0.001$, ICLE-S: $p = 0.04$). This reflects the typical lexicalization patterns for motion events in English, in which the use of manner verbs is dominant, and these are often combined with more than one path. The data suggest that native speakers of French, Italian, and Spanish clearly focus on manner when it is at issue and describe paths of motion in rather simple constructions.

The data for path verbs show very different patterns. Table 6 shows the percentages for path verbs. In the learner corpora, about three quarters of the path verbs were used with one path, while this is the case for 65% of the path verbs in the BNC. The relative frequencies for two or more paths are quite similar in the ICLE and in the BNC. Again, there is no significant difference between the learner groups ($p = 0.76$). In contrast to the significant differences found for manner verbs, the difference between the learner corpora and the native speaker corpora is not significant either (ICLE-F: $p = 0.21$, ICLE-I: $p = 0.43$, ICLE-S: $p = 0.43$).

The results for simple motion verbs and paths are not much different from those for path verbs. The results are displayed in Table 7.

Table 6. Relative frequencies of path verbs used with paths (number of tokens in parentheses)

	French learners (ICLE-F)	Italian learners (ICLE-I)	Spanish learners (ICLE-S)	Native English speakers (BNC)
0	14% (69)	19% (78)	19% (85)	26% (224)
1	76% (397)	74% (299)	74% (325)	65% (556)
2	9% (45)	7% (27)	7% (29)	8% (67)
3 or more	1% (1)	–	–	1% (2)

Table 7. Relative frequencies of simple motion verbs used with paths (number of tokens in parentheses)

	French learners (ICLE-F)	Italian learners (ICLE-I)	Spanish learners (ICLE-S)	Native English speakers (BNC)
0	24% (66)	13% (29)	20% (43)	23% (81)
1	66% (181)	77% (168)	71% (154)	64% (230)
2	10% (26)	10% (21)	9% (20)	12% (44)
3 or more	<1% (1)	–	–	1% (2)

More simple motion verbs than path verbs were used with more than one path. This is not only the case in the learner corpora, but also in the native speaker data. This is probably due to the path feature that is implicit in path verbs, so that these verbs are less likely to be used with additional paths than other verb types. Similar to the differences presented for path verbs, there is no significant difference in the use of simple motion verbs with paths between the three learner groups ($p = 0.38$). The difference between the learner data and the native speaker is not significant either (ICLE-F: $p = 0.74$, ICLE-I: $p = 0.16$, ICLE-S: $p = 0.57$).

Overall, the results show that there are significant differences between the learner corpora and the native speaker data with regard to the relative frequencies of manner verbs and associated paths. This was not the case for path verbs and simple motion verbs where the results for native speakers and EFL learners were more similar, and the difference was not significant. It seems that the learners have not (yet) acquired the typical English lexicalization patterns that provide the option to combine manner verbs with more than one path.

As described above, the use of path descriptions (especially more than one) with manner verbs is not very frequent in the ICLE data. Thus, motion descriptions as in (16) and (17) are used very rarely:

(16) *They are completely exhausted when they come back home and, overcome with sleepiness, **flop down into** an armchair in front of TV in order to stop thinking about their job or the other problems of their everyday life.* (ICLE-F)

(17) *Once I was **chasing for** a parking space, **around** a public building in L.A.* (ICLE-I)

While native speakers of English often code manner in the verb and use a chain of paths outside the verb (Slobin 1996b), Romance learners of English show a tendency to restrict the expression of direction with manner verbs to one path or omit path or Ground information altogether.

4. Summary

The analysis of corpus data has shown that in their written L2 production, Romance learners of English use lexicalization patterns that are different from those typically used by native speakers of English for motion event descriptions.

The first major difference that the data revealed refers to the diversity of verb types, i.e. manner verbs, path verbs, and simple motion verbs. While there was no significant difference between the learner groups, the differences between each of the learner corpora and the BNC were significant. Moreover, when manner of motion is expressed by a manner verb in the learner corpora, the verbs describing manner of motion are to a large extent rather neutral in the manner that they convey, while in the native speaker data, more specific notions of manner are employed. Many examples from the ICLE subcorpora show that the context makes the use of a manner-of-motion verb obligatory.

The lexicalization patterns for motion events in English provide an easily accessible way to use a motion verb of whatever category. This is thought to be one of the reasons why English has developed a large lexicon of manner-of-motion verbs, while many other languages rely on more neutral descriptions of manner within the verb:

> To be sure, both language types have "expressive" manner verbs, used when exceptional manner is in focus – verbs with meanings such as 'limp' and 'dash' and 'jump' and the like. But – to my initial surprise – I've discovered that V-languages seem to have far fewer expressive manner verbs than S-languages. It is as if the availability of the combined slot for motion and manner in S-languages has encouraged speakers to elaborate the entries in this slot (Slobin 2000: 113).

The second part of the analysis aimed at revealing similarities and differences in the number of verb tokens. The number of manner verbs was more than twice as high in the BNC data as compared to the ICLE data. By contrast, the relative frequency of simple motion verbs was considerably higher in the ICLE subcorpora (30% in the Spanish subcorpus, 31% in the French and Italian subcorpora respectively) than in the BNC (23%). The relative frequencies for path verbs were almost the same in the learner data and in the native speaker data. Again, there was no significant difference between the learner corpora.

In contrast to the low number of manner verbs and the high number of path verbs in Romance languages, English not only has a large lexicon of manner verbs, but also a rich inventory of path verbs,

> all of Romance descent: *cross, descend, ascend, enter, exit, penetrate, pierce*. In that respect, English participates in Romance lexicalization patterns as well. But the basic, commonly used MOTION verbs are mostly MANNER lexicalizations. Thus

> English can still be validly said to represent the type of a language lexicalizing the MANNER of a MOTION in a monomorphematic MOTION verb
> (Wienold and Schwarze 2002: 4).

Detailed path descriptions were rarely used in the learner essays. The analysis of paths in combination with motion verbs revealed interesting results. While there was no significant difference between the learner data and the native speaker data with regard to paths used in combination with simple motion verbs and path verbs, the difference in the frequencies of paths used in combination with manner verbs was significant. This leads to the assumption that these learners of English have not acquired the typical English lexicalization patterns that provide the option to combine manner verbs with more than one path. They rather show a tendency to restrict the expression of direction with manner verbs to one path or omit it altogether.

5. Discussion

In many ways the work presented in this chapter is based on Talmy's typology of verb-framed and satellite-framed languages. However, the approach taken here focuses on the learnability of lexicalization patterns. The results of the analysis of English interlanguage show lexicalization patterns that have been observed to be typical for verb-framed languages.

Former research has taken different approaches to find converging evidence for Talmy's typology, concentrating on some major distinctions between the two language types. The domain of manner has received much attention in this context. In general, it cannot be taken for granted that the different lexicalization patterns observed for the two types of languages correspond to those that occur in interlanguage. Since the essays were written in English (S-language), and not in French, Spanish, or Italian (i.e. V-languages), learners of EFL are to a certain extent forced to adopt the lexicalization patterns of English when describing motion events.

However, the data presented in this study show converging evidence in favor of Talmy's typology in that Romance learners of EFL and native speakers of English describe motion events in very different ways. The interlanguage of Romance learners of English differs from English L1 patterns in ways that are similar to the differences that have been observed for the two types of languages, especially with regard to manner-of-motion and the encoding of path outside the verb. Hence, it can be concluded from the analysis that the interlanguage patterns observed in this study rather correspond to the patterns that have been claimed to be typical for V-languages in general and for Romance languages in particular. These corpus-based observations converge on the same conclusion as previous results retrieved from other methodological approaches. The distinction between S-languages and V-languages seems to be psychologically real, as it shows up in very different linguistic situations.

Romance learners of EFL seem to have difficulties in acquiring lexicalization patterns that are different from the dominant patterns in their native languages. Thus, they are not only faced with the grammatical constraints in their native languages (e.g. Braun 1976), but also with lexical constraints, since English, as outlined above (Slobin 2000), seems to have more manner verbs than many other languages. For native speakers of English it is natural to acquire different lexical items describing a manner of motion and to use verbs for detailed descriptions of manner because they are "trained" to use these lexical items during L1 acquisition:

> [Verb-framed] languages are remarkably consistent in *dis*preferring manner verbs [...]. Yet these languages do have verbs meaning "fly" and "emerge suddenly" in various manners. [...] I propose that speakers of the two language types differ in their *habitual attention* to manner of motion [...]. [Speakers of the two language types] also differ in their attention to the *internal structure* of this domain. Speakers of S-languages have been trained, by their language, to make more distinctions of motor pattern, rate, affect, and evaluation of movement, in comparison with speakers of V-languages (113).

This has also been shown for other lexical categories. For example, Bowerman and Choi (2001) note that in English children express single morphemes with meanings like *up*, *down*, *in*, or *out* from the one-word stage on, while the meanings of these particles can often not be expressed as single lexical items in many other languages:

> The meanings of these little words seem so straightforward that it is easy to suppose they reflect an inevitable conceptual parsing of the world. But although all languages provide ways to talk about the situations for which English speakers use these words, they do not necessarily have morphemes with translation-equivalent meanings (480).

While in English, there "is no additional 'cost' to adding richer manner expressions" (Slobin 2000: 113), this option is not available in the same way to native speakers of Romance languages and therefore difficult to express in a foreign language like English. For speakers of French, Spanish, or Italian, the encoding of motion events in a foreign language like English requires attention to additional aspects that are seemingly unimportant (and hence omitted) in V-languages. Thus, the overall typical patterns of English contrast with patterns that seem to be typical for verb-framed-languages, even when speakers of these languages express motion events in English.

The grammatical constraints described in the introduction (Braun 1976) seem to be responsible for the difficulties that Romance learners of EFL experience when they are faced with the simultaneous encoding of manner and path in a clause. The grammatical constraints seem to be the crucial point in dispreferring manner and in dispreferring combinations of manner verbs and directional descriptions even in their L2 production. Hence, the results of previous research and the results from the present corpus-based approach point into the same directions: there is converging evidence for the typological distinction of verb-framed and satellite-framed languages because these patterns are not only observed in L1 production, but also show up in interlanguage.

Cross-linguistic influence and interlanguage theory in the domain of motion events needs more converging evidence in order to give more weight to the findings presented in this study. Further research should address this issue from additional perspectives. Experimental and corpus-based approaches should be carried out in order to analyze these patterns in the interlanguage of native speakers of English acquiring a Romance language or another language of the verb-framed type. Since the results derived here speak for the transfer of lexicalization patterns to the interlanguage of Romance learners of English, it can be assumed that similar results can be found in an analysis from the opposite perspective. That is, since native speakers of English use lexicalization patterns for motion events that are different from those used by native speakers of Romance languages, it can be expected that English native speakers learning Romance languages produce ungrammatical patterns. Given the grammatical constraints for the lexicalization of motion events in Romance languages, English native speakers can be expected to have difficulties in acquiring the combinations of manner verbs and spatial PPs that are grammatical in Romance languages. Furthermore, research should address this issue with regard to languages of the same typological pattern, e.g. English and German.[2] Since German – like English – belongs to the satellite-framed language type and similar patterns of manner and path conflation have been observed, native speakers of German should have fewer difficulties in acquiring typical English lexicalization patterns.

References

Bowerman, Melissa and Soonja Choi. 2001. Shaping meanings for language: universal and language-specific in the acquisition of spatial semantic categories. In M. Bowerman & S. C. Levinson, eds., *Language Acquisition and Conceptual Development*, 475–511. Cambridge: Cambridge University Press.

2. An analysis of the German subcorpus of the ICLE is currently being carried out in order to support the results retrieved from this study.

Braun, Theodore E. 1976. Motion and change of place in French and English verbs. *The French Review* 49: 388–92.

Cadierno, Teresa. 2004. Expressing motion events in a second language: A cognitive typological perspective. In M. Achard & S. Niemeier, eds., *Cognitive Linguistics, Second Language Acquisition, and Foreign Language Teaching*, 13–49. Berlin: Mouton de Gruyter.

Ellis, Rod. 1994. *The Study of Second Language Acquisition*. Oxford: Oxford University Press.

Gries, Stefan Th., Beate Hampe, & Doris Schönefeld. 2005. Converging evidence: Bringing together experimental and corpus data on the association of verbs and constructions. *Cognitive Linguistics* 16(4): 635–76.

Navarro, Samuel & Elena Nicoladis. 2005. Describing motion events in adult L2 Spanish narratives. In D. Eddington, ed., *Selected Proceedings of the 6th Conference on the Acquisition of Spanish and Portuguese as First and Second Languages*, 102–7. Somerville, MA: Cascadilla Proceedings Project.

Odlin, Terence. 1989. *Language Transfer*. Cambridge: Cambridge University Press.

Selinker, Larry. 1972. Interlanguage. *International Review of Applied Linguistics* 10: 209–31.

Slobin, Dan I. 1996a. From "thought and language" to "thinking for speaking". In J. J. Gumperz & S. C. Levinson, eds., *Rethinking Linguistic Relativity*, 70–96. Cambridge: Cambridge University Press.

Slobin, Dan I. 1996b. Two ways to travel: Verbs of motion in English and Spanish. In M. Shibatani & S. A. Thompson, eds., *Grammatical Constructions: Their Form and Meaning*, 195–219. Oxford: Oxford University Press.

Slobin, Dan I. 1997. Mind, code, and text. In J. Bybee, J. Haiman, & S. A. Thompson, eds., *Essays on Language Function and Language Type: Dedicated to T. Givón*, 437–67. Amsterdam & Philadelphia: Benjamins.

Slobin, Dan I. 2000. Verbalized events. A dynamic approach to linguistic relativity and determinism. In S. Niemeier & R. Dirven, eds., *Evidence for Linguistic Relativity*, 107–38. Amsterdam & Philadelphia: Benjamins.

Slobin, Dan I. 2004. Relating narrative events in translation. In H. B. Schyldkrot, ed., *Perspectives on Language and Language Development: Essays in Honor of Ruth A. Berman*, 115–30. Dordrecht: Kluwer.

Talmy, Leonard. 1985. Lexicalization patterns: Semantic structure in lexical forms. In T. Shopen, ed., *Language Typology and Semantic Description. Vol. 3: Grammatical Categories and the Lexicon*, 57–149. Cambridge: Cambridge University Press.

Talmy, Leonard. 1991. Path to realization. *Proceedings of the Seventeenth Annual Meeting of the Berkeley Linguistics Society:* 480–519.

Talmy, Leonard. 2000. *Toward a Cognitive Semantics: Vol. II: Typology and Process in Concept Structuring*. Cambridge, MA: MIT Press.

Tesnière, Lucien. 1959. *Élements de Syntaxe Structurale*. Paris: Librairie C. Klincksieck.

Wienold, Götz & Christoph Schwarze. 2002. *The Lexicalization of Movement Concepts in French, Italian, Japanese and Korean: Towards a Realistic Typology*. Konstanz: Fachgruppe Sprachwissenschaft der Universität.

Corpora

The British National Corpus, version 3 (BNC XML Edition) (2007): Distributed by Oxford University Computing Services on behalf of the BNC Consortium. URL: http://www.natcorp.ox.ac.uk/

Granger, Sylviane, Estelle Dagneaux, & Fanny Meunier. 2002. *The International Corpus of Learner English*. Louvain-la-Neuve: Presses Universitaires de Louvain.

Appendix

List of all intransitive motion verbs used for the analysis

abandon, access, advance, approach, approximate, arrive, ascend, back, balance, barge, board, boat, bob, bolt, bounce, bound, brush, bump, burst, buzz, charge, chase, circle, clamber, climb, coast, come, continue, course, crash, crawl, creep, cross, cut, cycle, dance, dart, dash, decamp, depart, descend, desert, dip, disembark, dive, dodge, draw, drift, drive, drop, edge, embark, emigrate, enter, entrain, escape, exit, fall, falter, flap, flee, flit, float, flop, flounce, flounder, flow, fly, force, ford, forge, frisk, funnel, gallop, get, glide, go, grope, hasten, head, hike, hobble, hop, hug, hurdle, hurl, hurry, hustle, immigrate, jaunt, jig, jog, joggle, journey, jump, lap, launch, leap, leave, limp, loiter, loop, lope, lumber, lunge, lurch, manoeuvre/maneuver, march, meander, migrate, mince, mooch, move, near, orbit, overstep, pace, pad, paddle, parade, pass, patter, pedal, penetrate, pitch, plane, plod, plonk, plop, plummet, plunge, pop, pounce, pound, power, prance, proceed, progress, promenade, pull, put oneself, race, raft, ram, rampage, range, rattle, reach, recede, reel, retire, retrace, retreat, return, revert, revolve, ride, rise, roll, rotate, row, run, rush, sail, saunter, scale, scoot, scorch, scramble, scud, scuff, scurry, scuttle, set, shamble, shift, shoot, shoulder, shrink, shuffle, sidle, sink, skate, ski, skid, skim, skip, skitter, skulk, sled/sledge, slide, slink, slip, slither, slosh, slouch, slump, sneak, spin, spring, sprint, spurt, squeeze, stagger, stalk, stamp, steal, step, stomp, storm, straggle, stream, stride, stroll, struggle, strut, stumble, stump, surf, surface, surge, swagger, swan, swarm, sway, sweep, swerve, swim, swing, swirl, swish, swoop, taxi, tear, teeter, thread, throw, thunder, tilt, tip, tiptoe, toddle, toil, tool, top, topple, toss, totter, tour, trail, traipse, tramp, trample, transfer, travel, traverse, tread, trek, trespass, trickle, trip, trot, truck, trudge, trundle, tumble, turn, twirl, twist, twitch, vault, veer, voyage, waddle, wade, walk, wallow, waltz, wander, waver, weave, wend, wheel, whip, whirl, whistle, wiggle, wind, wing, withdraw, wobble, work, wrench, wriggle, zoom

PART 3

Multi-methodological approaches to the study of discourse

Differences in the use of emotion metaphors in expert-lay communication

Converging evidence from two complementary studies*

Anke Beger
Flensburg University

In this chapter I traverse the empirical cycle to analyze the use of conceptual metaphors for anger, love, and sadness in authentic discourse between experts and laypersons. The results gained by examining corpus data of expert-lay communication in psychology guide me in formulating my hypothesis regarding the factors that account for the differences between experts and laypersons in metaphor use. Following the empirical cycle, this hypothesis is then tested by collecting evidence from a methodologically different study in which data are elicited in guided interviews with laypersons. Relating the evidence from the two studies leads to a refinement of my initial hypothesis about the aspects contributing to the differences in the use of emotion metaphors between experts and laypersons.

Keywords: conceptual metaphors, discourse of counseling, emotion concepts

1. Introduction

Within the framework of Cognitive Metaphor Theory (CMT) (Lakoff and Johnson 1980, 1999; Lakoff 1993), emotion metaphors figure prominently as one of the best-researched domains (Kövecses 1986, 1988, 1990, 1995, 2000, 2008; Lakoff 1987, Lakoff and Kövecses 1987). While earlier works on (emotion) metaphors establish rather general theories, often gained by introspection or unsystematic observations, more recent research in CMT tends to investigate the occurrence

* I am very grateful for the useful comments from two anonymous referees, whose feedback helped to substantially improve an earlier version of this chapter. Of course, any remaining insufficiencies are my responsibility alone.

and function of metaphors in different discourse settings based on corpus material (see e.g. Cameron and Low 2004, Deignan 2005, Semino 2008, Musolff and Zinken 2009). The importance of metaphors in therapy is well-known (see e.g. Lyddon et al. 2001), yet, there are only a few studies that examine conceptual metaphors in the discourse of counseling. Moreover, emotion metaphors are not the primary target of those few studies. Although Chapman (2009: 68), for example, recognizes the importance of emotions in therapy and thus dedicates a subchapter to emotion metaphors, her qualitative analysis does not focus on a particular emotion or phenomenon but points out different potential functions of (linguistic) metaphors in the talk between therapist and client. A more quantitative study is provided by Angus and Korman (2002), who investigate conceptual metaphors in brief experiential psychotherapy. Yet, their focus is on metaphor themes, not on individual emotions. The study closest to researching emotion metaphors in the discourse of counseling is probably McMullen and Conway's (2002) investigation of patients' use of conventional metaphors when talking about depression. Since usually the emotion of sadness and depression are inextricably linked to each other, the results of their study are equally intriguing and important for the present chapter.

With the exception of the investigation conducted by McMullen and Conway, there seems to be little research on emotion metaphors in the discourse of counseling. This chapter analyzes conceptual metaphors for the target domains ANGER, LOVE, and SADNESS. It explores differences in the use of emotion metaphors between experts and laypersons in the discourse of counseling. For this purpose, two complementary studies were conducted. I demonstrate how we can profit from applying two methodologically different studies to analyze the emotion metaphors experts and laypersons use in authentic discourse situations. The first study (Section 3) draws on performance data of experts and laypersons in psychology guides, and the second study (Section 4) uses elicited data from laypersons outside the discourse of counseling. While I traverse the empirical cycle using the example of the application of emotion metaphors in these two studies, I formulate and refine my hypothesis about the factors that contribute to the differences in the metaphor use between experts and laypersons. This example of converging evidence attests to the necessity of drawing on different kinds of evidence in linguistic research (cf. Schönefeld, this volume), which are discussed in Section 5.

2. Methodology

Before outlining the two complementary studies and discussing their results, as well as the implications for the hypothesis, some brief comments on methodological issues are in order.

2.1 Experts vs. Laypersons

In investigating expert-lay communication, the terms *expert* and *layperson* must be made explicit. The problem of defining these terms is well known, especially in studies of languages for special purposes (LSP). Although there is a general consensus about the inappropriateness of binary approaches (cf. Richardt 2005: 93, 94) and experts and laypersons are viewed as endpoints of a continuum, researchers are forced to simplify the complexity of this problem for methodological reasons. In LSP, the criterion for distinguishing laypersons from experts is either the latter's academic degree in the respective science (see e.g. Richardt 2005: 99), or, as Bromme and Rambow (1998: 50) put it, "training of sufficient duration and specialized knowledge which is socially codified".[1] While the latter definition is still rather vague, the former is hard to apply in this study. The web pages analyzed offer counseling or advice. In an attempt to establish professional credibility, such web sites often advertise that their counselors hold some degree or qualification that enables them to deal with emotional difficulties. Though the truth of these claims cannot really be verified, it is assumed in this study that laypersons believe in the expertise of counselors on such web pages; otherwise they would probably not turn to them for help. According to Nothdurft (1994: 15), the asymmetry of knowledge between expert and layperson in counseling and the fact that experts have more distance from laypersons' problems define them as *experts*. Given the anonymity of the Internet, which makes it impossible to verify claims of degrees in psychology and similar fields on the one hand, and the phenomenon that people turn to those pages despite this fact on the other hand, Nothdurft's definition of the term *expert* seems more adequate for the present investigation. Thus, I resort to a functional, discourse-pragmatic definition of *expert* versus *layperson*. I treat those interlocutors publicly offering advice on emotions and having distance from the psychological problem at hand as *experts*. In turn, everyone who does not match these criteria is considered a *layperson*.

2.2 Metaphor analysis

The present chapter is not concerned with the quantity of metaphorically used words in the entire discourse under investigation. Rather, the frequency of individual *conceptual metaphors* in relation to each other and to all *metaphorical expressions* for anger, love or sadness is of crucial interest. This, however, does not lessen the importance of identifying all metaphorically used words in the corpus. Therefore I adopted the "metaphor identification procedure" (MIP), devised by the Pragglejaz Group

1. Translation from German into English by the author.

(2007) to use an explicit and reliable method, instead of relying on intuition. In the following, I exemplify the application of MIP on a short excerpt of corpus data:

(1) The next time you feel the *anger starting to surge*, take just a couple of seconds – or a few minutes or longer – to realize what is happening, think briefly about the event or person who is *triggering the anger*, then decide if you really want to let your subconscious continue on its programmed path(...).[2]

Following the procedure proposed by the Pragglejaz Group (2007: 3), I first read the entire text written by this expert and established the meaning (step 1): The author is trying to prevent the layperson from being overcome by anger and is giving advice on how to react in a particular situation.[3] Next (step 2), I determined the lexical units of the text-discourse that, in this case, are identical with the individual words. After that, the meaning in context was established for each lexical unit (step 3a). I exemplify this only for those lexical units that were marked as metaphorical (*surge*, *take*, *triggering*, *programmed*, *path*) and that were recognized as referring to one of the target domains: *surge* and *triggering*. In the given context, *surge* could be paraphrased as 'to increase' and *triggering* could mean 'causing anger'. According to the Oxford English Dictionary, both words have a more basic meaning, which is also more concrete: "to rise and fall or toss on the waves; to ride (at anchor, or along over the waves); To rise in great waves or billows, as the sea; to swell or heave with great force, as a large wave; to move tempestuously" and "to pull (depress, etc.) the trigger of (a gun or other device)" (step 3b). The contextual and the basic meanings contrast with each other in that emotions are neither fluids, nor guns. However, the contextual meaning of *surge* and *trigger* can be understood in comparison with the basic meaning (step 3c): Increasing anger can be understood in terms of fluids rising inside a container. Yet, anger or the event of showing angry behavior can also be understood as being a gun that can be triggered by another person. Thus, I marked *surge* as well as *triggering* as metaphorical (step 4). Since I am interested in only metaphors for the three different target domains, all other metaphorical units were excluded from further analyses.

After identifying the relevant, metaphorically used words in the discourse, their source domains were determined. Looking back at the examples, it is obvious that the source domains correspond to the basic meanings of the words. Thus, for excerpt (1) metaphors for anger draw on the source domains FLUIDS and WEAPONS. The point about conceptual metaphors is that there are systematic cross-domain mappings (cf. Lakoff 1993: 244). Linguistic metaphors like those identified

---

2. Taken from the experts' corpus. The sources of all linguistic examples can be found in the Appendix.

3. As the interviews consist of spoken language, they were first transcribed.

for anger in Example (1) are often not isolated phenomena. Rather, as Lakoff and Johnson (1980: 7) suggest, there seem to be many linguistic metaphors that share a systematic mapping. Thus, all metaphorical expressions belonging to the same source domains were grouped systematically to formulate the respective conceptual metaphors they instantiate (cf. Jäkel 2003: 142). Given that both investigations are exploratory studies, I did not exclude from the analysis any special kind of metaphor (e.g. novel vs. conventional metaphors) described thus far. Furthermore, I did not differentiate between novel, conventional, grammatical, or lexical metaphors until that point in order to get a general impression of the perspective on anger, love, and sadness expressed by the metaphors of both, experts and laypersons. Yet, a conceptual metaphor was formulated only if at least three linguistic metaphors realizing it were detected in the corpus data. As a consequence, there is a considerable number of uncategorized metaphorical expressions. To lessen the subjectivity of the classification of metaphorical expressions, all identified linguistic metaphors for anger, love, and sadness were given to a second linguist with expertise in conceptual metaphors. He also assigned all linguistic metaphors to what he believed to be the corresponding conceptual metaphor. An inter-rater agreement test (Krippendorff's alpha) showed an agreement of 97%. The problematic cases were resolved through subsequent discussion.

Finally, for each emotion the frequency of the individual conceptual metaphors in relation to all metaphorical expressions was determined in the three corpora (experts, laypersons of the Internet study, and laypersons of the interviews). Furthermore, the conceptual metaphors were analyzed with regard to their interrelation, that is, whether they are linked to each other, as is the case for ANGER IS HEAT and ANGER IS A HOT FLUID (cf. Lakoff 1987: 383).[4] It was also examined whether conceptual metaphors that are not directly connected to each other share important aspects, e.g. the conceptualization of anger as something dangerous implied by both, ANGER IS A PRISON and ANGER IS INSANITY. Finally, an analysis of variance ($\alpha = 0.05$) was conducted to determine whether the different groups under investigation differ significantly in their use of the individual conceptual metaphors.

3. Study 1: Performance data

The first investigation was carried out in the spring of 2008. The goal was to discover the types of conceptual metaphors experts and laypersons draw on when they communicate about issues concerning anger, love, and sadness. The focus of

4. Lakoff originally called the conceptual metaphor ANGER IS THE HEAT OF A FLUID IN A CONTAINER. Kövecses (2000: 21) later uses the name adopted here. For a discussion of that matter see e.g. Soriano (2004: 298) and Goatly (2007: 246).

the study was on differences between the metaphorical conceptualizations of experts and laypersons.

3.1 Corpus

In order to gain quantifiable results from authentic discourses about the target domains ANGER, LOVE, and SADNESS, English psychology guides available on the Internet were investigated (Beger 2008). There are various web sites containing sections for people to turn to for advice regarding their emotional problems. The investigation focused on those web pages where a permanent team of experts or a single expert answers questions about emotional problems. Most of these sites were accessed in the spring of 2008, but the corpus was slightly enlarged in the spring of 2009 (for details, cf. Beger 2011).

The data analyzed are similar to counseling interviews, although they consist of written, instead of typically spoken, language. Furthermore, in contrast to counseling interviews, the Internet dialogs are of a very restricted length, namely one turn of each interlocutor. In addition to this question-plus-answer discourse, some longer textual passages about problems concerning anger, love, and sadness written by experts for an anonymous audience of laypersons were included in the corpus. Of course, the additional data of experts add to the general asymmetry displayed by the discourse data, in which typically relatively short contributions by laypersons are followed by more elaborate answers from experts. As a result, the share of the experts of the corpus is larger than the share of the laypersons (see below).

Other sociolinguistic factors like age, gender, or social status of the interlocutors were not accounted for when the study was conducted. Even though there are sometimes hints in the corpus data regarding the gender and even the age of contributors, this information is not reliable. The laypersons posing questions on the web sites investigated remain anonymous and can therefore lie regarding their age, gender, or any other personal information.

The corpus investigated consists of 43,080 words. Of the three subcorpora, the love corpus is the smallest, containing 567 sentences produced by experts and 212 sentences from laypersons. The anger corpus comprises 673 sentences of expert language and 131 sentences from laypersons. As the largest subcorpus, sadness involves 777 sentences produced by experts and 197 sentences by laypersons.

3.2 Results

3.2.1 *Anger*

The most frequent conceptual metaphor that experts and laypersons employ is ANGER IS A HOT FLUID IN A CONTAINER. This finding supports the claim of Lakoff

(1987: 383) that ANGER IS A HOT FLUID IN A CONTAINER is the central metaphor for anger. However, laypersons draw on this concept less often than experts (see Table 1). The difference between these groups is significant for F(1,28) – 16.2.

Although ANGER IS AN EXPLOSION can be viewed as being directly linked to ANGER IS A HOT FLUID IN A CONTAINER, and both can be subsumed under the general metaphor ANGER IS HEAT, the three metaphors were analyzed separately. This procedure reveals an interesting insight. If the more specific mappings of both ANGER IS AN EXPLOSION and ANGER IS A HOT FLUID IN A CONTAINER are subsumed under the single metaphor ANGER IS HEAT, which displays a rather general mapping, the qualitative difference between the two conceptual metaphors would go unnoticed. Although the heated fluid is dangerous in that it threatens to either escape the container or make the container explode, it can still be suppressed or cooled off. Thus, in this case the conceptualization implies a certain degree of control over anger on the part of the angry person. This is not the case in ANGER IS AN EXPLOSION, where the person concerned has already lost control over the emotion – with severe consequences, as the following examples taken from the laypersons' data suggest:

Table 1. Observed frequencies (n_o = number of occurrences) and percentage (rounded off) of instances of conceptual metaphors for anger in relation to all metaphorical expressions for that emotion detected in each of the three subcorpora

	Experts		Laypersons		Interviewees	
ANGER IS...	n_o	%	n_o	%	n_o	%
A HOT FLUID IN A CONTAINER	22	25.7	7	17.9	17	22.7
A WEAPON	12	11.4	1	2.6	0	0
HEAT	11	10.5	1	2.6	8	10.7
A VEIL	5	4.5	0	0	0	0
AN EXPLOSION	5	4.5	5	12.8	6	8.0
COMING FROM A SOURCE	5	4.5	1	2.6	4	5.3
A LIVING BEING	4	3.8	0	0	0	0
A DANGEROUS ANIMAL	4	3.8	0	0	0	0
A MOBILE ENTITY	3	2.9	1	2.6	3	4.0
AN OPPONENT	2	1.9	1	2.6	0	0
INSANITY	2	1.9	7	17.9	3	4.0
A MOVABLE OBJECT	2	1.9	0	0	0	0
A CONTAINER	1	1.0	2	5.1	3	4.0
A PRISON/CAGE	1	1.0	0	0	3	4.0
INTERFERING WITH ACCURATE PERCEPTION	0	0	0	0	5	6.7
Uncategorized	21	20.0	13	33.3	23	30.6
n (total)	105		39		75	

(2) Then sometimes *he* snaps out of it, or *blows up* again.
(3) It [the anger] keeps building up inside and soon I feel like *I will explode.*
(4) How can I regain control over all of this anger I feel inside me without *exploding at those* who seem to care about me the most?

While both, examples (2) and (3), indicate that the angry person explodes due to the unbearable intensity of anger, Example (3) additionally reveals the connection of ANGER IS AN EXPLOSION to ANGER IS A HOT FLUID IN A CONTAINER. The ANGER FLUID is *building up* inside of the CONTAINER, i.e. the human body, so that the person concerned feels that he cannot stand the PRESSURE caused by ANGER for much longer. This example demonstrates that the explosion of the container results from the increasing pressure produced by the HEAT of the ANGER FLUID. In Example (4), anger is also conceptualized as being inside a person. This individual not only fears EXPLODING and thus representing a danger to herself, but she is worried that she may hurt persons she is close to. The explosion referenced in Example (4) is directed *at* someone. According to Lakoff's (1987: 397–405) cognitive model of anger, this example constitutes a nonprototypical case. The angry person seems to be unable to perform a retributive act against the wrongdoer who caused the emotion and now fears her anger may be directed towards someone else.

Looking at the two metaphors separately brings to light that while experts more often refer to the schema of the rising liquid or building pressure inside the human body, laypersons focus on the negative consequences when the anger becomes too intense, i.e. the explosion of the BODY CONTAINER. There is a significant difference between experts and laypersons regarding their application of ANGER IS AN EXPLOSION, with $F(1,28) = 14.1$. Furthermore, more than half of the instances of ANGER IS HEAT detected in the experts' data actually highlights the aspect that the emotion can be reduced by *cooling it off/down* (see Table 2).

Table 2. Total metaphorical expressions instantiating ANGER IS HEAT (taken from experts' corpus)

ANGER IS HEAT	
***reducing* anger**	***increasing* anger or neutral**
and some techniques to *cool off*	both partners are *hot-tempered*
Cooling off your anger is often a first step	if you're in a *heated discussion*
In the *cooling-off period*	*simmering* in your withdrawal
don't use this *cooling off period* to dwell on	your *anger flares* out of control
Cool down	warning signs of an *emotional*
after a few successful "*cool downs*"	*flare-up*

While the examples in Table 2 suggest that anger is controllable and less dangerous, the conceptualization of ANGER AS AN EXPLOSION implies the opposite. Although Lakoff (1987: 401) points out that, according to our folk model of anger, loss of control over the emotion and retribution are part of the prototypical anger scenario, these two stages seem to be particular troubling for laypersons. Moreover, experts rather avoid metaphorical expressions belonging to the last two stages of the prototypical anger scenario. Perceiving anger as something dangerous or even uncontrollable is in general more prominent in the laypersons' data than in the experts', as is evident in the following paragraphs.

Another conceptual metaphor occurring frequently in the laypersons' data is ANGER IS INSANITY. Expressions that can be assigned to ANGER IS INSANITY account for 17.9% of all metaphorical expressions about ANGER, making this metaphor one of the most frequent detected in the laypersons' corpus. Both ANGER IS INSANITY and ANGER IS AN EXPLOSION conceptualize anger as a dangerous emotion that can impair one's health. While the latter involves a loss of physical health, ANGER IS INSANITY interferes with one's mental health. A person who has lost his or her mental health cannot function normally. Thus, a person who is very angry has lost the ability to function normally (cf. Lakoff 1987: 391). The following examples are extracted from the laypersons' corpus:

(5) Why does he *get so mad* at us when he never does anything himself?
(6) She *drives me crazy* because she judges people before she knows them.

In Example (5) the insane behavior can be directed even towards other individuals. Conversely, another person is also able to cause the loss of mental health, as is evidenced in Example (6). It is interesting to note that, in opposition to the laypersons, experts draw on ANGER IS INSANITY only very rarely, rendering 1.8% of all metaphorical expressions instantiating this conceptual metaphor. The laypersons, on the other hand, draw not only on ANGER IS INSANITY significantly more often ($F = 9.33$), but also on ANGER IS AN EXPLOSION. Together these two conceptual metaphors account for 30.7% of all metaphorical expressions in the laypersons' data. This indicates that almost a third of all metaphorical expressions for anger employed by the laypersons imply that the emotion is a threat to a person's health that is beyond one's control. Obviously, particularly the two final stages of the prototypical anger scenario (cf. Lakoff 1987: 401) are experienced as something that requires treatment.

However, in the subcorpus of the experts we find metaphorical expressions pertaining to conceptual metaphors that entail that the angry person can regain control over the emotion. ANGER IS A WEAPON is such a conceptual metaphor. A weapon is something we are in control of. We decide if and when to pull the trigger, what target to direct the weapon against, etc. Utterances like Example (7) and Example (1) from above demonstrate this:

(7) You have always *a target* that your *anger is directed against...*

Although Example (1) indicates that the angry person is not always the one in control of the weapon (as an event or another person can trigger the anger), it also implies that the individual experiencing this emotion can indeed regain control over the events. Of all metaphorical expressions about anger in the experts' corpus, 11.4% could be assigned to ANGER IS A WEAPON, whereas only 2.6% of the laypersons' metaphorical expressions pertain to this concept, rendering a significant difference between the two groups of F = 7.1.

A metaphor in which anger is not conceptualized as something explicitly dangerous is ANGER IS A VEIL. Examples pertaining to this conceptual metaphor were detected only in the data of the experts. Although only 4.5% of the metaphorical expressions for anger found in the experts' corpus instantiate ANGER IS A VEIL, it is still significantly different from the laypersons' corpus data (F = 8.0). ANGER IS A VEIL conceptualizes anger as an object capable of concealing other emotions. Depending on their actual position, some emotion objects can be hidden by others, as is illustrated by the following examples:

(8) *Anger is* nothing more than *a cover for* hurt, frustration or fear – or all three.

(9) ...you might find that *behind the anger* are more pertinent feelings, such as disappointment, sadness, fear, and so on

(10) As you pay attention to your internal process, you can move *past the anger* to deeper emotions.

All of these examples point out that anger is not the actual problem. Instead, the unexposed emotions constitute the true cause of the problem, which is hidden by the effect, namely anger. Experts approach anger in an analytical fashion. Therefore they look beyond the effects of anger and focus on the presumed causes of the laypersons' problems. Their knowledge about the human psyche seems to involve the notion that anger is an emotion that results from suppressing other emotions. Perhaps they use the metaphor ANGER IS A VEIL to make laypersons aware of this, in order to enable them to tackle the underlying problem.

3.2.2 *Love*

According to the corpus evidence, LOVE IS A CONTAINER is the conceptual metaphor employed most frequently by the experts. As illustrated in Table 3, 16.1% of the metaphorical expressions about love detected in the experts' corpus instantiate this metaphor. Differing significantly from the experts' application of LOVE IS A CONTAINER with $F(1,19) = 14.2$, laypersons draw on that concept almost twice as often. Although it is not their most frequently employed metaphor, LOVE IS A CONTAINER seems to play an important role in the laypersons' conceptualization of this emotion. According to this metaphor, love is an external room or space that we enter when we experience the emotion. More important, though, is the notion of how we enter the LOVE CONTAINER:

(11) ...but *we fell in love* after going out for three weeks.
(12) ...and I eventually *fell head over heels in love* for him, and forgot about my ex.

Both examples illustrate that a common way to enter the LOVE CONTAINER is the passive event of falling into it. While Example (11) demonstrates the additional aspect that two people can enter the container together, which means that they share the emotion of love, Example (12) emphasizes the intensity. As we see in the conclusion (5.), the use of these expressions indicates that the persons talking experience the emotion as something they have no control over. This view of love might be exactly what constitutes the laypersons' problems with the emotion or romantic relationships.

Table 3. Observed frequencies (n_o = number of occurrences) and percentage (rounded off) of instances of conceptual metaphors for LOVE in relation to all metaphorical expressions for that emotion detected in each of the three subcorpora

	Experts		Laypersons		Interviewees	
	n_o	%	n_o	%	n_o	%
LOVE IS A CONTAINER	8	16.1	8	29.6	21	16.4
LOVE IS A STRUCTURED OBJECT	17	15.2	1	3.7	10	7.8
LOVE IS A LIVING BEING	12	10.7	0	0	0	0
LOVE IS A MOVABLE OBJECT	9	8.0	1	3.7	0	0
LOVE IS A UNITY	9	8.0	9	33.3	43	33.6
LOVE IS AN ECONOMIC EXCHANGE	7	6.3	0	0	1	0.8
LOVE IS A MOBILE ENTITY	7	6.3	0	0	1	0.8
LOVE IS A JOURNEY	7	6.3	3	11.1	2	1.6
THE OBJECT OF LOVE IS APPETIZING FOOD	3	2.7	0	0	0	0
LOVE IS A HIDDEN OBJECT	3	2.7	1	3.7	1	0.8
LOVE IS A MAGNETIC FORCE	2	1.8	1	3.7	8	6.3
LOVE IS HEAT	1	0.9	0	0	2	1.6
LOVE IS INSANITY	1	0.9	0	0	2	1.6
LOVE IS A DRUG	0	0	0	0	5	3.9
LOVE IS A NATURAL FORCE	0	0	0	0	7	5.5
uncategorized	16	15.0	3	11.1	25	19.5
n (total)	112		27		128	

Yet, considering how often instances of LOVE IS A CONTAINER occur in both data sets, the metaphor seems to be important for the folk model of love, even though it was previously neglected in linguistic research.[5],[6] Furthermore, LOVE, contrary to ANGER, does not appear to belong to the general metaphor THE BODY IS A CONTAINER FOR THE EMOTIONS, in the way well-known examples like "She was *overflowing with love*" (Kövecses 2000: 26) suggest.

More important than the differences in the conceptualizations of the different emotions, however, are the distinctions between the metaphors for a single emotion when experts and laypersons are compared for their use. The most frequent conceptual metaphor occurring in the data of the laypersons is LOVE IS A UNITY OF PARTS. The instances of this metaphor account for one third of all metaphorical expressions for love employed by the laypersons. Considering that only 8% of all metaphorical expressions of the experts can be assigned to this metaphor, laypersons and experts significantly differ ($F = 9.0$) in their use of LOVE IS A UNITY OF PARTS.

In LOVE IS A UNITY OF PARTS, the parts that form a whole correspond to the lovers in a relationship. In the ideal case they share the feeling of love, probably to an equal degree, and live in a state of harmony (cf. Kövecses 1988: 56). Correspondingly, when this UNITY breaks apart, one of the lovers no longer loves the other one. The following utterances taken from the laypersons' corpus exemplify this:

(13) Since then they moved in together and *are inseparable*.
(14) It just *tore us apart* as it was more out of spite than real love for the guy I lived with

The positive aspects suggested by the LOVE IS A UNITY OF PARTS metaphor are shown in Example (13). Being *inseparable* implies that their relationship is intact, which means that they probably love each other to the same degree. Still, another implication of LOVE IS A UNITY OF PARTS is demonstrated in Example (14) in which the UNITY of the lovers is destroyed. Additionally, in this case passivity reappears. The lovers do not actively break up their UNITY but are torn apart by something else. Although this metaphor occurs frequently in the Internet data, Kövecses (2000: 27) overgeneralizes when referring to LOVE IS A UNITY OF TWO COMPLEMENTARY PARTS as the central metaphor of love. The data examined indicate a difference in the conceptualization of love between experts and laypersons. While

5. At this stage of research in metaphor and thought, it is not clear if metaphors are processed by activating two different conceptual domains (cf. Steen 2009, this volume). Thus, we cannot be certain if source domains of conceptual metaphors actually are indications of how people understand particular target domains. For a more detailed discussion, see Steen (2009, this volume).

6. Kövecses (1988: 56–71), e.g., does not mention this conceptual metaphor in what he calls 'the typical model of love'.

the preferred metaphor of laypersons is LOVE IS A UNITY OF PARTS, one of the most frequent metaphors experts draw on appears less romantic.

The second most frequent expert metaphor of love is LOVE IS A STRUCTURED OBJECT. In the experts' corpus, 15.2% of all metaphorical expressions about love instantiate this conceptual metaphor. In the laypersons' corpus, expressions pertaining to LOVE IS A STRUCTURED OBJECT account for only 3.7% of all metaphorical expressions, yielding a significant difference (F = 15.8) between the two groups. Kövecses (1988: 80) points out that "the structured object might be a machine, a tool, a house".

As the examples in Table 4 demonstrate, LOVE IS A STRUCTURED OBJECT highlights several aspects of love or romantic relationships, which contradict the implications of the conceptual metaphors examined thus far. First, in contrast to the sentimental view of love conveyed in LOVE IS A UNITY OF PARTS, the romantic relationship is compared with a machine here, displaying a functional approach to love. Second, instead of passively and incidentally forming a UNITY or falling into the LOVE CONTAINER, the lovers actively *build* and *maintain* their relationships, which requires time and energy as well as conscious planning (cf. Kövecses 1988: 81). Furthermore, problems in a relationship can be solved just as machines can be *repaired*.

Table 4. Total of metaphorical expressions instantiating LOVE IS A STRUCTURED OBJECT (taken from the experts' corpus)

LOVE IS A STRUCTURED OBJECT	n
your chances of actually *building the relationship* you want	1
and *build relationships* that cannot fail	1
building great *relationships* with emotional intelligence	1
skills we need needed to *build* great *relationships*	1
empowers you to *build* healthy *new relationships*	1
which emotional intelligence skills help *build* and *maintain* great *relationships*	2
of vital importance to *building* and *maintaining* healthy *relationships*	2
this *damages* the *relationship*	1
the surface symptoms of their *dysfunctional relationships*	1
like anything in life, *relationships* must be *tended to* and *renovated* to be *kept at full capacity*, call it *love spring cleaning*	4
I know you are looking for *ways to repair*	1
the question to really ask yourself then is not how you can *fix it*	1
	17

Another expert metaphor that counters the romantic attitude towards love displayed by the laypersons' metaphors is LOVE IS AN ECONOMIC EXCHANGE. Of all metaphorical expressions employed by the experts, 6.3% instantiate this conceptual metaphor, which places LOVE IS AN ECONOMIC EXCHANGE in position five in the ranking of the most frequently employed metaphors. The following utterances of experts exemplify this conceptual metaphor:

(15) Success, happiness, and the ability to *give and receive love* all hinge on our relationships.
(16) You wanted *a lot more out of this relationship* and now that it's gotten this far you figure it can only get better right?

The first Example (15) suggests that love is a valuable commodity that is exchanged between the lovers and refers to the lovers in a relationship as business partners involved in economic transactions. The partners also seem to expect a certain amount of love from their partner, as Example (16) indicates. If one of the lovers withholds a certain amount of love from their partner, the romantic relationship is seen as functioning improperly. Interestingly, metaphorical expressions belonging to LOVE IS AN ECONOMIC EXCHANGE are completely absent in the laypersons' corpus. This marks a significant difference (F = 5.1) between the expert and the layperson group.

3.2.3 *Sadness*

When it comes to the feeling of sadness, both experts and laypersons most frequently employ the same metaphor, SADNESS IS DOWN. Yet, there is a significant difference with F(1,20) = 14.8 in their use of this metaphor. While instances of SADNESS IS DOWN account for only 34.2% of the total number of metaphorical expressions for sadness in the experts' data, laypersons seem to draw on this metaphor almost exclusively (see Table 5). In the laypersons' corpus, 81.3% of all metaphorical expressions pertain to SADNESS IS DOWN. The only metaphorical expressions in the laypersons' corpus that do not belong to SADNESS IS DOWN were used by a single person. According to Lakoff and Johnson (1980: 15), the metaphor SADNESS IS DOWN is closely linked to our physical experience while feeling this emotion, which is indicated by the drooping posture we display when feeling sad.[7] The following examples taken from the laypersons' corpus illustrate the mapping of the physiological results of sadness onto the emotion itself, displayed by the physical basis of SADNESS IS DOWN:

(17) I am feeling kind of *low* right now.
(18) I have decided not to contact my ex because that *gets me down* as well.
(19) However, she's been getting quite *depressed* lately.

7. For a more general account on metaphors relating to spatial orientations (and thus sensory experiences) as their source domains, see e.g. Lakoff and Johnson (1999).

Table 5. Observed frequencies (n_o = number of occurrences) and percentage (rounded off) of instances of conceptual metaphors for sadness in relation to all metaphorical expressions for sadness in the three subcorpora

	Experts		Laypersons		Interviewees	
SADNESS IS...	n_o	%	n_o	%	n_o	%
DOWN	26	34.2	13	81.3	8	23.5
A MOBILE ENTITY	16	21.1	2	12.5	0	0
AN ENEMY	9	11.8	0	0	0	0
A MOVABLE OBJECT	6	8.0	0	0	0	0
A CONTAINER	6	8.0	0	0	7	20.6
A SUBSTANCE	4	5.3	1	6.3	1	2.9
A LIVING BEING	3	4.0	0	0	3	8.8
DARKNESS	3	4.0	0	0	1	2.9
A NATURAL FORCE	0	0	0	0	7	20.6
uncategorized	3	4.0	0	0	7	20.6
n (total)	76		16		34	

An increase of sadness is experienced as being physically nearer to the ground. One can be just low in one's physical position as in Example (17), or even down to the ground as Example (18) suggests. Additionally, Example (18) shows that another person is able to evoke sadness. In Example (19), being physically pressed down to the ground is mapped onto the emotion of intense sadness. Gibbs (1994: 414) states that adults associate being down with dependence, helplessness, and inferiority, which he considers the source of the metaphor SADNESS IS DOWN.

Nevertheless, experts also draw on conceptual metaphors that are not closely linked to spatial orientation. The second highest number of metaphorical expressions in the language data of the experts can be assigned to the metaphor SADNESS IS A MOBILE ENTITY. Although this is also true for the laypersons, there is a significant difference (F = 7.9) between the two groups, as only 12.5% of all the laypersons' metaphorical expressions for sadness pertain to this conceptual metaphor. The following utterances are taken from the experts' corpus:

(20) When *sadness comes*, we need to allow ourselves to feel it fully.
(21) So it is okay for her to wish *her sadness will return*, but instead of trying to WILL *its return*, it is more effective to INVITE *it to return at its own leisure.*

The examples reveal that sadness is conceptualized as a self-propelled entity. In Example (21), the emotion comes to us whenever it wants to. When sadness is present, we feel sad. In general, this metaphor suggests that a person does not have much influence on the emotion sadness, as the given example shows. Considering that every fifth metaphorical expression for sadness in the experts' data can be assigned the conceptual content SADNESS IS A MOBILE ENTITY, one may wonder why experts so frequently choose to conceptualize sadness as the active part and the person feeling sad as the passive part. Yet, it may be helpful for those who suffer from this emotion to be assured by experts that being sad is not their fault, as sadness decides when to come to a person. Furthermore it may be comforting to know that sadness is not a permanent emotional state. It may appear at some point, but it will also vanish again.

A closely connected conceptualization of sadness is the metaphor SADNESS IS AN ENEMY. More than every tenth metaphorical expression of experts about sadness pertains to this concept. This metaphor conceptualizes sadness as an opponent to fight with or even eliminate, as the following examples taken from the experts' data illustrate:

(22) When joy comes into our life we experience it freely, but when sadness or grief is present, we often *struggle with them*

(23) First, it's not about trying to *eliminate* sadness or 'fix' it in some way. The first step is to *not back away from it*, but really be aware of the sensations and thoughts that spin the feeling

(24) Healing is in the ability to breathe in softness and love rather than trying to *kill off or exile the sadness to an inner fortress*. So, instead of building a more rigid, taller fortress, I propose *embracing the sadness* in our lives and sending love to ourselves.

Example (22) shows that we tend to fight the emotion of sadness. However, the interesting point about this concept is that although experts use the metaphor SADNESS IS AN ENEMY, they do not necessarily advise laypersons to actually fight the emotion. As Example (23) demonstrates, it is *not* about *eliminating* sadness, *nor* are the addressed individuals supposed to *back away* from the emotion. Instead, it is proposed to accept the emotion that is often fought against. This is even taken one step further in Example (24) in which a sad person is advised to *embrace* the emotion he or she thought of as an opponent. The data of the laypersons reveal that indeed none of them employs the conceptual metaphor SADNESS IS AN ENEMY, and yet, experts seem to assume that this is how laypersons (unconsciously) understand the emotion. According to the corpus evidence, experts then attempt to reframe this conceptualization of sadness by suggesting to conceive of sadness as a friend, or to simply accept the presence of sadness as a companion.

3.3 Discussion

The analysis of the Internet data suggests that experts and laypersons indeed differ in their conceptualizations of anger, love, and sadness. The results for anger show that laypersons tend to employ conceptual metaphors highlighting negative aspects of the emotion. A considerable number of the metaphorical expressions for anger identified in the laypersons' corpus focuses on the loss of control and health caused by the emotion. Considering that loss of control and retribution are part of our cultural folk theory of anger (cf. Lakoff and Johnson 1987: 398), it might be rather unexpected that those final stages of the prototypical anger scenario seem to be problematic for the laypersons. Yet, there may be various reasons for the laypersons' fear of a loss of control. For example, some laypersons might have experienced that the intensity of their retributive acts outweighs the intensity of the offenses and seriously endangers other people. There are several possible non-prototypical cases that would explain the laypersons' difficulties with the loss of control over the emotion of anger (cf. Lakoff 1987: 401–405). The experts, drawing less frequently on metaphors involving the loss of control, seem to respond to the laypersons' concerns by offering different metaphors. On the one hand, they use metaphors that refer to the laypersons' concerns about losing control, emphasizing possibilities of restraining anger. On the other hand, they introduce ANGER IS A VEIL, which conveys that anger is an emotion that hides more basic problems. In both cases, the expert advice proposes behavior that does not fall under the prototypical anger scenario. This implies that the stage of loss of control and the stage of retribution in Lakoff's (1987: 401) prototypical scenario are indeed dangerous and should be avoided.

The concept LOVE in the metaphors of the laypersons seems to view the emotion of love in a quite romantic fashion. First of all, the emotion passively happens to a person. Moreover, once one is in a romantic relationship, a symbiosis with a partner can be formed. Both conceptualizations imply that experiencing love or having a romantic relationship is just something that magically happens. Yet, one of the most frequent conceptual metaphors of the experts highlights exactly the opposite, focusing on the active role lovers should play in a romantic relationship. Furthermore, love is conceptualized as a valuable good in an economic transaction between the lovers, leaving not much space for romanticism. These findings suggest that experts might employ conceptual metaphors to give the laypersons a perspective on love that enables them to actively approach this emotion and their problems with romantic relationships.

Laypersons seem to be even more restricted in their view of an emotion when it comes to sadness. While they almost exclusively draw on a metaphor that is linked to spatial orientation, experts employ a variety of conceptual metaphors.

About a third of the expert metaphors suggest accepting or befriending the emotion of sadness. The experts may assume that this perspective helps the laypersons to come to terms with sadness. Furthermore, the experts' advice of acknowledging and welcoming sadness might be explained by the cultural attitude toward this emotion. Sadness is an emotion that we are not supposed to experience or show too frequently. The word *sadness* and the clinical term *depression* are often used interchangeably, which evidences the close relationship between the two. As people displaying sadness may be considered by others as depressive or close to depression, as a result sadness might tend to be suppressed out of fear of social stigmatization. Being aware of this, experts may encourage laypersons to accept their feelings of sadness in order to avoid the consequences of suppressed emotions.

In summary, I hypothesize that the differences observed in the use of metaphors between experts and laypersons are due to the professional knowledge of the experts. Their expertise leads to an application of a broader variety of metaphors for anger, love, and sadness in order to help the laypersons in adopting a less troubling perspective on the emotions.

4. Study 2: Elicited data

Carried out in the spring of 2009, the second study aimed at moving further through the empirical cycle by testing the hypothesis developed on the basis of the study presented in the previous section (cf. Schönefeld, Section 4, this volume). Since the laypersons' share of the corpus in the first study was comparatively small, I focused on obtaining language data from laypersons. Furthermore, I am interested in the different conceptualizations of emotions between experts and laypersons, but the laypersons of the first study constitute only a very specific sub-group of laypersons, namely those who were troubled by the emotion under investigation at the time the study was conducted. Consequently, I tried to collect comparable data from laypersons outside the discourse of counseling. However, it proved to be difficult to find naturally occurring language data from laypersons who are talking about anger, love, and sadness at times when they are not experiencing difficulties with these emotions. Therefore, I opted for a different method and elicited spoken data in guided interviews. My expectation was to find concepts of anger, love, and sadness similar to those of the first study that clearly distinguish the laypersons' use of conceptual metaphors from the experts' application of metaphor. Thus, this second study was carried out to collect more evidence about the phenomenon of distinctions in the metaphor use of experts and laypersons. This evidence from two methodologically different analyses was expected to converge on the assumptions, namely that there are differences in the application of metaphors between experts and laypersons and that these distinctions in metaphor use result from the experts' specialized knowledge.

4.1 Corpus

The corpus of the interviews consists of four and a half hours of spoken data, gained by interviewing 15 people randomly chosen, aged 23 to 66. The sole criterion was that they be native English speakers. The duration of the individual interviews varied from twelve and a half minutes to 30 minutes. Since the purpose of this second study is to explore all metaphorical expressions that might possibly occur, the design of the questionnaire was chosen accordingly.[8] Multiple-choice questions were considered incompatible with the aims of the study. Questions that are too open proved to be a problem, however. I opted for an in-between solution and designed a questionnaire consisting of two parts and a prefixed question to prepare the subjects for the topic. The first part (questions 2–10) comprises three questions on each emotion. The second part (questions 11–13) consciously triggers metaphors for different purposes. Only questions 2–10 were transcribed and included in the metaphor analysis.

4.2 Results

4.2.1 *Anger*

For the emotion of anger, the results of the Internet data study are also present in the interviews (see Table 2). Instances of the general metaphor ANGER IS HEAT account for every third metaphorical expression the interviewees used to relate to anger. The specific case in which heat is applied to a fluid, generating the conceptual metaphor ANGER IS A HOT FLUID IN A CONTAINER, is the metaphor most frequently employed. With 22.7%, more than every fifth metaphorical expression for anger used by the interviewees pertains to this conceptual metaphor. These results corroborate Lakoff and Kövecses' suggestion that ANGER IS A HOT FLUID IN A CONTAINER is indeed the central metaphor for anger.

Although interviewees, experts, and laypersons share the conceptualization of anger as HEAT, noteworthy differences in their use of metaphors are evident. One of the most interesting distinctions is that the interviewed persons do not use any metaphorical expressions that could be assigned to ANGER IS A VEIL. With $F(1, 29) = 10.3$, the difference between experts and laypersons is significant regarding their

8. The questions in the questionnaire can be found in the Appendix. A more detailed description of the interview design and performance, including a discussion of the observer's paradox, can be found in Beger (2011).

use of ANGER IS A VEIL. Above, this conceptual metaphor was interpreted as an analytical tool of the experts; the interview data are compatible with the hypothesis that ANGER IS A VEIL is used only by experts to perform some kind of therapeutic reframing.

Furthermore, there are conceptual metaphors, which both experts and interviewees employ far less frequently than laypersons in the Internet data. Expressions instantiating ANGER IS INSANITY, for example, account for only 4% of all metaphorical expressions about anger found in the data of the interviews. In the corpus of laypersons in the first study, however, this is one of the conceptual metaphors most frequently exploited (see Table 1).

4.2.2 *Love*

Turning to the emotion of love, we find a mixed picture. Of all metaphorical expressions used by the interviewees to talk about love, 16.4% could be assigned to LOVE IS A CONTAINER. This supports the observation that love is more often conceptualized as an entity outside the body rather than conceptualized as being a fluid inside the body container. Yet, in the data of the interviewees, LOVE IS A CONTAINER is not the most commonly used metaphor.

Instead, instances of LOVE IS A UNITY occurred most frequently in the interviewees' corpus. With 33.6% of all metaphorical expressions, they draw on this metaphor as often as the laypersons in the Internet study (see Table 3). By far less often employed by the interviewees, but still ranking in third place, is LOVE IS A STRUCTURED OBJECT. Rather unexpectedly, the interview subjects draw on this metaphor more than twice as often as the group of Internet laypersons. The instances that can be assigned to LOVE IS A STRUCTURED OBJECT account for 7.8% of all metaphorical expressions uttered by the interviewees. As discussed above, LOVE IS A STRUCTURED OBJECT refers to the lovers in a relationship as active parts, whereas many other conceptual metaphors ascribe passive roles to the lovers. The relative importance of this metaphor to interview subjects seems to be inconsistent with the hypothesis that laypersons tend to view love as a passive experience. A closer look at the data reveals that love is understood as a process involving different stages. Interestingly, the laypersons in the Internet study seem to skip one of these stages. The experts as well as the interviewees include in their talk a stage of love in which emotional intensity decreases and gives way to a more dispassionate attitude. In contrast, the Internet laypersons seeking emotional guidance do not employ metaphorical expressions conceptualizing the decreasing intensity of love. The differences between the two groups of laypersons are discussed in more detail in Section 5.

4.2.3 *Sadness*

Although SADNESS IS DOWN is also the most frequently occurring metaphor in the interview data, the instances of this conceptual metaphor account for only 23.5% of all metaphorical expressions for sadness uttered by the interviewees. The difference of the use of this conceptual metaphor between the two layperson groups is significant with F(1,20) = 7.4. Additionally, SADNESS IS A CONTAINER and SADNESS IS A NATURAL FORCE are almost equally often employed by the interviewees. Even more interesting is the fact that those metaphors are completely absent in the corpus of the laypersons of the first study (see Table 5).

Instances of SADNESS IS A NATURAL FORCE account for one fifth of all metaphorical expressions for this emotion. The metaphor appears for the first time in the interviews and highlights the danger of the emotion, as is illustrated in the following examples:

(25) "So I was pretty *devastated* but I wasn't angry."
(26) "They are *not-getting-off-the-floor-kind-of-devastated*."

The physical destruction of a natural force is mapped onto the psychological state of human beings in Example (25) and (26). People experience sadness as a natural force over which they have no control. Furthermore, sadness is perceived as being quite dangerous. In Example (26), the state of being devastated by the emotion of sadness is described in greater detail to illustrate that a sad person is not only down on the ground, but even unable to get up again. Thus, the metaphor SADNESS IS DOWN is also employed in the metaphorical expression of Example (26).

Metaphorical expressions that can be assigned to SADNESS IS A CONTAINER also account for 20.6% of all metaphorical instances in the data of the interviewees. In contrast to SADNESS IS A NATURAL FORCE, instances of SADNESS IS A CONTAINER suggest that the experiencer may have a certain degree of control over the emotional state, as the following utterances of the interviewees demonstrate:

(27) "But if they are wanting to *get out of that sadness* faster, then they have to surround themselves with friends and things to do all the time."
(28) "*Let* yourself *go through those emotions*."
(29) "(...) that you don't ever, you're not *moving forward* and *moving out of it*, then you gotta probably find something new, you know, in your life to distract you a little bit or *pull you out of your cell*, you know, find a new hobby or (...)."

Examples (27) and (29) illustrate that a sad person can actively leave the container. While Example (27) describes how to speed up that process, Example (29) suggests several things that can help one to exit the SADNESS CONTAINER. In Example (28), however, the sad person seems to be rather passive. Still, the example is reminiscent of the experts' advice not to fight sadness, but to accept the emotion, as was shown in connection with SADNESS IS AN ENEMY.

It has become evident in this short presentation of conceptual metaphors employed by the laypersons of the second study that they use a variety of conceptual metaphors that highlight quite different aspects of the emotion of sadness. This general result was somewhat unexpected, considering the restricted set of metaphorical conceptualizations of sadness found in the data of the Internet laypersons. After a brief discussion of the results of the interview study, the diverging results of the two studies are discussed in Section 5.

4.3 Discussion

Although instances of ANGER IS AN EXPLOSIVE and ANGER IS INSANITY together only account for 12% of all metaphorical expressions used by the laypersons of the Internet study, their conceptualization of anger does not necessarily feature the aspects of danger and lack of control less frequently than the conceptual metaphors of the interview layperson group suggests. The metaphors ANGER IS A PRISON/CAGE and ANGER IS INTERFERENCE WITH ACCURATE PERCEPTION, which could not be illustrated here in more detail for reasons of space, also imply these aspects.

The results for LOVE, however, are intriguing. Instances of LOVE IS A STRUCTURED OBJECT appear twice as often as in the corpus of the Internet laypersons. This indicates that the differences in the use of metaphors between experts and laypersons observed in the first study are not as great when we broaden the group of laypersons. Additionally, the distinct frequencies in which the two different layperson groups draw on LOVE IS A STRUCTURED OBJECT suggest that the differences between experts and the laypersons of the first study cannot entirely be ascribed to the expertise of the professionals. However, looking at the other metaphors used by the laypersons of the second study, we find the same romantic view of LOVE displayed by the metaphor LOVE IS A UNITY OF PARTS, which is equally frequently employed by both groups of laypersons. Also, the aspects of passivity and inevitability encountered in the Internet data are reflected in LOVE IS A CONTAINER. The interviewees do not draw on this conceptual metaphor as often as the laypersons of the first study, but their application of LOVE IS A NATURAL FORCE and LOVE IS A MAGNETIC FORCE (see Table 4) suggests a similar perspective on love.

Since the interviewed persons also constitute a group of laypersons, we would expect to find similar results. In the case of LOVE IS A STRUCTURED OBJECT we saw that this assumption in not confirmed. Moreover, the results for SADNESS of the two groups of laypersons differ so strongly that statements about *the* use of metaphors seem to be almost impossible. Instead, the results of the two distinct groups of laypersons indicate that the application of metaphors might be determined by the present situation of an individual. The conceptualization of sadness differs depending on whether the person suffers from the emotion or just talks about it. Instances of SADNESS IS DOWN account only for a quarter of all metaphorical expressions for sadness in the interviewees' corpus. Furthermore, a variety of conceptual metaphors is employed, implying that different aspects of sadness are highlighted. Indeed, instances of SADNESS IS A CONTAINER suggest that the interviewees' perspective on the emotion includes aspects of actively dealing with sadness. This is a concept of sadness already encountered in the experts' use of sadness metaphors. As a consequence, the initial hypothesis that differences in the metaphor use between experts and laypersons can be exclusively ascribed to the expertise of the former must be refined.

5. Bringing together both studies: Summary and conclusion

Considering the new evidence of the second study, it is clear that expertise alone does not account for differences in the application of emotion metaphors. Instead, it seems that concepts of anger, love, or sadness change once emotional problems occur. The level of emotional involvement is the main factor that distinguishes the two groups of laypersons. While the Internet data involve laypersons affected by problems with the emotions they talk about, the interview subjects are presumably not experiencing these emotions at the time of the interview.

Both groups of laypersons show a similar conceptualization of the emotion of anger, except for one interesting distinction: the interviewees draw far less frequently on ANGER IS INSANITY. Since we all seem to undergo similar stages when angry (cf. Lakoff 1987), it is not surprising that the laypersons of the interviews, as well as the laypersons currently troubled by the emotion, highlight negative aspects of anger, like loss of control and danger. Yet, the interviewees do not seem to conceptualize anger as "losing one's mind" as frequently as the Internet laypersons. Nevertheless, significant differences between the interviewees and the experts exist. The occurrence of the metaphor ANGER IS A VEIL, possibly employed as a therapeutic tool by the experts, is absent not only in the laypersons' data of the Internet study, but also in the interviewees' data. This indicates that the hypothesis based on the evidence of the first study is not disconfirmed. Expertise is probably a major factor contributing to differences in the use of emotion metaphors between experts and laypersons. However, the evidence of the second study suggests that expertise is not the only aspect to take into account when interpreting the distinctive metaphor use of experts and laypersons.

While the laypersons' problems with anger encountered in the Internet data seems to result from a lack of an analytical perspective on the emotion, their main difficulty with love seems to be that their conceptualization of this emotion omits an important stage in the development of romantic relationships: While at the beginning of a romantic relationship people seem to perceive love as a very intense emotion beyond their control, the intensity of the emotion decreases after a while and control is re-established. This is the point at which a romantic relationship starts to be conceptualized as requiring active work and both partners' energy to be able to sustain the relationship. In short, the view of love changes from a somewhat irrational and romantic one into a more sober perspective (cf. Beger 2011: 68–69). The latter is exactly what is implied by the metaphor LOVE IS A STRUCTURED OBJECT. Instances of this conceptual metaphor, however, occur only very rarely in the corpus of the laypersons who are troubled with love. In contrast to this, LOVE IS A STRUCTURED OBJECT is one of the metaphors experts draw on most frequently. These results suggested that this conceptual metaphor might be specific for experts. Yet, bringing in the new evidence provided by the second study, we see that LOVE IS A STRUCTURED OBJECT is indeed part of our folk understanding of love. Considering that the interviewees employ LOVE IS A STRUCTURED OBJECT more than twice as often as the Internet layperson group, it follows that emotional involvement prevents the troubled laypersons from adopting a more rational view of love. Experts probably employ this conceptual metaphor frequently to offer the laypersons the rational perspective on love they are presently lacking. For the same reason, experts seem to use LOVE IS AN ECONOMIC EXCHANGE. This converging evidence of the use of LOVE metaphors corroborates what has been indicated by the results for ANGER. Although the experts' specialized knowledge accounts for a large part of the differences between experts and laypersons regarding their use of emotion metaphors, the emotional state of the laypersons must also be taken into account. Thus, the evidence collected in the second study leads to a refinement of the initial hypothesis.

In the analysis of SADNESS, the need to refine the hypothesis becomes even more evident, as the differences between the two groups of laypersons are greater yet. The abundant use of SADNESS IS DOWN found in the Internet laypersons' talk might indicate that they have trouble not only with the emotion of sadness, but that they are already suffering from depression. As mentioned above, McMullen and Conway (2002) investigated the metaphors of patients diagnosed with depression. According to their study (2002: 171), the most frequent metaphor employed by the clients is DEPRESSION IS DESCENT, which is similar to SADNESS IS DOWN in the sense that expressions of being *down* or *low* are also central to DEPRESSION IS DESCENT. The distinct mental conditions of the two layperson groups can explain the large differences in their use of conceptual metaphors.

Bringing together the results of the two studies first of all reveals that experts and laypersons employ different conceptual metaphors in the discourse of counseling. These differences were observed in the first study and corroborated by the evidence of the second study. Based on the observations of the Internet study, it was hypothesized that these differences are attributable to the experts' role in the given discourse, and in particular their specialized knowledge they apply to fulfill their role in the discourse of counseling. The experts are supposed to solve people's problems with emotions, doing so by offering the troubled laypersons alternative perspectives on anger, love, or sadness. To support this kind of therapeutic reframing, the experts apply, consciously or unconsciously, certain kinds of conceptual metaphors that result from their expertise and represent emotions in a more rational fashion. On the other hand, the converging evidence of both studies brings to light that care should be taken in making statements about the laypersons' use of metaphors in general. Instead, the two different studies suggest that the laypersons' application of emotion metaphors depends highly on their involvement with these emotions. Emotional problems seem to restrict a person's view of their particular emotional situations, which is reflected in the narrow range of conceptual metaphors used. This was apparent most notably in the differences between the two groups of laypersons when talking about sadness. The new evidence collected in the second study makes it possible to avoid overgeneralizations about laypersons. Instead, it is now possible to differentiate between laypersons in general, in contrast to those presently suffering from the emotions under investigation.

The converging evidence of both studies reveals important differences in the conceptualization of anger, love, and sadness between the two groups of laypersons. Rather than relying on a single method for the analysis of laypersons' metaphors, the application of two distinct discovery procedures contributes to a better understanding of the phenomenon under investigation.

However, some questions about the use of emotion metaphors in expert-lay communication remain and others are raised. As only a small sample of data was analyzed, the first question is whether larger studies can confirm/replicate the results of these exploratory studies. Assuming that this is the case, it would be interesting to explore whether laypersons seeking advice actually adopt some of the perspectives on the emotions suggested by the conceptual metaphors offered by the experts. To what extent do they understand the advice administered in the shape of conceptual metaphors in the first place? And will they actually internalize the constructive aspects highlighted by the experts, benefiting from this metaphorical reframing in order to modify their future behavior? To see how useful conceptual metaphors can actually be as therapeutic devices, some comprehensive long-term studies would have to be conducted. For that purpose, it might be helpful to record counseling/therapy sessions and combine these data with follow-up interviews after the sessions as well as after the end of the therapy. If individuals suffering from emotional problems not only understand expert metaphors such as

ANGER IS A VEIL, but also are able to integrate them in their concepts of emotions, counselors and therapists might benefit from using conceptual metaphors as a therapeutic device.

References

Angus, Lynne & Yifaht Kormann. 2002. Conflict, coherence and change in brief psychotherapy: A metaphor theme analysis. In S. Fussel, ed., *The Verbal Communication of Emotions*, 151–167. Mahwah, NJ & London: Lawrence Erlbaum Associates.

Beger, Anke. 2008. Metaphors of Anger, Love and Sadness in Psychology Guides and Movies: A Comparison. BA Thesis, Flensburg University.

Beger, Anke. 2011. *ANGER, LOVE and SADNESS Revisited: Studying Emotion Metaphors in Authentic Discourse between Experts and Laypersons*. Flensburg: Flensburg University Press.

Beger, Anke & Olaf Jäkel. 2009. ANGER, LOVE and SADNESS revisited: Differences in emotion metaphors between experts and laypersons in the genre psychology guides. In C. Polzin-Haumann et al., eds., *Metaphor und Wissenstransfer – Metaphor and Knowledge Transfer (metaphorik.de 16)*, 87–108. Hannover: Wehrhahn Verlag.

Bromme, Rainer & Riklew Rambow. 1998. Die Verständigung zwischen Experte und Laie. Das Beispiel der Architektur. In W. Schulz, ed., *Expertenwissen. Soziologische, psychologische und pädagogische Perspektiven*, 49–67. Opladen: Leske + Budrich.

Cameron, Lynne & Graham Low. 2004. Figurative variation in episodes of educational talk and text. *European Journal of English Studies* 8 (3): 355–373.

Chapman, Rochelle D. 2009. The Use of Metaphor in Counseling: A Discourse Analysis. MA Thesis, University of British Columbia, Vancouver.

Deignan, Alice. 2005. *Metaphor and Corpus Linguistics*. Amsterdam & Philadelphia: Benjamins.

Gibbs, Raymond W. 1994. *The Poetics of Mind: Figurative Thought, Language, and Understanding*. Cambridge: Cambridge University Press.

Gibbs, Raymond W. 2008. *The Cambridge Handbook of Metaphor and Thought*. Cambridge & New York: Cambridge University Press.

Goatly, Andrew. 2007. *Washing the Brain* – Metaphor and Hidden Ideology. Amsterdam & Philadelphia: Benjamins.

Jäkel, Olaf. 2003. *Wie Metaphern Wissen schaffen. Die kognitive Metapherntheorie und ihre Anwendung in Modell-Analysen der Diskursbereiche Geistestätigkeit, Wirtschaft, Wissenschaft und Religion*. Hamburg: Dr. Kovač.

Kövecses, Zoltán. 1986. *Metaphors of Anger, Pride, and Love: A Lexical Approach to the Structure of Concepts*. Amsterdam & Philadelphia: Benjamins.

Kövecses, Zoltán. 1988. *The Language of Love: The Semantics of Passion in Conversational English*. Lewisburg, London, & Toronto: Bucknell University Press.

Kövecses, Zoltán. 1990. *Emotion Concepts*. New York: Springer-Verlag.

Kövecses, Zoltán. 1995. Anger: Its language, conceptualization, and physiology in the light of cross-cultural evidence. In J. R. Taylor & R. E. MacLaury, eds., *Language and the Cognitive Construal of the World*, 181–196. Berlin & New York: Mouton de Gruyter.

Kövecses, Zoltán. 2000. *Metaphor and Emotion: Language, Culture, and Body in Human Feeling*. Cambridge: Cambridge University Press.

Kövecses, Zoltán. 2008. Metaphor and emotion. In R. W. Gibbs, ed., *The Cambridge Handbook of Metaphor and Thought*, 380–397. Cambridge & New York: Cambridge University Press.

Lakoff, George. 1987. Case study 1: Anger. In G. Lakoff. 1987. *Women, Fire, and Dangerous Things: What Categories Reveal about the Mind*, 380–415. Chicago: The University of Chicago Press.

Lakoff, George. 1993. The contemporary theory of metaphor. In A. Ortony, ed., *Metaphor and Thought*, 202–251. Cambridge: Cambridge University Press.

Lakoff, George & Mark Johnson. 1980. *Metaphors We Live By*. Chicago: The University of Chicago Press.

Lakoff, George & Mark Johnson. 1999. *Philosophy in the Flesh: The Embodied Mind and Its Challenge to Western Thought*. New York: Basic Books.

Lakoff, George & Zoltán Kövecses. 1987. The cognitive model of anger inherent in American English. In D. Holland & N. Quinn, eds., *Cultural Models in Language and Thought*, 195–221. Cambridge: Cambridge University Press.

Lyddon, William J., Alison L. Clay, & Cheri L. Sparks. 2001. Metaphor and change in counseling. *Journal of Counseling & Development* 79: 269–274.

McMullen, Linda M. & John B. Conway. 2002. Conventional metaphors for depression. In S. R. Fussel, ed., *The Verbal Communication of Emotions*, 167–183. Mahwah, NJ & London: Lawrence Erlbaum Associates.

Musolff, Andreas & Jörg Zinken. 2009. A discourse-centred perspective on metaphorical meaning and understanding. In A. Musolff & J. Zinken, eds., *Metaphor and Discourse*, 1–11. Hampshire: Palgrave Macmillan.

Nothdurft, W., M. Reitemeier & P. Schröder. 1994. *Beratungsgespräche. Analyse asymmetrischer Dialoge*. Tübingen: Narr.

Oxford English Dictionary. http://dictionary.oed.com/entrance.dtl

Pragglejaz Group. 2007. MIP: A method for identifying metaphorically used words in discourse. *Metaphor and Symbol* 22 (1): 1–39.

Richardt, Susanne. 2005. *Metaphor in Languages for Special Purposes: The Function of Conceptual Metaphor in Written Expert Language and Expert-Lay Communication in the Domains of Economics, Medicine and Computing*. Frankfurt am Main: Peter Lang.

Semino, Elena. 2008. *Metaphor in Discourse*. Cambridge: Cambridge University Press.

Soriano, Cristina M. 2004. The Conceptualization of Anger in English and Spanish: A Cognitive Approach. PhD Thesis, University of Murcia.

Steen, Gerard. 2009. Three kinds of metaphor in discourse: A linguistic taxonomy. In A. Musolff & J. Zinken, eds., *Metaphor and Discourse*, 25–40. Hampshire: Palgrave Macmillan.

Appendix

I. Sources of linguistic examples

(02) http://www.netwellness.org/question.cfm/40379.htm (13.04.2009)
(03) http://www.laurieslovelogic.com/questions/82.htm (13.04.2009)
(04) http://womentodaymagazine.com/advice/consumed_with_anger.html (27.03.2008)

(05) http://www.teengrowth.com/index.cfm?action=info_advice&ID_Advice =2217&category=emotions&catdesc=Emotions&subdesc=Anger (30.03.08)
(06) http://www.teengrowth.com/index.cfm?action=info_advice&ID_Advice =43830&category=emotions&catdesc=Emotions&subdesc=Anger (30.03.08)
(07) http://www.mentalhelp.net/poc/view_doc.php?type=doc&id=5804&cn=116 (11.04.08)
(08) http://www.drphil.com/articles/article/224 (29.03.08)
(09) http://www.guidetopsychology.com/anger.htm#8 (11.04.08)
(10) http://www.councilforrelationships.org/articles/handling-anger_9-5-05.htm (29.03.2008)
(11) http://www.lovingyou.com/content/advice/archive.php?M=11&D=14&Y=03 (16.05.2008)
(12) http://www.wayneandtamara.com/topicgrief.htm (31.03.2008)
(13) http://www.wayneandtamara.com/topicgrief.htm (31.03.08)
(14) http://www.kissmegoodnight.com/dating-advice-and-tips/dating-get-man-to-commit.shtml (16.05.2008)
(15) http://www.helpguide.org/mental/improve_relationships.htm (22.04.08)
(16) http://www.lovesickfools.com/articles/stale_relationships.html (27.03.08)
(17) http://www.itsteens.com/index.php?a=advice&t=read&id=935&PHPSESSID=0232465ff476c5acf7b126b3a7c9e1e2 (30.03.08)
(18) http://www.mentalhelp.net/poc/view_doc.php?type=advice&id=679&at =1&cn=5&d=1 (30.03.08)
(19) http://www.mentalhelp.net/poc/view_doc.php?type=advice&id=2639&at =1&cn=289&d=1 (30.03.08)
(20) http://mind.skserver.org/2006/02/04/effectively-dealing-with-sadness/ (11.03.08)
(21) http://www.persoal-development.com/chuck/feeling-sad.htm (12.04.08)
(22) http://mind.skserver.org/2006/02/04/effectively-dealing-with-sadness/ (12.04.08)
(23) http://www.gilpincountynews.com/20050707/sally_column.htm (15.04.08)
(24) http://www.gilpincountynews.com/20050707/sally_column.htm (15.04.2008)
(25) Steven1[9] 13:16
(26) Dave 10:03
(27) Stacy 11:05

9. The names of the interviewees have been changed.

(28) Ruth 16:28
(29) Ruth 16:55

II. Questionnaire

Questions[10]

1. Please tell me how you feel today.
2. Think of the last time you were really angry. Try to describe the situation: what made you angry, what did you do and how did you feel?
3. How would you describe the emotion ANGER in general to someone who does not know what it is (like someone from Mars...)?
4. Imagine the following situation: A mother told her 13 year old son several times to clean up his room but he didn't do it. She gets angry but gives him a last chance. He's supposed to clean up his room before she comes back from shopping. Two hours later, she comes back and her son's room looks exactly the way it did before she left the house while he is sitting in front of his game pad. What do you think happens with the mother and her feelings now?
5. Tell me about your "first big love". How did it begin and how did it feel like during the first months?
6. Think of your worst romantic relationship and tell me about the ending of it.
7. Tell me a short story that you would call a typical love story.
8. Think of an event that made you feel very sad. Please describe the situation and what you felt.
9. Imagine your best friend has been feeling sad for weeks because her/his partner has left her/him. How would you describe her/his feelings?
10. Now, this best friend needs your advice. She/He wonders if it's natural to feel sad for so long and what she/he can do to feel better. What would you tell her/him?
11. Think of something that makes you angry and try to picture the anger. What does it look like (like a person/living being? Like water, air, fire? Like an object? Etc.)
12. When you try to picture love, what does this emotion look like?
13. Now, try to picture sadness...

10. For the complete questionnaire including instructions to the interviewer, see Beger 2011.

Index